りんね

RIN-NE

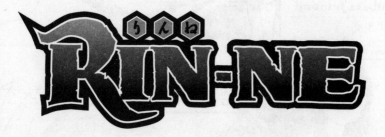

Story and Art by

Rumiko Takahashi

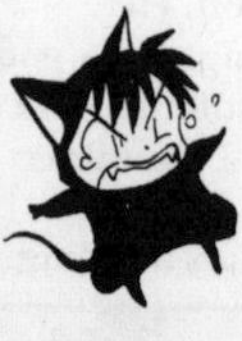

RIN-NE

Characters

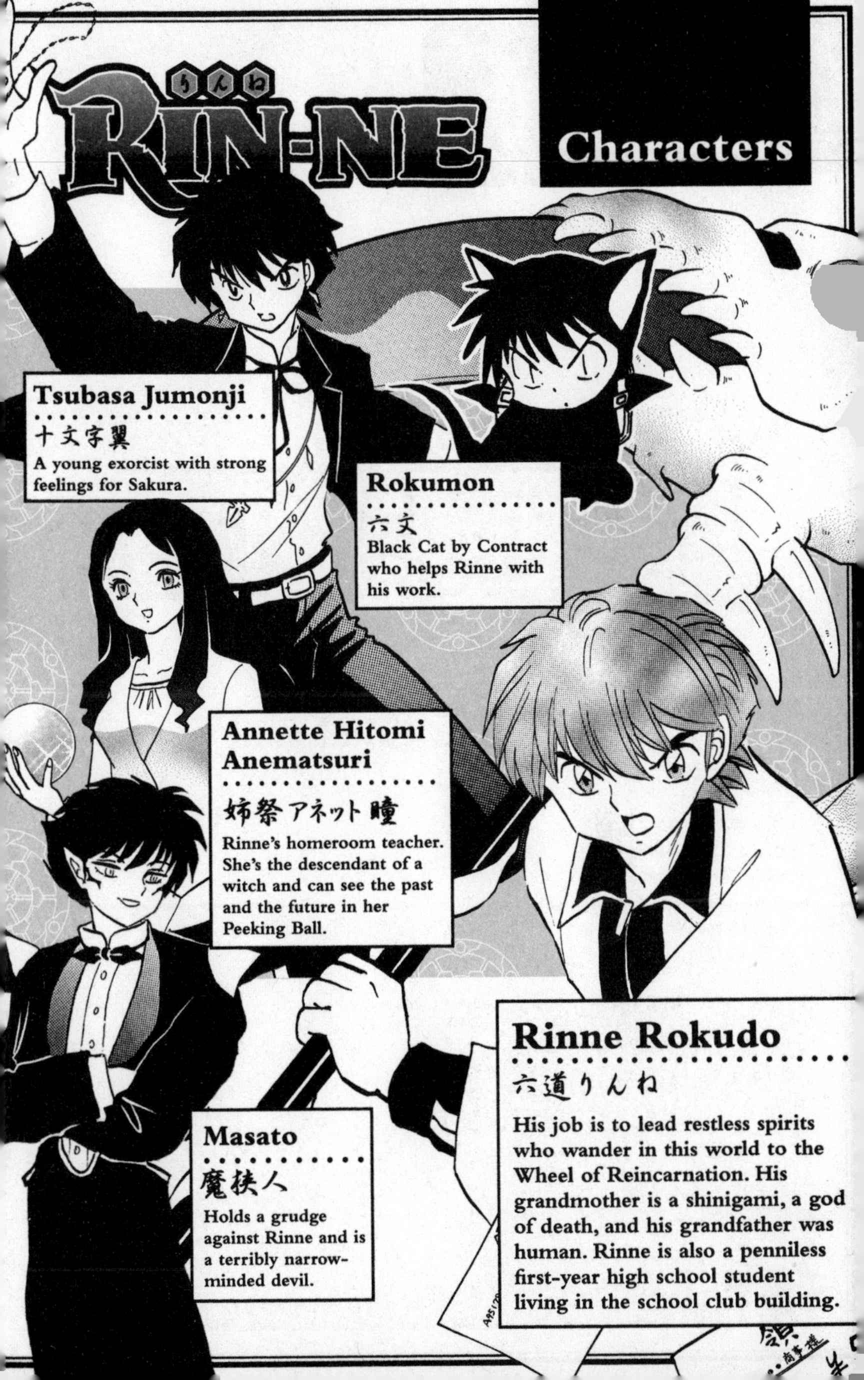

Tsubasa Jumonji

十文字翼

A young exorcist with strong feelings for Sakura.

Rokumon

六文

Black Cat by Contract who helps Rinne with his work.

Annette Hitomi Anematsuri

姉祭アネット瞳

Rinne's homeroom teacher. She's the descendant of a witch and can see the past and the future in her Peeking Ball.

Masato

魔挟人

Holds a grudge against Rinne and is a terribly narrow-minded devil.

Rinne Rokudo

六道りんね

His job is to lead restless spirits who wander in this world to the Wheel of Reincarnation. His grandmother is a shinigami, a god of death, and his grandfather was human. Rinne is also a penniless first-year high school student living in the school club building.

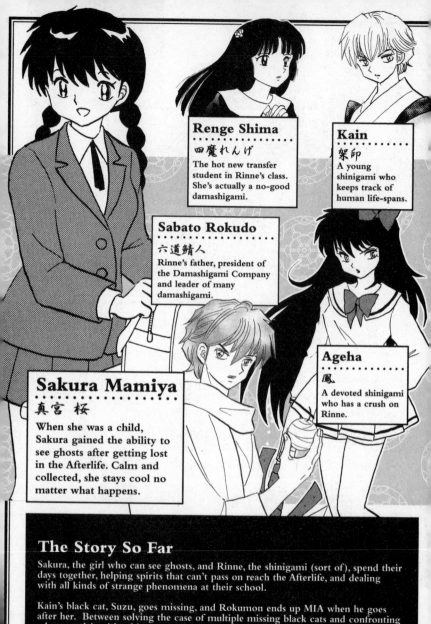

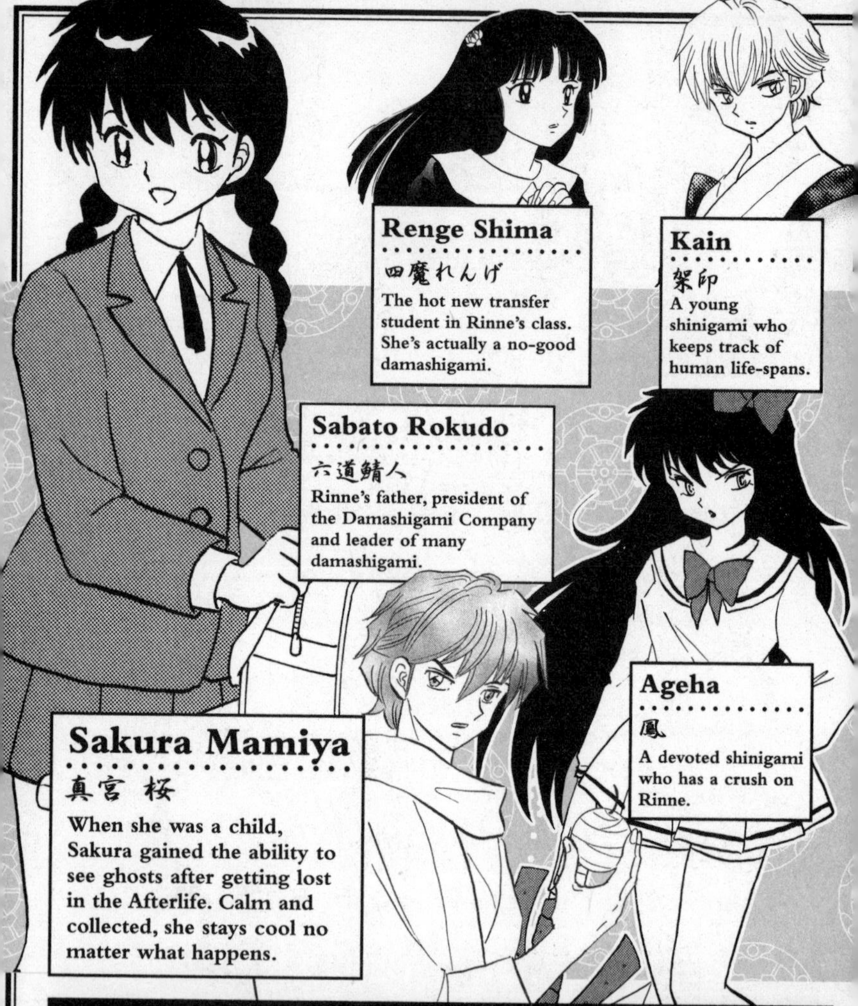
Renge Shima
四魔れんげ
The hot new transfer student in Rinne's class. She's actually a no-good damashigami.
Kain
架印
A young shinigami who keeps track of human life-spans.
Sabato Rokudo
六道鯖人
Rinne's father, president of the Damashigami Company and leader of many damashigami.
Ageha
鳳
A devoted shinigami who has a crush on Rinne.
Sakura Mamiya
真宮 桜
When she was a child, Sakura gained the ability to see ghosts after getting lost in the Afterlife. Calm and collected, she stays cool no matter what happens.

The Story So Far

Sakura, the girl who can see ghosts, and Rinne, the shinigami (sort of), spend their days together, helping spirits that can't pass on reach the Afterlife, and dealing with all kinds of strange phenomena at their school.

Kain's black cat, Suzu, goes missing, and Rokumon ends up MIA when he goes after her. Between solving the case of multiple missing black cats and confronting a kappa spirit with a bizarre grudge against Tsubasa, Rinne's as busy as ever. Now summer has arrived, bringing with it an increase in supernatural activity, and Rinne's crazy days of poverty and overwork are ramping up!

RIN-NE

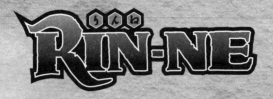

Contents

CHAPTER 289: THE GODDESS OF WISDOM

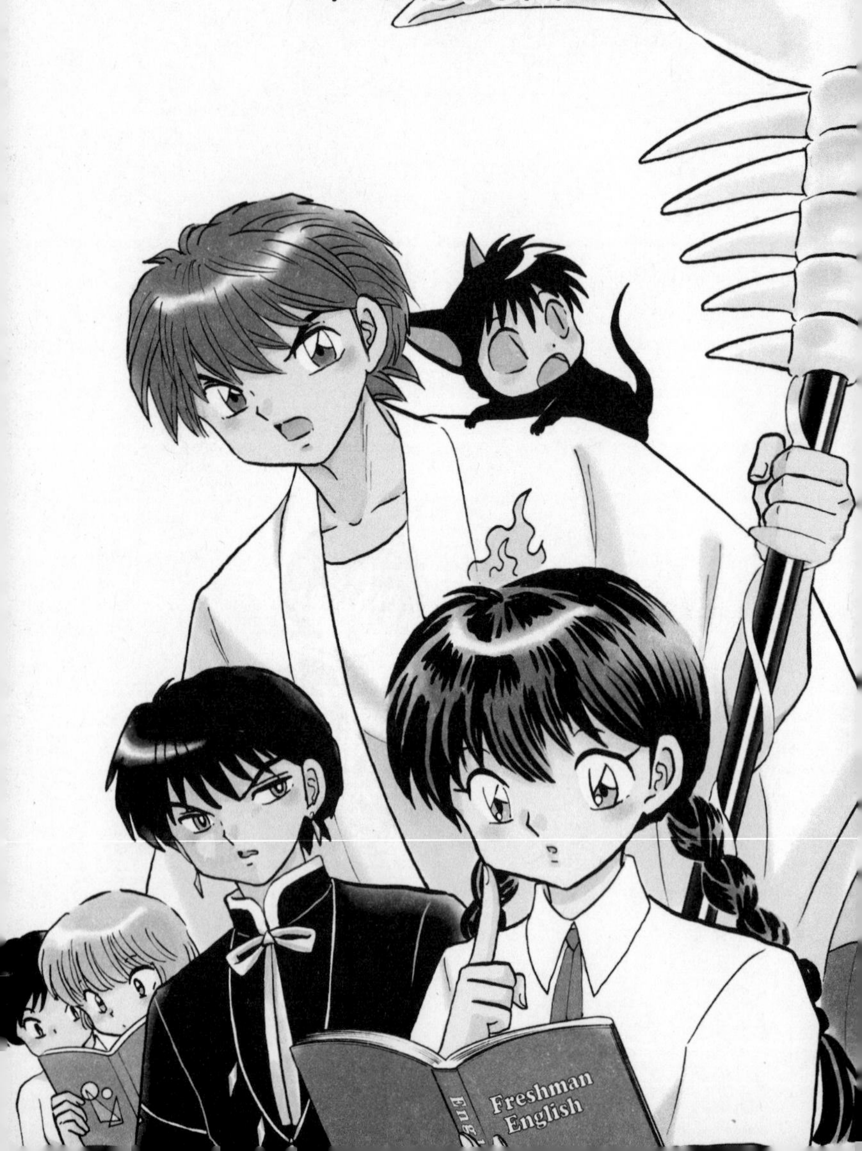

Freshman English

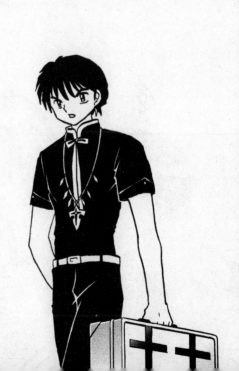

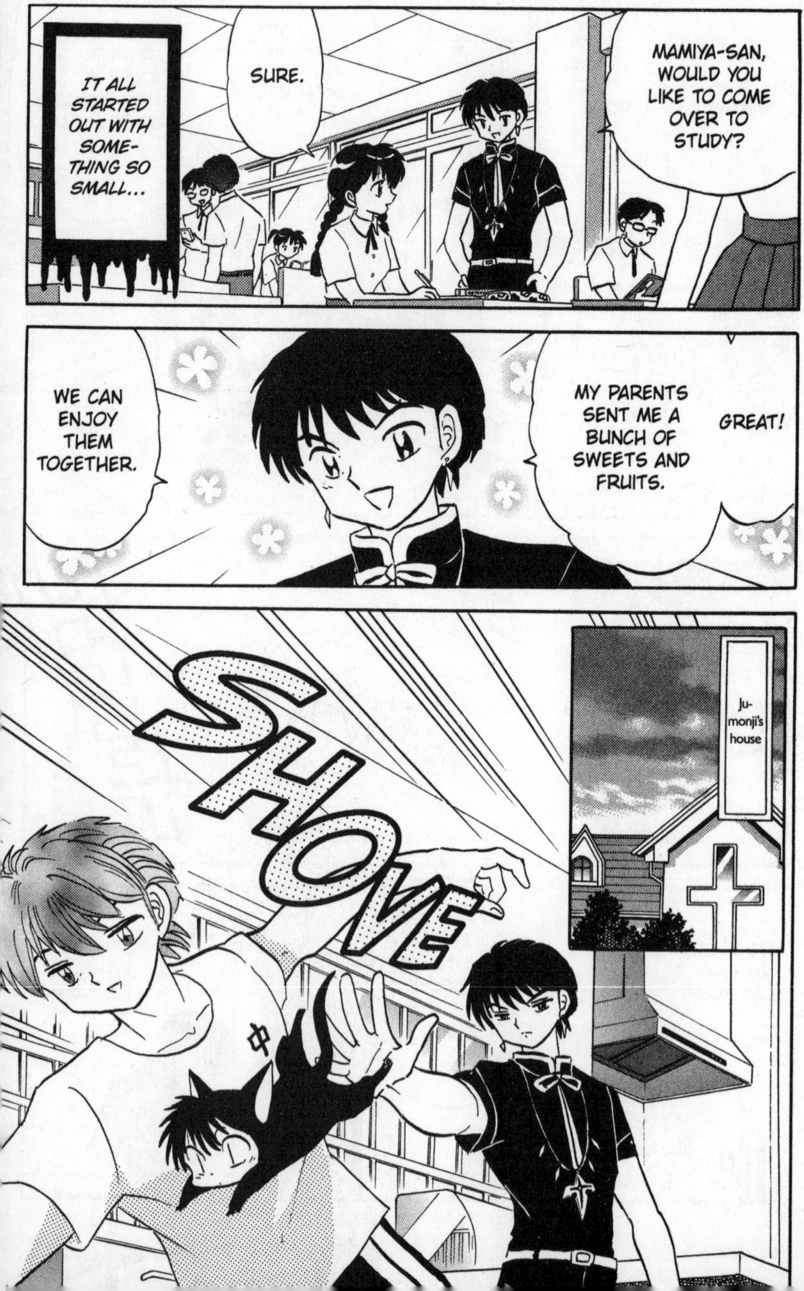
MAMIYA-SAN, WOULD YOU LIKE TO COME OVER TO STUDY?
SURE.
IT ALL STARTED OUT WITH SOME-THING SO SMALL...
GREAT!
MY PARENTS SENT ME A BUNCH OF SWEETS AND FRUITS.
WE CAN ENJOY THEM TOGETHER.
Ju-monji's house
SHOVE

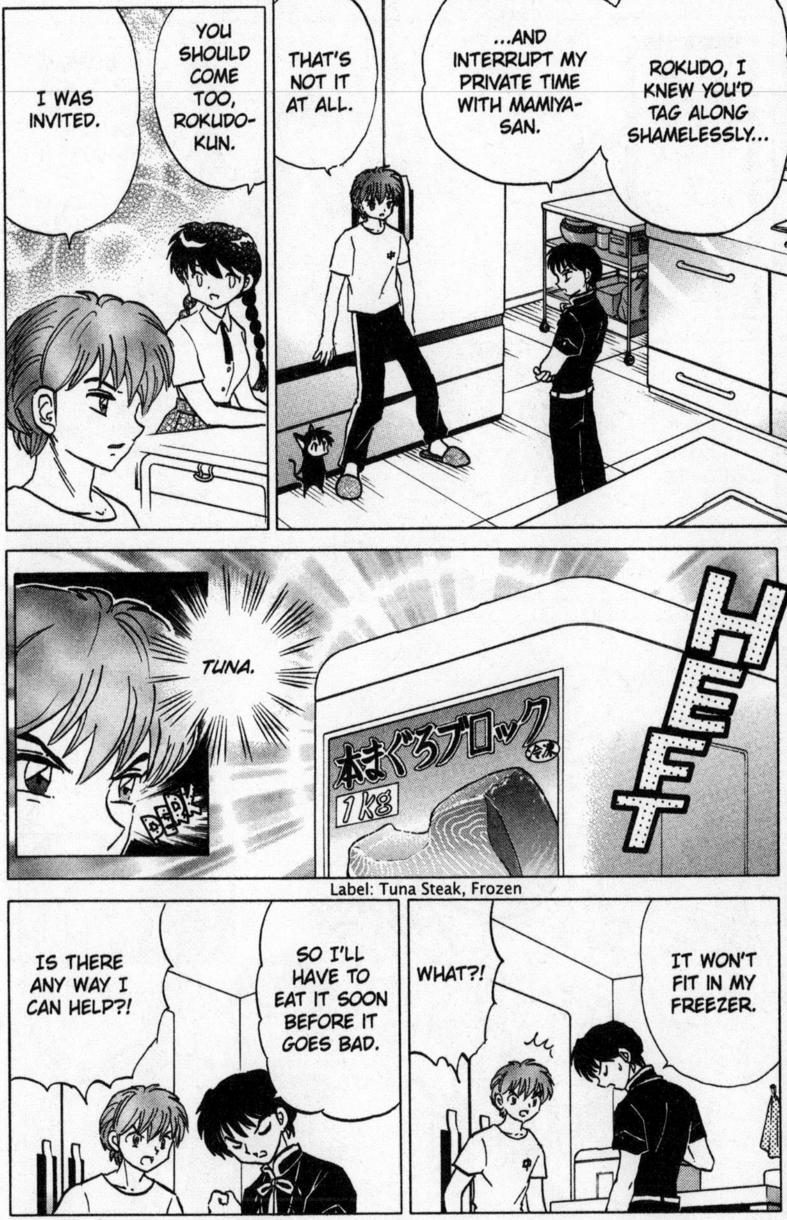
ROKUDO, I KNEW YOU'D TAG ALONG SHAMELESSLY...
...AND INTERRUPT MY PRIVATE TIME WITH MAMIYA-SAN.
THAT'S NOT IT AT ALL.
YOU SHOULD COME TOO, ROKUDO-KUN.
I WAS INVITED.
HEFT
本まぐろブロック
冷凍
1kg
TUNA.
Label: Tuna Steak, Frozen
IT WON'T FIT IN MY FREEZER.
WHAT?!
SO I'LL HAVE TO EAT IT SOON BEFORE IT GOES BAD.
IS THERE ANY WAY I CAN HELP?!

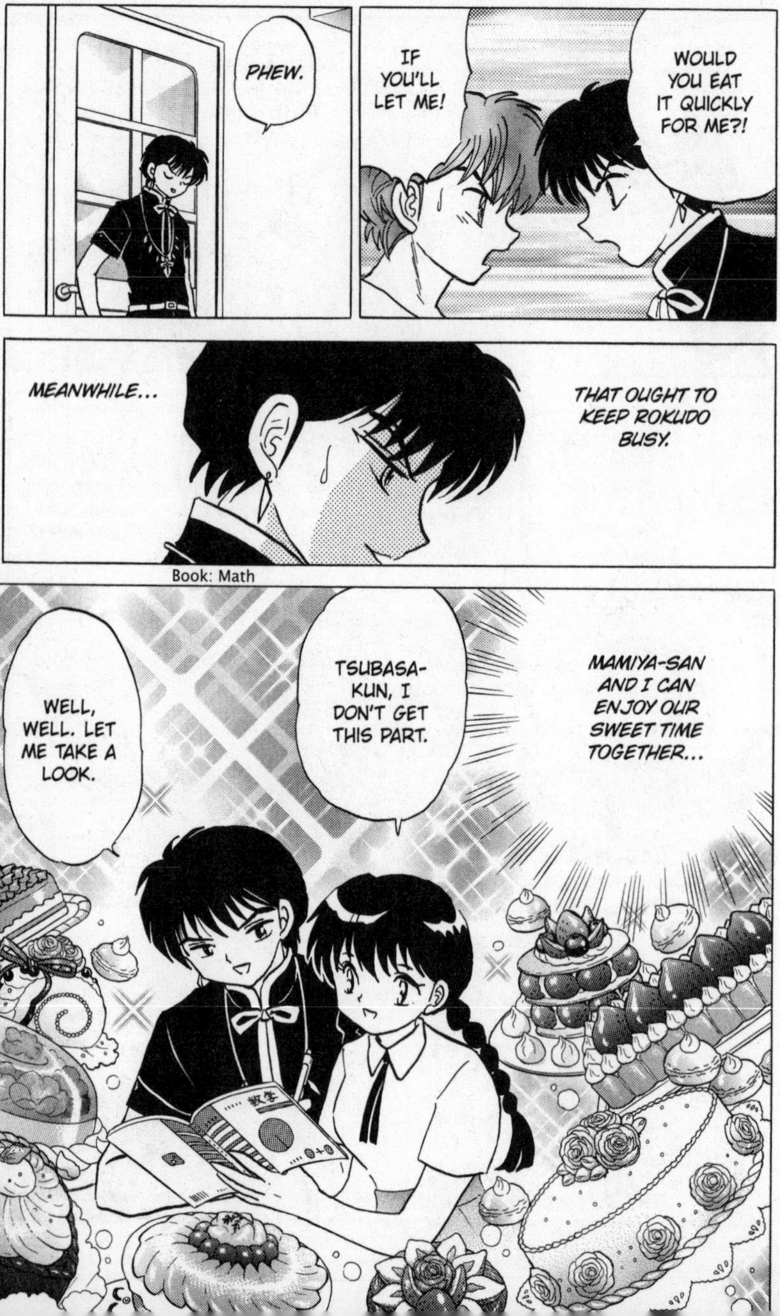
WOULD YOU EAT IT QUICKLY FOR ME?!
IF YOU'LL LET ME!
PHEW.
THAT OUGHT TO KEEP ROKUDO BUSY.
MEANWHILE...
MAMIYA-SAN AND I CAN ENJOY OUR SWEET TIME TOGETHER...
TSUBASA-KUN, I DON'T GET THIS PART.
WELL, WELL. LET ME TAKE A LOOK.
Book: Math

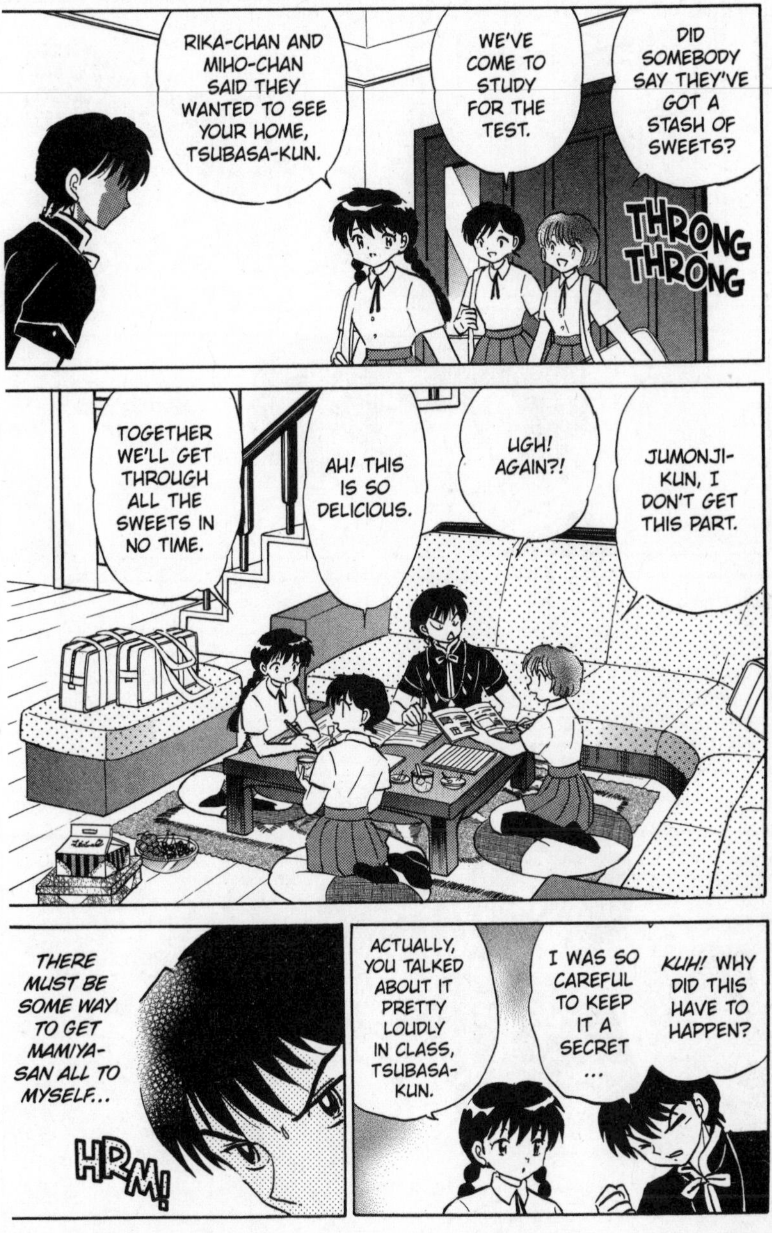
DID SOMEBODY SAY THEY'VE GOT A STASH OF SWEETS?
WE'VE COME TO STUDY FOR THE TEST.
RIKA-CHAN AND MIHO-CHAN SAID THEY WANTED TO SEE YOUR HOME, TSUBASA-KUN.
THRONG THRONG
JUMONJI-KUN, I DON'T GET THIS PART.
UGH! AGAIN?!
AH! THIS IS SO DELICIOUS.
TOGETHER WE'LL GET THROUGH ALL THE SWEETS IN NO TIME.
KUH! WHY DID THIS HAVE TO HAPPEN?
I WAS SO CAREFUL TO KEEP IT A SECRET ...
ACTUALLY, YOU TALKED ABOUT IT PRETTY LOUDLY IN CLASS, TSUBASA-KUN.
THERE MUST BE SOME WAY TO GET MAMIYA-SAN ALL TO MYSELF...
HRM!

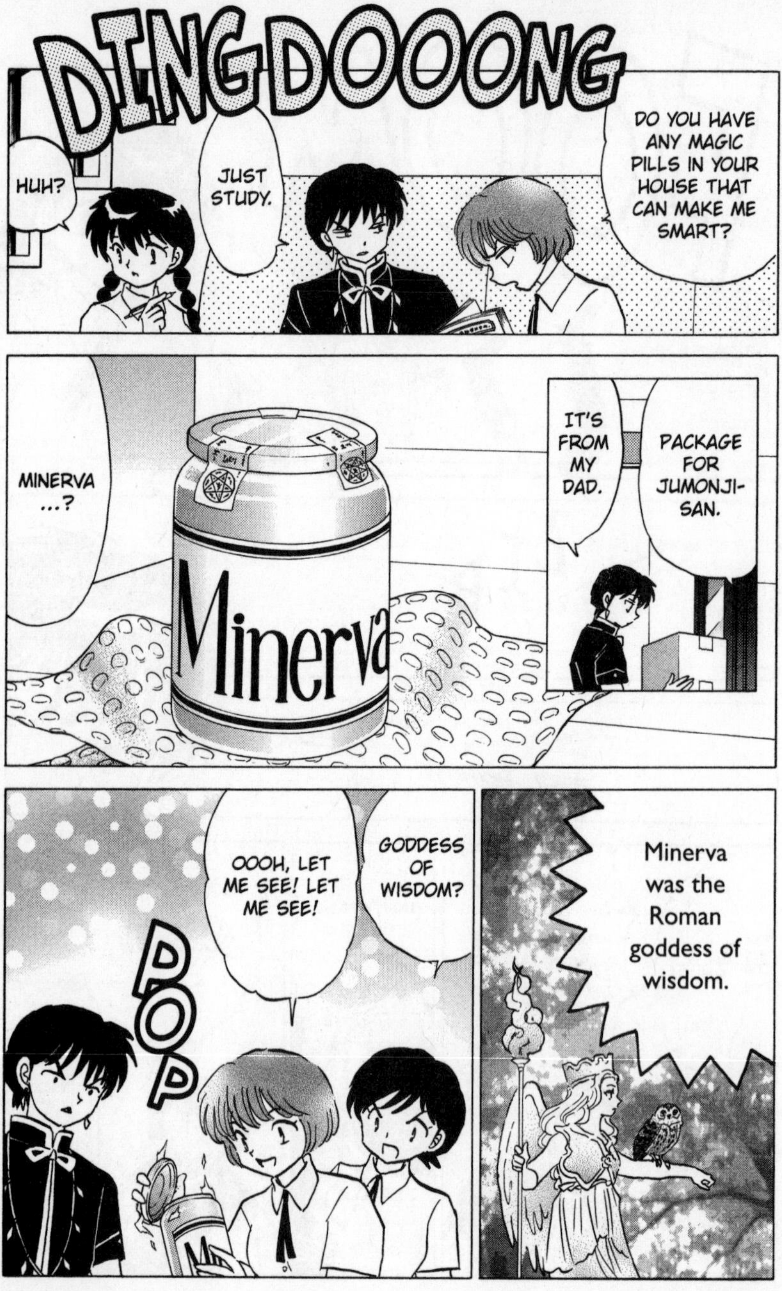
DO YOU HAVE ANY MAGIC PILLS IN YOUR HOUSE THAT CAN MAKE ME SMART?
JUST STUDY.
HUH?
DINGDOOONG
PACKAGE FOR JUMONJI-SAN.
IT'S FROM MY DAD.
Minerva
MINERVA ...?
Minerva was the Roman goddess of wisdom.
GODDESS OF WISDOM?
OOOH, LET ME SEE! LET ME SEE!
POP

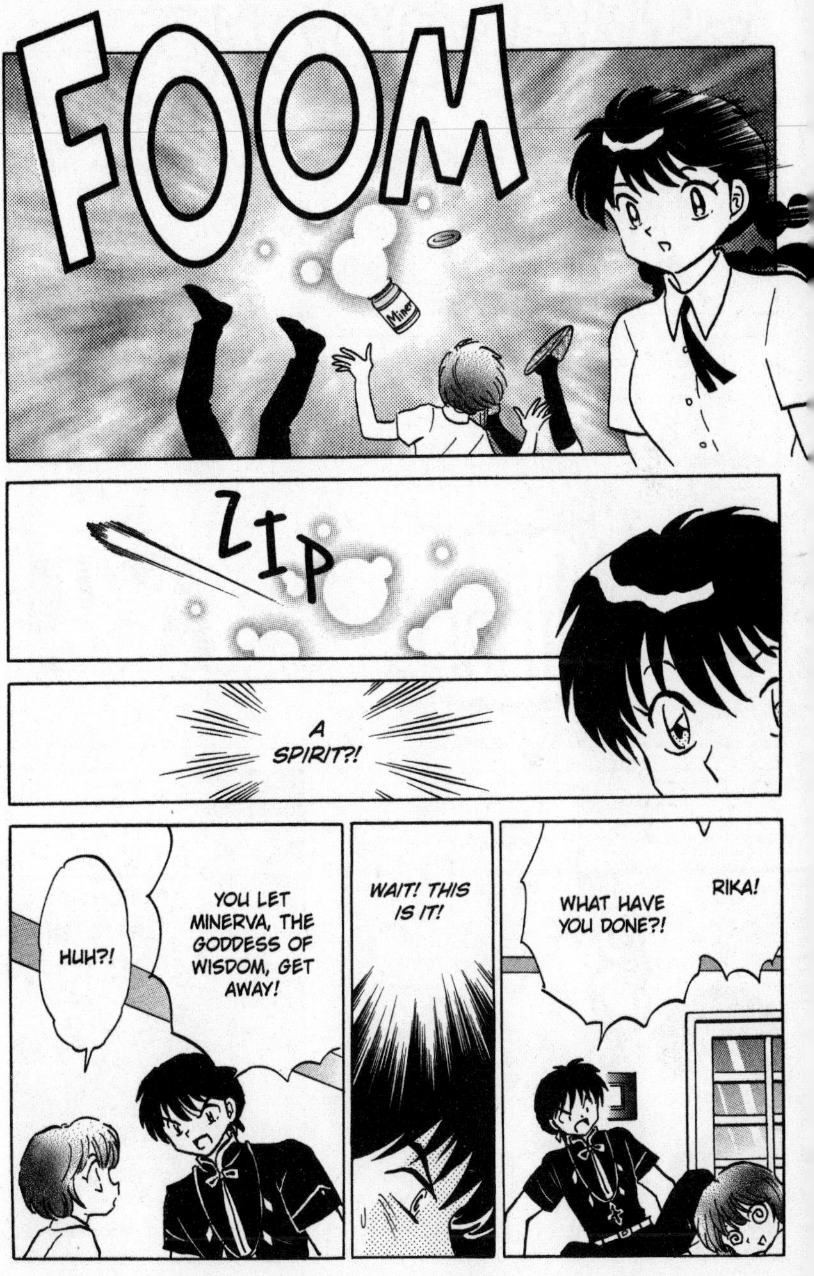
FOOM
Miner
ZIP
A SPIRIT?!
RIKA!
WHAT HAVE YOU DONE?!
WAIT! THIS IS IT!
YOU LET MINERVA, THE GODDESS OF WISDOM, GET AWAY!
HUH?!

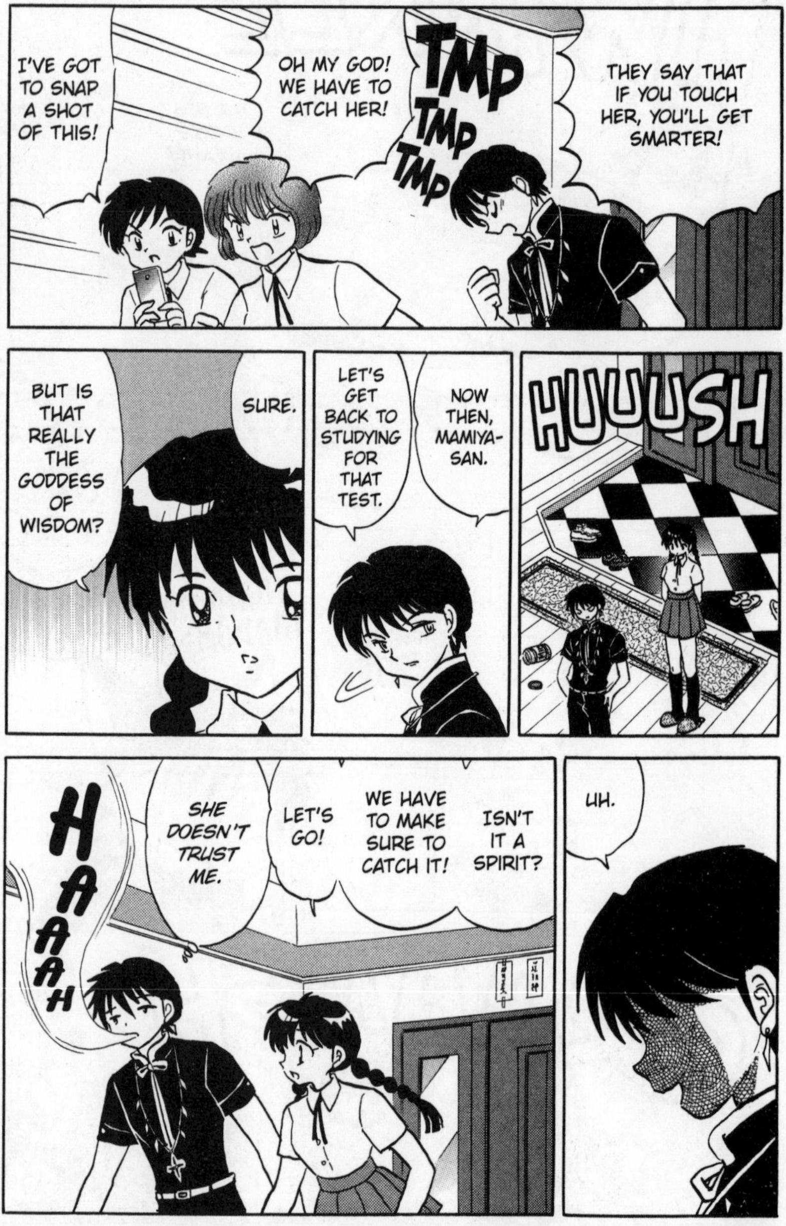
THEY SAY THAT IF YOU TOUCH HER, YOU'LL GET SMARTER!
TMP TMP TMP
OH MY GOD! WE HAVE TO CATCH HER!
I'VE GOT TO SNAP A SHOT OF THIS!
HUUUSH
NOW THEN, MAMIYA-SAN.
LET'S GET BACK TO STUDYING FOR THAT TEST.
SURE.
BUT IS THAT REALLY THE GODDESS OF WISDOM?
UH.
ISN'T IT A SPIRIT?
WE HAVE TO MAKE SURE TO CATCH IT!
LET'S GO!
SHE DOESN'T TRUST ME.
HAAAAH

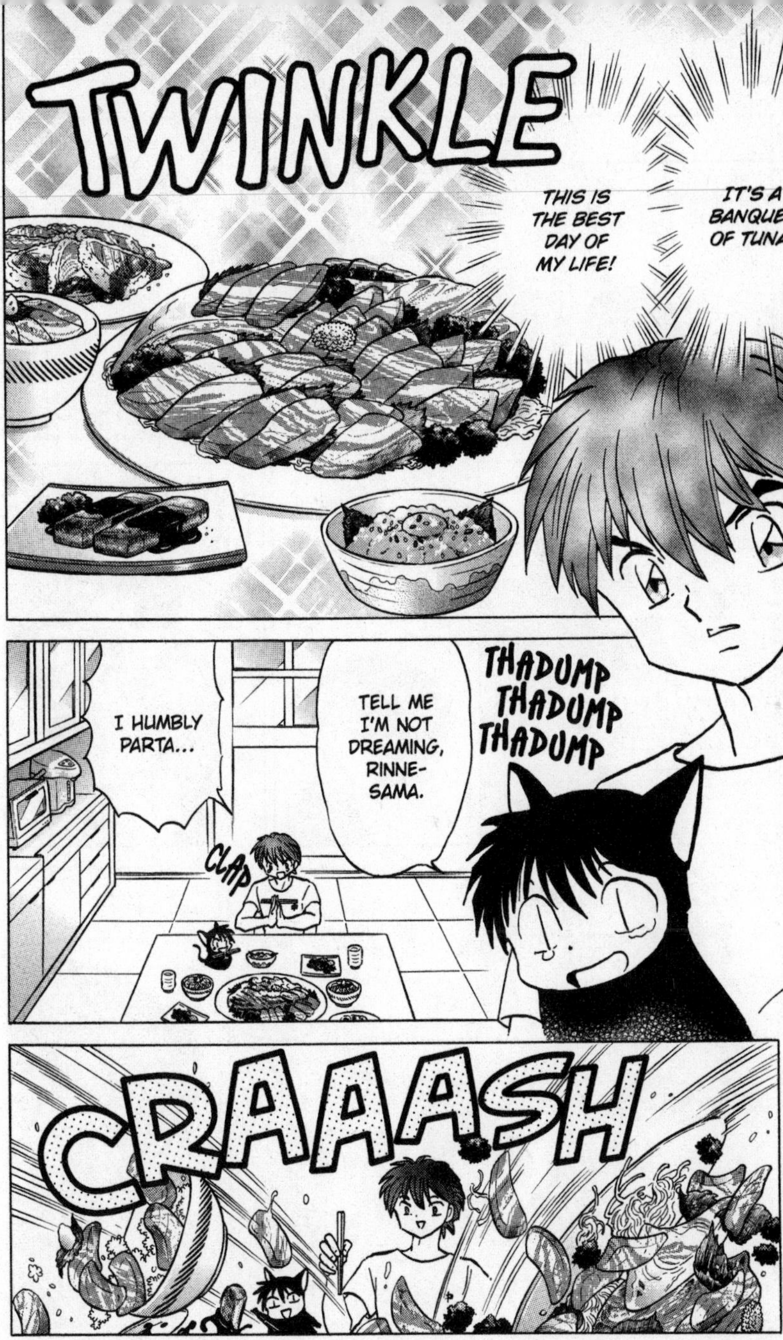
TWINKLE
IT'S A BANQUET OF TUNA.
THIS IS THE BEST DAY OF MY LIFE!
THADUMP THADUMP THADUMP
TELL ME I'M NOT DREAMING, RINNE-SAMA.
I HUMBLY PARTA...
CLAP
CRAAASH

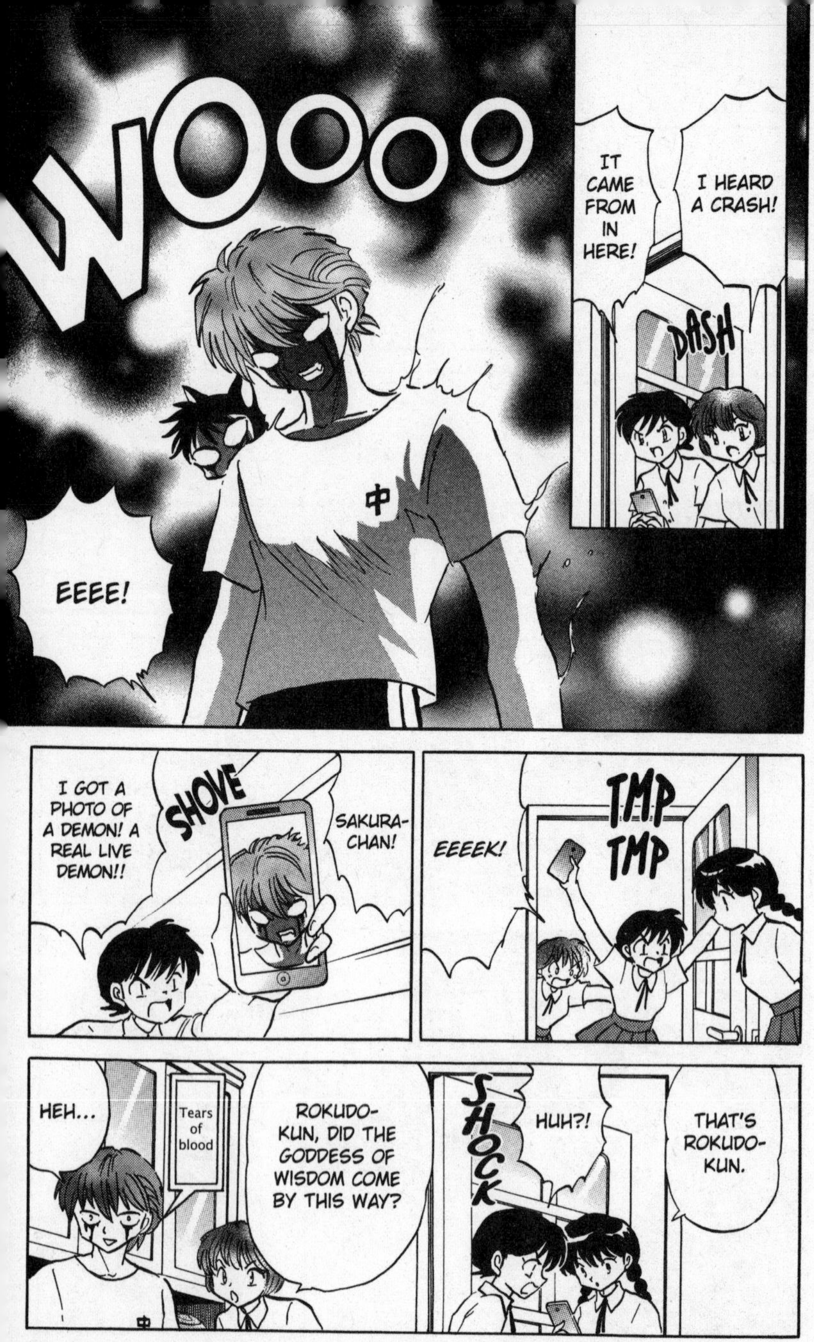
I HEARD A CRASH!
IT CAME FROM IN HERE!
DASH
WOOOOO
EEEE!
TMP TMP
EEEEK!
SAKURA-CHAN!
SHOVE
I GOT A PHOTO OF A DEMON! A REAL LIVE DEMON!!
THAT'S ROKUDO-KUN.
HUH?!
SHOCK
ROKUDO-KUN, DID THE GODDESS OF WISDOM COME BY THIS WAY?
Tears of blood
HEH...

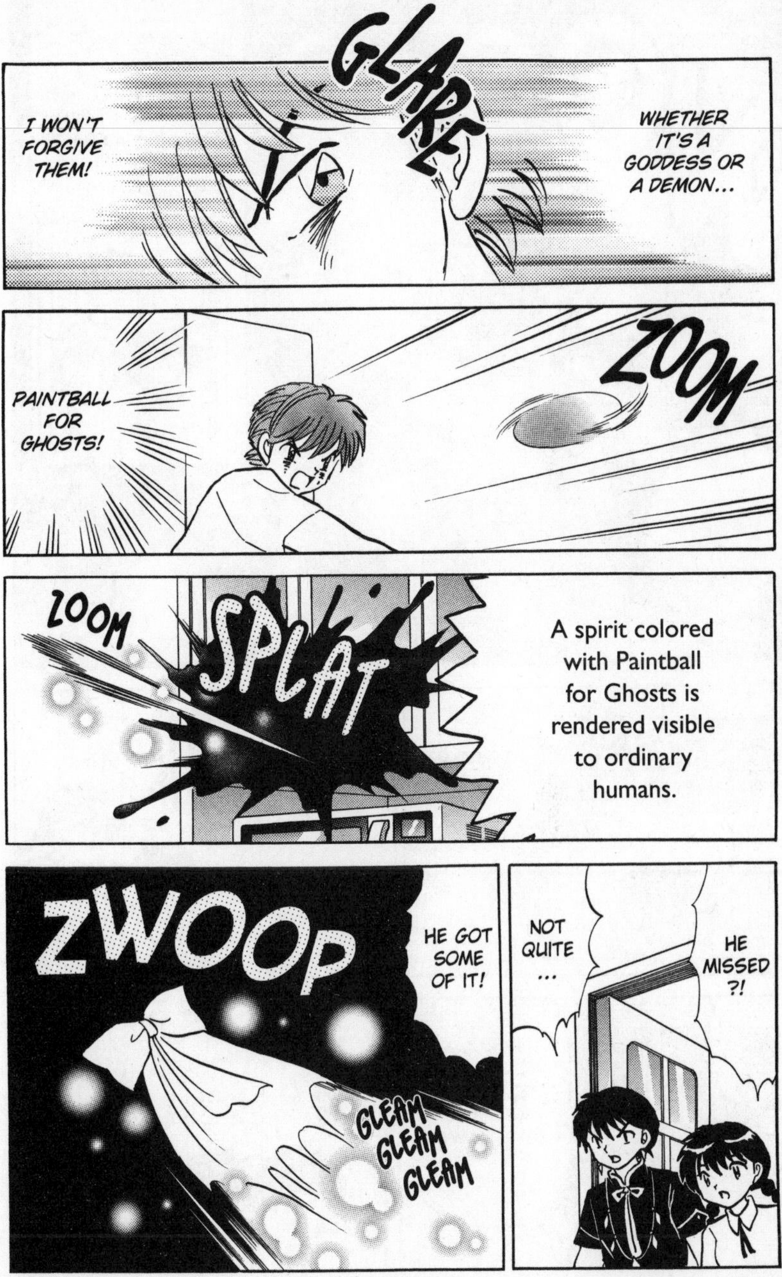
WHETHER IT'S A GODDESS OR A DEMON...
GLARE
I WON'T FORGIVE THEM!
ZOOM
PAINTBALL FOR GHOSTS!
A spirit colored with Paintball for Ghosts is rendered visible to ordinary humans.
SPLAT
ZOOM
HE MISSED?!
NOT QUITE...
HE GOT SOME OF IT!
ZWOOP
GLEAM GLEAM GLEAM

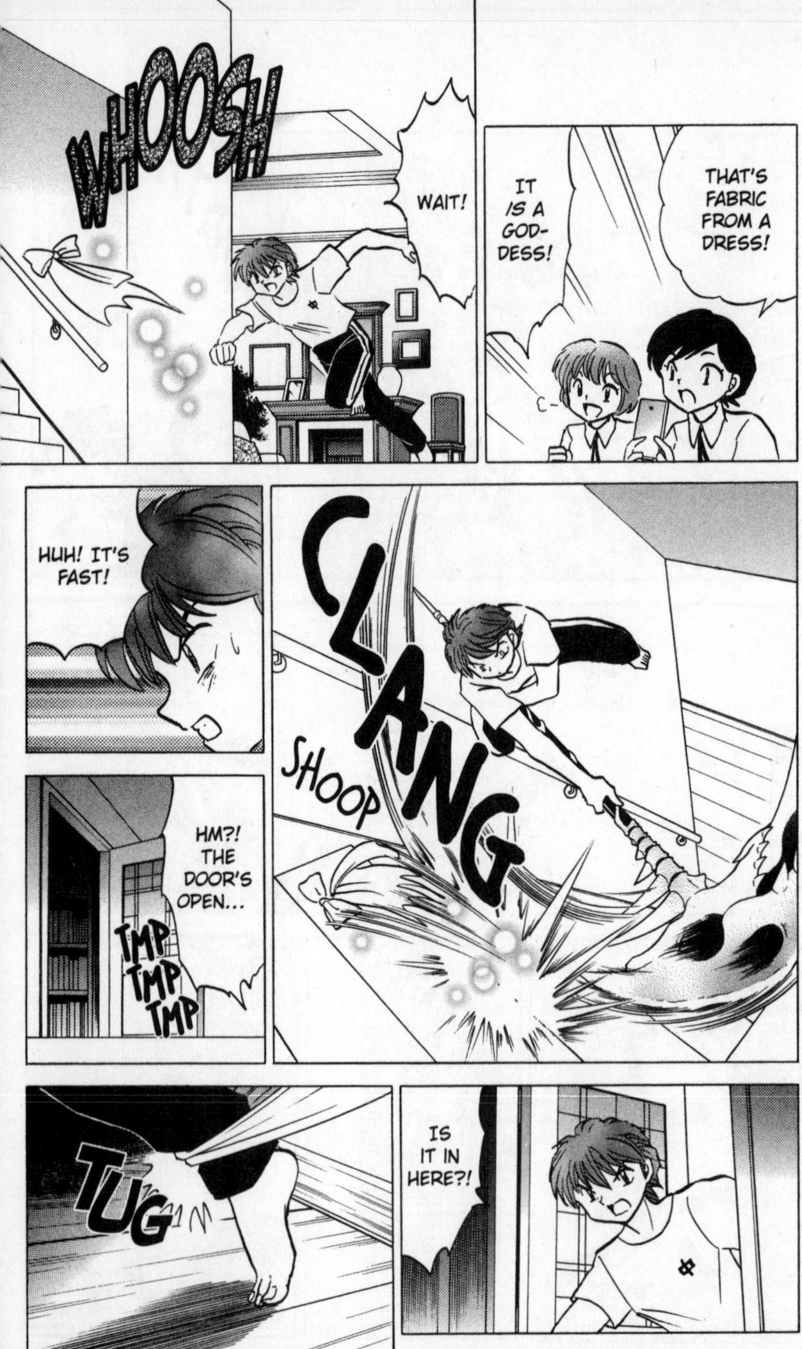
THAT'S FABRIC FROM A DRESS!
IT IS A GODDESS!
WAIT!
WHOOSH
CLANG
SHOOP
HUH! IT'S FAST!
HM?! THE DOOR'S OPEN...
TMP TMP TMP
IS IT IN HERE?!
TUG

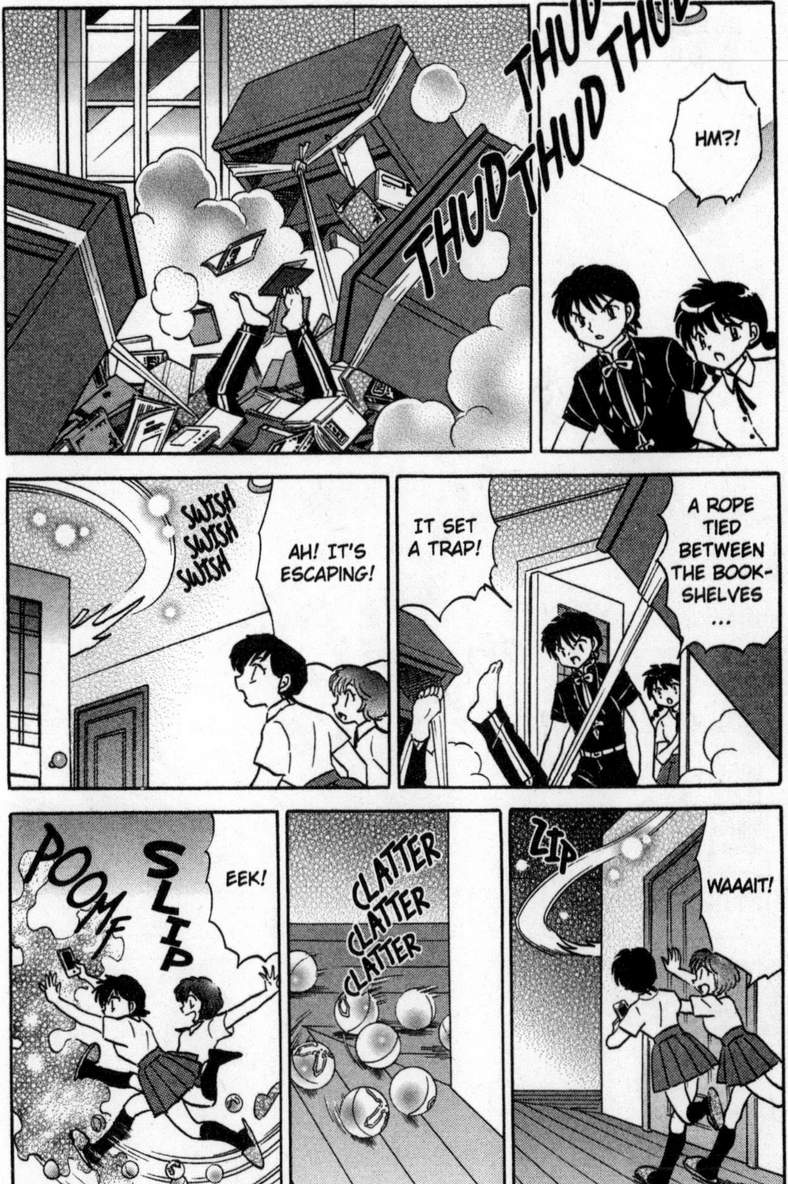
HM?!
THUD THUD THUD THUD THUD
A ROPE TIED BETWEEN THE BOOK-SHELVES ...
IT SET A TRAP!
AH! IT'S ESCAPING!
SWISH SWISH SWISH
WAAAIT!
ZIP
CLATTER CLATTER CLATTER
EEK!
SLIP
POOMF

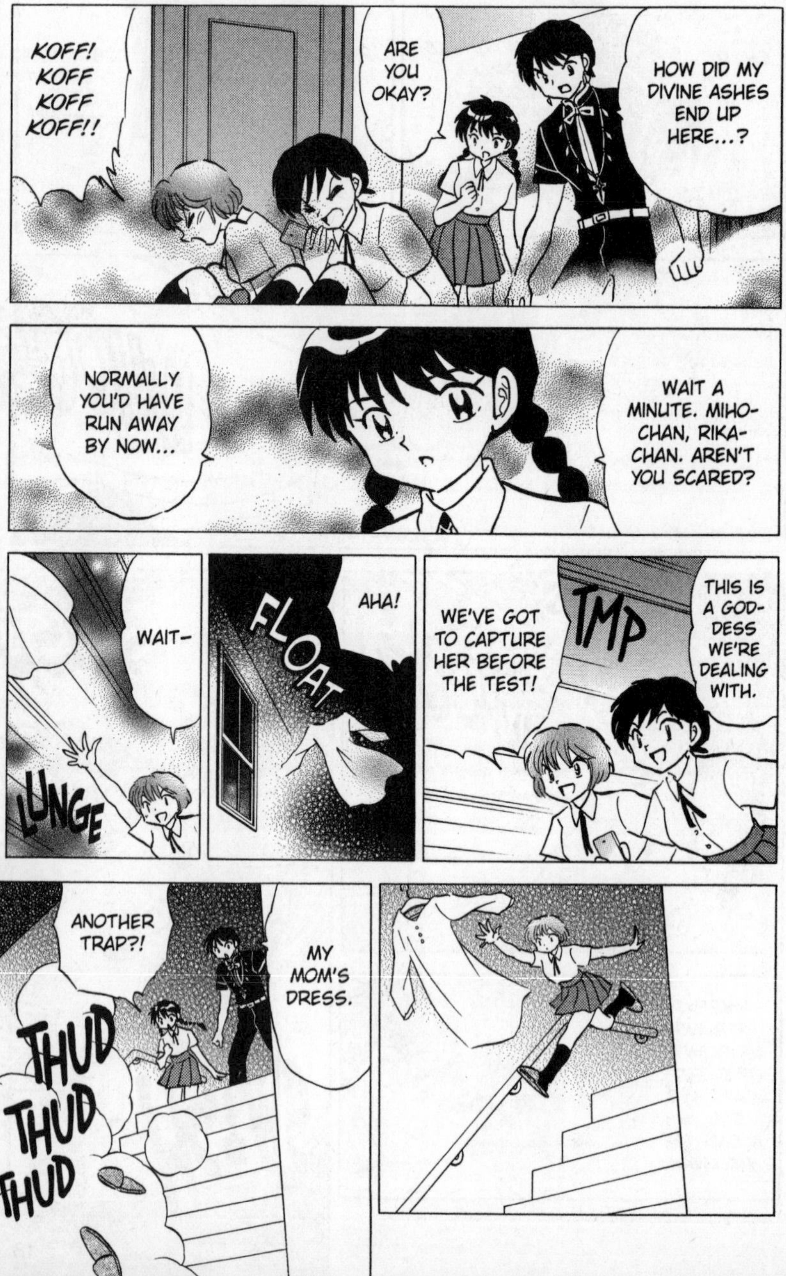
HOW DID MY DIVINE ASHES END UP HERE...?
ARE YOU OKAY?
KOFF! KOFF KOFF KOFF!!
WAIT A MINUTE. MIHO-CHAN, RIKA-CHAN. AREN'T YOU SCARED?
NORMALLY YOU'D HAVE RUN AWAY BY NOW...
THIS IS A GOD-DESS WE'RE DEALING WITH.
WE'VE GOT TO CAPTURE HER BEFORE THE TEST!
TMP
AHA!
FLOAT
WAIT-
LUNGE
MY MOM'S DRESS.
ANOTHER TRAP?!
THUD THUD THUD

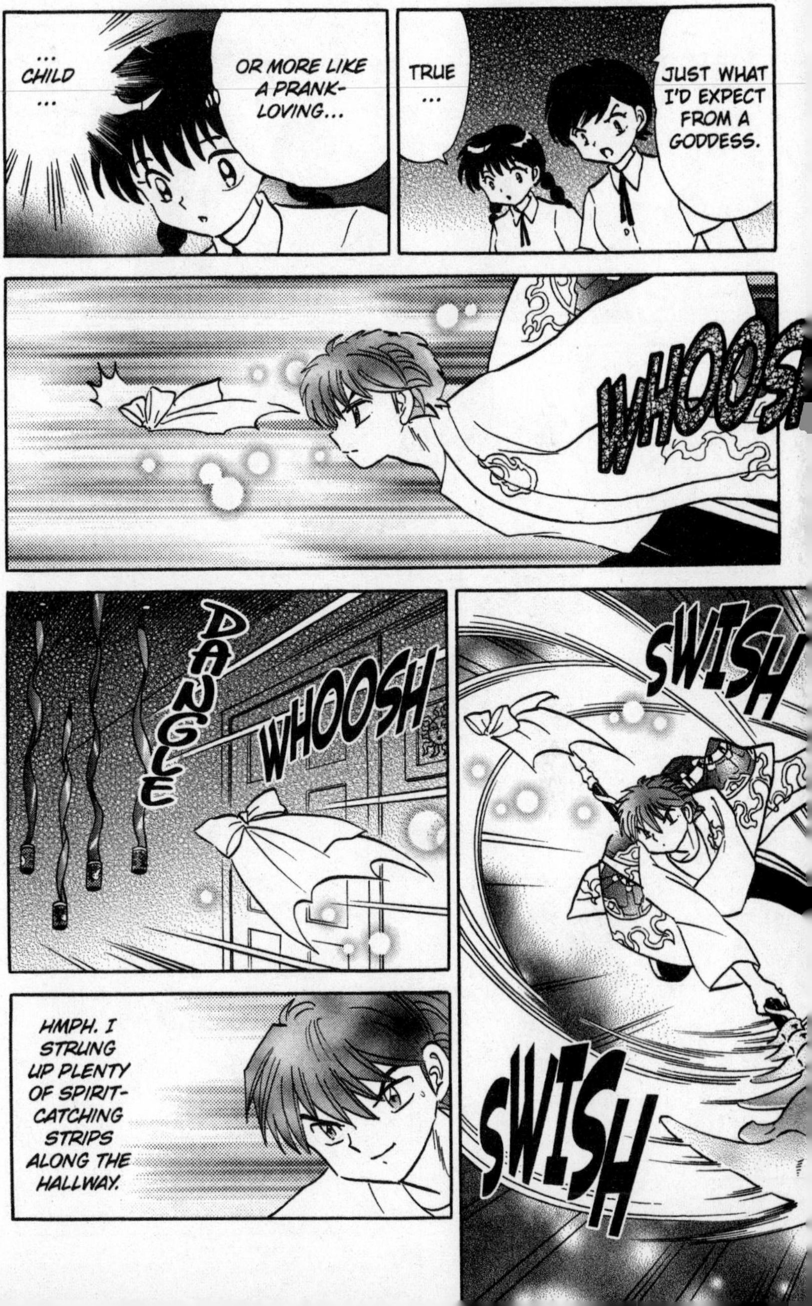
JUST WHAT I'D EXPECT FROM A GODDESS.
TRUE ...
OR MORE LIKE A PRANK-LOVING...
... CHILD ...
WHOOS
SWISH
SWISH
DANGLE
WHOOSH
HMPH. I STRUNG UP PLENTY OF SPIRIT-CATCHING STRIPS ALONG THE HALLWAY.

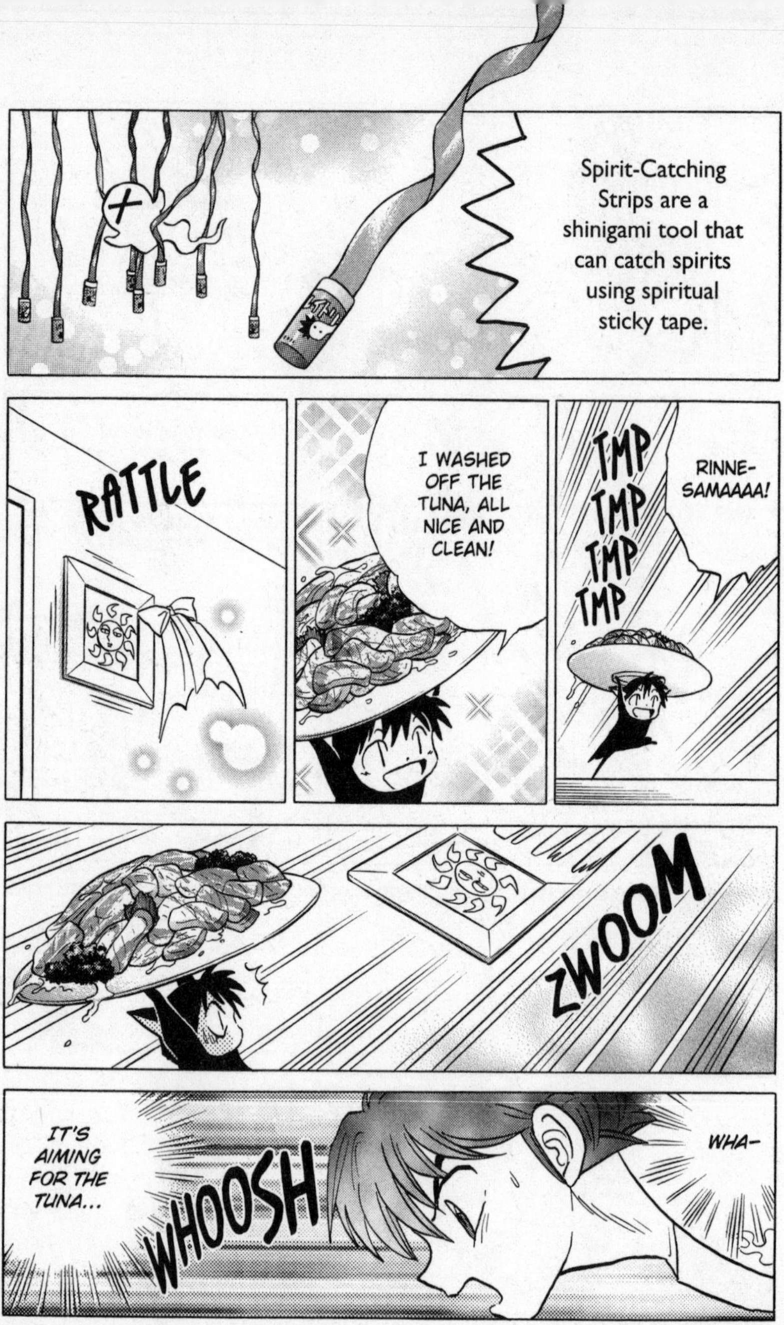
Spirit-Catching Strips are a shinigami tool that can catch spirits using spiritual sticky tape.
RINNE-SAMAAAA!
TMP TMP TMP TMP
I WASHED OFF THE TUNA, ALL NICE AND CLEAN!
RATTLE
ZWOOM
WHA-
WHOOSH
IT'S AIMING FOR THE TUNA...

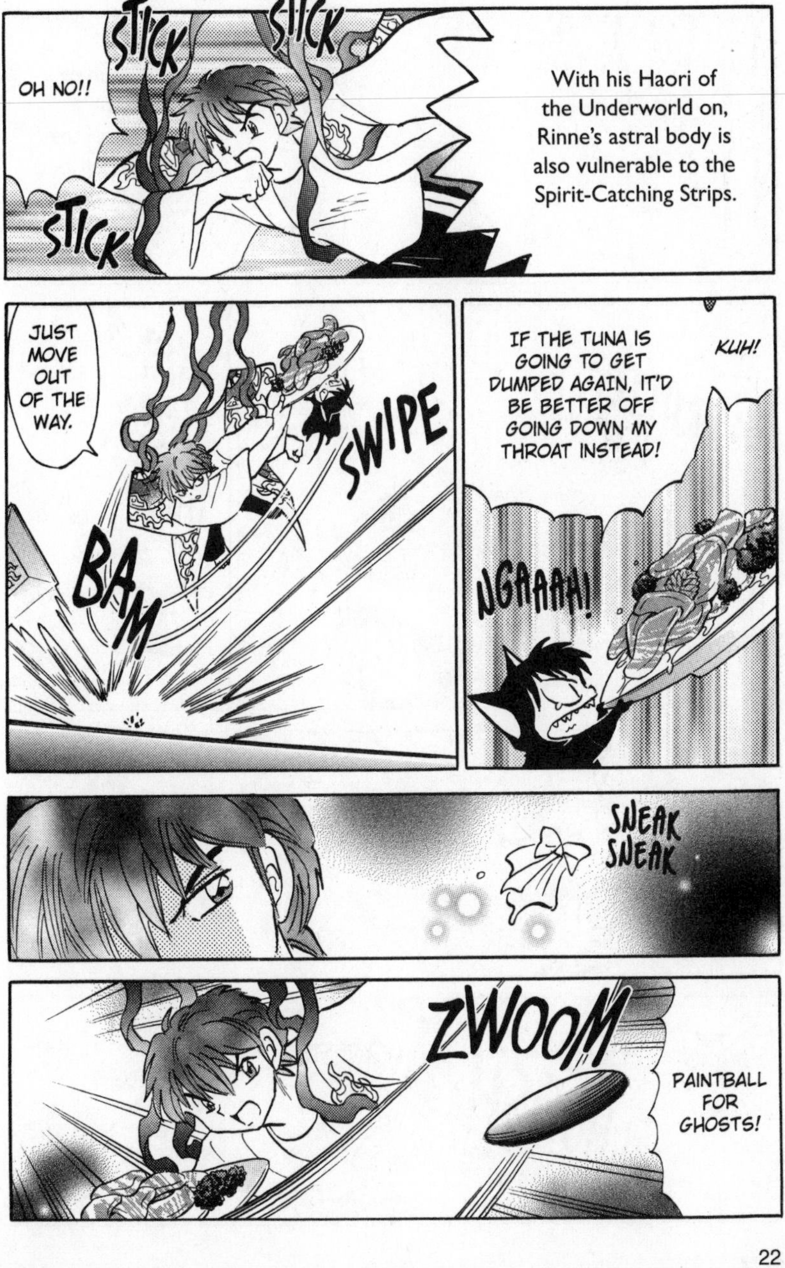
With his Haori of the Underworld on, Rinne's astral body is also vulnerable to the Spirit-Catching Strips.
STICK
STICK
OH NO!!
STICK
KUH!
IF THE TUNA IS GOING TO GET DUMPED AGAIN, IT'D BE BETTER OFF GOING DOWN MY THROAT INSTEAD!
NGAAAH!
SWIPE
JUST MOVE OUT OF THE WAY.
BAM
SNEAK SNEAK
PAINTBALL FOR GHOSTS!
ZWOOM

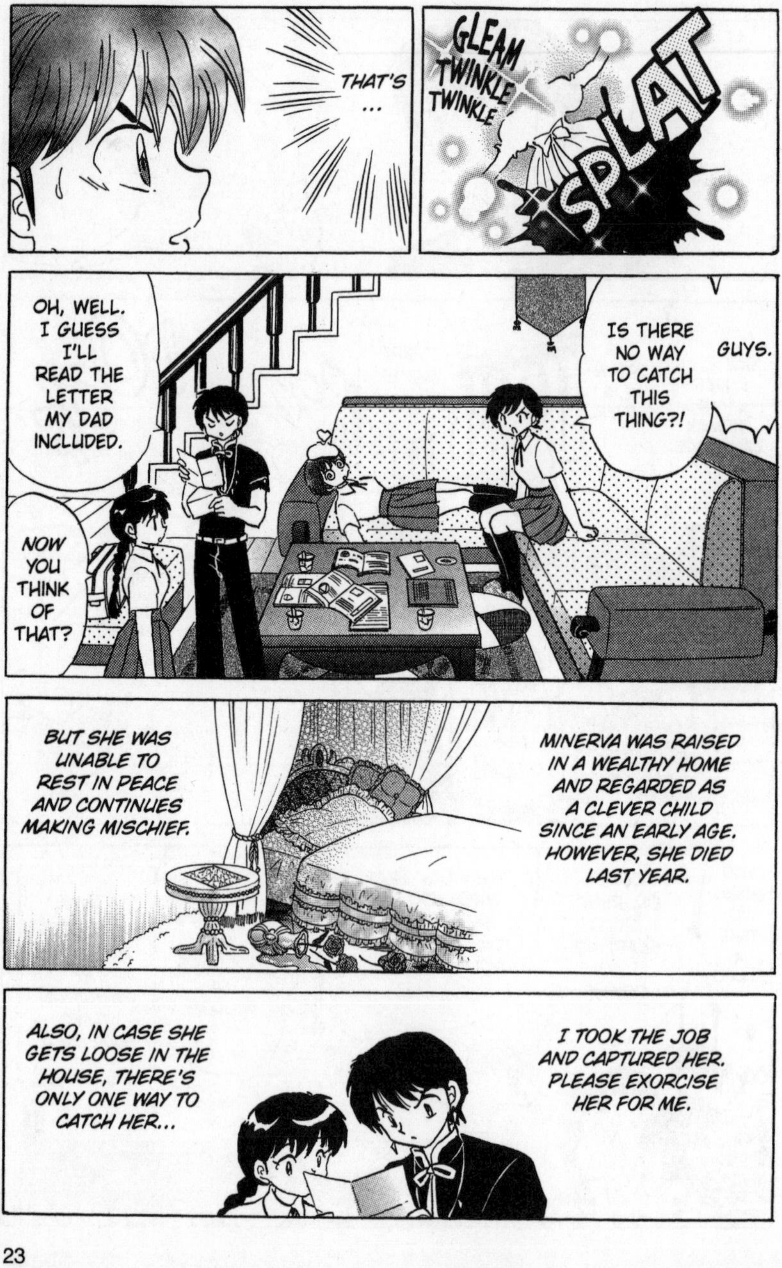
GLEAM
TWINKLE
TWINKLE
SPLAT
THAT'S ...
GUYS.
IS THERE NO WAY TO CATCH THIS THING?!
OH, WELL. I GUESS I'LL READ THE LETTER MY DAD INCLUDED.
NOW YOU THINK OF THAT?
MINERVA WAS RAISED IN A WEALTHY HOME AND REGARDED AS A CLEVER CHILD SINCE AN EARLY AGE. HOWEVER, SHE DIED LAST YEAR.
BUT SHE WAS UNABLE TO REST IN PEACE AND CONTINUES MAKING MISCHIEF.
I TOOK THE JOB AND CAPTURED HER. PLEASE EXORCISE HER FOR ME.
ALSO, IN CASE SHE GETS LOOSE IN THE HOUSE, THERE'S ONLY ONE WAY TO CATCH HER...

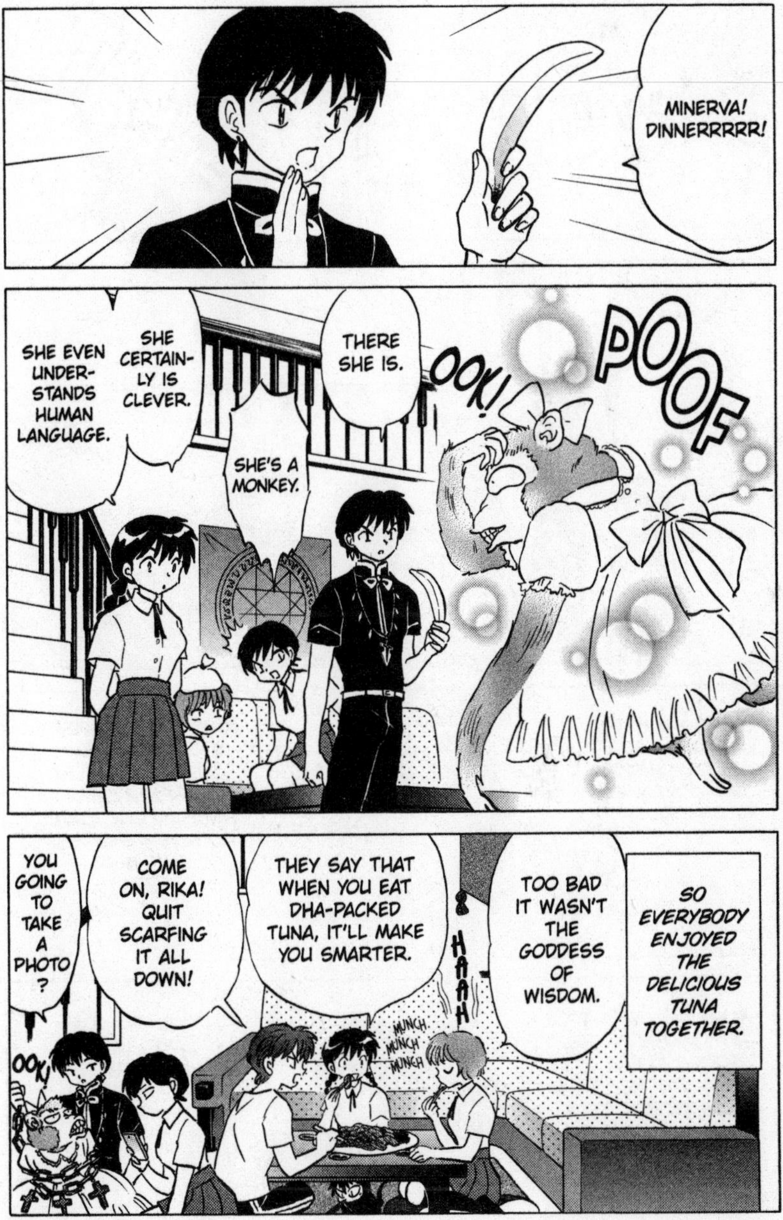
MINERVA! DINNERRRRR!
POOF
OOK!
THERE SHE IS.
SHE'S A MONKEY.
SHE CERTAIN-LY IS CLEVER.
SHE EVEN UNDER-STANDS HUMAN LANGUAGE.
SO EVERYBODY ENJOYED THE DELICIOUS TUNA TOGETHER.
TOO BAD IT WASN'T THE GODDESS OF WISDOM.
HAAAH
THEY SAY THAT WHEN YOU EAT DHA-PACKED TUNA, IT'LL MAKE YOU SMARTER.
MUNCH MUNCH MUNCH
COME ON, RIKA! QUIT SCARFING IT ALL DOWN!
YOU GOING TO TAKE A PHOTO?
OOK!

CHAPTER 290: THE BELL OF LOVE

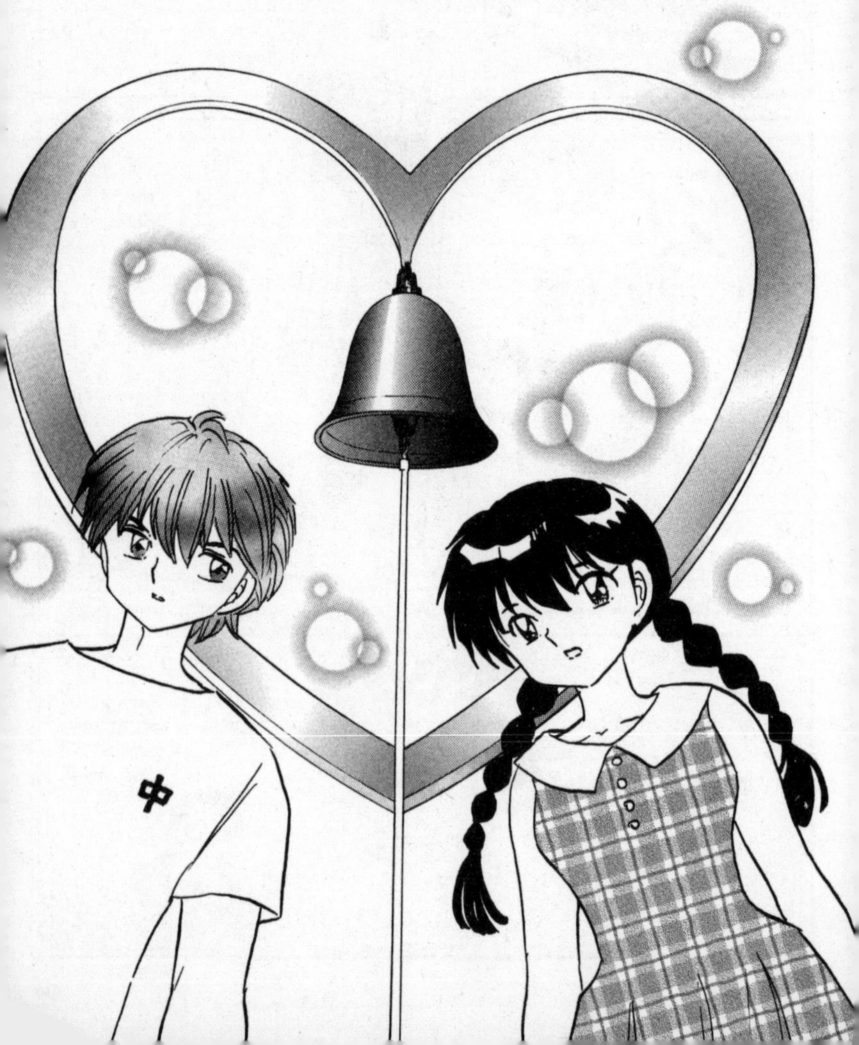
中

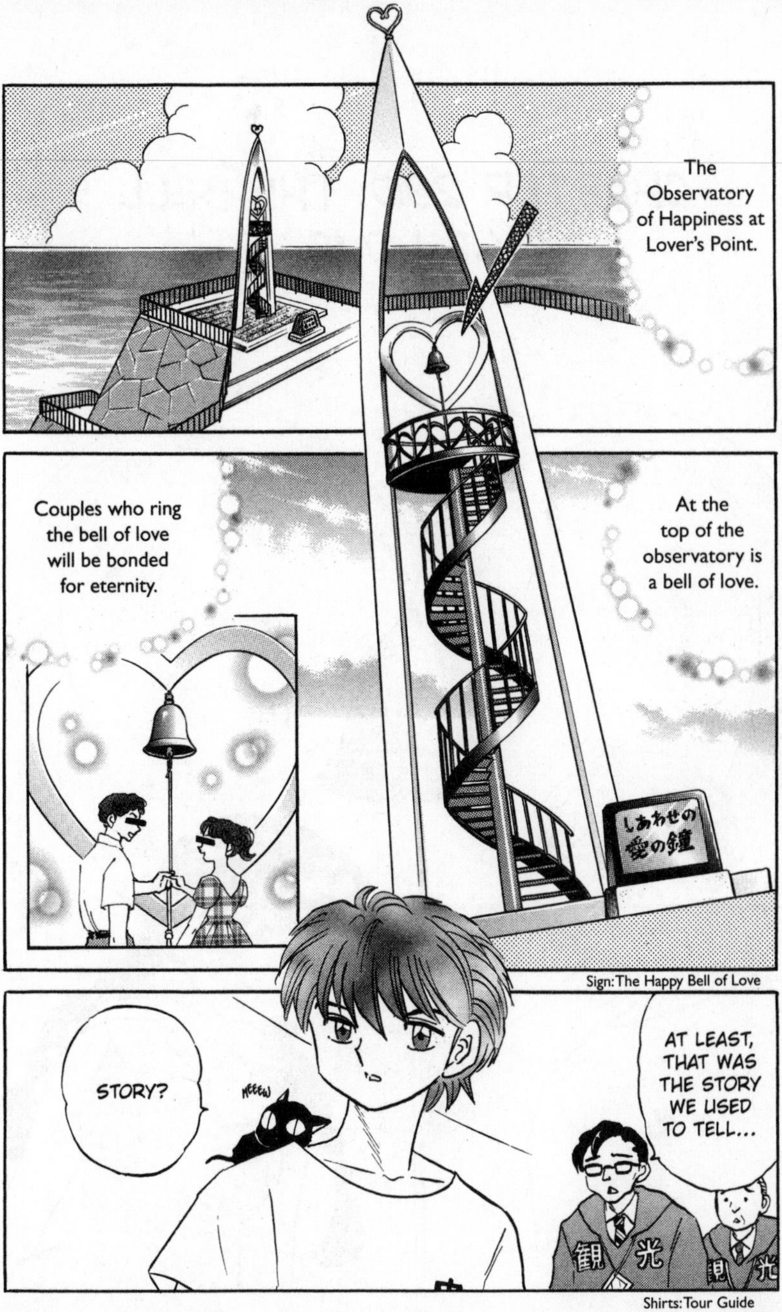
The Observatory of Happiness at Lover's Point.
At the top of the observatory is a bell of love.
Couples who ring the bell of love will be bonded for eternity.
しあわせの愛の鐘
AT LEAST, THAT WAS THE STORY WE USED TO TELL...
MEEEW
STORY?
観光
観光
Sign: The Happy Bell of Love

Shirts: Tour Guide

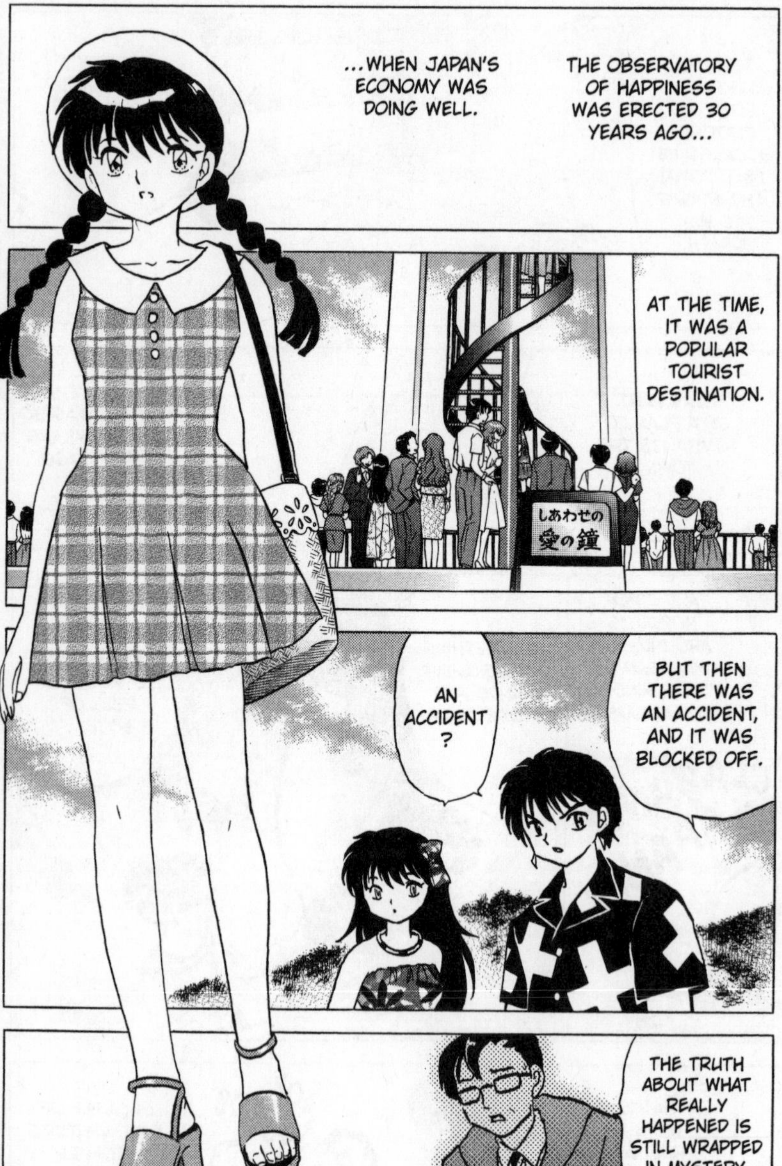
THE OBSERVATORY OF HAPPINESS WAS ERECTED 30 YEARS AGO...
...WHEN JAPAN'S ECONOMY WAS DOING WELL.
AT THE TIME, IT WAS A POPULAR TOURIST DESTINATION.
しあわせの
愛の鐘
BUT THEN THERE WAS AN ACCIDENT, AND IT WAS BLOCKED OFF.
AN ACCIDENT?
THE TRUTH ABOUT WHAT REALLY HAPPENED IS STILL WRAPPED IN MYSTERY, BUT...

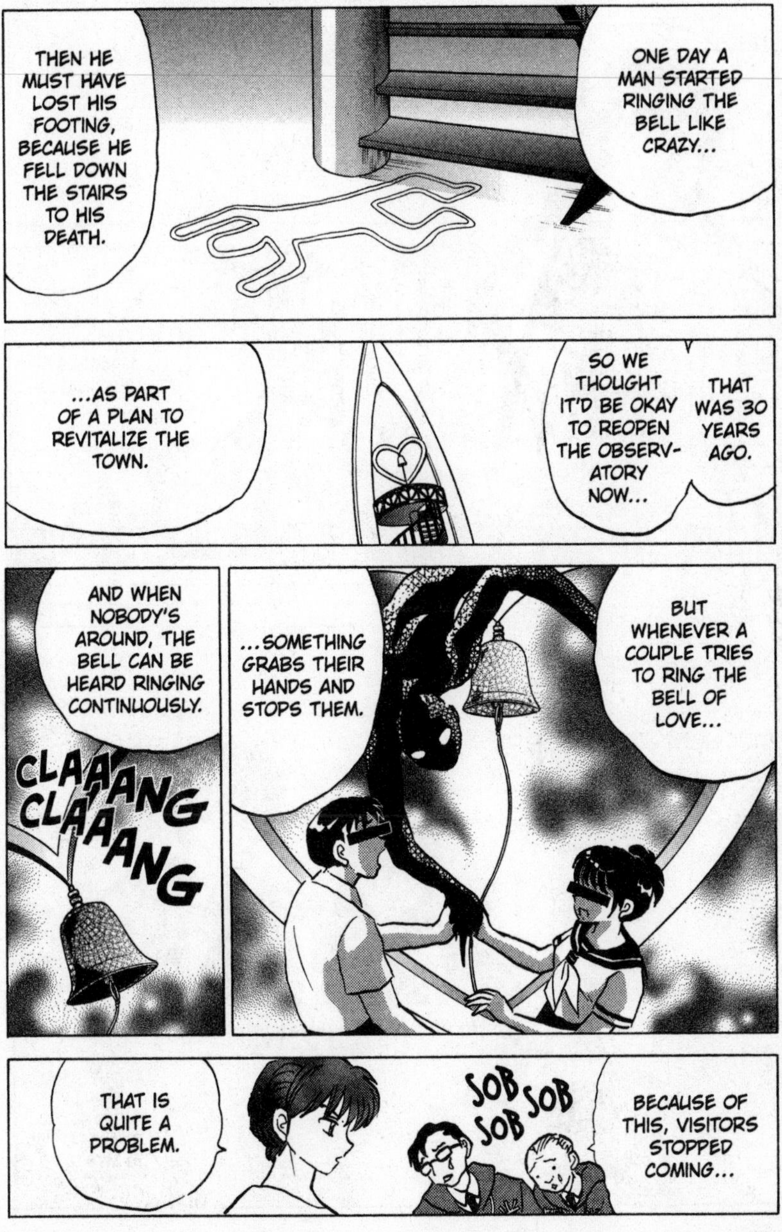
ONE DAY A MAN STARTED RINGING THE BELL LIKE CRAZY...
THEN HE MUST HAVE LOST HIS FOOTING, BECAUSE HE FELL DOWN THE STAIRS TO HIS DEATH.
THAT WAS 30 YEARS AGO.
SO WE THOUGHT IT'D BE OKAY TO REOPEN THE OBSERV-ATORY NOW...
...AS PART OF A PLAN TO REVITALIZE THE TOWN.
BUT WHENEVER A COUPLE TRIES TO RING THE BELL OF LOVE...
...SOMETHING GRABS THEIR HANDS AND STOPS THEM.
AND WHEN NOBODY'S AROUND, THE BELL CAN BE HEARD RINGING CONTINUOUSLY.
CLAAANG CLAAAANG
BECAUSE OF THIS, VISITORS STOPPED COMING...
SOB SOB SOB
THAT IS QUITE A PROBLEM.

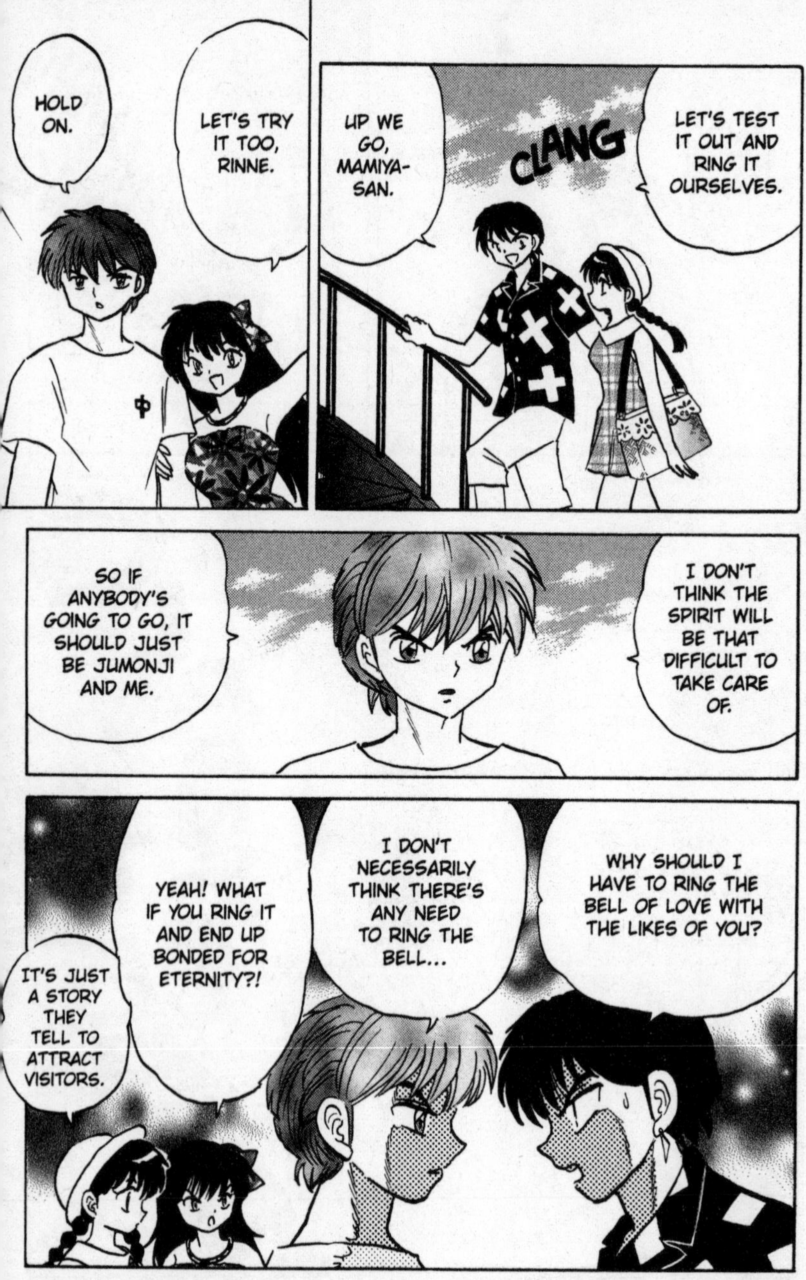
LET'S TEST IT OUT AND RING IT OURSELVES.
CLANG
UP WE GO, MAMIYA-SAN.
LET'S TRY IT TOO, RINNE.
HOLD ON.
I DON'T THINK THE SPIRIT WILL BE THAT DIFFICULT TO TAKE CARE OF.
SO IF ANYBODY'S GOING TO GO, IT SHOULD JUST BE JUMONJI AND ME.
WHY SHOULD I HAVE TO RING THE BELL OF LOVE WITH THE LIKES OF YOU?
I DON'T NECESSARILY THINK THERE'S ANY NEED TO RING THE BELL...
YEAH! WHAT IF YOU RING IT AND END UP BONDED FOR ETERNITY?!
IT'S JUST A STORY THEY TELL TO ATTRACT VISITORS.

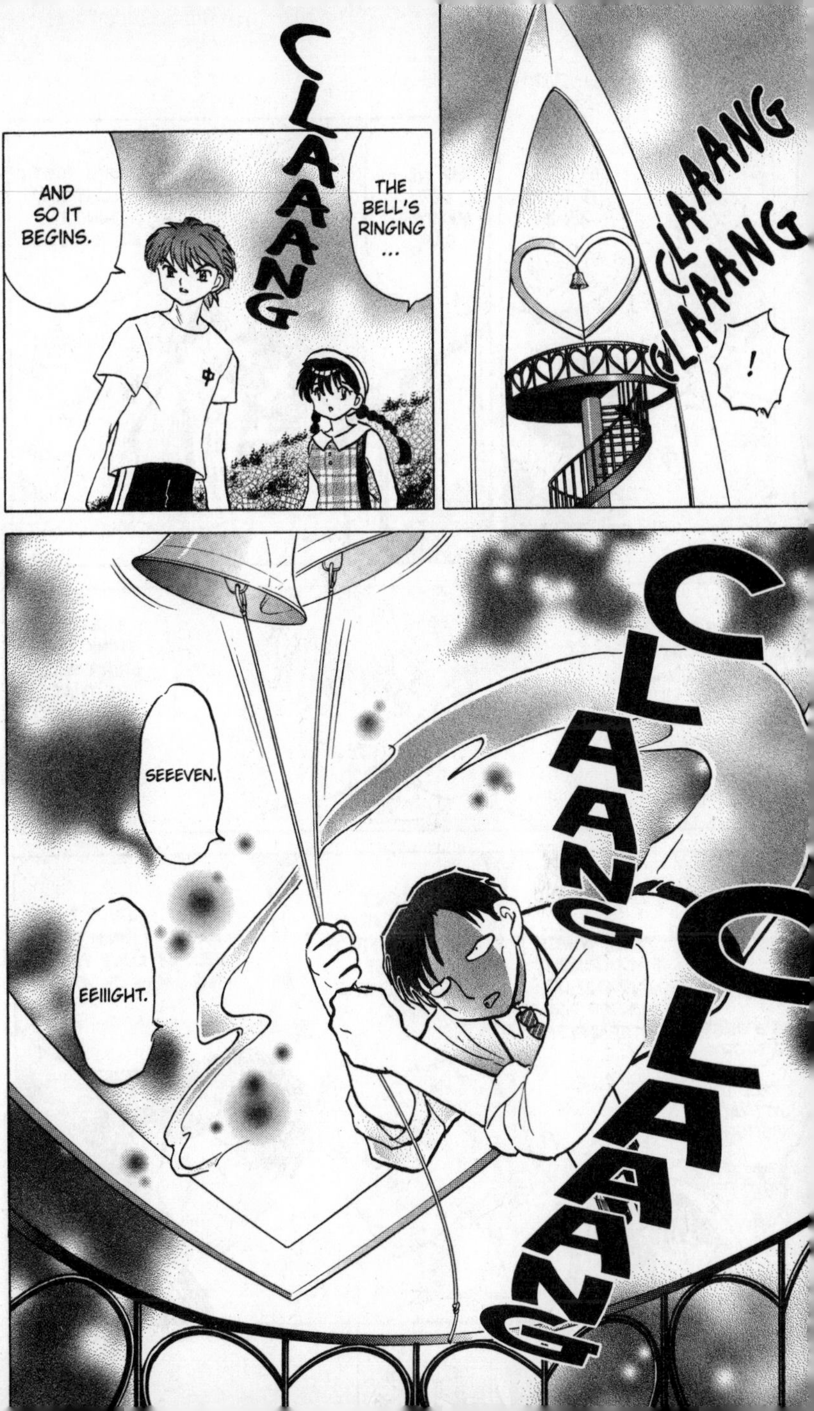
CLAAANG
CLAAANG
CLAAANG
!
CLAAANG
THE BELL'S RINGING...
AND SO IT BEGINS.
CLAAANG
CLAAANG
SEEEVEN.
EEIIIGHT.

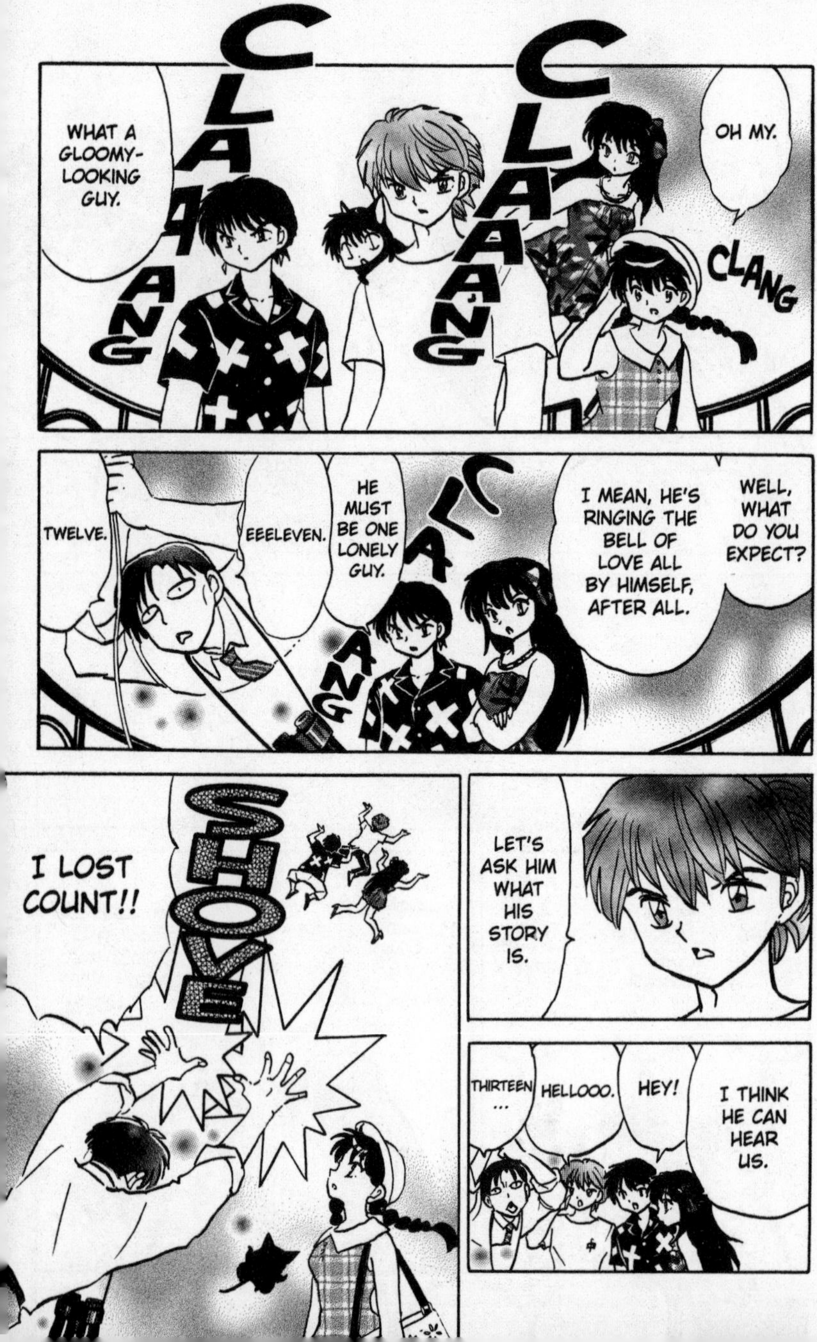
OH MY.
CLANG
CLAAANG
CLAAANG
WHAT A GLOOMY-LOOKING GUY.
WELL, WHAT DO YOU EXPECT?
I MEAN, HE'S RINGING THE BELL OF LOVE ALL BY HIMSELF, AFTER ALL.
CLAANG
HE MUST BE ONE LONELY GUY.
EEELEVEN.
TWELVE.
LET'S ASK HIM WHAT HIS STORY IS.
I THINK HE CAN HEAR US.
HEY!
HELLOOO.
THIRTEEN...
SHOVE
I LOST COUNT!!

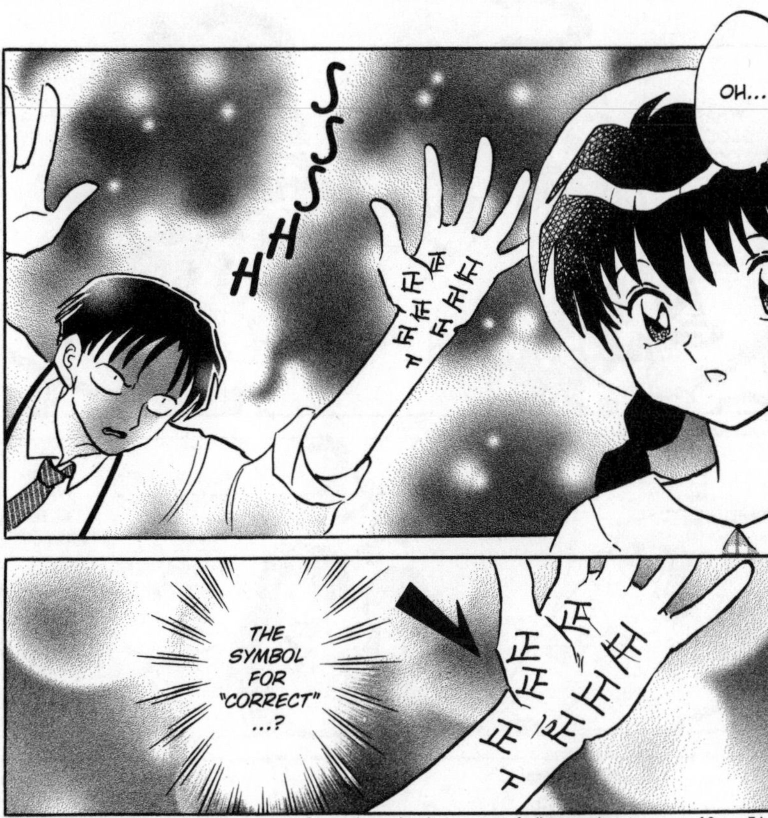
OH...
SSSHHH
THE SYMBOL FOR "CORRECT" ...?

The Japanese symbol for "correct" is written in five strokes and is also a system of tallying numbers in groups of five.—Ed.

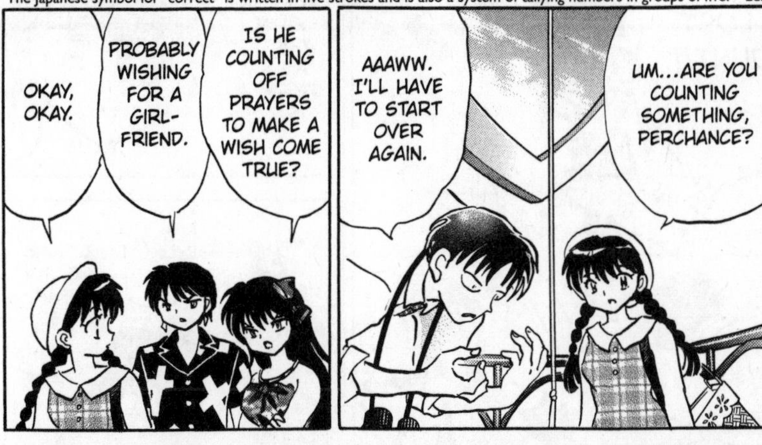
UM...ARE YOU COUNTING SOMETHING, PERCHANCE?
AAAWW. I'LL HAVE TO START OVER AGAIN.
IS HE COUNTING OFF PRAYERS TO MAKE A WISH COME TRUE?
PROBABLY WISHING FOR A GIRL-FRIEND.
OKAY, OKAY.

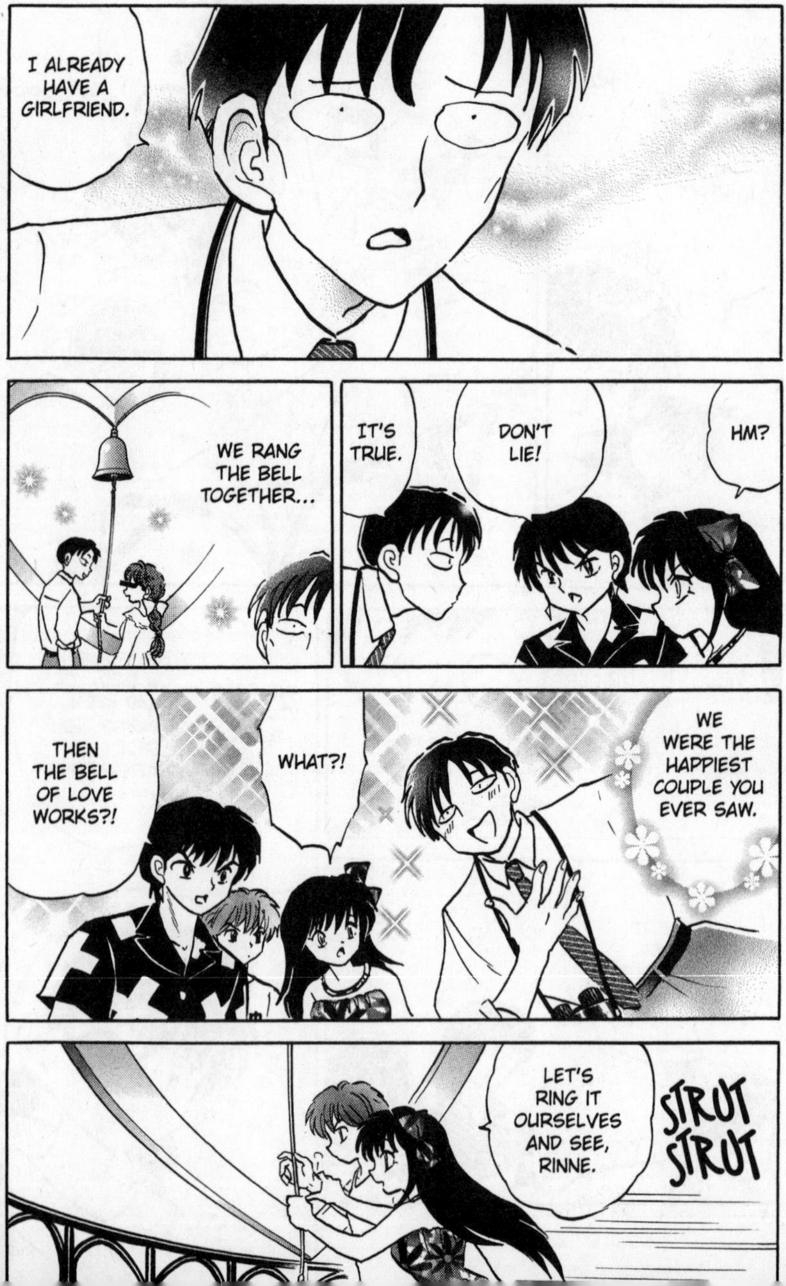
I ALREADY HAVE A GIRLFRIEND.
HM?
DON'T LIE!
IT'S TRUE.
WE RANG THE BELL TOGETHER...
WE WERE THE HAPPIEST COUPLE YOU EVER SAW.
WHAT?!
THEN THE BELL OF LOVE WORKS?!
STRUT STRUT
LET'S RING IT OURSELVES AND SEE, RINNE.

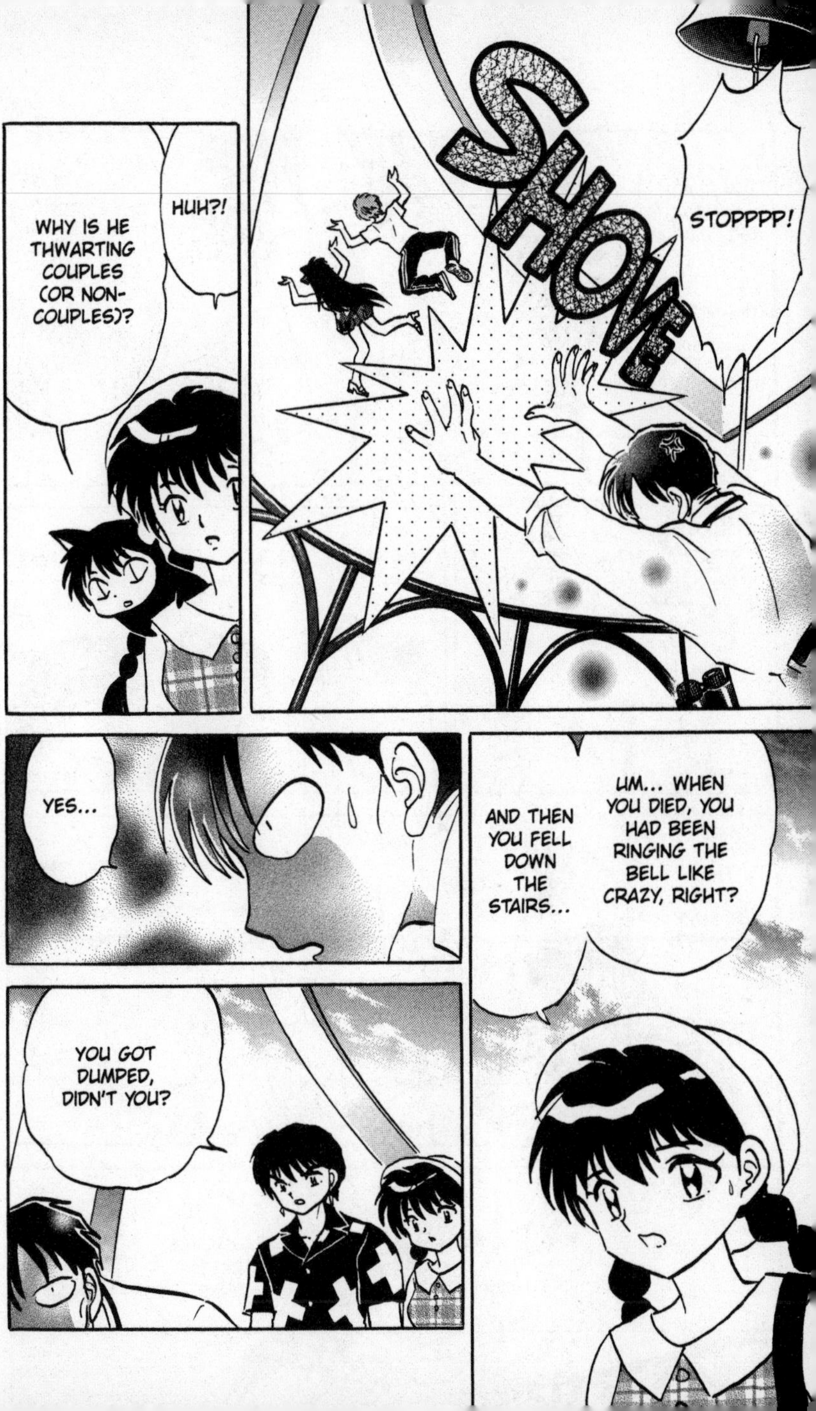
STOPPPP!
SHOVE
HUH?!
WHY IS HE THWARTING COUPLES (OR NON-COUPLES)?
UM... WHEN YOU DIED, YOU HAD BEEN RINGING THE BELL LIKE CRAZY, RIGHT?
AND THEN YOU FELL DOWN THE STAIRS...
YES...
YOU GOT DUMPED, DIDN'T YOU?

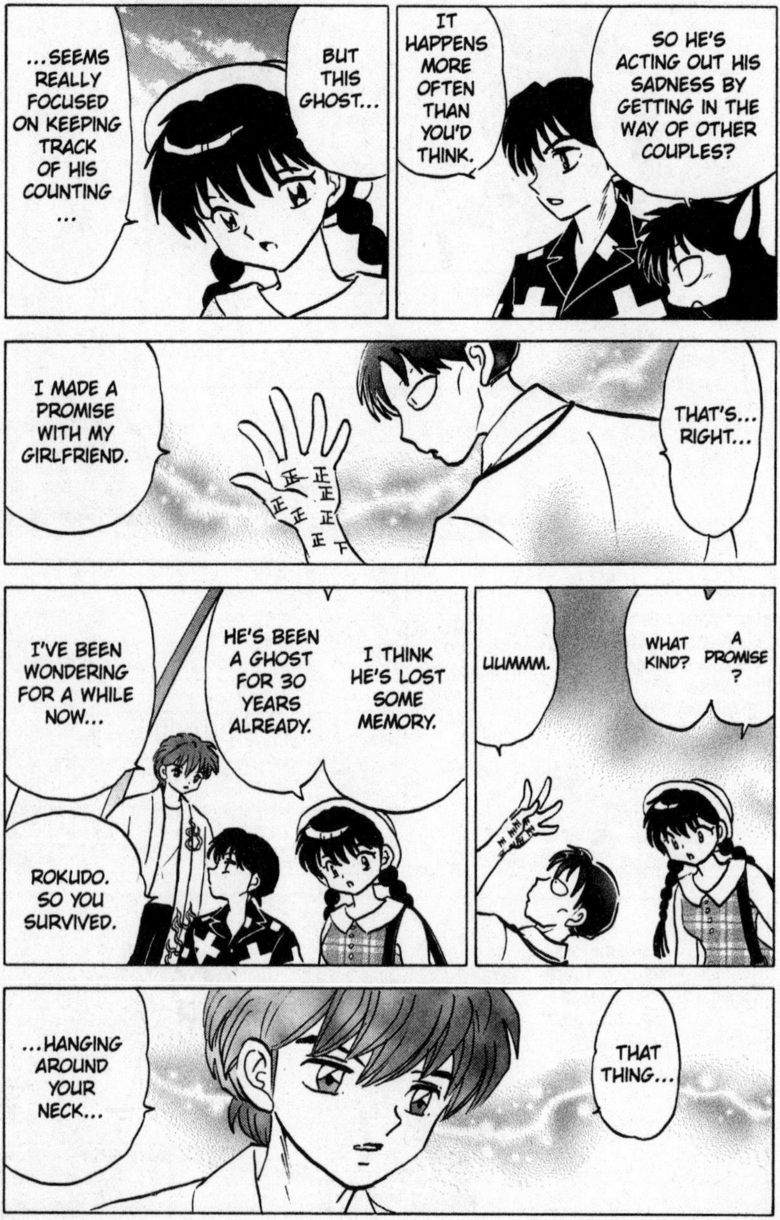
SO HE'S ACTING OUT HIS SADNESS BY GETTING IN THE WAY OF OTHER COUPLES?
IT HAPPENS MORE OFTEN THAN YOU'D THINK.
BUT THIS GHOST...
...SEEMS REALLY FOCUSED ON KEEPING TRACK OF HIS COUNTING ...
THAT'S... RIGHT...
I MADE A PROMISE WITH MY GIRLFRIEND.
A PROMISE?
WHAT KIND?
UUMMM.
HE'S BEEN A GHOST FOR 30 YEARS ALREADY.
I THINK HE'S LOST SOME MEMORY.
ROKUDO. SO YOU SURVIVED.
I'VE BEEN WONDERING FOR A WHILE NOW...
THAT THING...
...HANGING AROUND YOUR NECK...

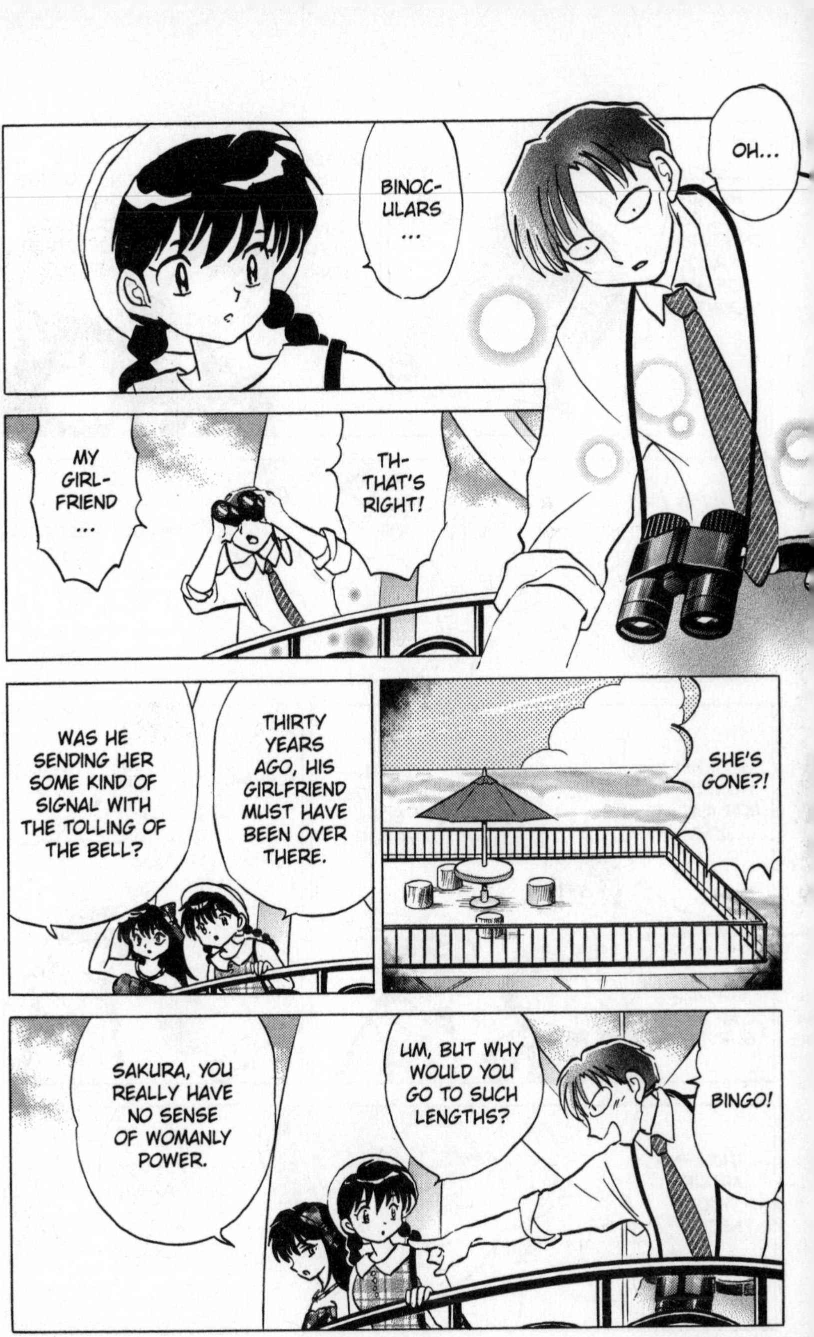
OH...
BINOC-ULARS ...
TH-THAT'S RIGHT!
MY GIRL-FRIEND ...
SHE'S GONE?!
THIRTY YEARS AGO, HIS GIRLFRIEND MUST HAVE BEEN OVER THERE.
WAS HE SENDING HER SOME KIND OF SIGNAL WITH THE TOLLING OF THE BELL?
BINGO!
UM, BUT WHY WOULD YOU GO TO SUCH LENGTHS?
SAKURA, YOU REALLY HAVE NO SENSE OF WOMANLY POWER.

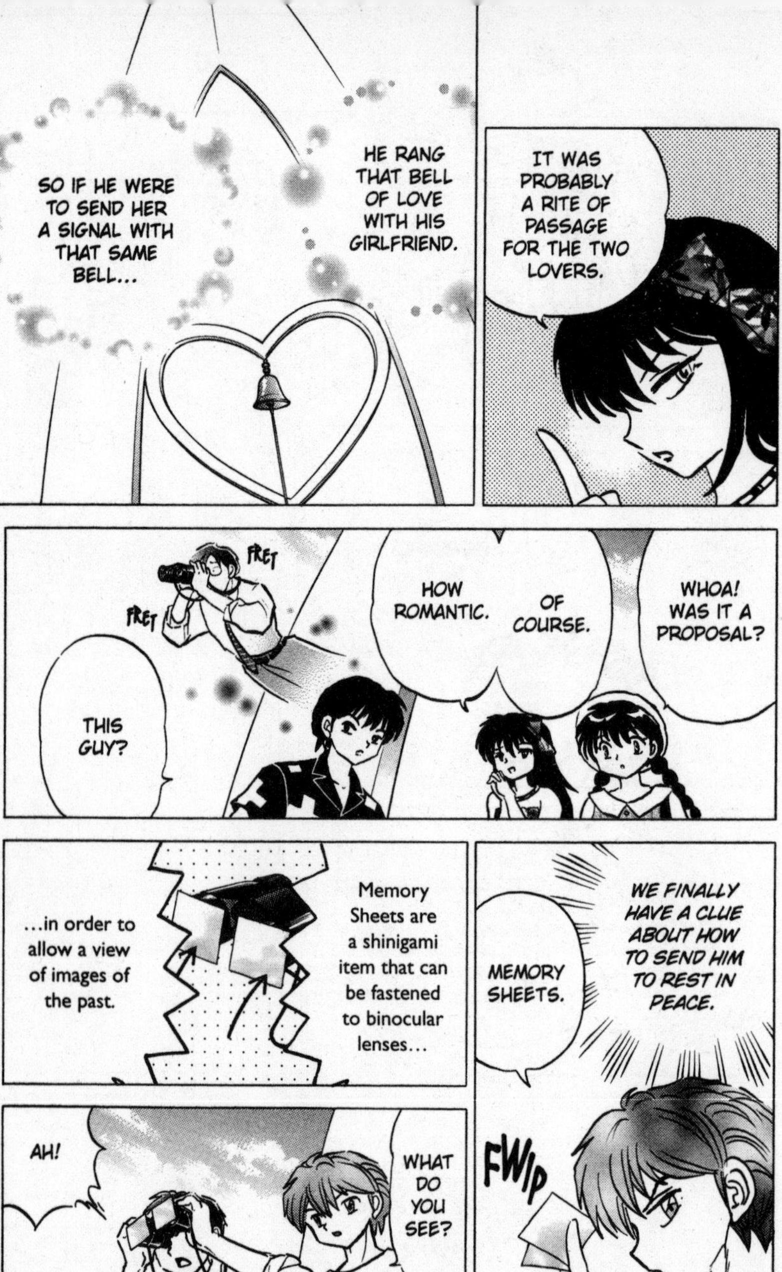
IT WAS PROBABLY A RITE OF PASSAGE FOR THE TWO LOVERS.
HE RANG THAT BELL OF LOVE WITH HIS GIRLFRIEND.
SO IF HE WERE TO SEND HER A SIGNAL WITH THAT SAME BELL...
WHOA! WAS IT A PROPOSAL?
OF COURSE.
HOW ROMANTIC.
FRET
FRET
THIS GUY?
WE FINALLY HAVE A CLUE ABOUT HOW TO SEND HIM TO REST IN PEACE.
MEMORY SHEETS.
FWIP
Memory Sheets are a shinigami item that can be fastened to binocular lenses...
...in order to allow a view of images of the past.
WHAT DO YOU SEE?
AH!

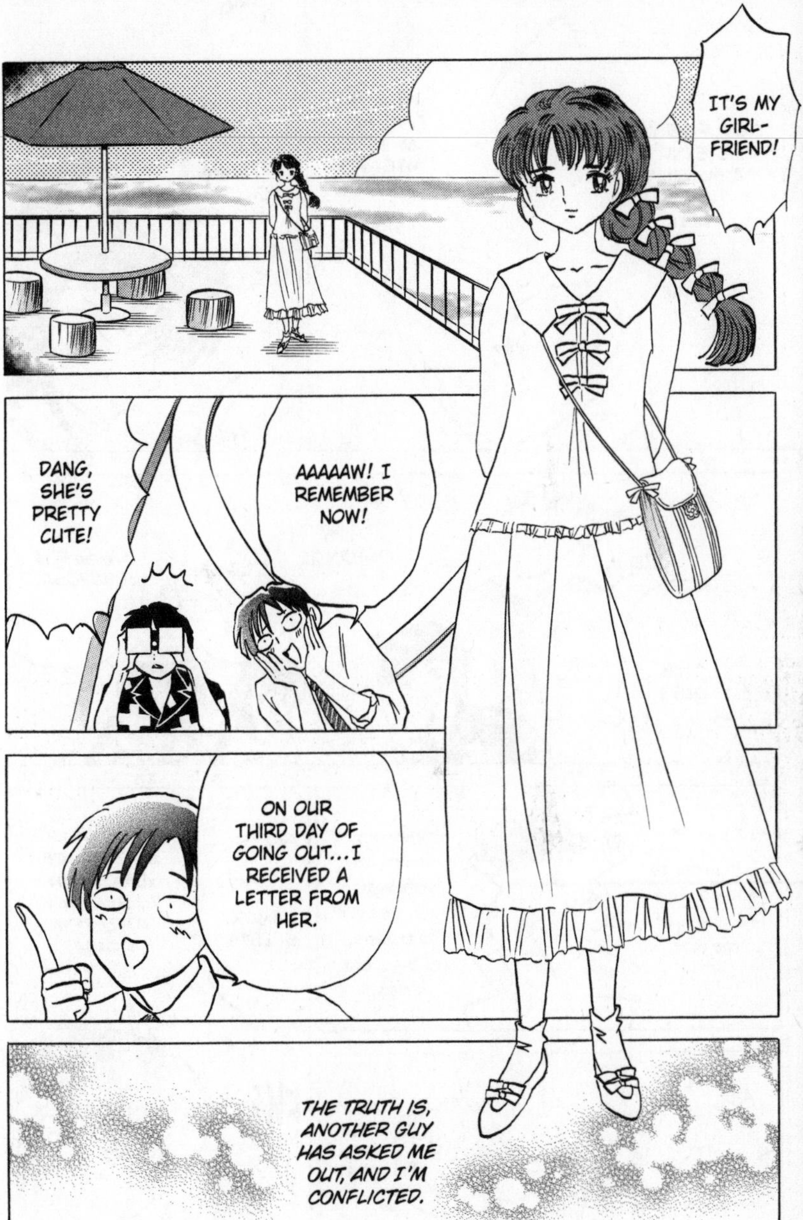
IT'S MY GIRL-FRIEND!
AAAAAW! I REMEMBER NOW!
DANG, SHE'S PRETTY CUTE!
ON OUR THIRD DAY OF GOING OUT...I RECEIVED A LETTER FROM HER.
THE TRUTH IS, ANOTHER GUY HAS ASKED ME OUT, AND I'M CONFLICTED.

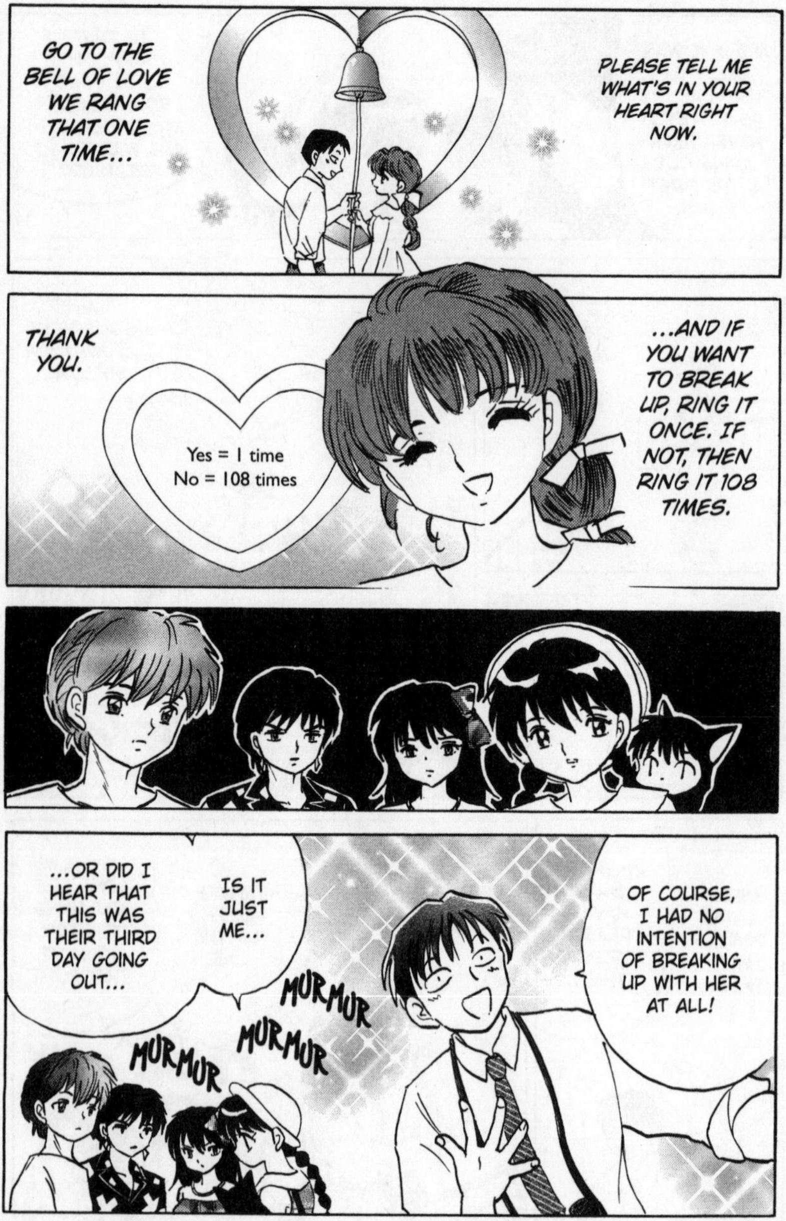
PLEASE TELL ME WHAT'S IN YOUR HEART RIGHT NOW.
GO TO THE BELL OF LOVE WE RANG THAT ONE TIME...
...AND IF YOU WANT TO BREAK UP, RING IT ONCE. IF NOT, THEN RING IT 108 TIMES.
Yes = 1 time
No = 108 times
THANK YOU.
OF COURSE, I HAD NO INTENTION OF BREAKING UP WITH HER AT ALL!
IS IT JUST ME...
...OR DID I HEAR THAT THIS WAS THEIR THIRD DAY GOING OUT...
MURMUR
MURMUR
MURMUR

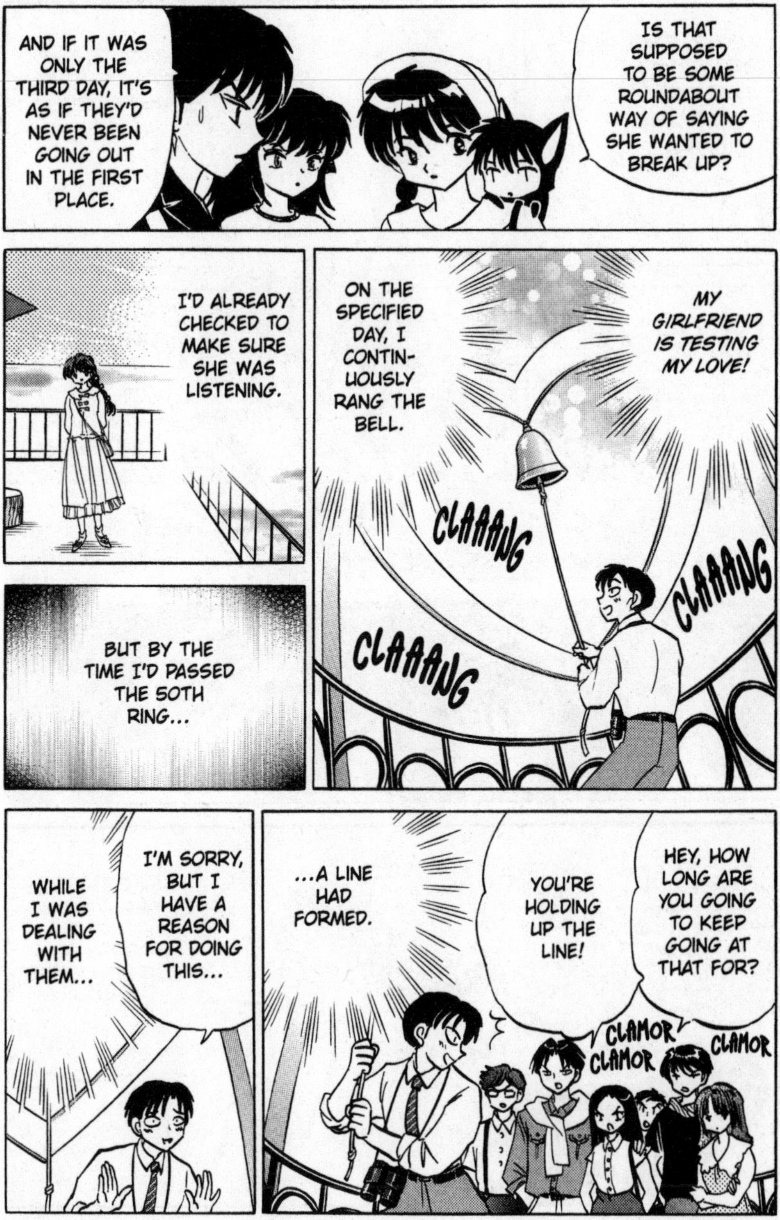
IS THAT SUPPOSED TO BE SOME ROUNDABOUT WAY OF SAYING SHE WANTED TO BREAK UP?
AND IF IT WAS ONLY THE THIRD DAY, IT'S AS IF THEY'D NEVER BEEN GOING OUT IN THE FIRST PLACE.
MY GIRLFRIEND IS TESTING MY LOVE!
ON THE SPECIFIED DAY, I CONTIN-UOUSLY RANG THE BELL.
CLAAANG
CLAAANG
CLAAANG
I'D ALREADY CHECKED TO MAKE SURE SHE WAS LISTENING.
BUT BY THE TIME I'D PASSED THE 50TH RING...
HEY, HOW LONG ARE YOU GOING TO KEEP GOING AT THAT FOR?
YOU'RE HOLDING UP THE LINE!
CLAMOR
CLAMOR CLAMOR
...A LINE HAD FORMED.
I'M SORRY, BUT I HAVE A REASON FOR DOING THIS...
WHILE I WAS DEALING WITH THEM...

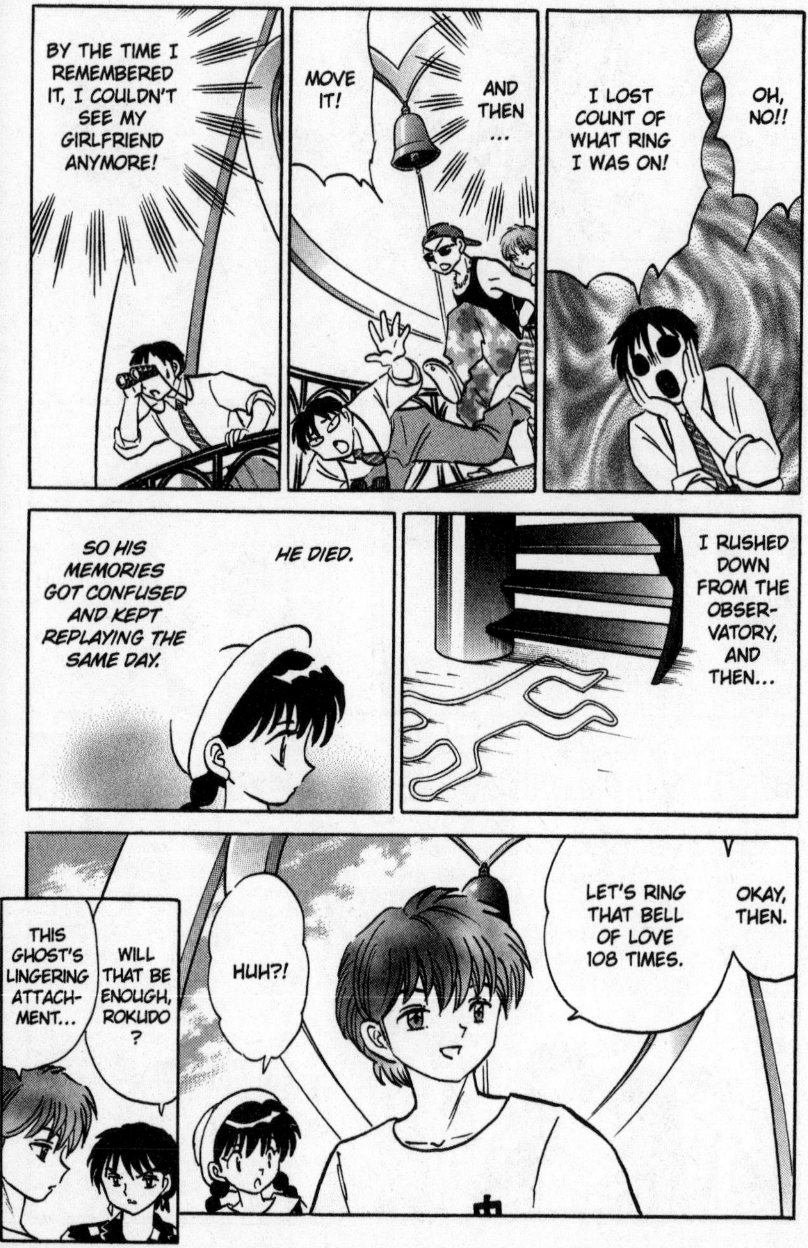
OH, NO!!
I LOST COUNT OF WHAT RING I WAS ON!
AND THEN...
MOVE IT!
BY THE TIME I REMEMBERED IT, I COULDN'T SEE MY GIRLFRIEND ANYMORE!
I RUSHED DOWN FROM THE OBSERVATORY, AND THEN...
HE DIED.
SO HIS MEMORIES GOT CONFUSED AND KEPT REPLAYING THE SAME DAY.
OKAY, THEN.
LET'S RING THAT BELL OF LOVE 108 TIMES.
HUH?!
WILL THAT BE ENOUGH, ROKUDO?
THIS GHOST'S LINGERING ATTACHMENT...

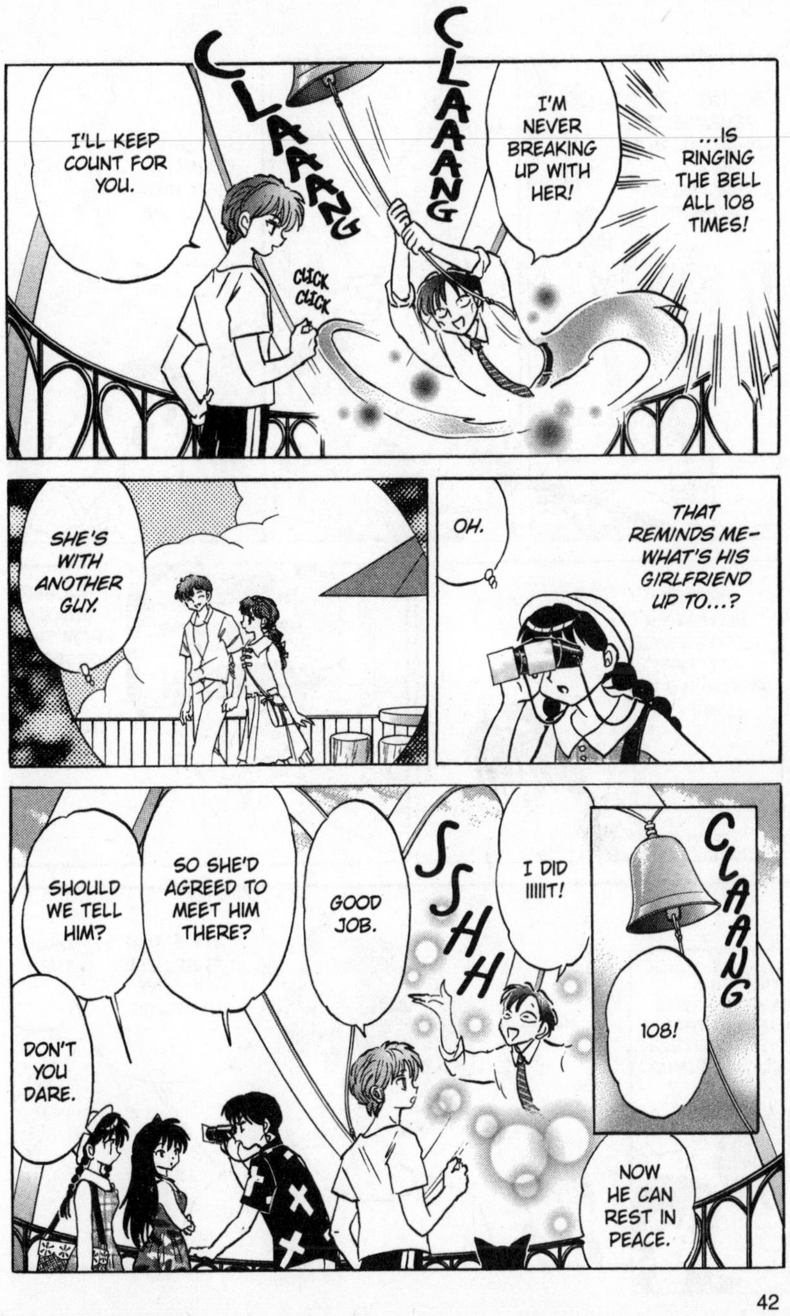
...IS RINGING THE BELL ALL 108 TIMES!
I'M NEVER BREAKING UP WITH HER!
CLAAANG
CLAAANG
I'LL KEEP COUNT FOR YOU.
CLICK CLICK
THAT REMINDS ME- WHAT'S HIS GIRLFRIEND UP TO...?
OH.
SHE'S WITH ANOTHER GUY.
CLAANG
108!
NOW HE CAN REST IN PEACE.
I DID IIIIIT!
SSHH
GOOD JOB.
SO SHE'D AGREED TO MEET HIM THERE?
SHOULD WE TELL HIM?
DON'T YOU DARE.

CHAPTER 291: SHORTCUT

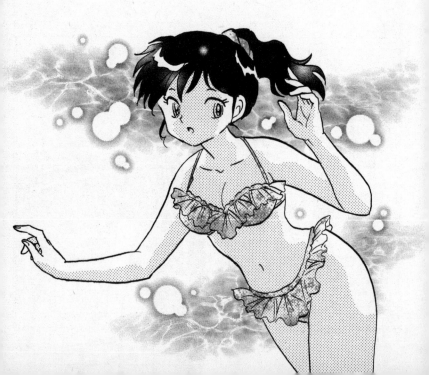

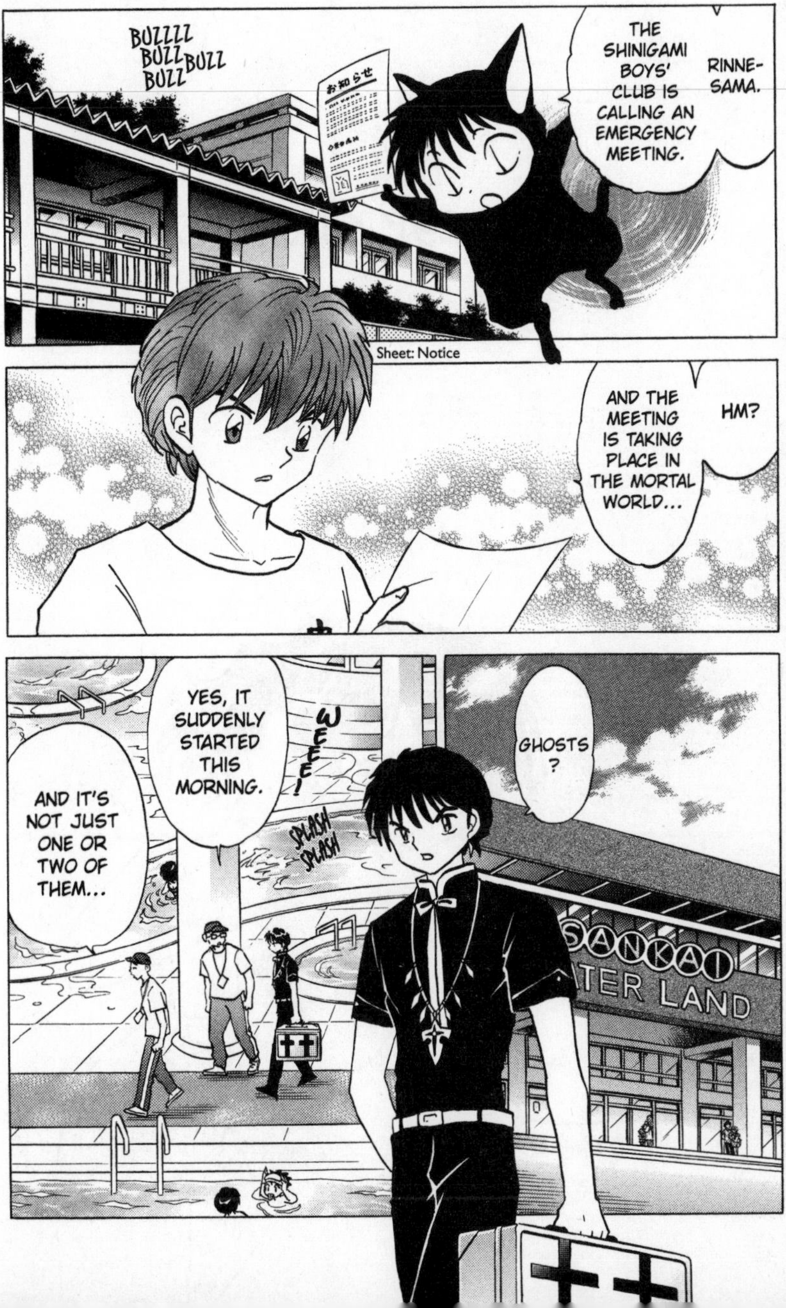
RINNE-SAMA.
THE SHINIGAMI BOYS' CLUB IS CALLING AN EMERGENCY MEETING.
お知らせ
BUZZZZ BUZZ BUZZ BUZZ
Sheet: Notice
HM?
AND THE MEETING IS TAKING PLACE IN THE MORTAL WORLD...
GHOSTS?
SANKAI
TER LAND
YES, IT SUDDENLY STARTED THIS MORNING.
WEEE!
SPLASH SPLASH
AND IT'S NOT JUST ONE OR TWO OF THEM...

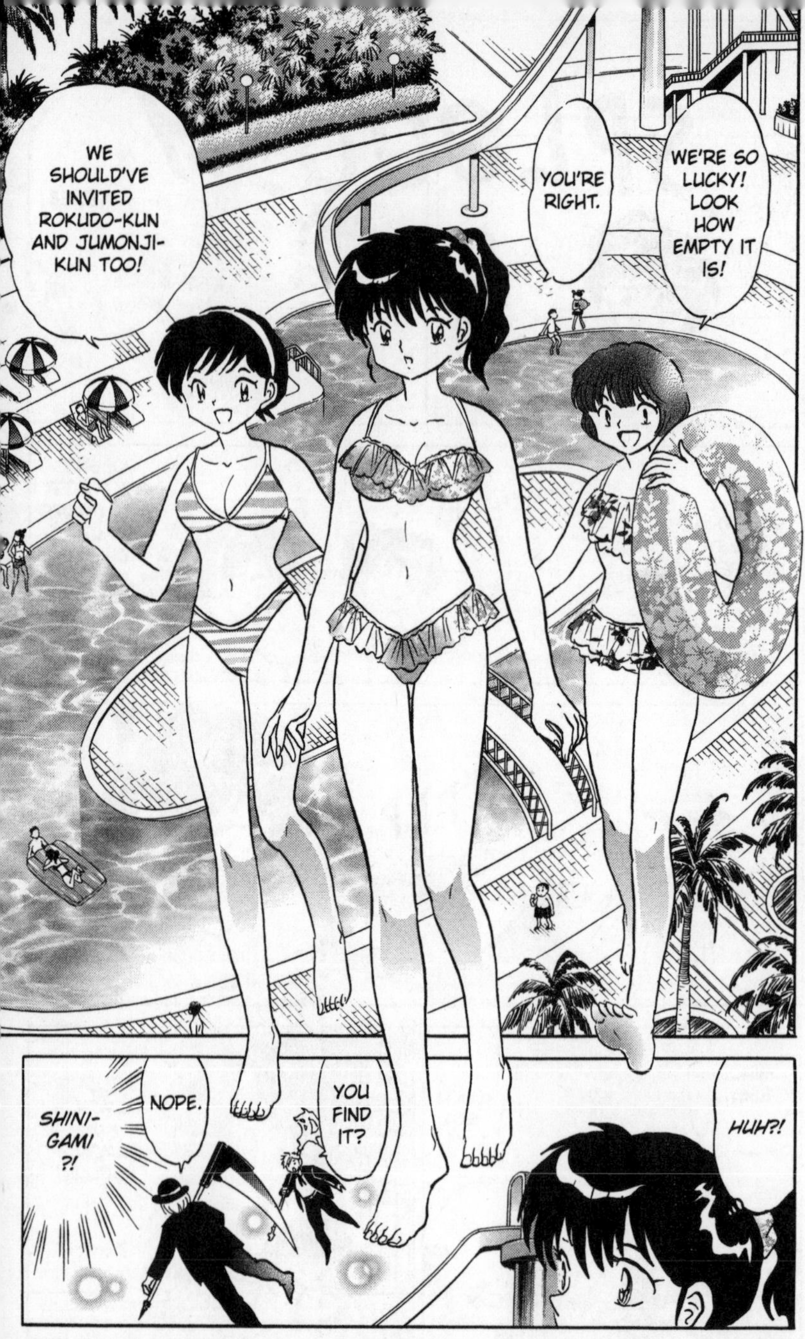
WE'RE SO LUCKY! LOOK HOW EMPTY IT IS!
YOU'RE RIGHT.
WE SHOULD'VE INVITED ROKUDO-KUN AND JUMONJI-KUN TOO!
HUH?!
YOU FIND IT?
NOPE.
SHINI-GAMI ?!

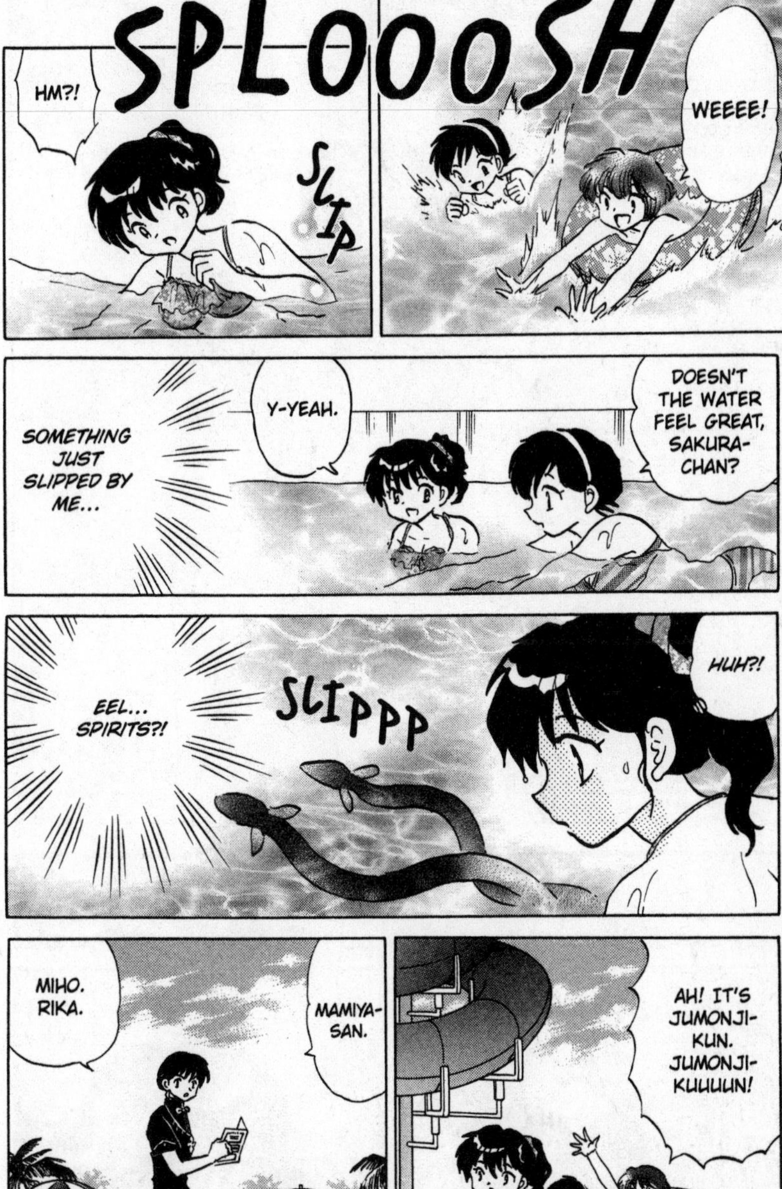
SPLOOOSH
WEEEE!
HM?!
SLIP
DOESN'T THE WATER FEEL GREAT, SAKURA-CHAN?
Y-YEAH.
SOMETHING JUST SLIPPED BY ME...
HUH?!
SLIPPP
EEL... SPIRITS?!
AH! IT'S JUMONJI-KUN. JUMONJI-KUUUUN!
MAMIYA-SAN.
MIHO. RIKA.

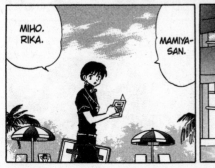

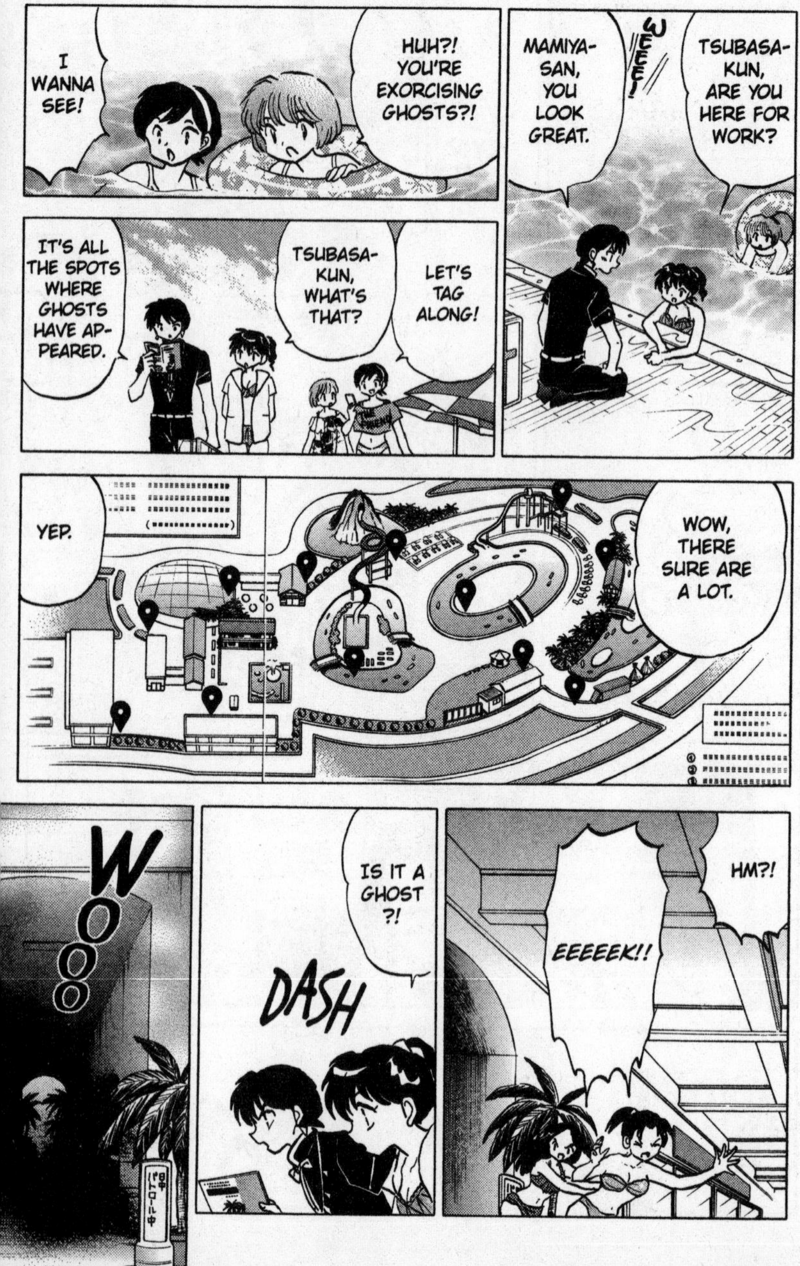
TSUBASA-KUN, ARE YOU HERE FOR WORK?
WEEE!
MAMIYA-SAN, YOU LOOK GREAT.
HUH?! YOU'RE EXORCISING GHOSTS?!
I WANNA SEE!
LET'S TAG ALONG!
TSUBASA-KUN, WHAT'S THAT?
IT'S ALL THE SPOTS WHERE GHOSTS HAVE APPEARED.
WOW, THERE SURE ARE A LOT.
YEP.
HM?!
EEEEEK!!
IS IT A GHOST?!
DASH
WOOO
パトロール中

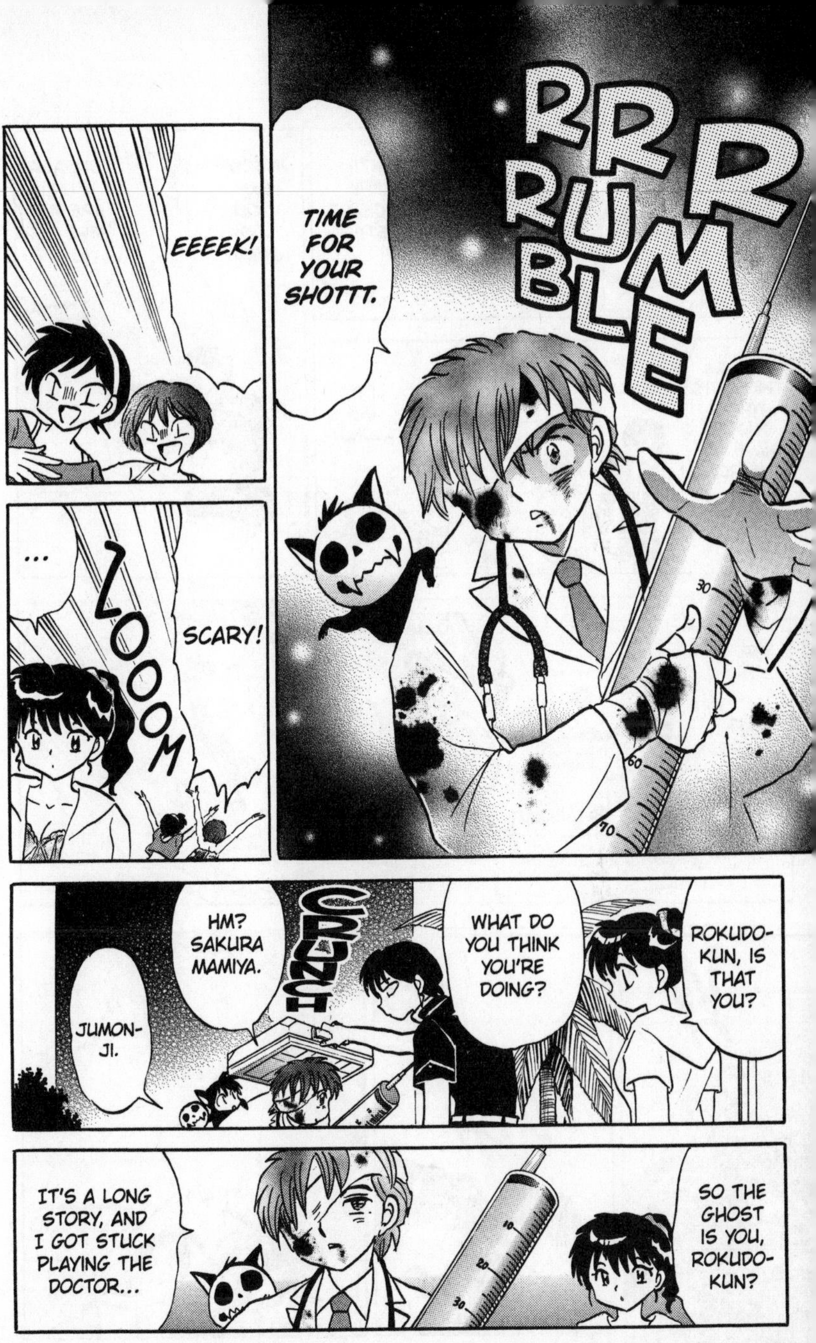
RRR RUMBLE
TIME FOR YOUR SHOTTT.
EEEEK!
SCARY!
ZOOOOM
...
ROKUDO-KUN, IS THAT YOU?
WHAT DO YOU THINK YOU'RE DOING?
CRUNCH
HM? SAKURA MAMIYA.
JUMON-JI.
SO THE GHOST IS YOU, ROKUDO-KUN?
IT'S A LONG STORY, AND I GOT STUCK PLAYING THE DOCTOR...

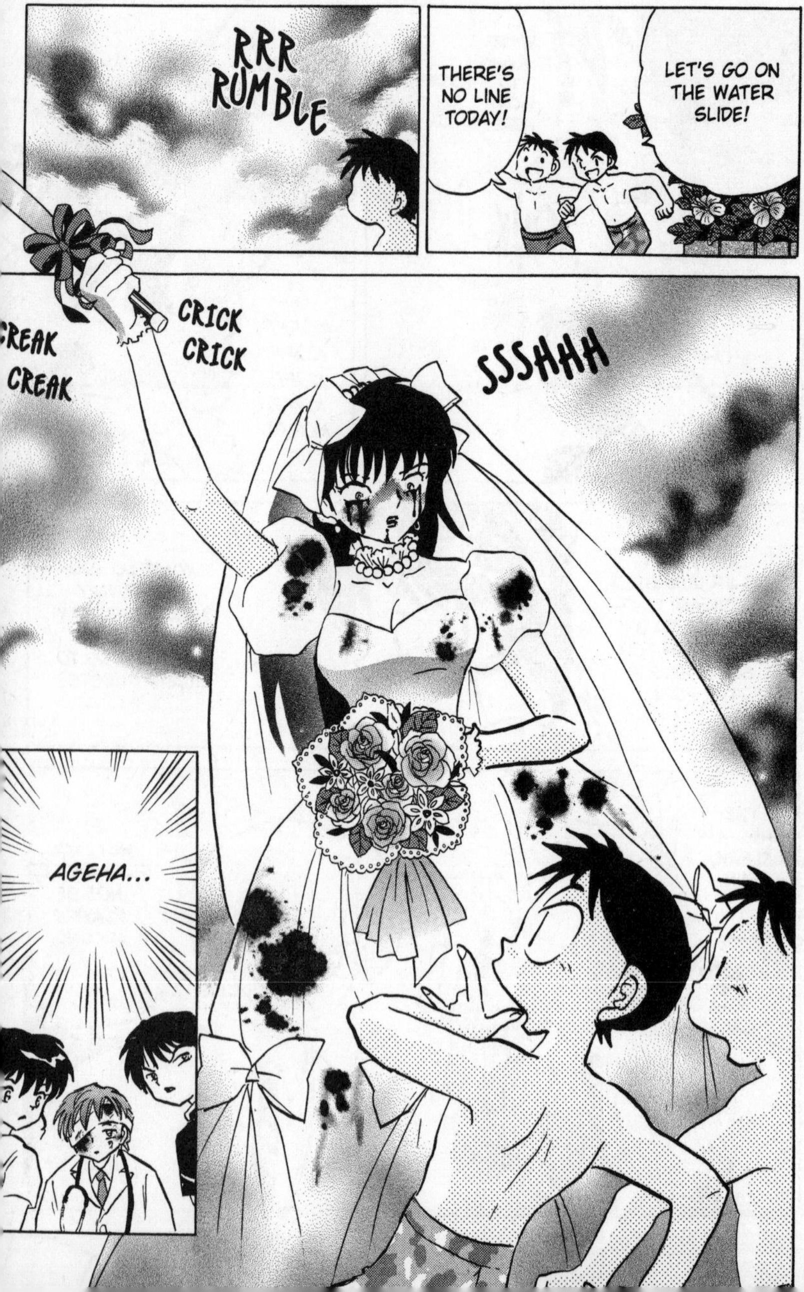
LET'S GO ON THE WATER SLIDE!
THERE'S NO LINE TODAY!
RRR RUMBLE
SSSHHH
CRICK CRICK
CREAK CREAK
AGEHA...

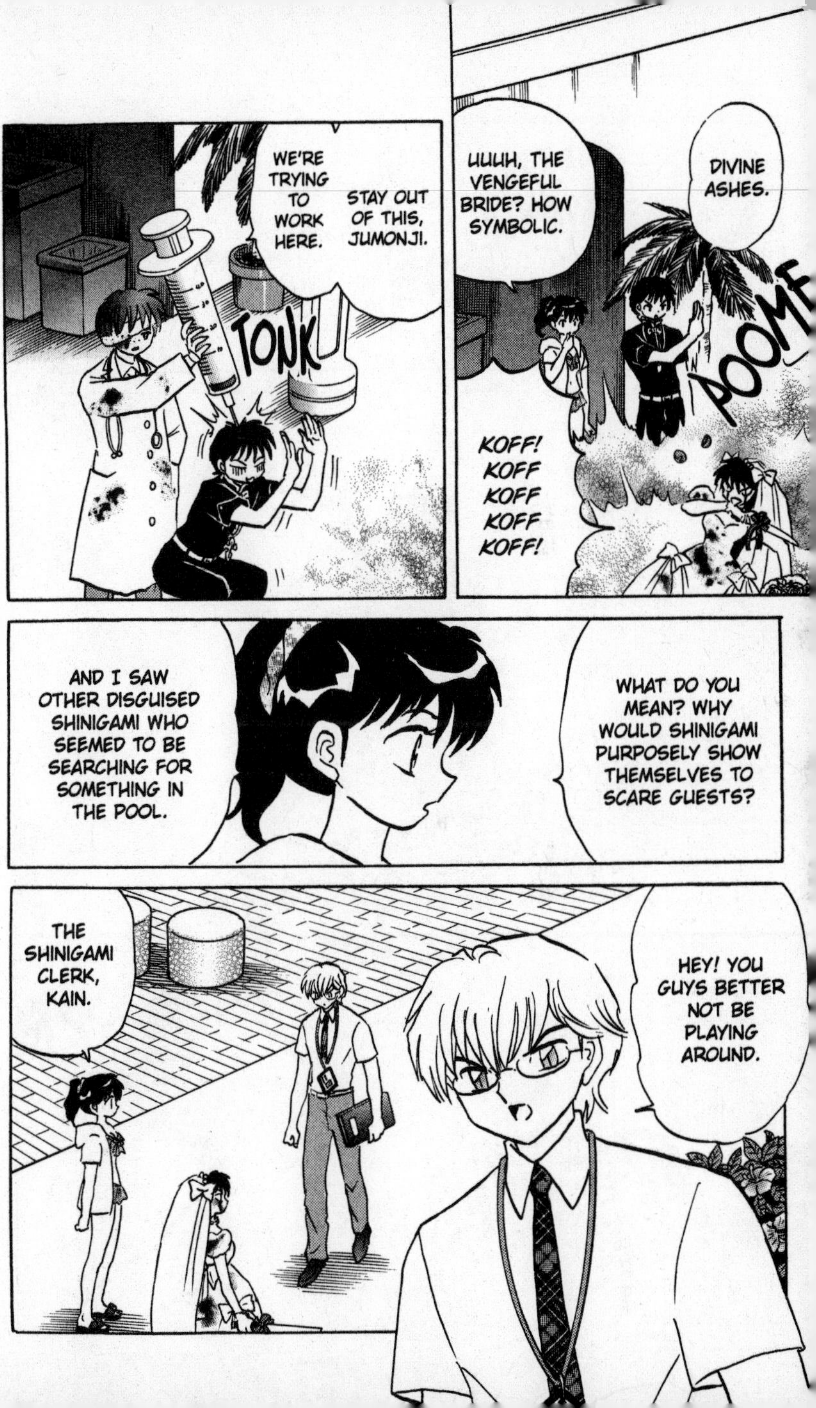
DIVINE ASHES.
UUUH, THE VENGEFUL BRIDE? HOW SYMBOLIC.
POOMF
KOFF! KOFF KOFF KOFF KOFF!
WE'RE TRYING TO WORK HERE.
STAY OUT OF THIS, JUMONJI.
TONK
WHAT DO YOU MEAN? WHY WOULD SHINIGAMI PURPOSELY SHOW THEMSELVES TO SCARE GUESTS?
AND I SAW OTHER DISGUISED SHINIGAMI WHO SEEMED TO BE SEARCHING FOR SOMETHING IN THE POOL.
HEY! YOU GUYS BETTER NOT BE PLAYING AROUND.
THE SHINIGAMI CLERK, KAIN.

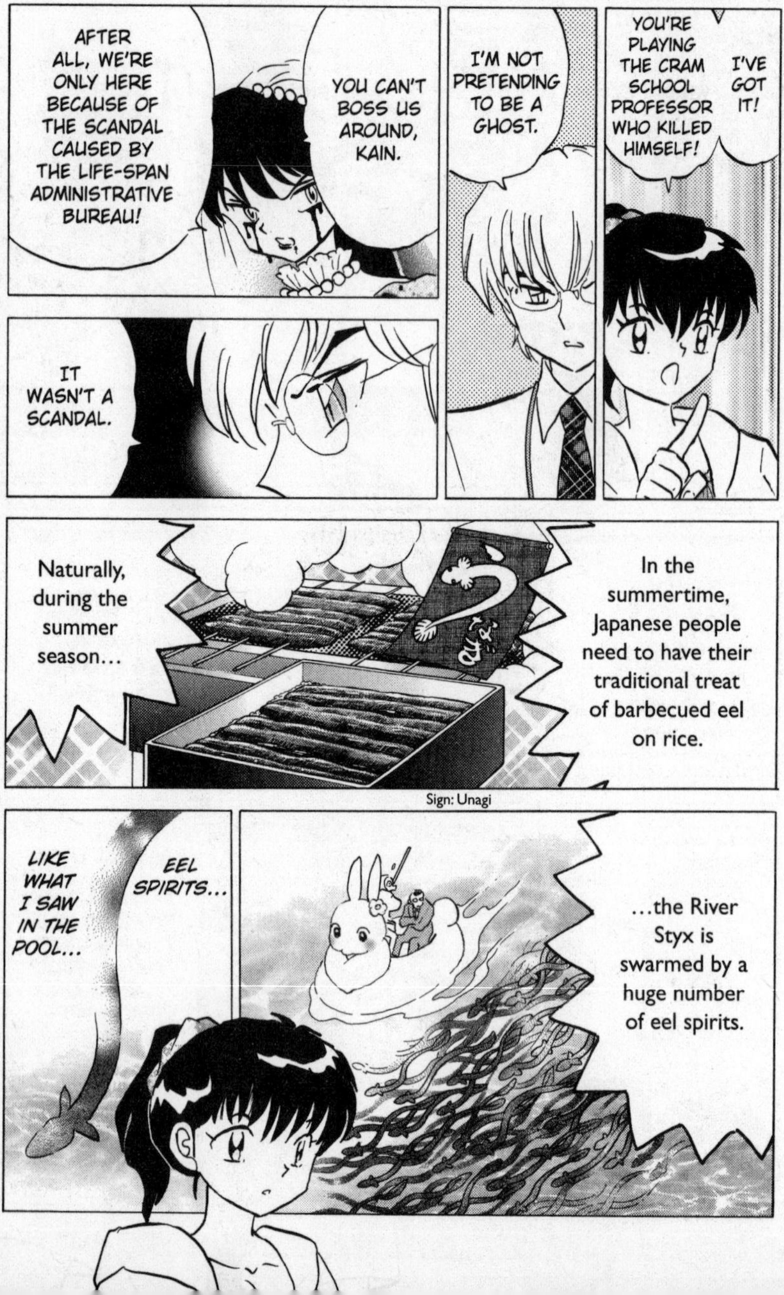
I'VE GOT IT!
YOU'RE PLAYING THE CRAM SCHOOL PROFESSOR WHO KILLED HIMSELF!
I'M NOT PRETENDING TO BE A GHOST.
YOU CAN'T BOSS US AROUND, KAIN.
AFTER ALL, WE'RE ONLY HERE BECAUSE OF THE SCANDAL CAUSED BY THE LIFE-SPAN ADMINISTRATIVE BUREAU!
IT WASN'T A SCANDAL.
In the summertime, Japanese people need to have their traditional treat of barbecued eel on rice.
Naturally, during the summer season…
Sign: Unagi
…the River Styx is swarmed by a huge number of eel spirits.
EEL SPIRITS…
LIKE WHAT I SAW IN THE POOL…

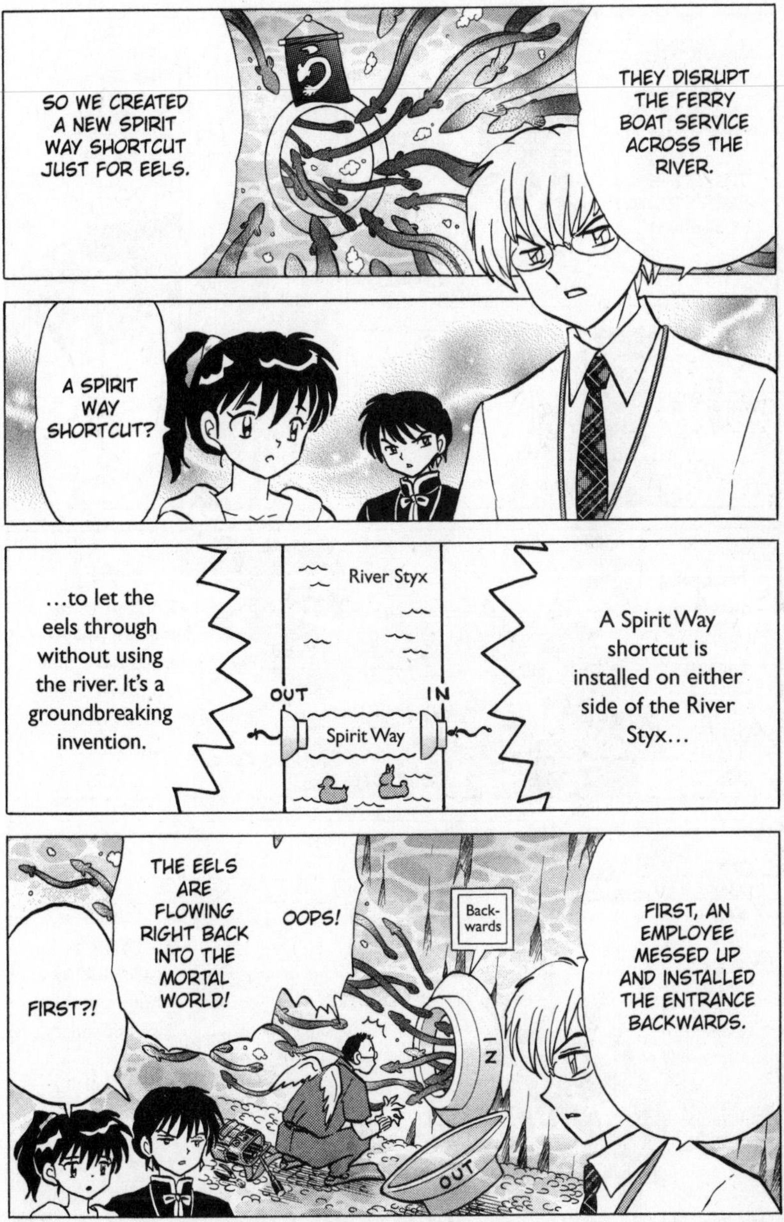
THEY DISRUPT THE FERRY BOAT SERVICE ACROSS THE RIVER.
SO WE CREATED A NEW SPIRIT WAY SHORTCUT JUST FOR EELS.
A SPIRIT WAY SHORTCUT?
A Spirit Way shortcut is installed on either side of the River Styx…
River Styx
IN
OUT
Spirit Way
…to let the eels through without using the river. It's a groundbreaking invention.
FIRST, AN EMPLOYEE MESSED UP AND INSTALLED THE ENTRANCE BACKWARDS.
Back-wards
OUT
OOPS!
THE EELS ARE FLOWING RIGHT BACK INTO THE MORTAL WORLD!
FIRST?!

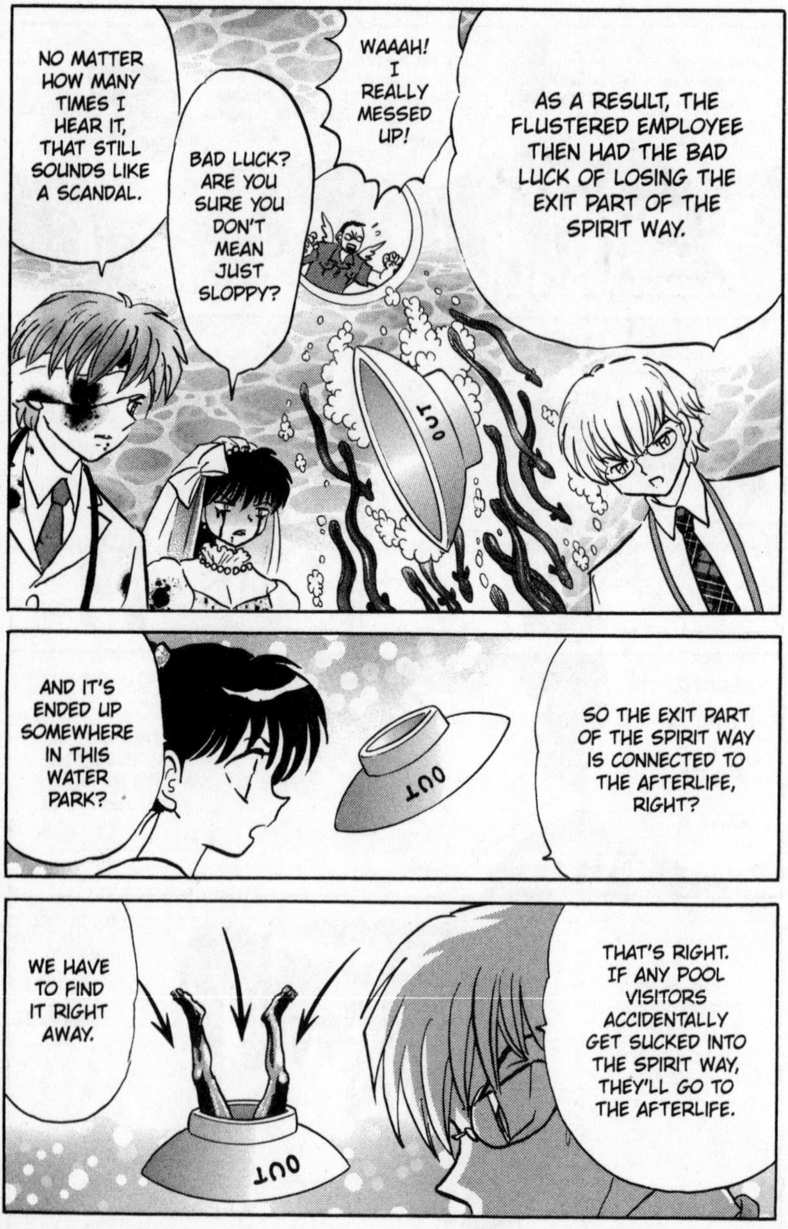
AS A RESULT, THE FLUSTERED EMPLOYEE THEN HAD THE BAD LUCK OF LOSING THE EXIT PART OF THE SPIRIT WAY.
WAAAH! I REALLY MESSED UP!
OUT
BAD LUCK? ARE YOU SURE YOU DON'T MEAN JUST SLOPPY?
NO MATTER HOW MANY TIMES I HEAR IT, THAT STILL SOUNDS LIKE A SCANDAL.
SO THE EXIT PART OF THE SPIRIT WAY IS CONNECTED TO THE AFTERLIFE, RIGHT?
OUT
AND IT'S ENDED UP SOMEWHERE IN THIS WATER PARK?
THAT'S RIGHT. IF ANY POOL VISITORS ACCIDENTALLY GET SUCKED INTO THE SPIRIT WAY, THEY'LL GO TO THE AFTERLIFE.
OUT
WE HAVE TO FIND IT RIGHT AWAY.

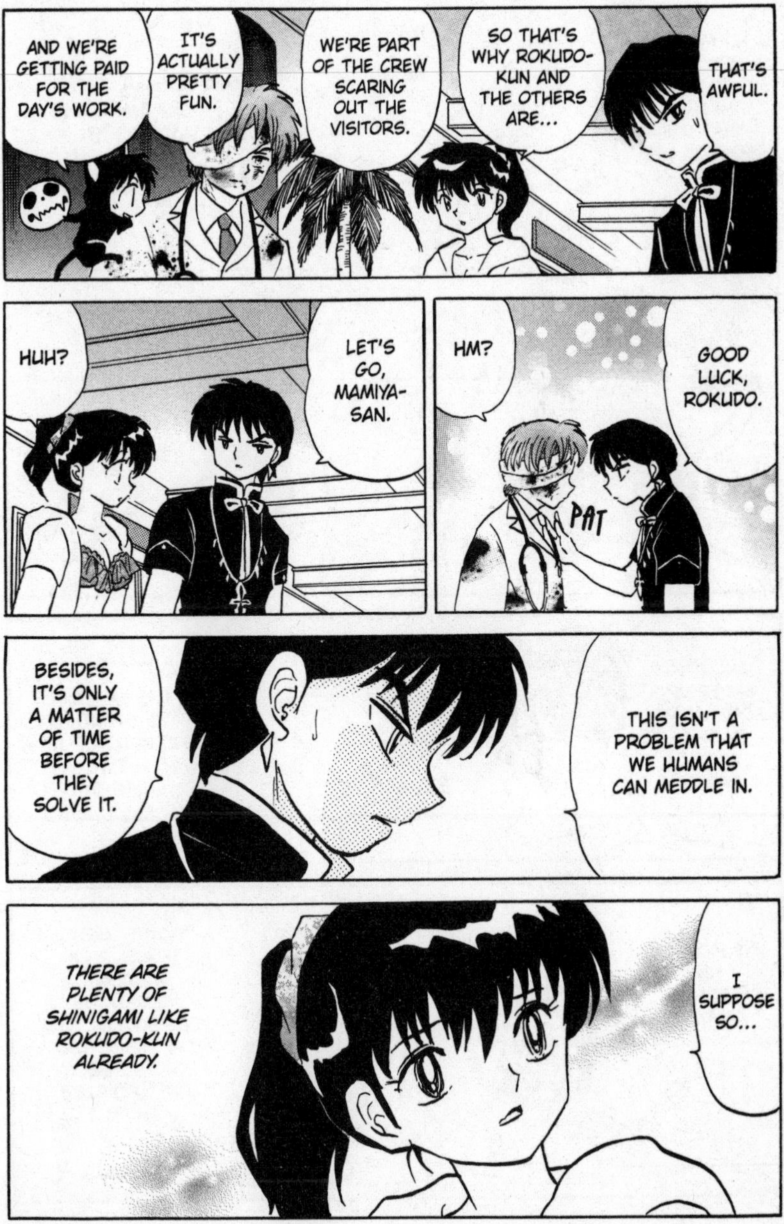
THAT'S AWFUL.
SO THAT'S WHY ROKUDO-KUN AND THE OTHERS ARE...
WE'RE PART OF THE CREW SCARING OUT THE VISITORS.
IT'S ACTUALLY PRETTY FUN.
AND WE'RE GETTING PAID FOR THE DAY'S WORK.
GOOD LUCK, ROKUDO.
HM?
PAT
LET'S GO, MAMIYA-SAN.
HUH?
THIS ISN'T A PROBLEM THAT WE HUMANS CAN MEDDLE IN.
BESIDES, IT'S ONLY A MATTER OF TIME BEFORE THEY SOLVE IT.
I SUPPOSE SO...
THERE ARE PLENTY OF SHINIGAMI LIKE ROKUDO-KUN ALREADY.

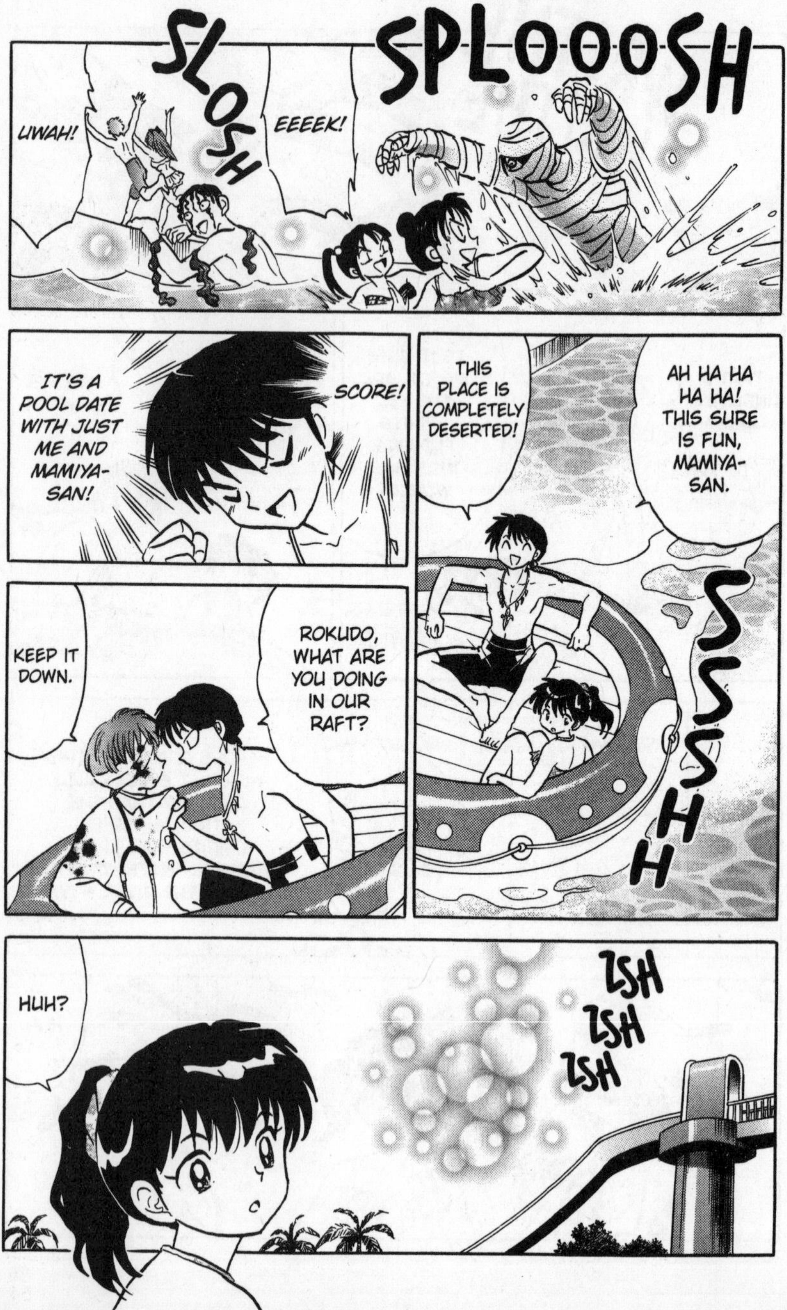
SPLOOOSH
EEEEK!
SLOSH
UWAH!
AH HA HA HA HA! THIS SURE IS FUN, MAMIYA-SAN.
THIS PLACE IS COMPLETELY DESERTED!
SSSHHH
SCORE!
IT'S A POOL DATE WITH JUST ME AND MAMIYA-SAN!
ROKUDO, WHAT ARE YOU DOING IN OUR RAFT?
KEEP IT DOWN.
ZSH
ZSH
ZSH
HUH?

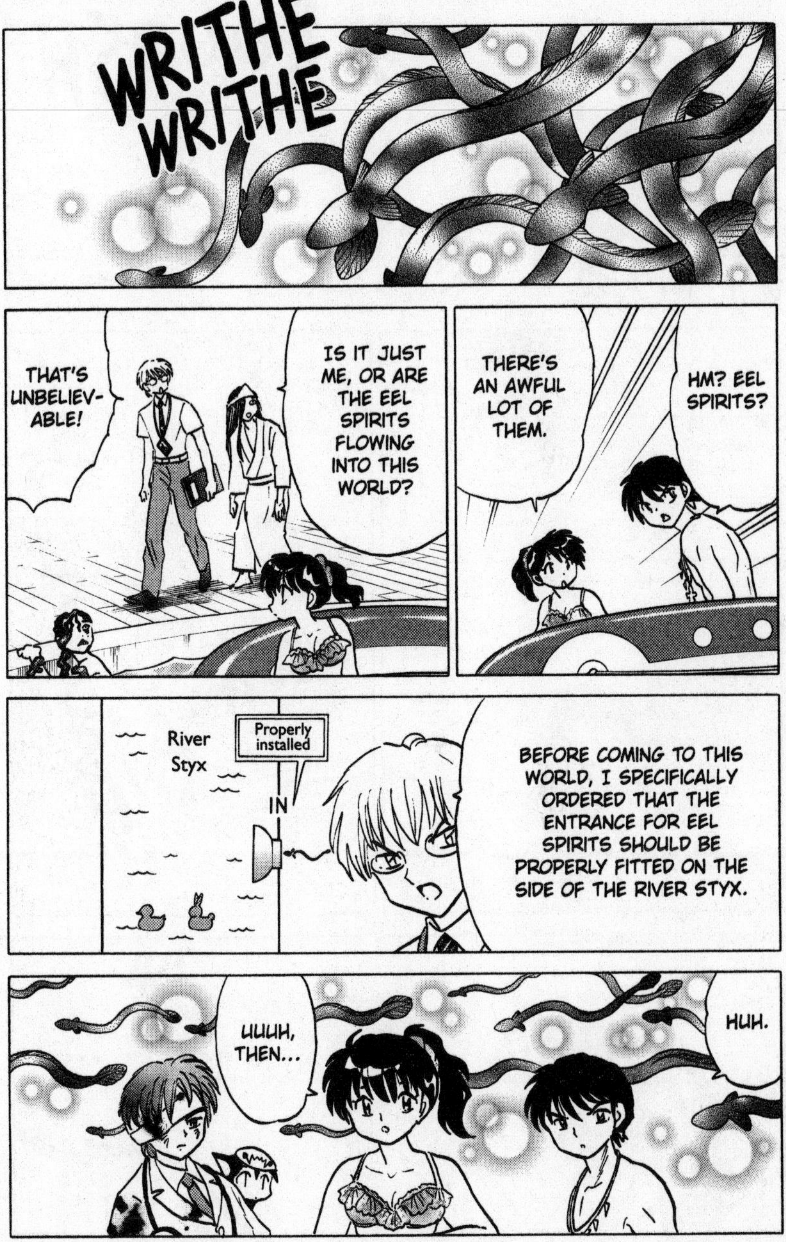
WRITHE WRITHE
HM? EEL SPIRITS?
THERE'S AN AWFUL LOT OF THEM.
IS IT JUST ME, OR ARE THE EEL SPIRITS FLOWING INTO THIS WORLD?
THAT'S UNBELIEV-ABLE!
BEFORE COMING TO THIS WORLD, I SPECIFICALLY ORDERED THAT THE ENTRANCE FOR EEL SPIRITS SHOULD BE PROPERLY FITTED ON THE SIDE OF THE RIVER STYX.
Properly installed
River Styx
IN
HUH.
UUUH, THEN...

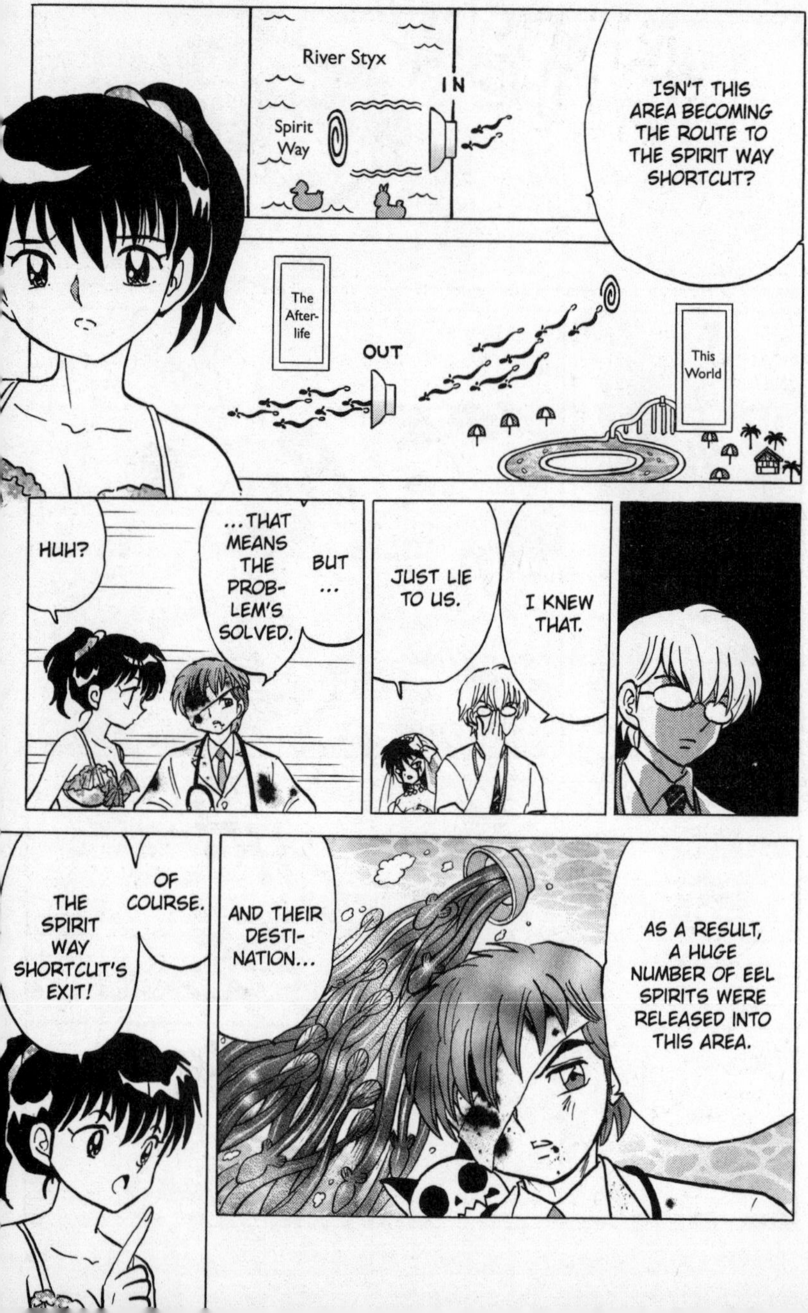
ISN'T THIS AREA BECOMING THE ROUTE TO THE SPIRIT WAY SHORTCUT?
IN
River Styx
Spirit Way
This World
OUT
The After-life
I KNEW THAT.
JUST LIE TO US.
BUT ...
...THAT MEANS THE PROB-LEM'S SOLVED.
HUH?
AS A RESULT, A HUGE NUMBER OF EEL SPIRITS WERE RELEASED INTO THIS AREA.
AND THEIR DESTI-NATION...
OF COURSE.
THE SPIRIT WAY SHORTCUT'S EXIT!

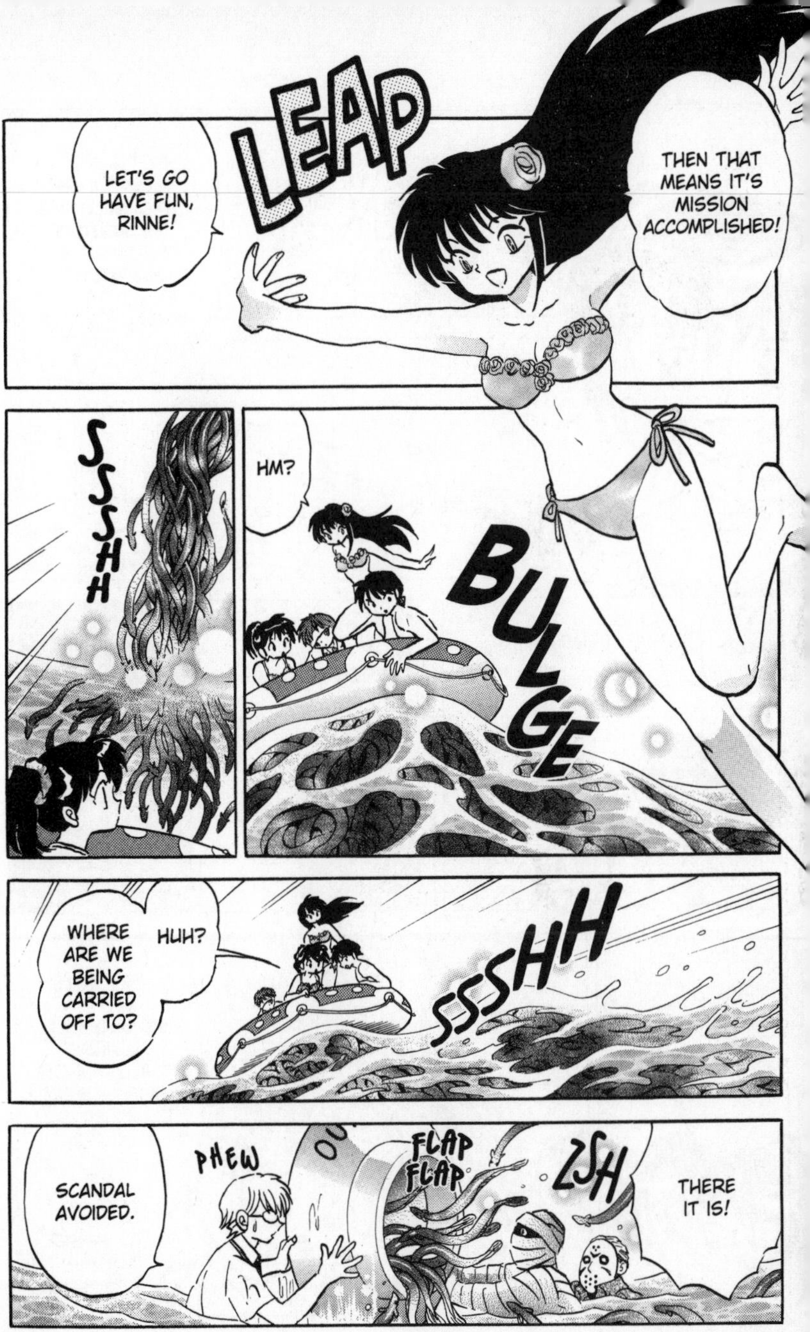
THEN THAT MEANS IT'S MISSION ACCOMPLISHED!
LEAP
LET'S GO HAVE FUN, RINNE!
HM?
BULGE
SSSHH
SSSHH
HUH?
WHERE ARE WE BEING CARRIED OFF TO?
THERE IT IS!
ZSH
FLAP FLAP
PHEW
SCANDAL AVOIDED.

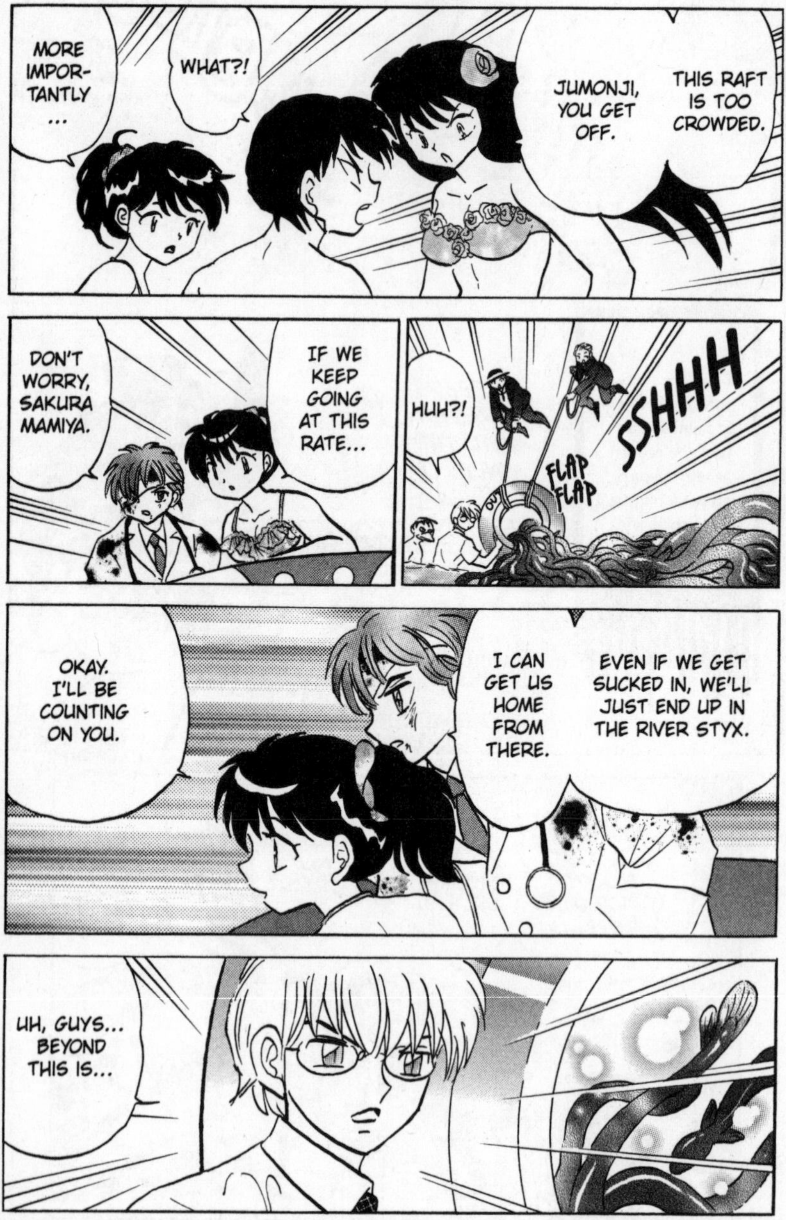
THIS RAFT IS TOO CROWDED.
JUMONJI, YOU GET OFF.
WHAT?!
MORE IMPORTANTLY ...
SSHHH
FLAP FLAP
OUT
HUH?!
IF WE KEEP GOING AT THIS RATE...
DON'T WORRY, SAKURA MAMIYA.
EVEN IF WE GET SUCKED IN, WE'LL JUST END UP IN THE RIVER STYX.
I CAN GET US HOME FROM THERE.
OKAY. I'LL BE COUNTING ON YOU.
UH, GUYS... BEYOND THIS IS...

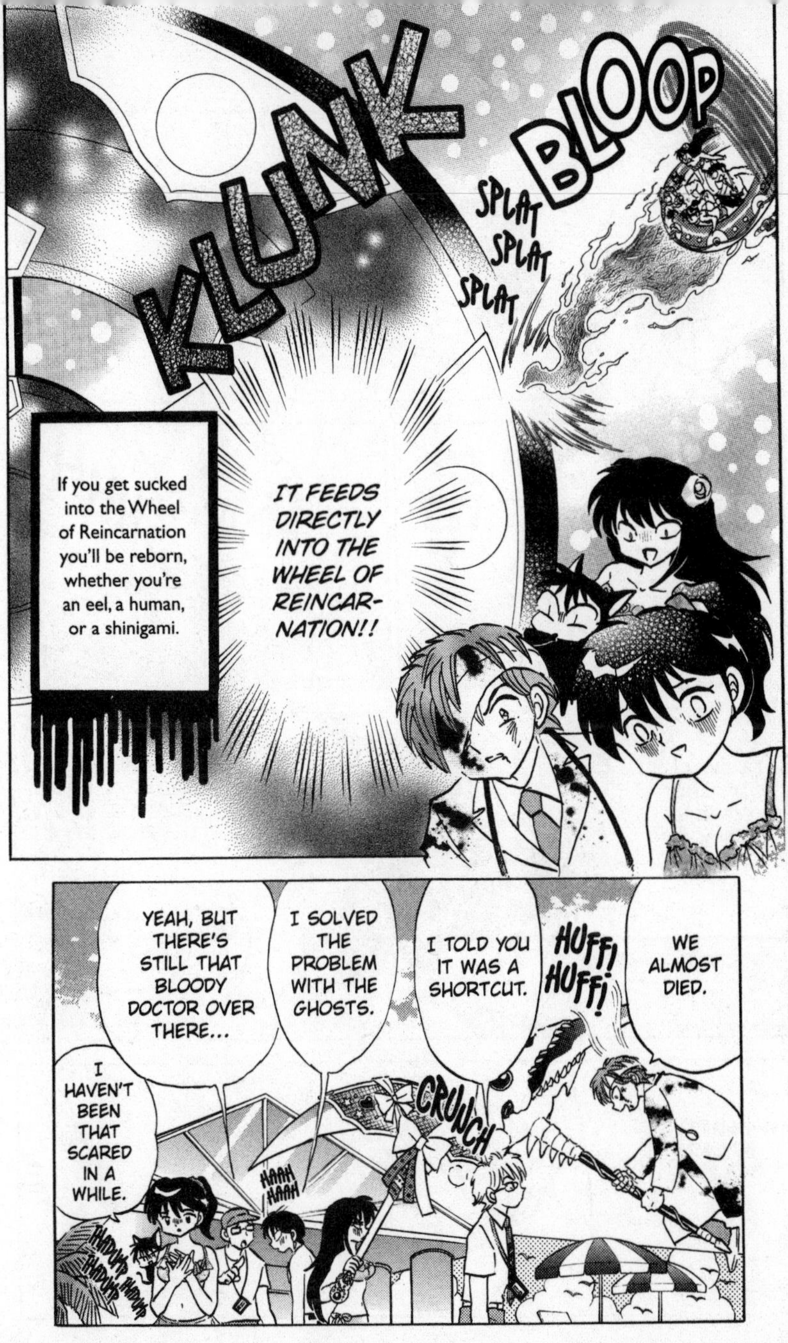
BLOOP
SPLAT
SPLAT
SPLAT
KLUNK
IT FEEDS DIRECTLY INTO THE WHEEL OF REINCAR-NATION!!
If you get sucked into the Wheel of Reincarnation you'll be reborn, whether you're an eel, a human, or a shinigami.
WE ALMOST DIED.
HUFF! HUFF!
I TOLD YOU IT WAS A SHORTCUT.
CRUNCH
I SOLVED THE PROBLEM WITH THE GHOSTS.
YEAH, BUT THERE'S STILL THAT BLOODY DOCTOR OVER THERE...
HAAH HAAH
I HAVEN'T BEEN THAT SCARED IN A WHILE.
THADUMP THADUMP THADUMP THADUMP

CHAPTER 292: I HATE BRAIDS

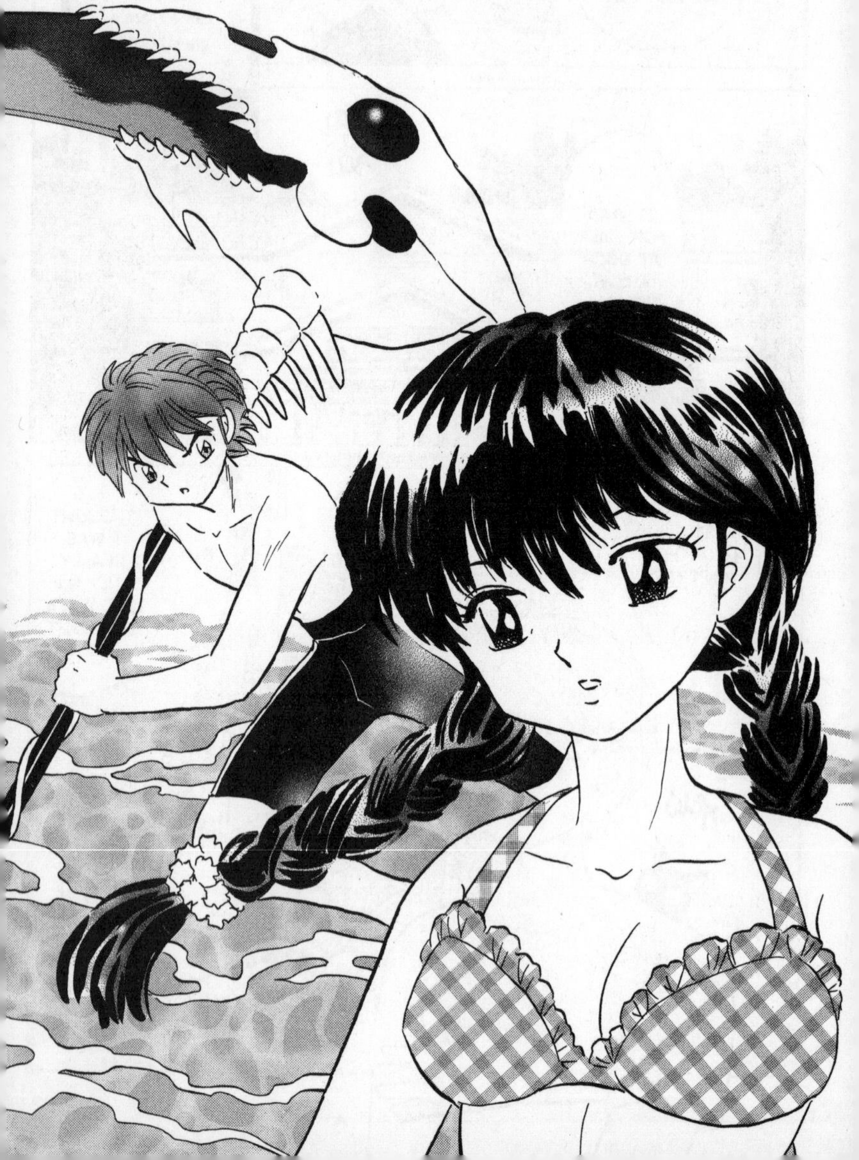

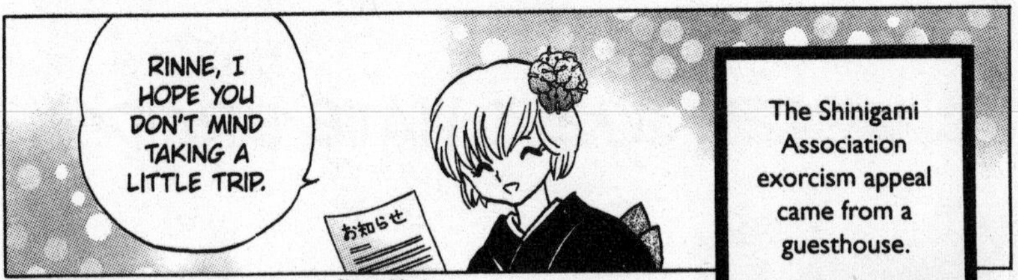
The Shinigami Association exorcism appeal came from a guesthouse.
RINNE, I HOPE YOU DON'T MIND TAKING A LITTLE TRIP.
お知らせ
Sheet: Notice

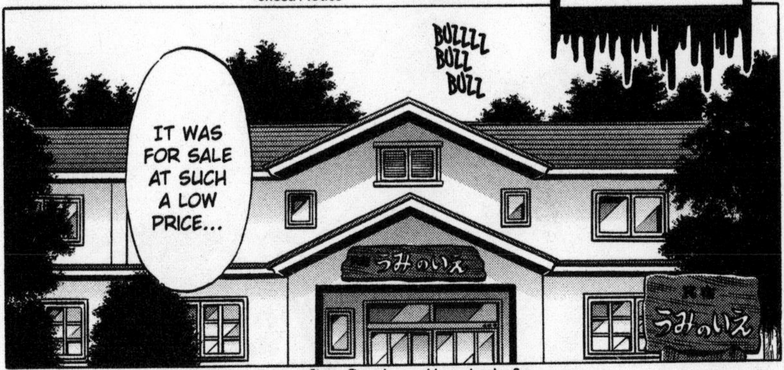
BUZZZZ BUZZ BUZZ
IT WAS FOR SALE AT SUCH A LOW PRICE...
うみのいえ
うみのいえ
Signs: Guesthouse; Home by the Sea

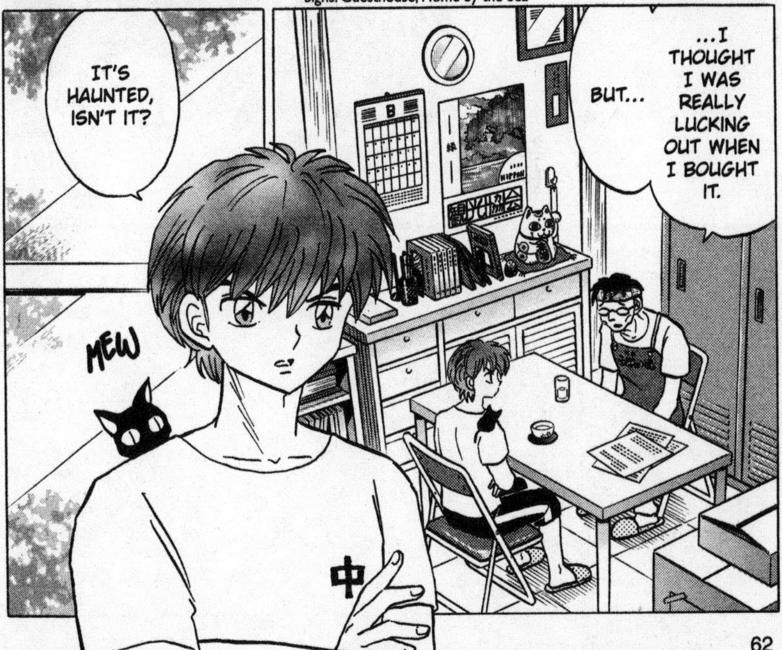
...I THOUGHT I WAS REALLY LUCKING OUT WHEN I BOUGHT IT.
BUT...
IT'S HAUNTED, ISN'T IT?
MEW

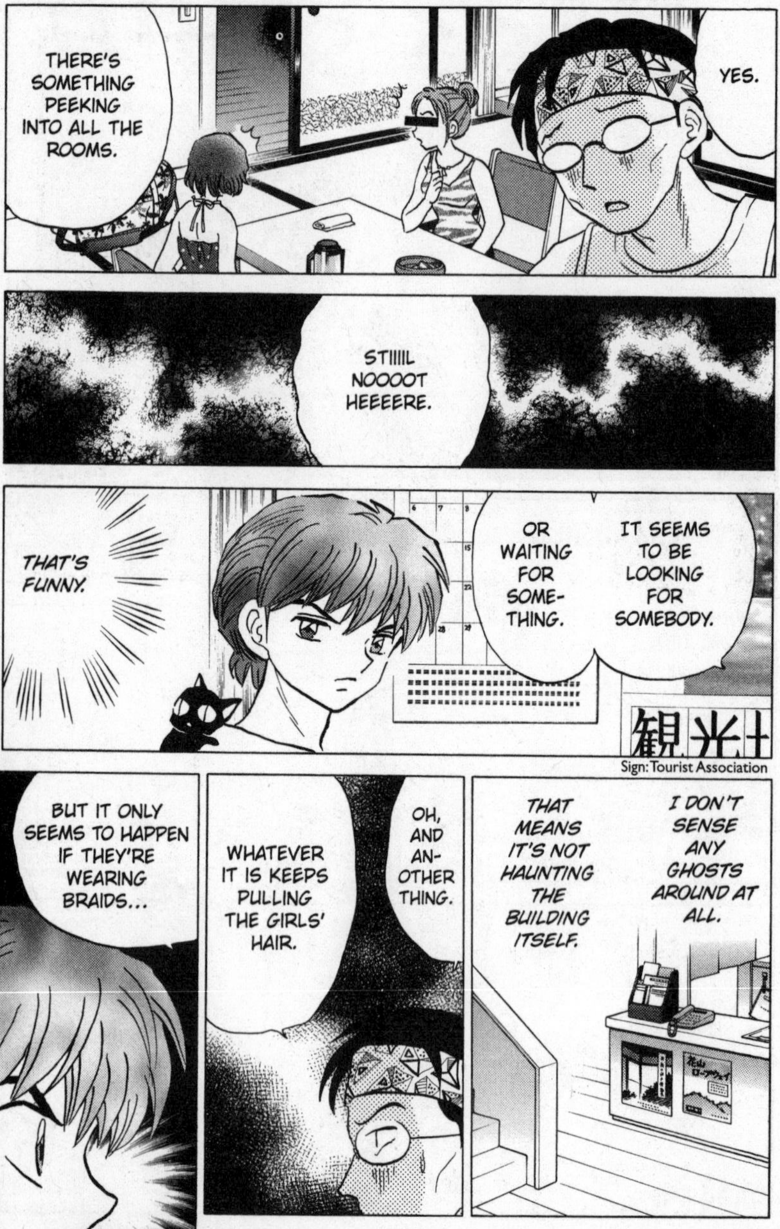
YES.
THERE'S SOMETHING PEEKING INTO ALL THE ROOMS.
STIIIIL NOOOOT HEEEERE.
IT SEEMS TO BE LOOKING FOR SOMEBODY.
OR WAITING FOR SOMETHING.
THAT'S FUNNY.
観光
Sign: Tourist Association
I DON'T SENSE ANY GHOSTS AROUND AT ALL.
THAT MEANS IT'S NOT HAUNTING THE BUILDING ITSELF.
OH, AND ANOTHER THING.
WHATEVER IT IS KEEPS PULLING THE GIRLS' HAIR.
BUT IT ONLY SEEMS TO HAPPEN IF THEY'RE WEARING BRAIDS...

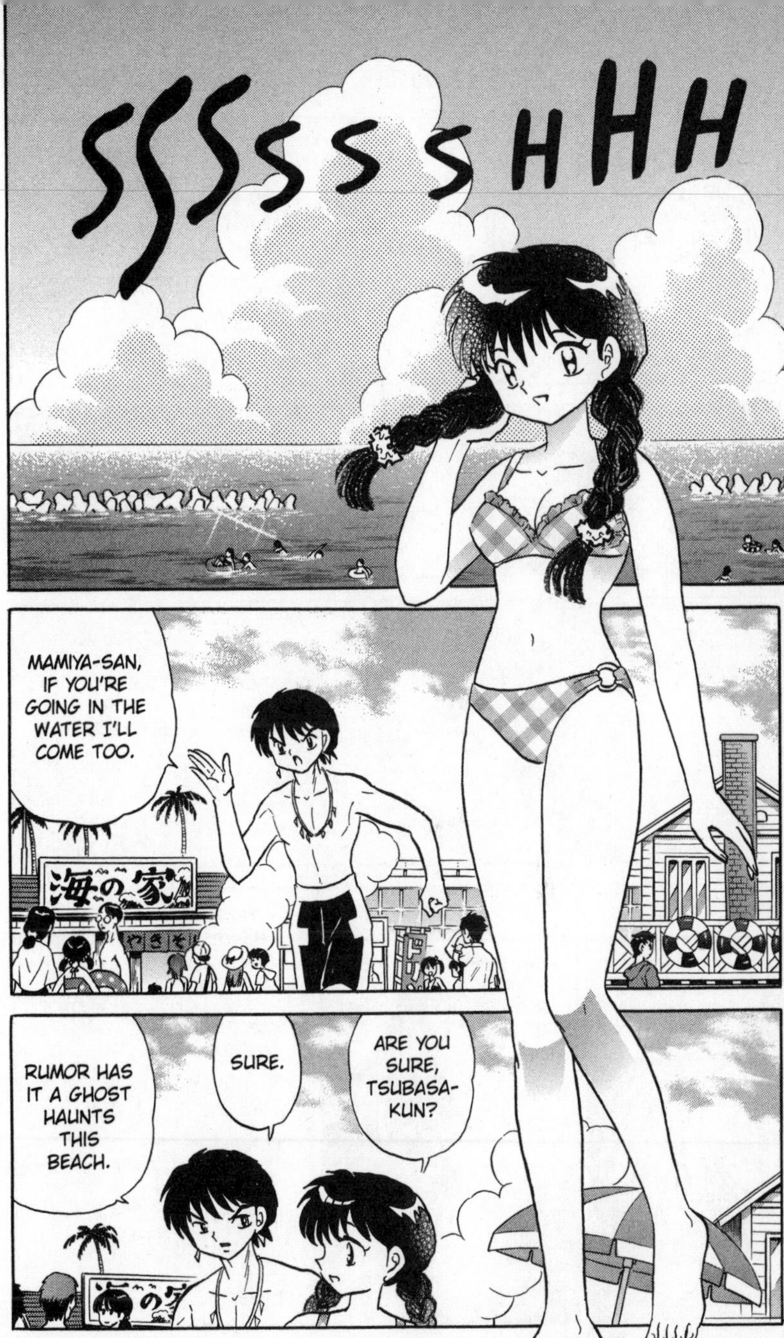
SSSSSSSHHH
MAMIYA-SAN, IF YOU'RE GOING IN THE WATER I'LL COME TOO.
海の家
ARE YOU SURE, TSUBASA-KUN?
SURE.
RUMOR HAS IT A GHOST HAUNTS THIS BEACH.

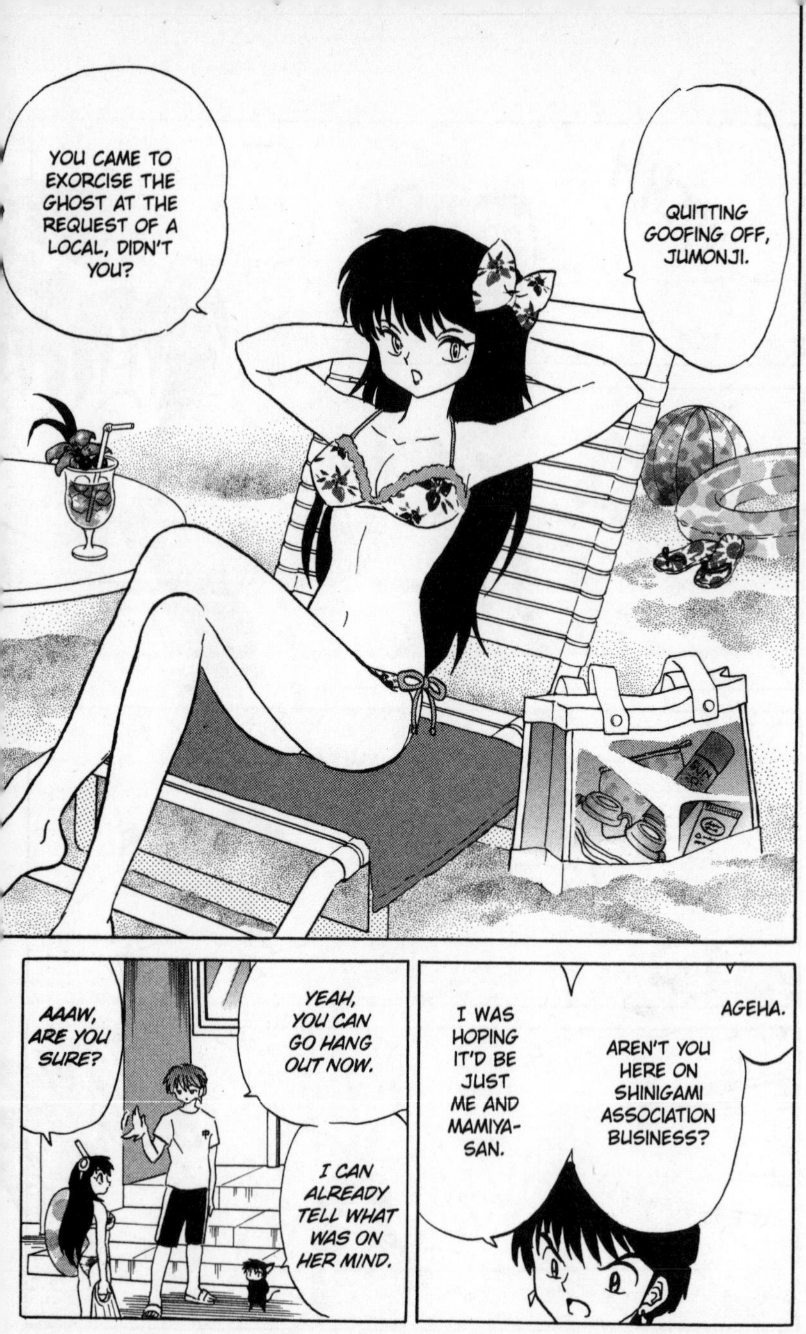
QUITTING GOOFING OFF, JUMONJI.
YOU CAME TO EXORCISE THE GHOST AT THE REQUEST OF A LOCAL, DIDN'T YOU?
AGEHA.
AREN'T YOU HERE ON SHINIGAMI ASSOCIATION BUSINESS?
I WAS HOPING IT'D BE JUST ME AND MAMIYA-SAN.
YEAH, YOU CAN GO HANG OUT NOW.
AAAW, ARE YOU SURE?
I CAN ALREADY TELL WHAT WAS ON HER MIND.

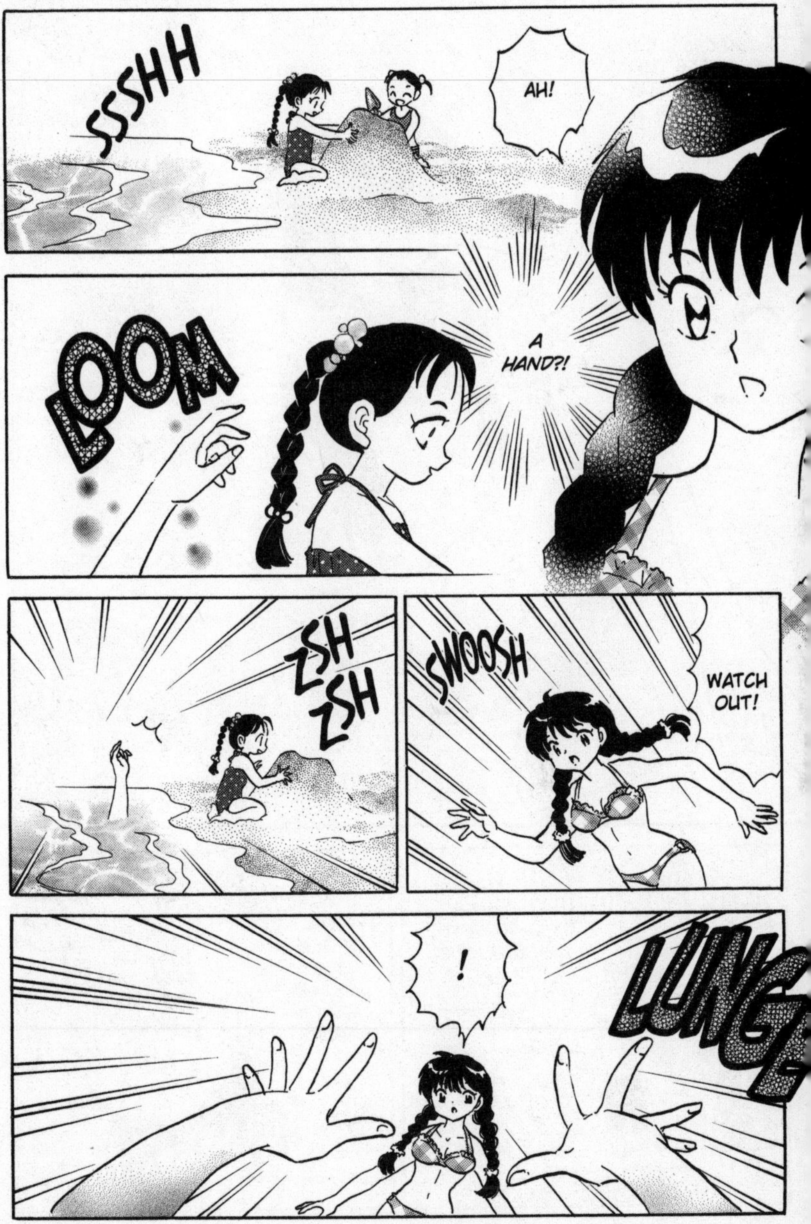
AH!
SSSHH
A HAND?!
LOOM
SWOOSH
WATCH OUT!
ZSH
ZSH
!
LUNGE

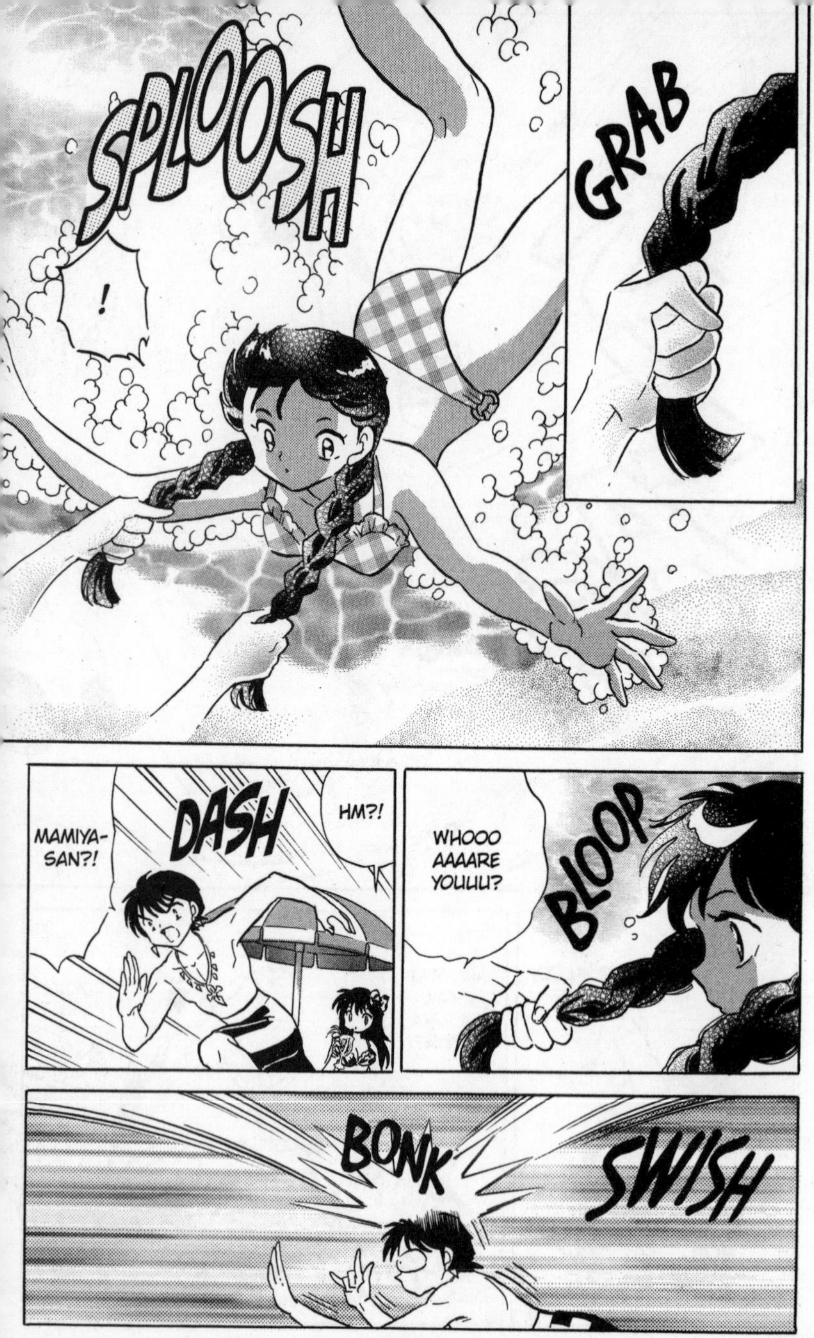
GRAB
SPLOOSH
!
WHOOO AAAARE YOUUU?
BLOOP
HM?!
DASH
MAMIYA-SAN?!
SWISH
BONK

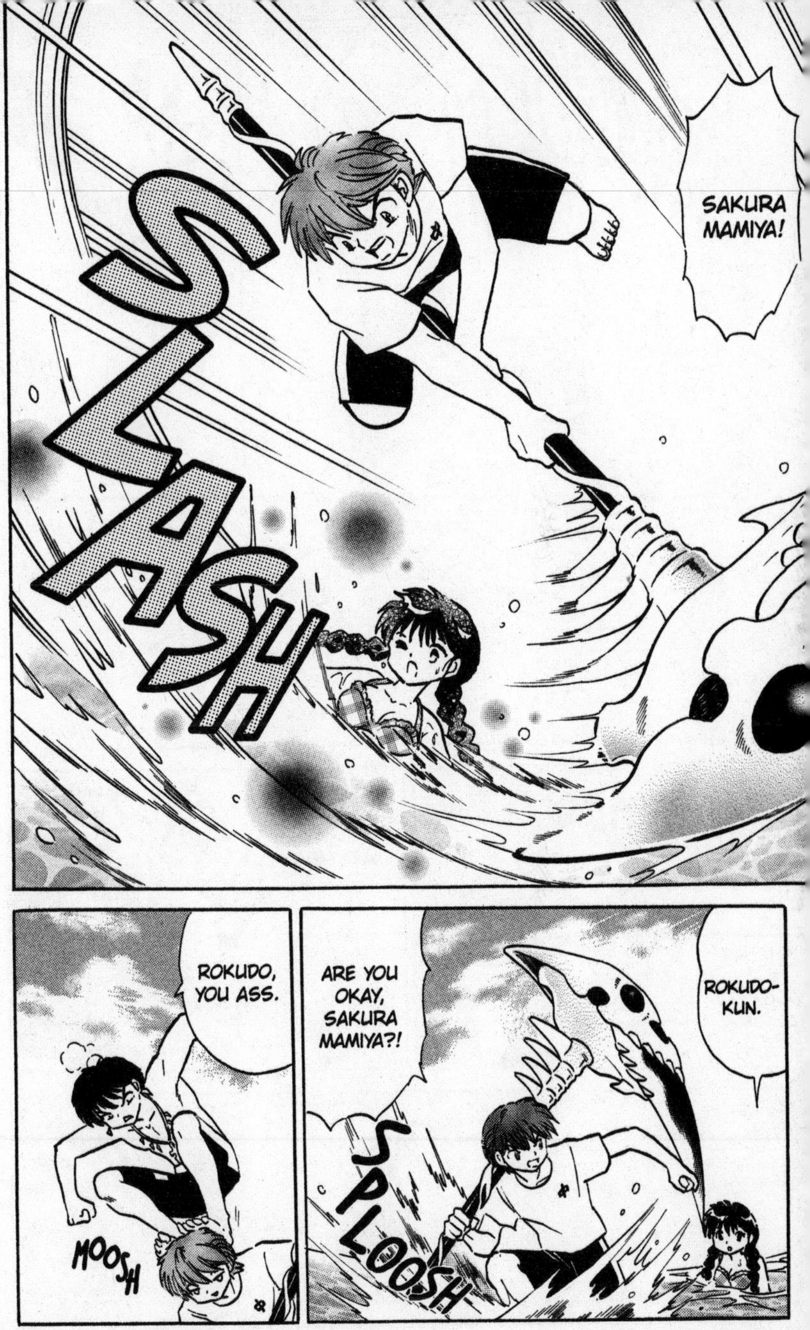
SAKURA MAMIYA!
SLASH
ROKUDO-KUN.
ARE YOU OKAY, SAKURA MAMIYA?!
SPLOOSH
ROKUDO, YOU ASS.
MOOSH

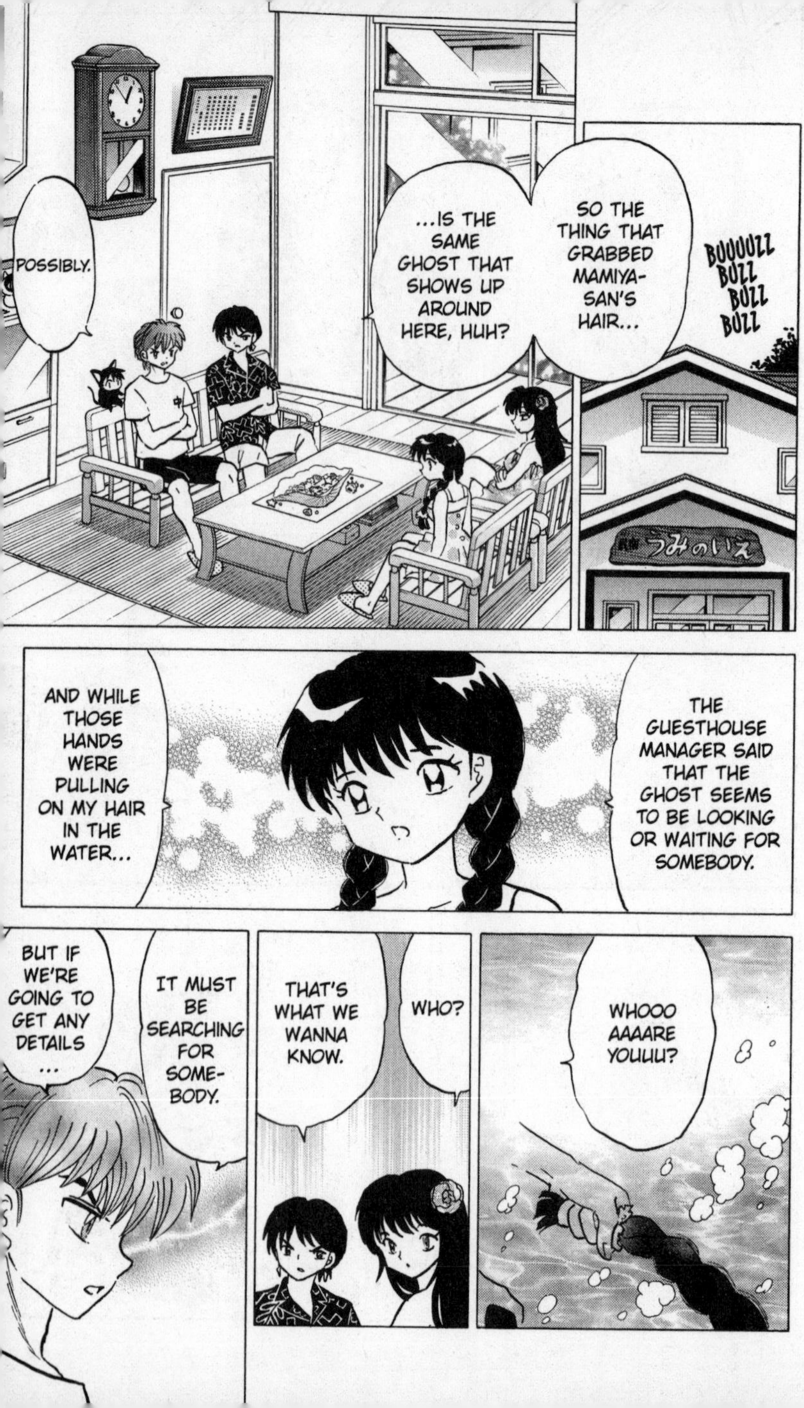
BUUUUZZ BUZZ BUZZ BUZZ
うみのいえ
SO THE THING THAT GRABBED MAMIYA-SAN'S HAIR...
...IS THE SAME GHOST THAT SHOWS UP AROUND HERE, HUH?
POSSIBLY.
THE GUESTHOUSE MANAGER SAID THAT THE GHOST SEEMS TO BE LOOKING OR WAITING FOR SOMEBODY.
AND WHILE THOSE HANDS WERE PULLING ON MY HAIR IN THE WATER...
WHOOO AAAARE YOUUU?
WHO?
THAT'S WHAT WE WANNA KNOW.
IT MUST BE SEARCHING FOR SOME-BODY.
BUT IF WE'RE GOING TO GET ANY DETAILS ...

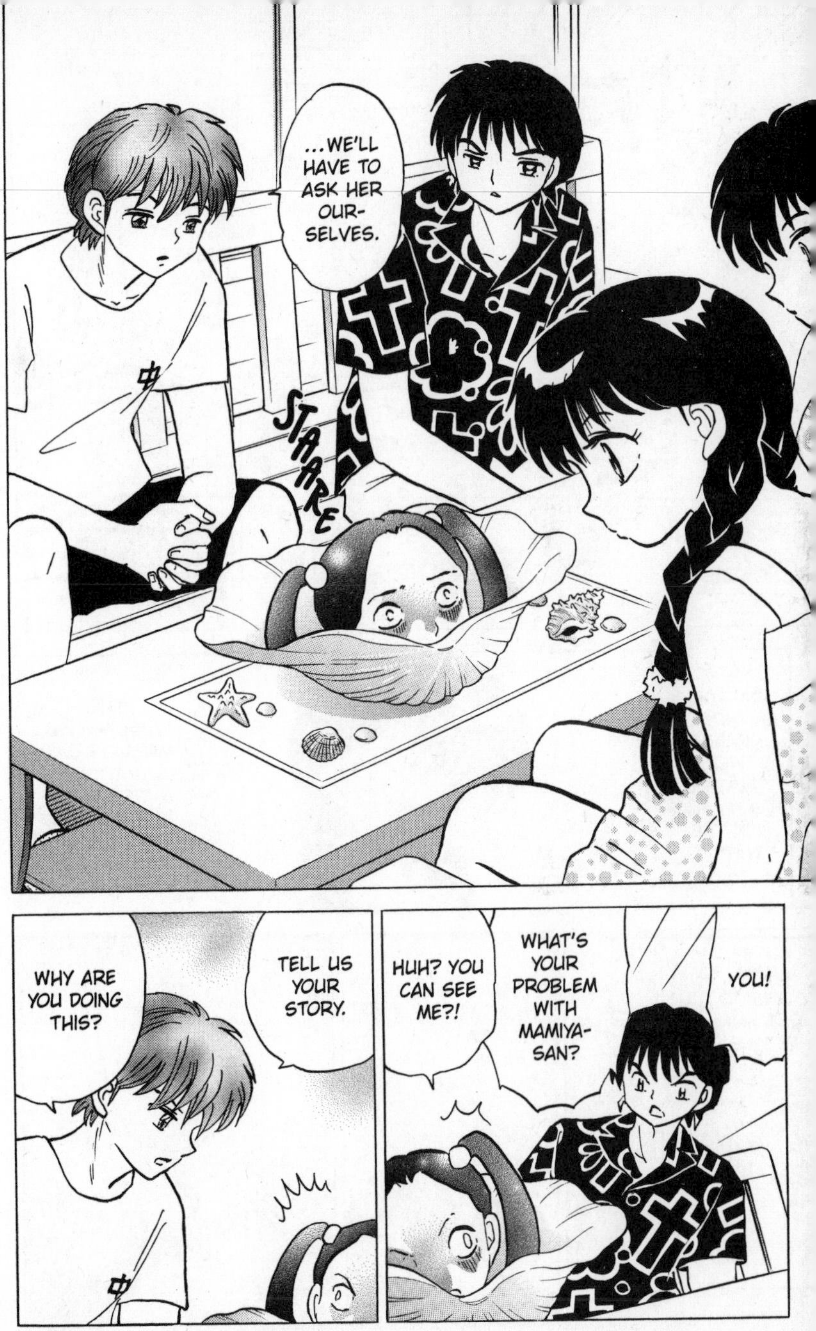
...WE'LL HAVE TO ASK HER OURSELVES.
STARE
YOU!
WHAT'S YOUR PROBLEM WITH MAMIYA-SAN?
HUH? YOU CAN SEE ME?!
TELL US YOUR STORY.
WHY ARE YOU DOING THIS?

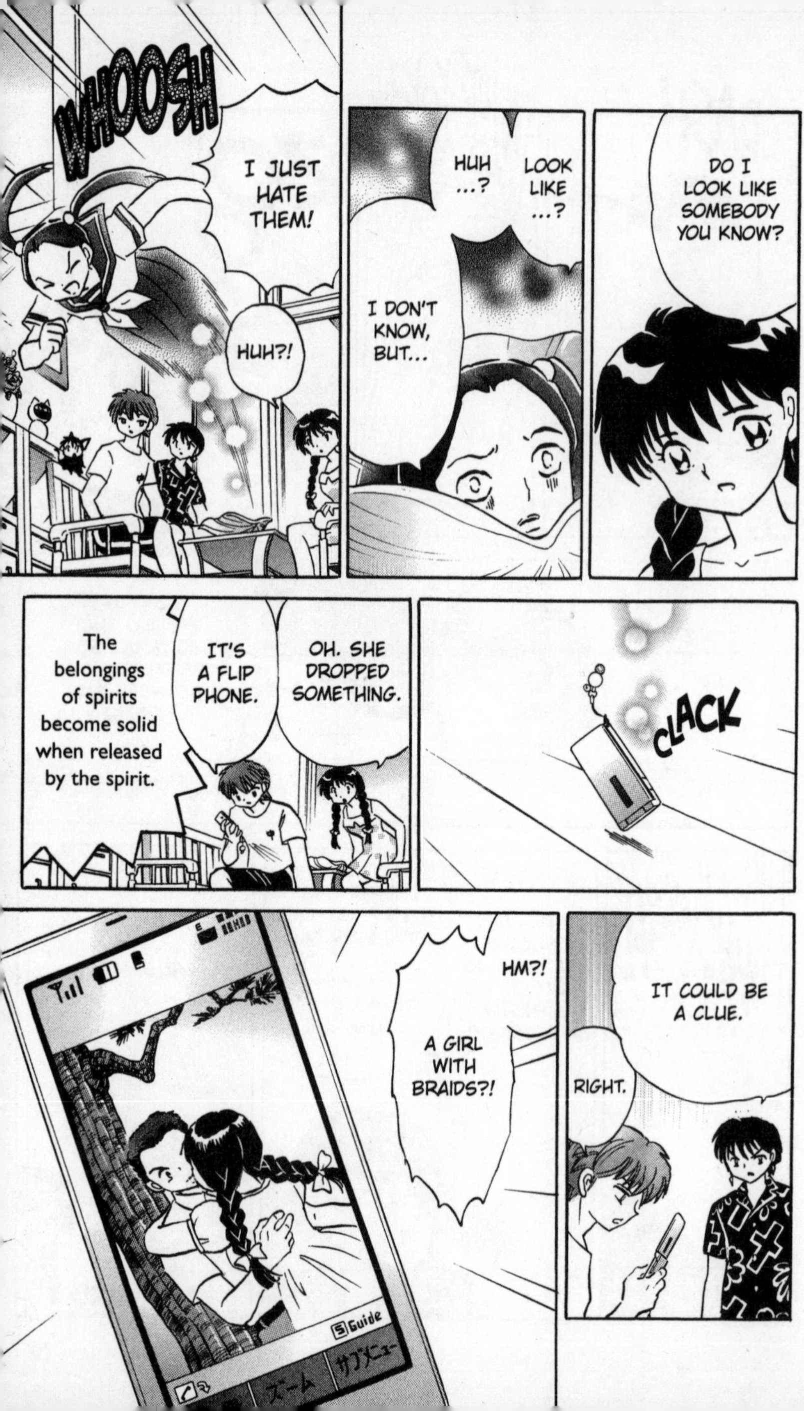
DO I LOOK LIKE SOMEBODY YOU KNOW?
LOOK LIKE ...?
HUH ...?
I DON'T KNOW, BUT...
WHOOSH
I JUST HATE THEM!
HUH?!
CLACK
OH. SHE DROPPED SOMETHING.
IT'S A FLIP PHONE.
The belongings of spirits become solid when released by the spirit.
IT COULD BE A CLUE.
RIGHT.
HM?!
A GIRL WITH BRAIDS?!
Guide
サブメニュー
ズーム

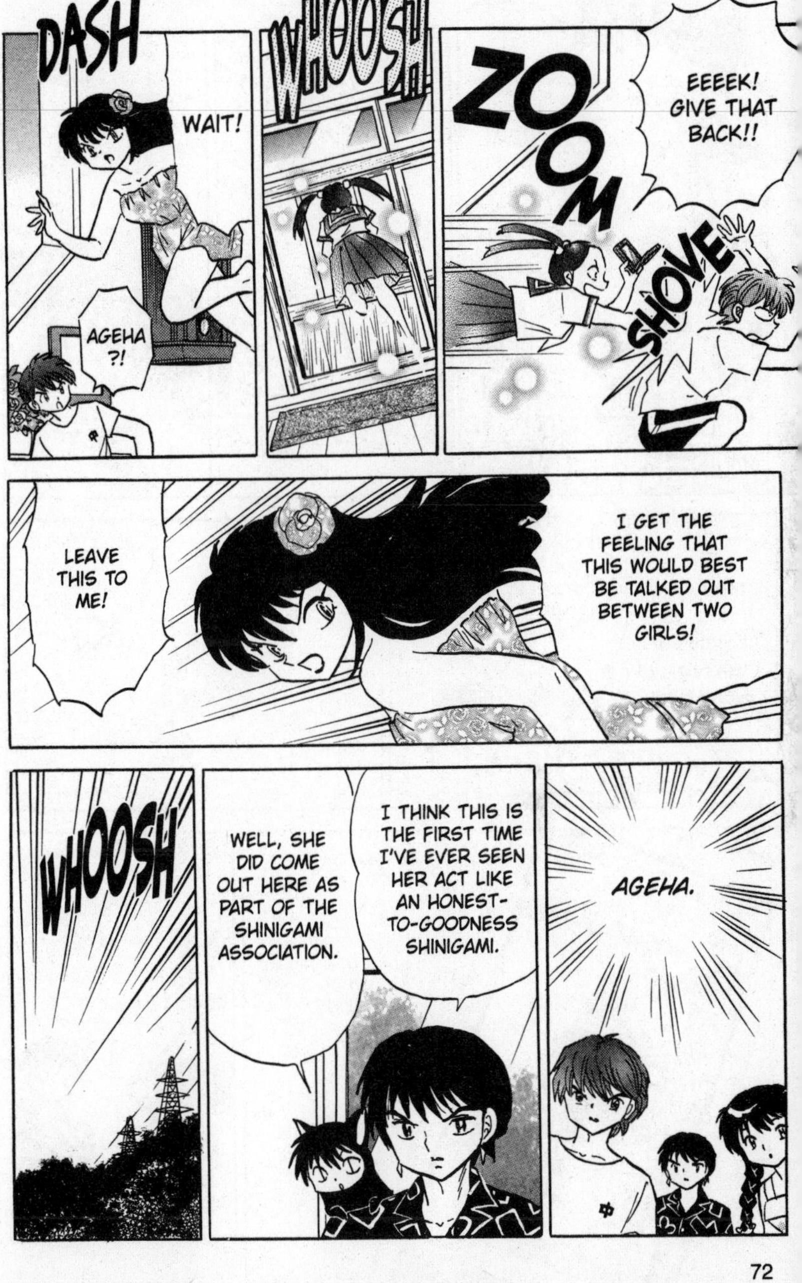
ZOOM
EEEEK! GIVE THAT BACK!!
SHOVE
WHOOSH
DASH
WAIT!
AGEHA ?!
I GET THE FEELING THAT THIS WOULD BEST BE TALKED OUT BETWEEN TWO GIRLS!
LEAVE THIS TO ME!
AGEHA.
I THINK THIS IS THE FIRST TIME I'VE EVER SEEN HER ACT LIKE AN HONEST-TO-GOODNESS SHINIGAMI.
WELL, SHE DID COME OUT HERE AS PART OF THE SHINIGAMI ASSOCIATION.
WHOOSH

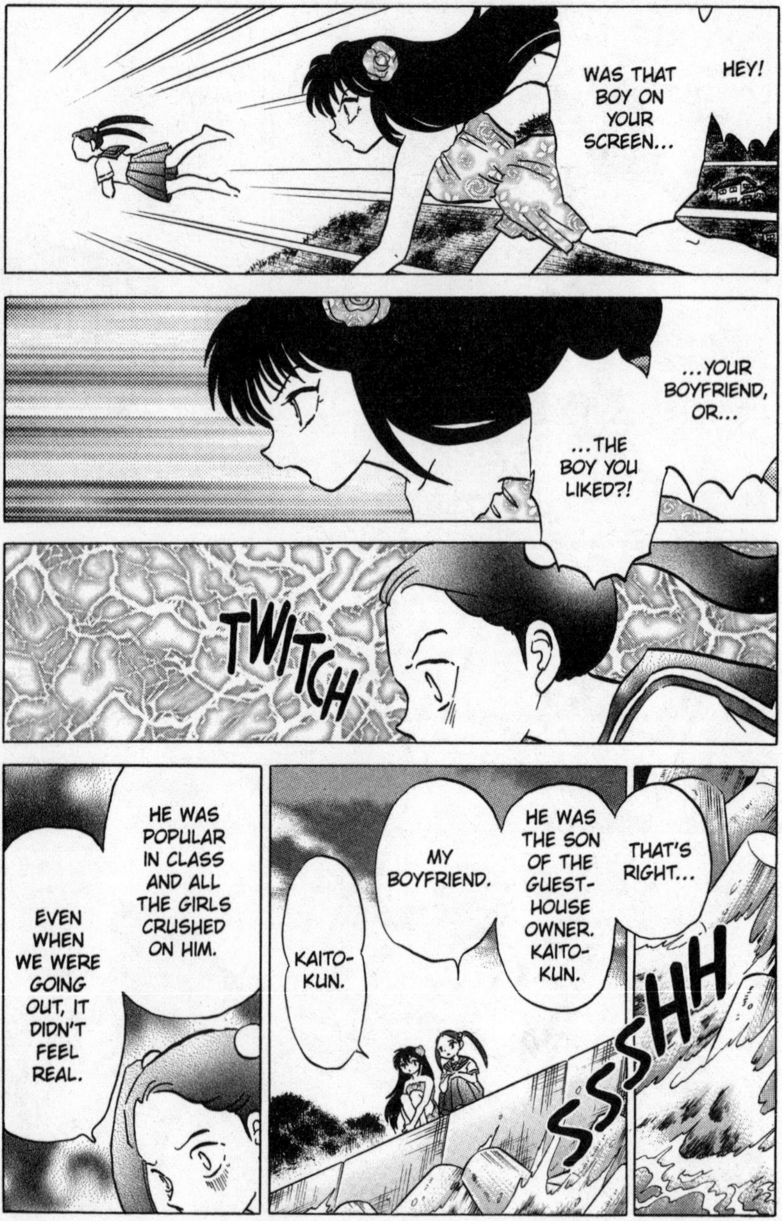
HEY!
WAS THAT BOY ON YOUR SCREEN...
...YOUR BOYFRIEND, OR...
...THE BOY YOU LIKED?!
TWITCH
THAT'S RIGHT...
SSSHH
HE WAS THE SON OF THE GUEST-HOUSE OWNER. KAITO-KUN.
MY BOYFRIEND.
KAITO-KUN.
HE WAS POPULAR IN CLASS AND ALL THE GIRLS CRUSHED ON HIM.
EVEN WHEN WE WERE GOING OUT, IT DIDN'T FEEL REAL.

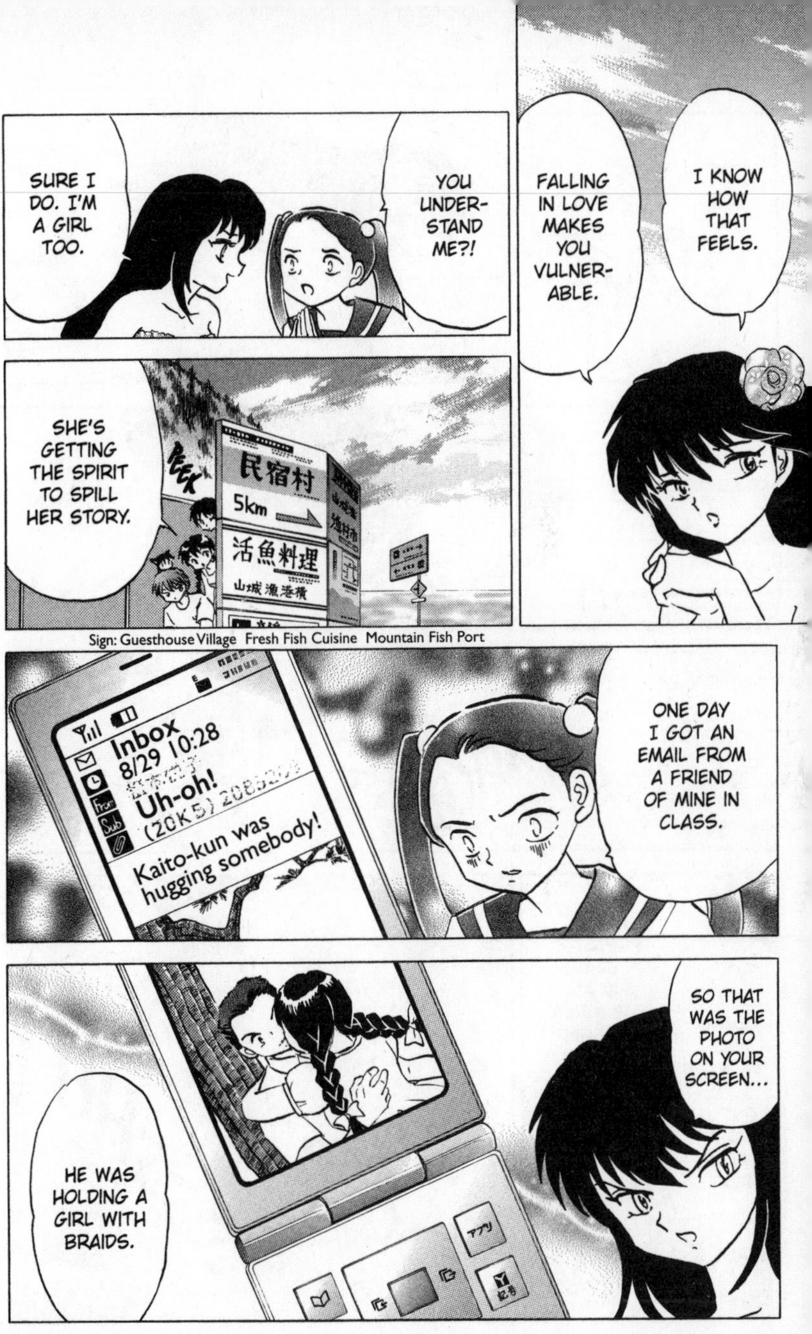
I KNOW HOW THAT FEELS.
FALLING IN LOVE MAKES YOU VULNERABLE.
YOU UNDERSTAND ME?!
SURE I DO. I'M A GIRL TOO.
民宿村
5km
活魚料理
山城漁港横
EEK
SHE'S GETTING THE SPIRIT TO SPILL HER STORY.
Sign: Guesthouse Village Fresh Fish Cuisine Mountain Fish Port
ONE DAY I GOT AN EMAIL FROM A FRIEND OF MINE IN CLASS.
Inbox
8/29 10:28
Uh-oh!
Kaito-kun was hugging somebody!
SO THAT WAS THE PHOTO ON YOUR SCREEN...
HE WAS HOLDING A GIRL WITH BRAIDS.

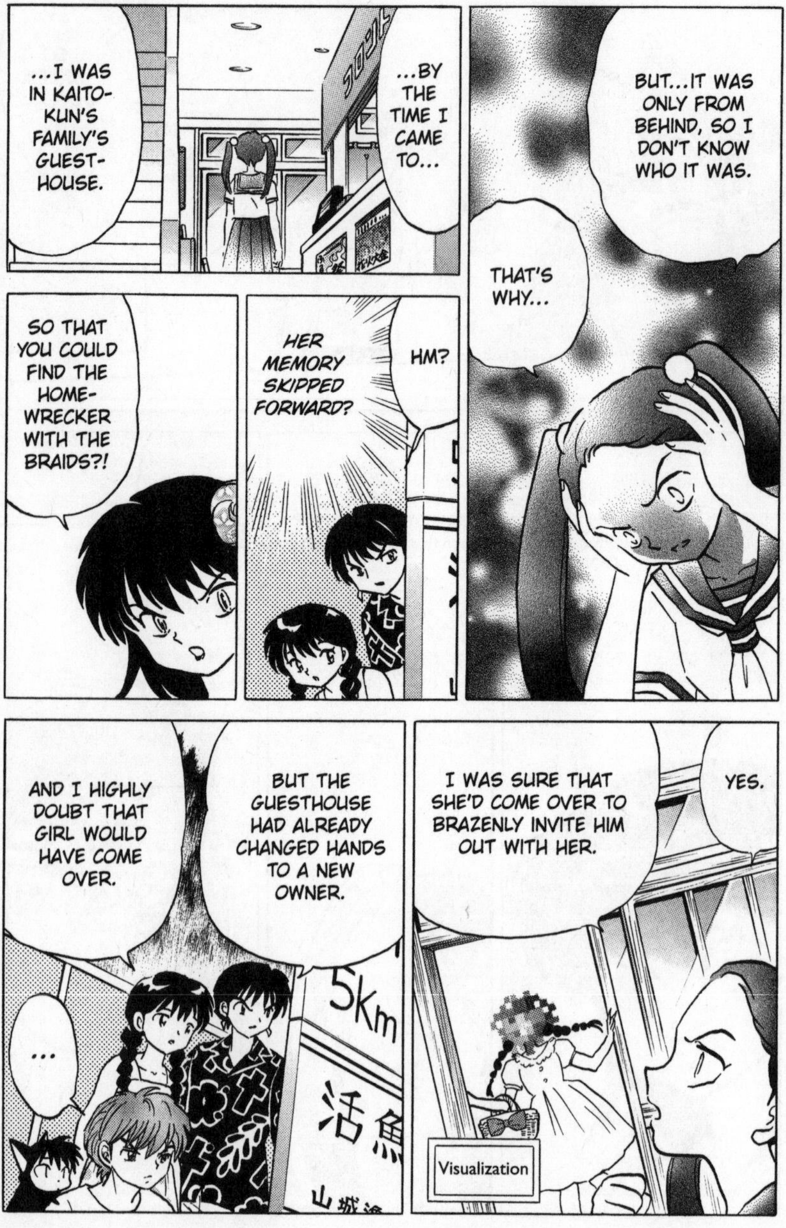

BUT...IT WAS ONLY FROM BEHIND, SO I DON'T KNOW WHO IT WAS.
THAT'S WHY...
...BY THE TIME I CAME TO...
...I WAS IN KAITO-KUN'S FAMILY'S GUEST-HOUSE.
HM?
HER MEMORY SKIPPED FORWARD?
SO THAT YOU COULD FIND THE HOME-WRECKER WITH THE BRAIDS?!
YES.
I WAS SURE THAT SHE'D COME OVER TO BRAZENLY INVITE HIM OUT WITH HER.
Visualization
BUT THE GUESTHOUSE HAD ALREADY CHANGED HANDS TO A NEW OWNER.
AND I HIGHLY DOUBT THAT GIRL WOULD HAVE COME OVER.
...
5Km
活魚

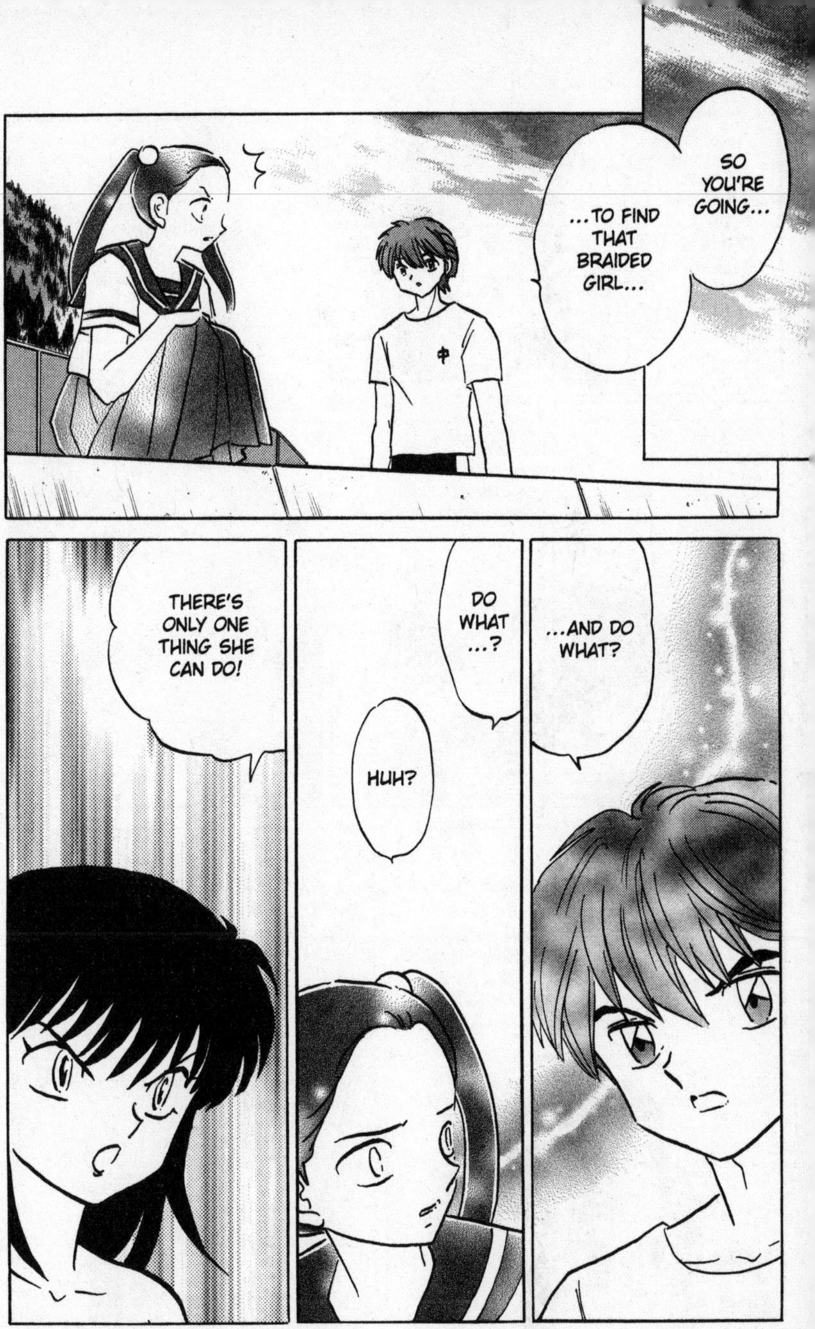
SO YOU'RE GOING...
...TO FIND THAT BRAIDED GIRL...
...AND DO WHAT?
DO WHAT ...?
HUH?
THERE'S ONLY ONE THING SHE CAN DO!

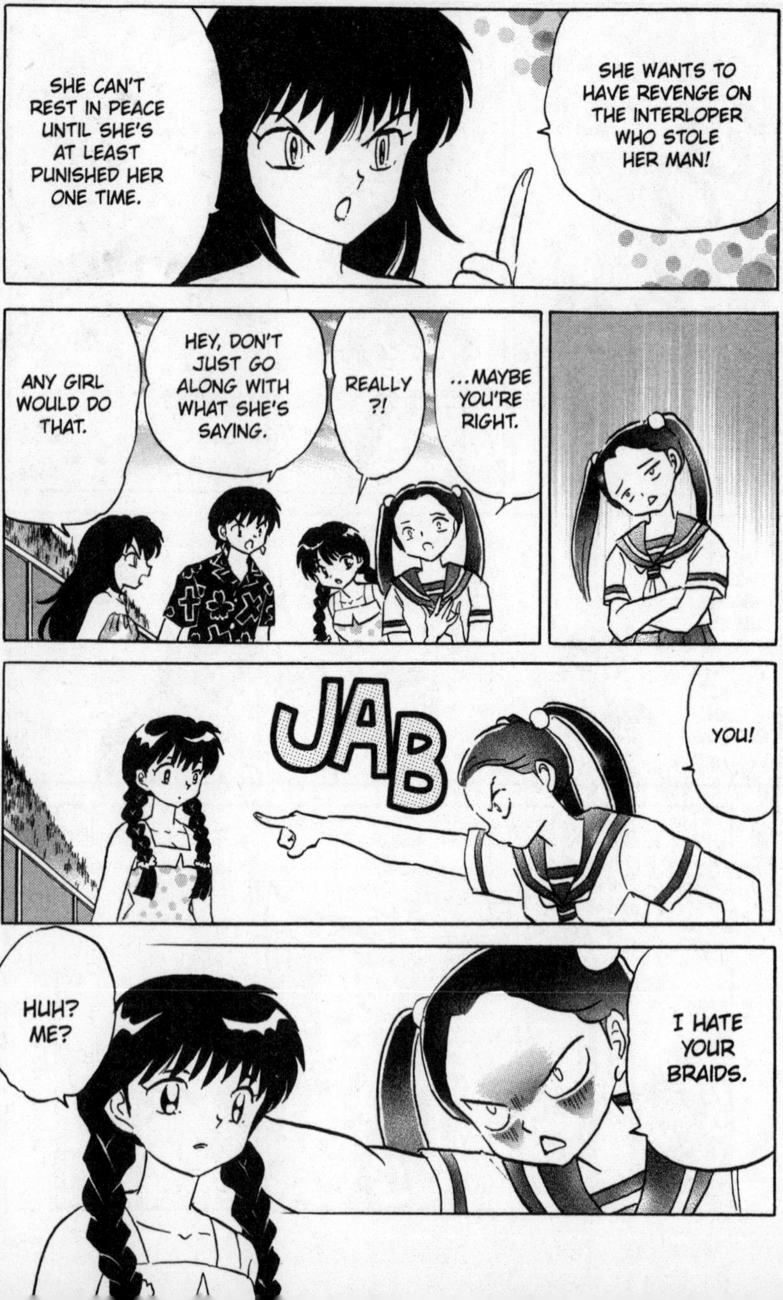
SHE WANTS TO HAVE REVENGE ON THE INTERLOPER WHO STOLE HER MAN!
SHE CAN'T REST IN PEACE UNTIL SHE'S AT LEAST PUNISHED HER ONE TIME.
...MAYBE YOU'RE RIGHT.
REALLY ?!
HEY, DON'T JUST GO ALONG WITH WHAT SHE'S SAYING.
ANY GIRL WOULD DO THAT.
YOU!
JAB
I HATE YOUR BRAIDS.
HUH? ME?

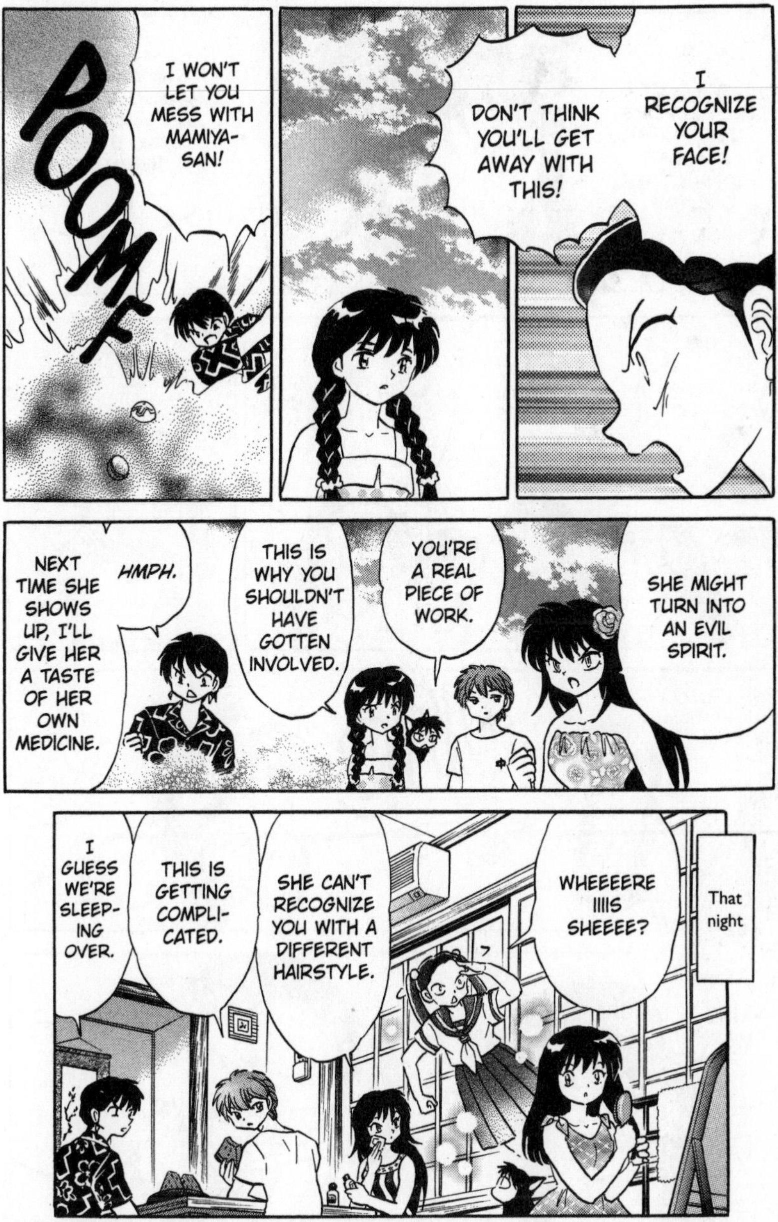
I RECOGNIZE YOUR FACE!
DON'T THINK YOU'LL GET AWAY WITH THIS!
I WON'T LET YOU MESS WITH MAMIYA-SAN!
POOMF
SHE MIGHT TURN INTO AN EVIL SPIRIT.
YOU'RE A REAL PIECE OF WORK.
THIS IS WHY YOU SHOULDN'T HAVE GOTTEN INVOLVED.
HMPH.
NEXT TIME SHE SHOWS UP, I'LL GIVE HER A TASTE OF HER OWN MEDICINE.
That night
WHEEEERE IIIS SHEEEE?
SHE CAN'T RECOGNIZE YOU WITH A DIFFERENT HAIRSTYLE.
THIS IS GETTING COMPLICATED.
I GUESS WE'RE SLEEPING OVER.

CHAPTER 293: REHEARSAL

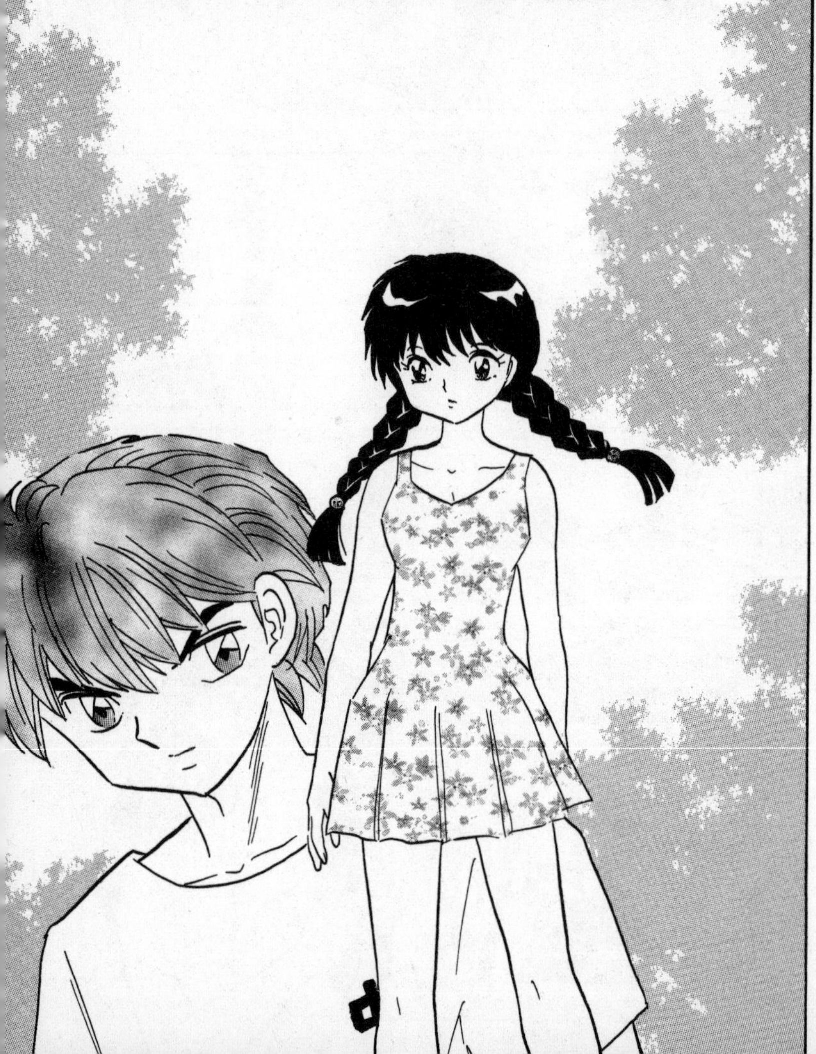

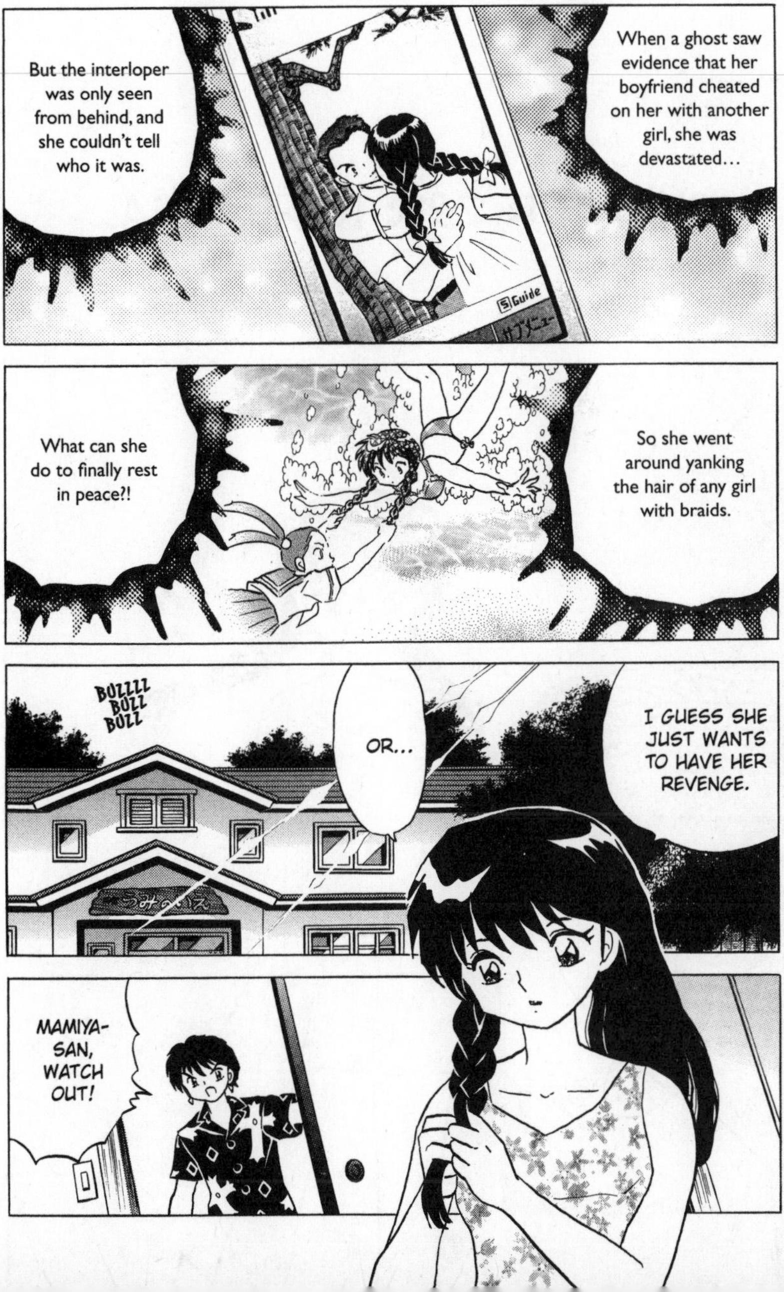
When a ghost saw evidence that her boyfriend cheated on her with another girl, she was devastated…
But the interloper was only seen from behind, and she couldn't tell who it was.
So she went around yanking the hair of any girl with braids.
What can she do to finally rest in peace?!
I GUESS SHE JUST WANTS TO HAVE HER REVENGE.
OR…
BUZZZZ BUZZ BUZZ
MAMIYA-SAN, WATCH OUT!

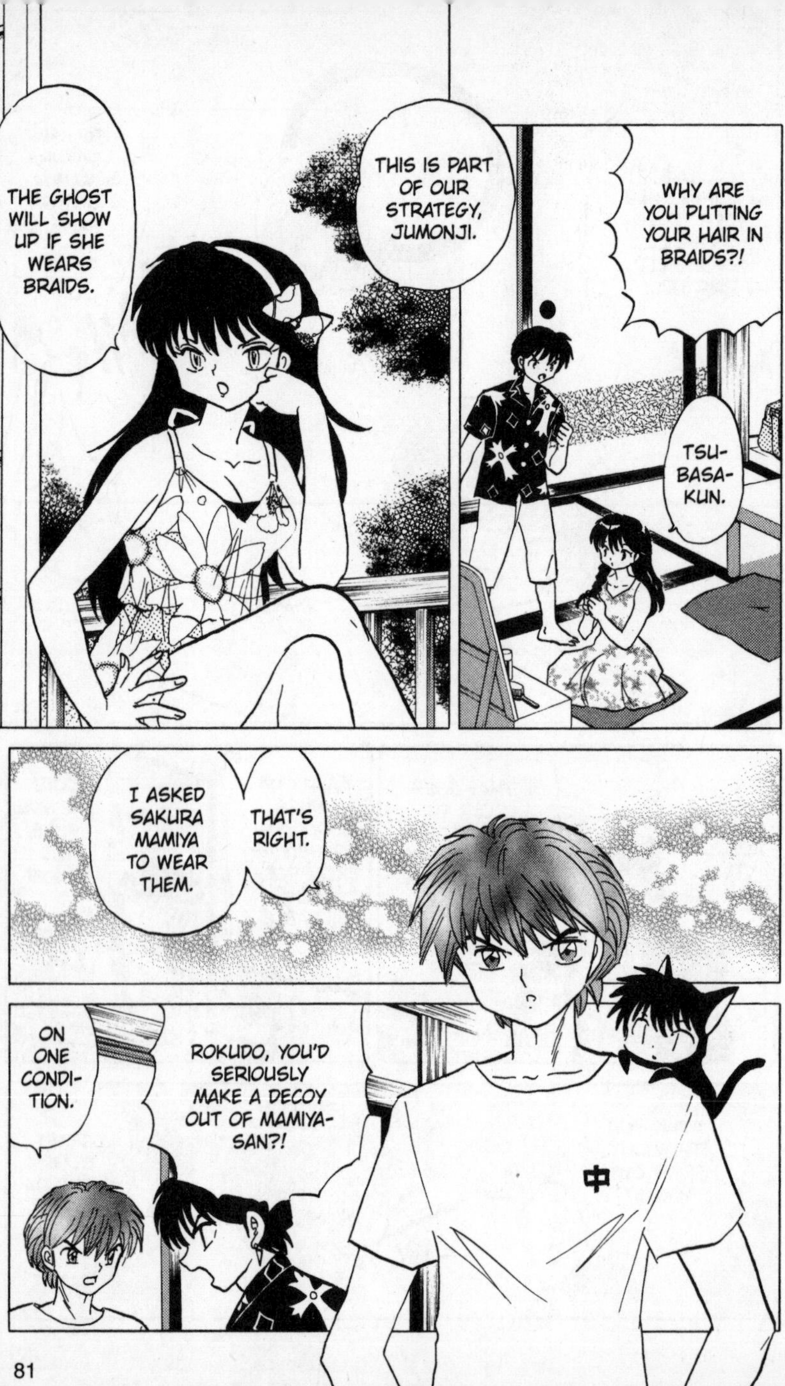
WHY ARE YOU PUTTING YOUR HAIR IN BRAIDS?!
TSU-BASA-KUN.
THIS IS PART OF OUR STRATEGY, JUMONJI.
THE GHOST WILL SHOW UP IF SHE WEARS BRAIDS.
THAT'S RIGHT.
I ASKED SAKURA MAMIYA TO WEAR THEM.
ROKUDO, YOU'D SERIOUSLY MAKE A DECOY OUT OF MAMIYA-SAN?!
ON ONE CONDI-TION.
中

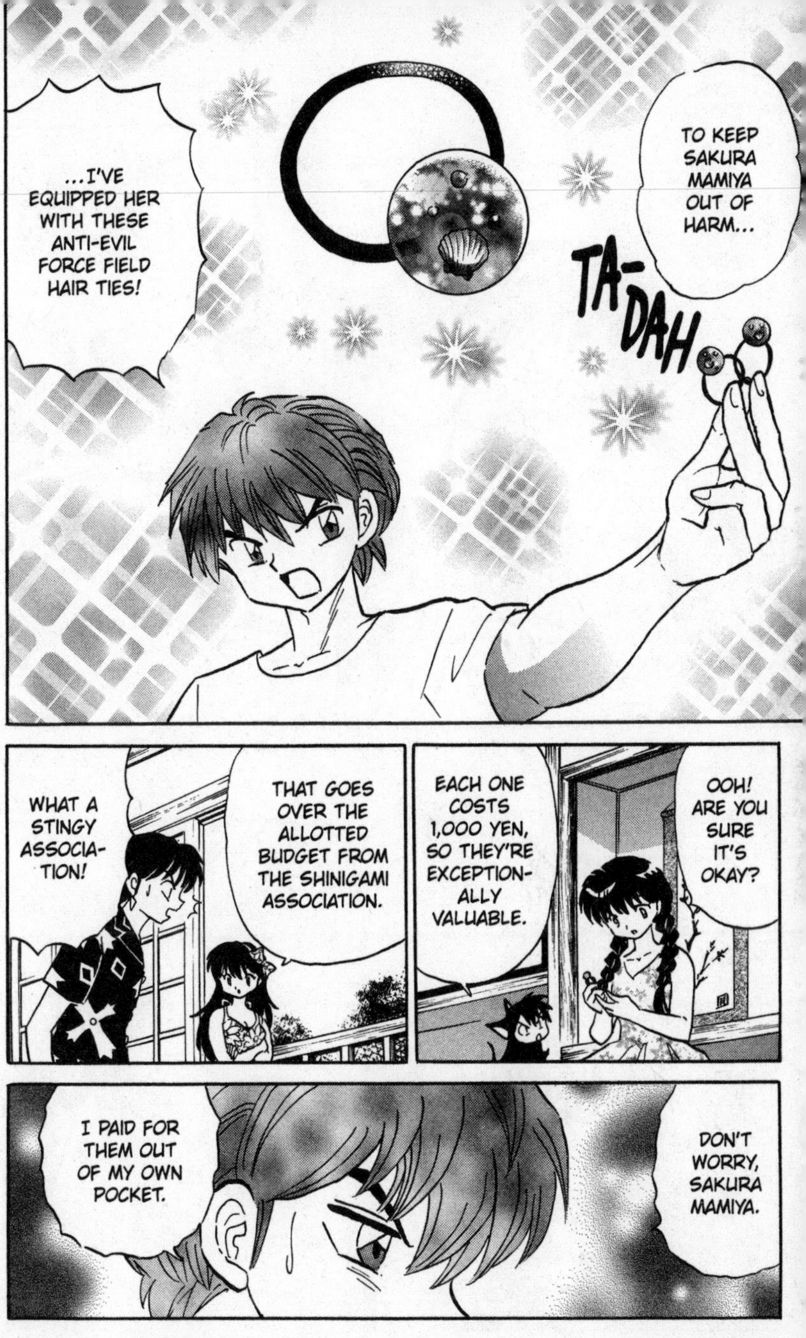
TO KEEP SAKURA MAMIYA OUT OF HARM...
TA-DAH
...I'VE EQUIPPED HER WITH THESE ANTI-EVIL FORCE FIELD HAIR TIES!
OOH! ARE YOU SURE IT'S OKAY?
EACH ONE COSTS 1,000 YEN, SO THEY'RE EXCEPTION-ALLY VALUABLE.
THAT GOES OVER THE ALLOTTED BUDGET FROM THE SHINIGAMI ASSOCIATION.
WHAT A STINGY ASSOCIA-TION!
DON'T WORRY, SAKURA MAMIYA.
I PAID FOR THEM OUT OF MY OWN POCKET.

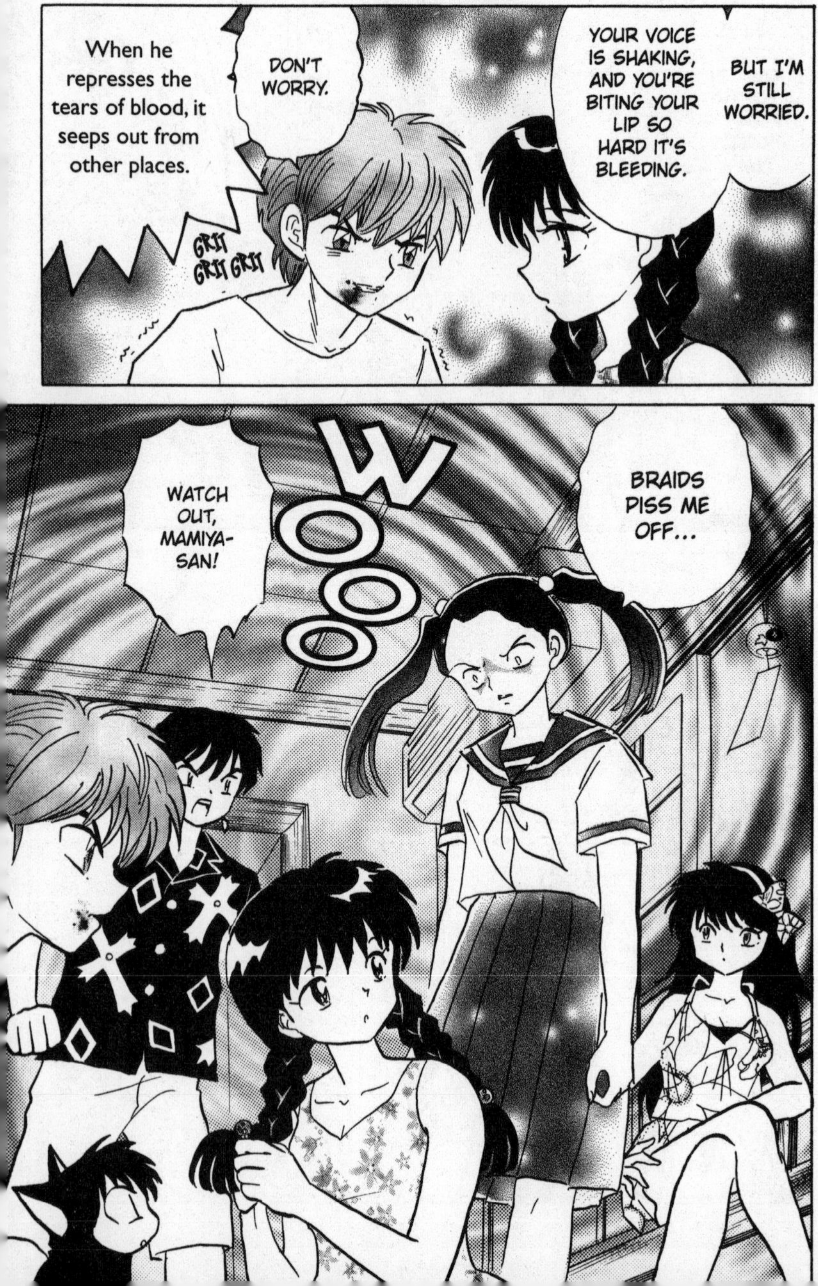

BUT I'M STILL WORRIED.
YOUR VOICE IS SHAKING, AND YOU'RE BITING YOUR LIP SO HARD IT'S BLEEDING.
DON'T WORRY.
GRIT GRIT GRIT
When he represses the tears of blood, it seeps out from other places.
BRAIDS PISS ME OFF...
WOOO
WATCH OUT, MAMIYA-SAN!

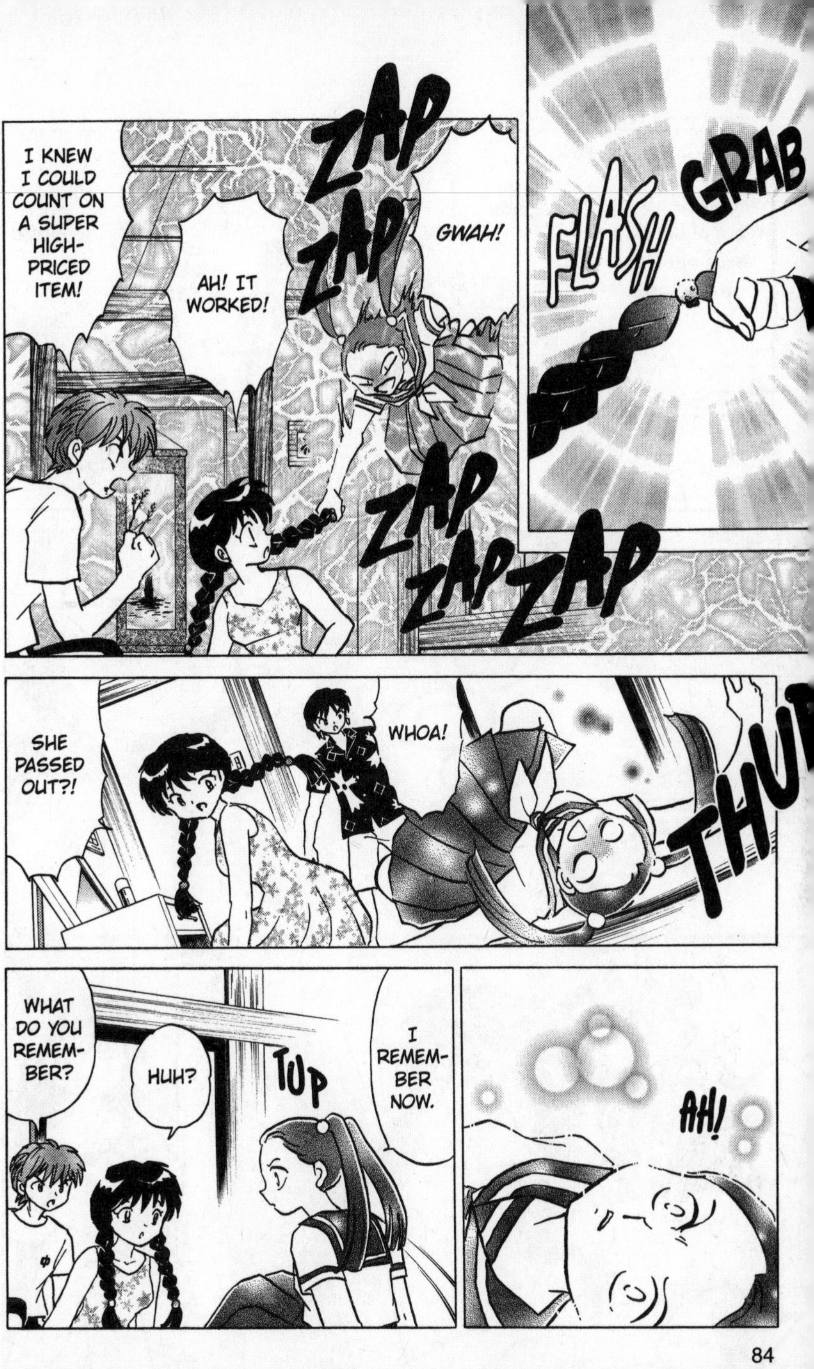
FLASH
GRAB
ZAP
ZAP
GWAH!
AH! IT WORKED!
I KNEW I COULD COUNT ON A SUPER HIGH-PRICED ITEM!
ZAP
ZAP
ZAP
ZAP
THU
WHOA!
SHE PASSED OUT?!
AH!
I REMEMBER NOW.
TUP
HUH?
WHAT DO YOU REMEMBER?

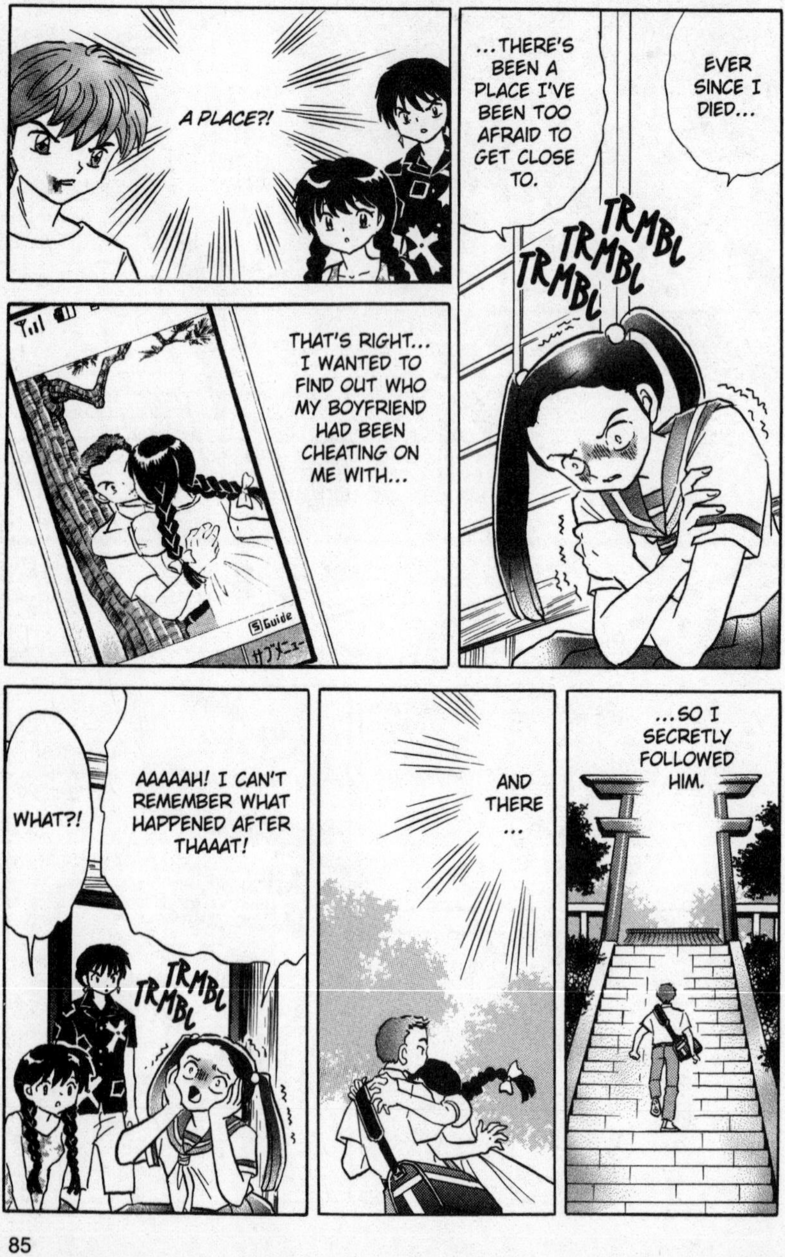
EVER SINCE I DIED...
...THERE'S BEEN A PLACE I'VE BEEN TOO AFRAID TO GET CLOSE TO.
TRMBL TRMBL TRMBL
A PLACE?!
Guide
サブメニュー
THAT'S RIGHT... I WANTED TO FIND OUT WHO MY BOYFRIEND HAD BEEN CHEATING ON ME WITH...
...SO I SECRETLY FOLLOWED HIM.
AND THERE ...
AAAAAH! I CAN'T REMEMBER WHAT HAPPENED AFTER THAAAT!
WHAT?!
TRMBL TRMBL

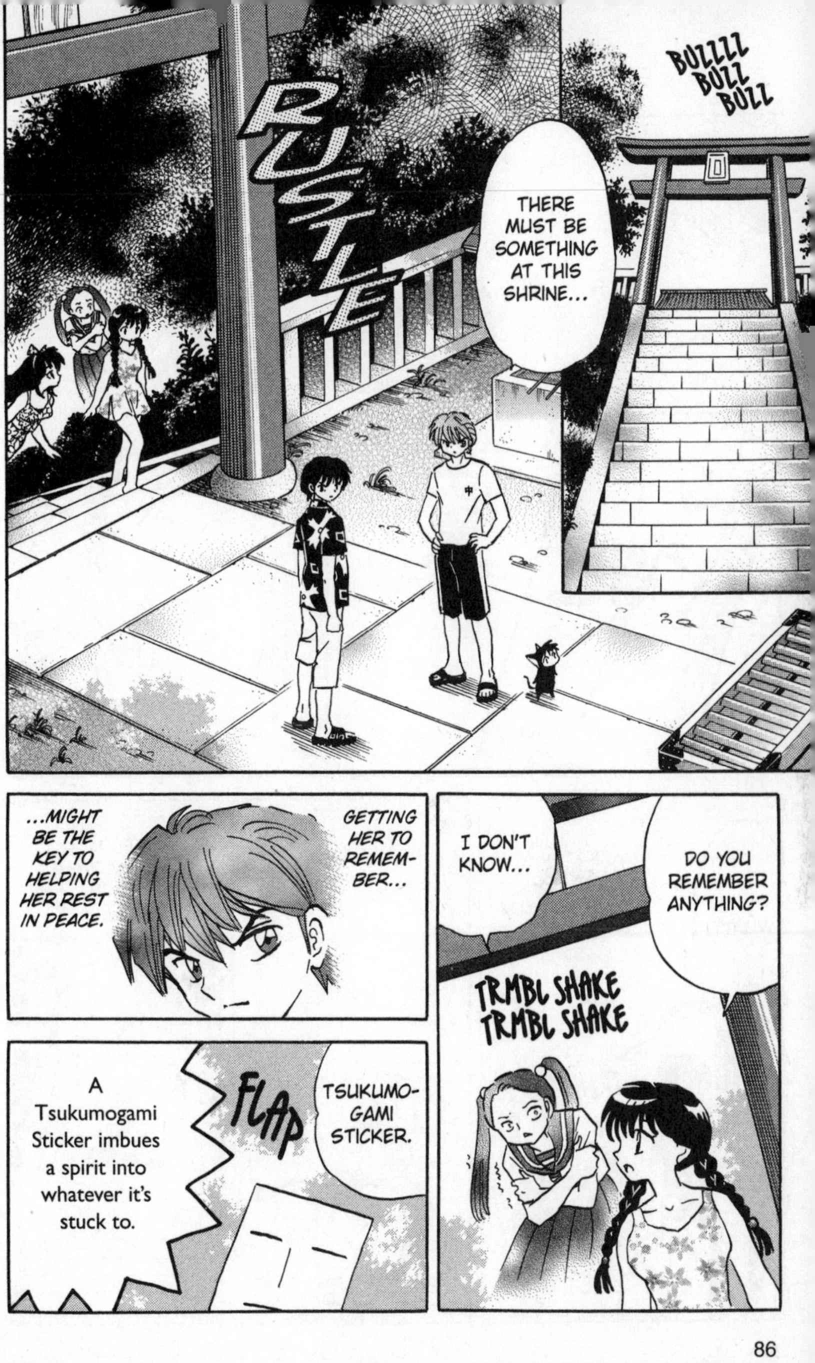
BUZZZZ BUZZ BUZZ
THERE MUST BE SOMETHING AT THIS SHRINE...
RUSTLE
DO YOU REMEMBER ANYTHING?
I DON'T KNOW...
TRMBL SHAKE TRMBL SHAKE
GETTING HER TO REMEMBER...
...MIGHT BE THE KEY TO HELPING HER REST IN PEACE.
TSUKUMOGAMI STICKER.
FLAP
A Tsukumogami Sticker imbues a spirit into whatever it's stuck to.

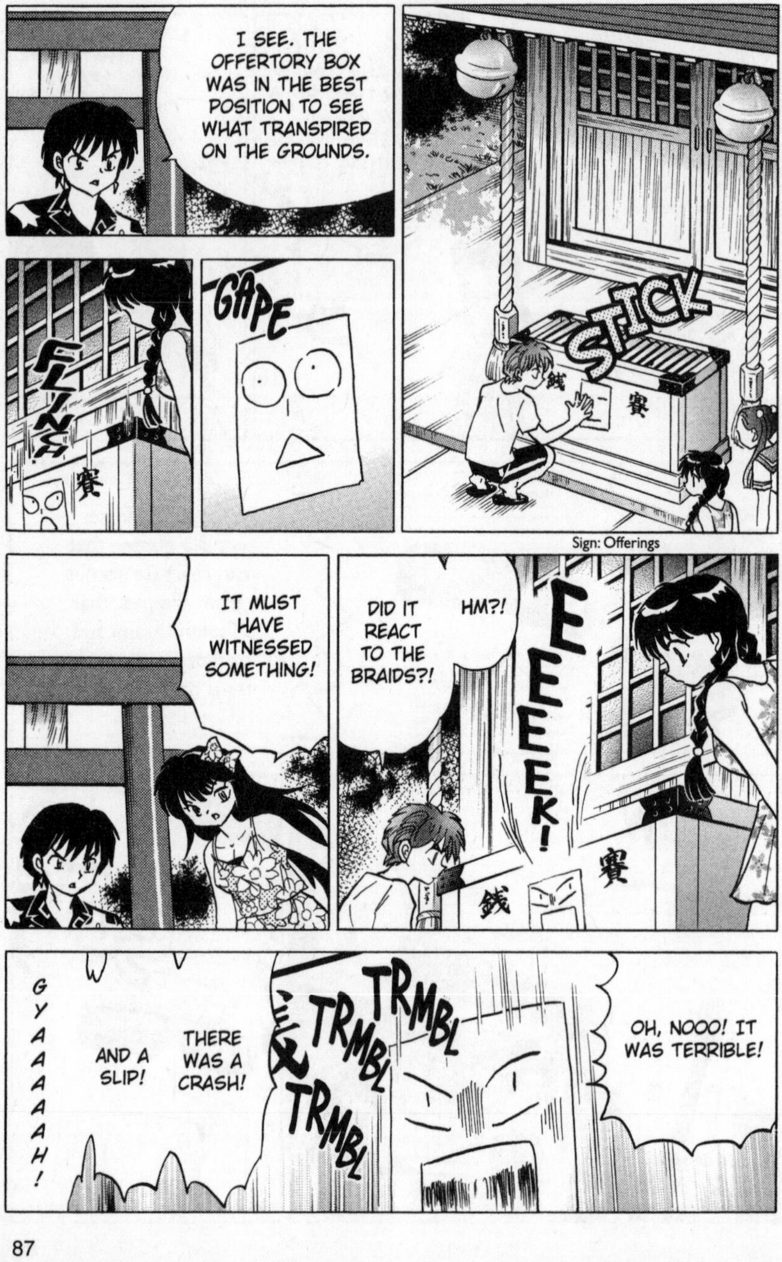
STICK
Sign: Offerings
I SEE. THE OFFERTORY BOX WAS IN THE BEST POSITION TO SEE WHAT TRANSPIRED ON THE GROUNDS.
GAPE
FLINCH
HM?!
DID IT REACT TO THE BRAIDS?!
EEEEEK!
IT MUST HAVE WITNESSED SOMETHING!
OH, NOOO! IT WAS TERRIBLE!
TRMBL
TRMBL
TRMBL
THERE WAS A CRASH!
AND A SLIP!
GYAAAAAAAH!

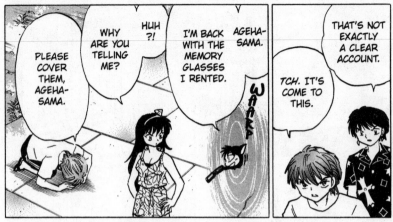

THAT'S NOT EXACTLY A CLEAR ACCOUNT.
TCH. IT'S COME TO THIS.
AGEHA-SAMA.
I'M BACK WITH THE MEMORY GLASSES I RENTED.
WAAARP
HUH?!
WHY ARE YOU TELLING ME?
PLEASE COVER THEM, AGEHA-SAMA.
Memory Glasses are 3D glasses that can recreate scenes from the past that Tsukumogami and other inarticulate items have witnessed.
Rental cost: 1,000 yen
Anaglyph Type
1,000 YEN?
THAT'S DEFINITELY OVER BUDGET.
SLAP
HM?!
GLOW
賽銭

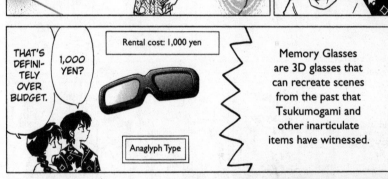

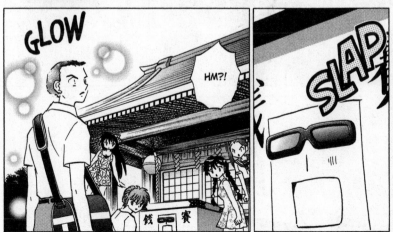

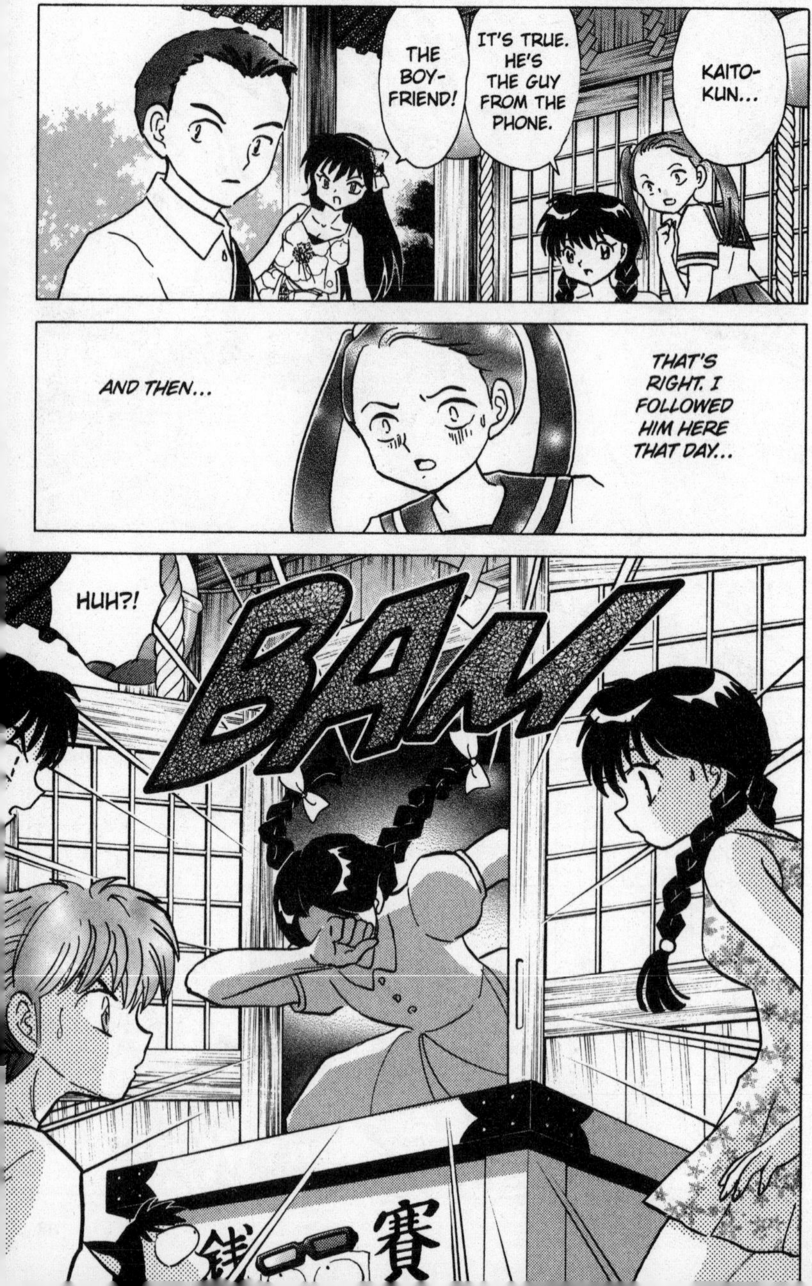
KAITO-KUN...
IT'S TRUE. HE'S THE GUY FROM THE PHONE.
THE BOY-FRIEND!
THAT'S RIGHT. I FOLLOWED HIM HERE THAT DAY...
AND THEN...
BAM
HUH?!

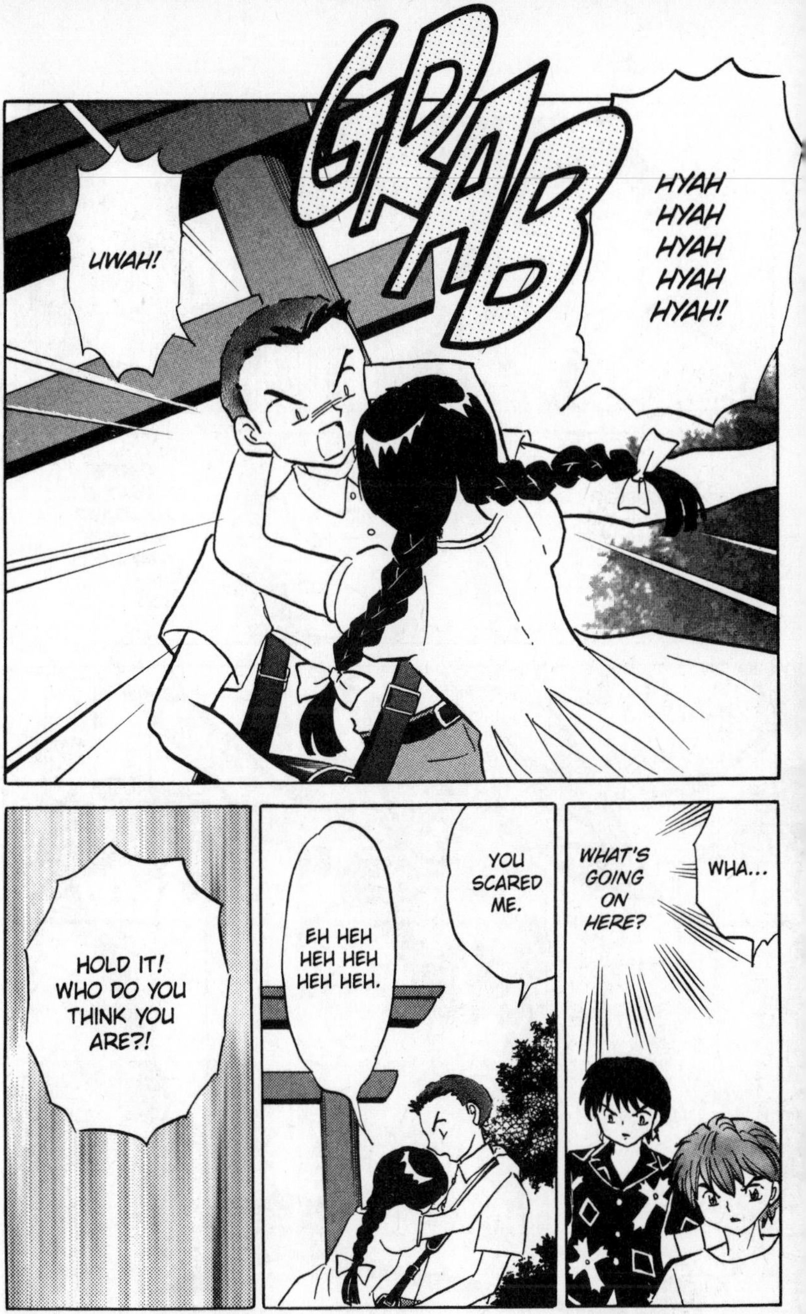
HYAH HYAH HYAH HYAH HYAH!
GRAB
UWAH!
WHA...
WHAT'S GOING ON HERE?
YOU SCARED ME.
EH HEH HEH HEH HEH HEH.
HOLD IT! WHO DO YOU THINK YOU ARE?!

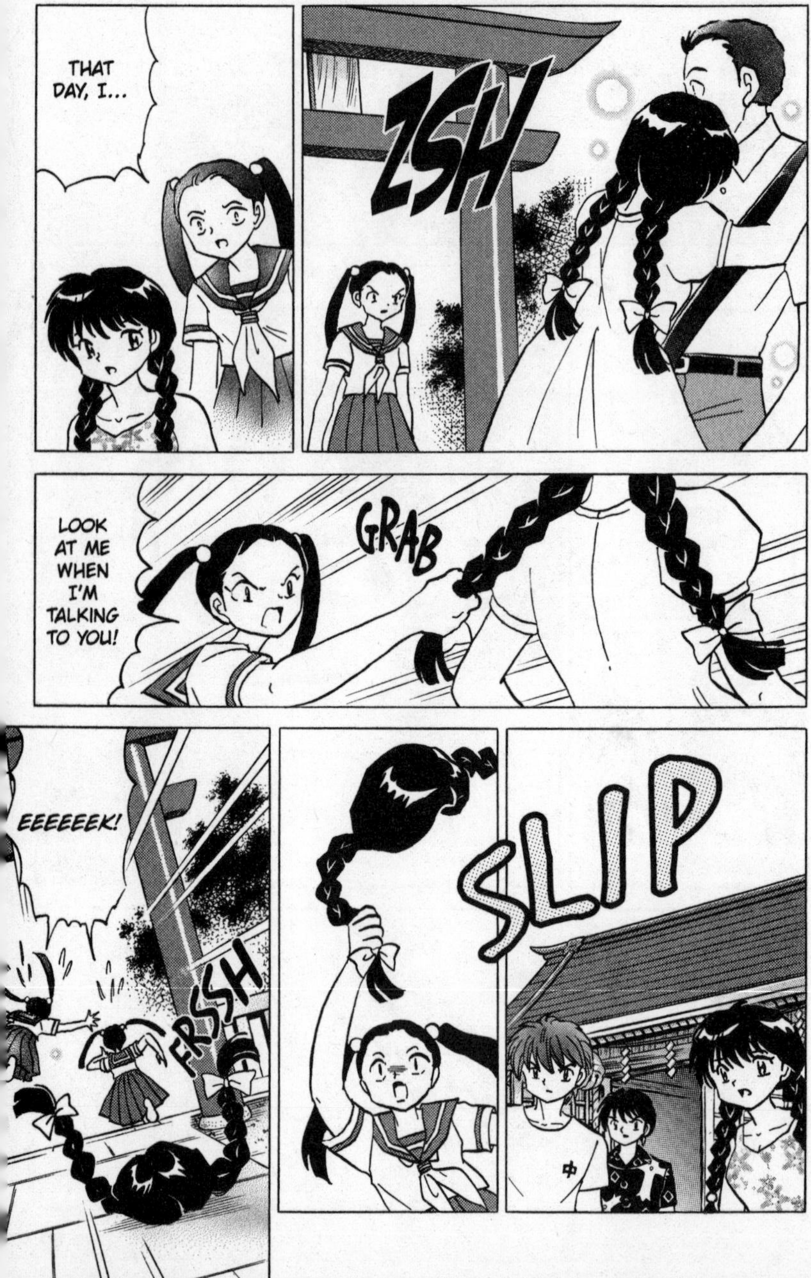
ZSH
THAT DAY, I...
GRAB
LOOK AT ME WHEN I'M TALKING TO YOU!
SLIP
EEEEEEK!
FRSSH

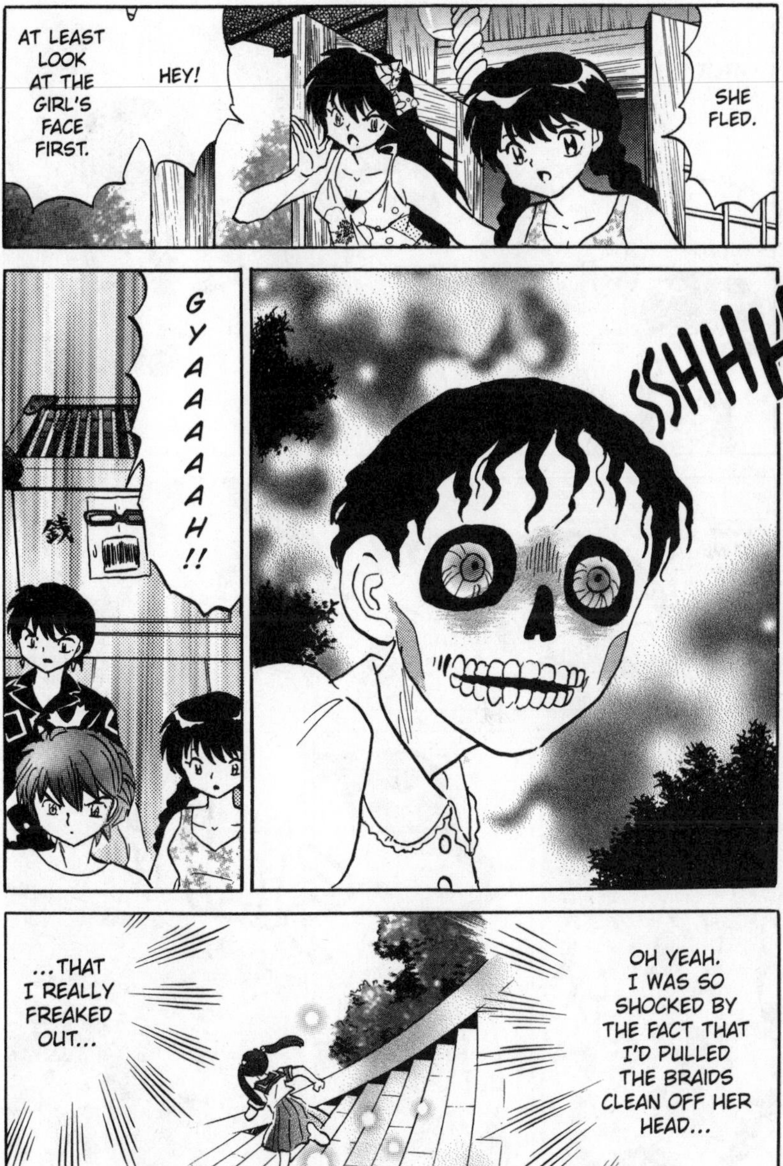
SHE FLED.
HEY!
AT LEAST LOOK AT THE GIRL'S FACE FIRST.
SSHHH
GYAAAAAAAH!!
OH YEAH. I WAS SO SHOCKED BY THE FACT THAT I'D PULLED THE BRAIDS CLEAN OFF HER HEAD...
...THAT I REALLY FREAKED OUT...

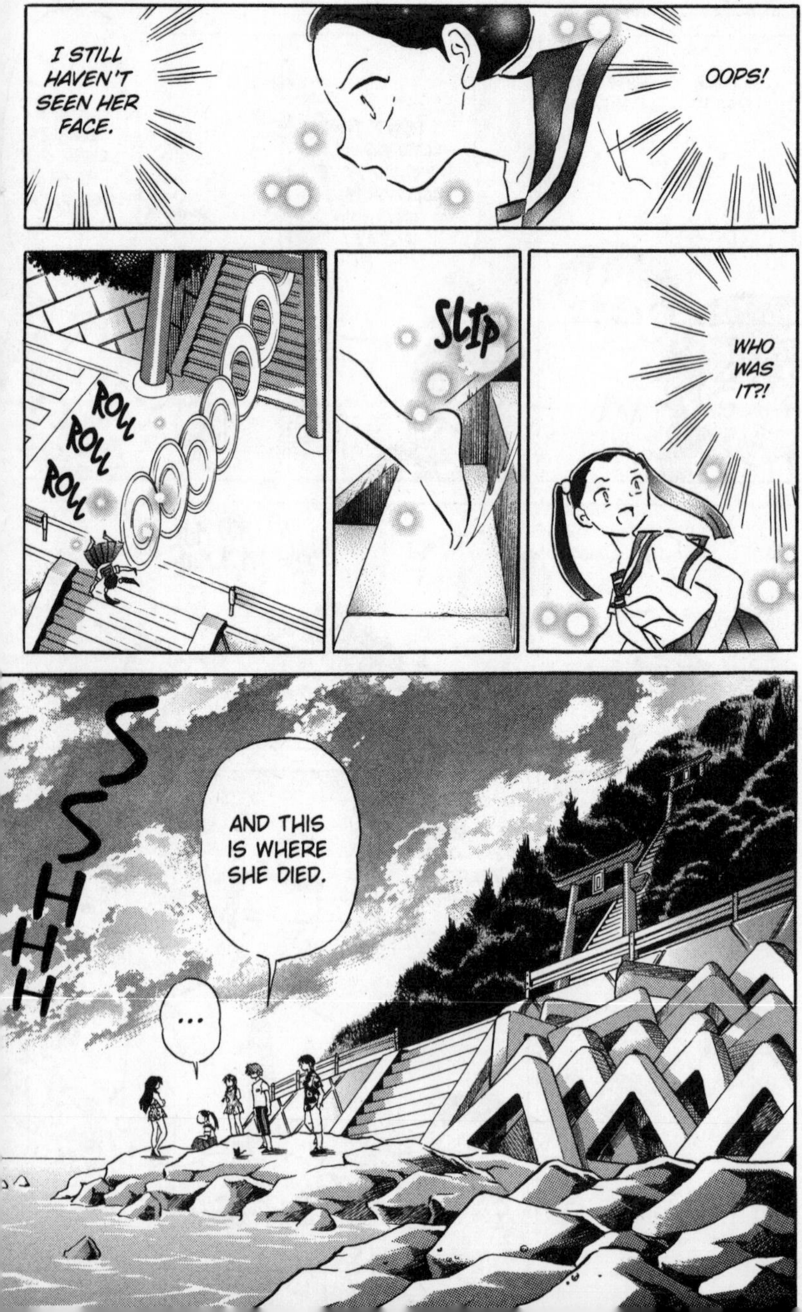

OOPS!
I STILL HAVEN'T SEEN HER FACE.
WHO WAS IT?!
SLIP
ROLL ROLL ROLL
AND THIS IS WHERE SHE DIED.
SSHHHH
...

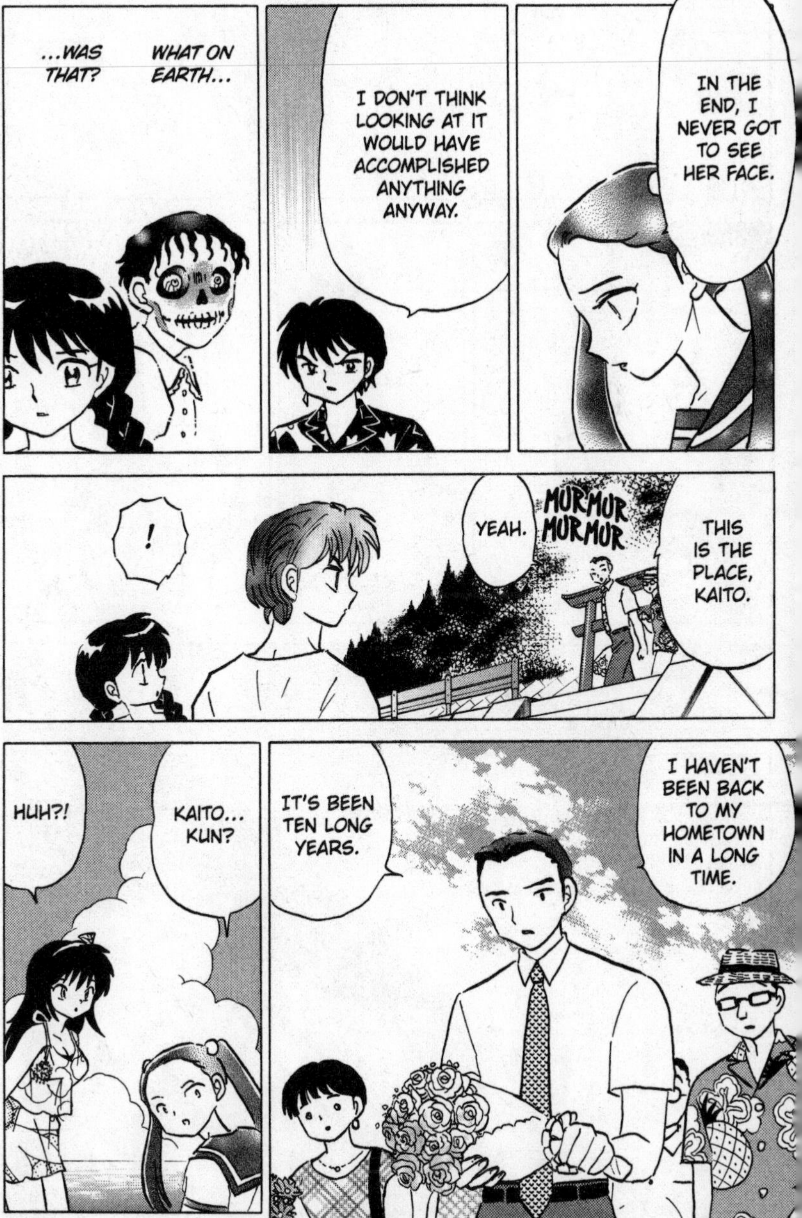
IN THE END, I NEVER GOT TO SEE HER FACE.
I DON'T THINK LOOKING AT IT WOULD HAVE ACCOMPLISHED ANYTHING ANYWAY.
WHAT ON EARTH...
...WAS THAT?
THIS IS THE PLACE, KAITO.
MURMUR MURMUR
YEAH.
!
I HAVEN'T BEEN BACK TO MY HOMETOWN IN A LONG TIME.
IT'S BEEN TEN LONG YEARS.
KAITO... KUN?
HUH?!

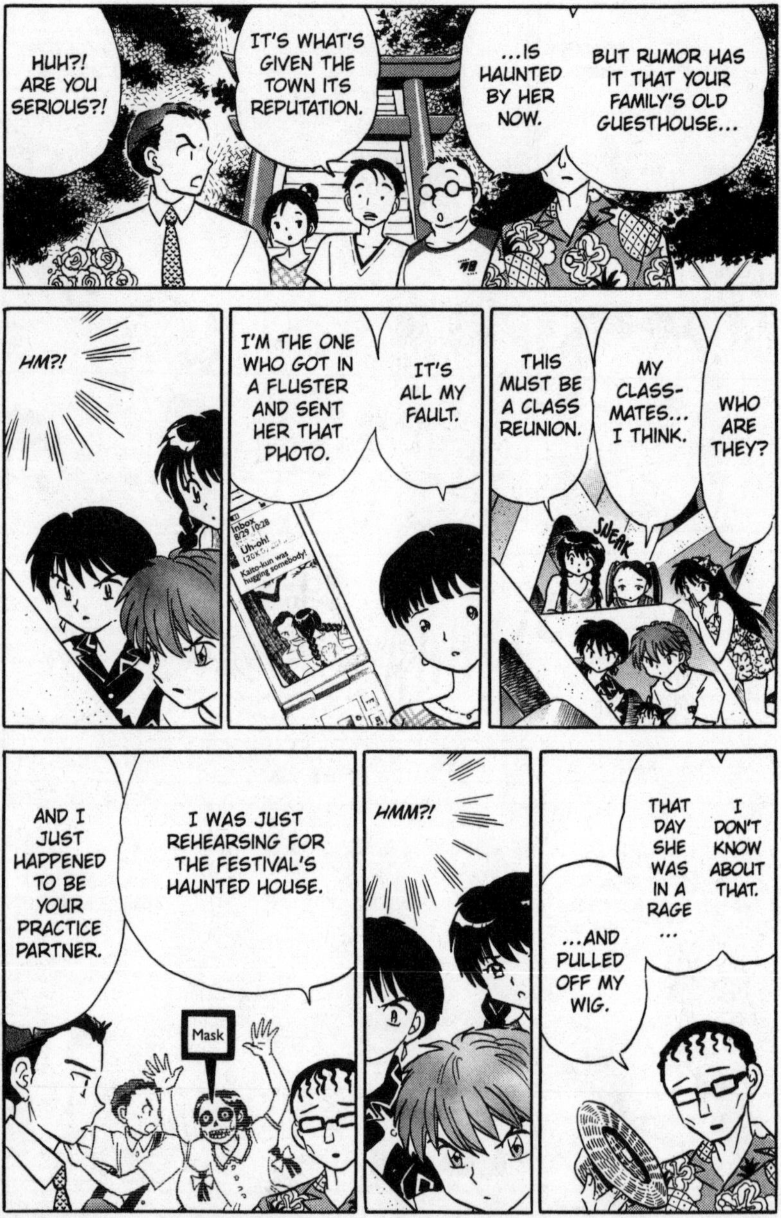
BUT RUMOR HAS IT THAT YOUR FAMILY'S OLD GUESTHOUSE...
...IS HAUNTED BY HER NOW.
IT'S WHAT'S GIVEN THE TOWN ITS REPUTATION.
HUH?! ARE YOU SERIOUS?!
WHO ARE THEY?
MY CLASSMATES... I THINK.
THIS MUST BE A CLASS REUNION.
SNEAK
IT'S ALL MY FAULT.
I'M THE ONE WHO GOT IN A FLUSTER AND SENT HER THAT PHOTO.
Inbox
8/29 10:28
Uh-oh!
Kaito-kun was hugging somebody!
HM?!
I DON'T KNOW ABOUT THAT.
THAT DAY SHE WAS IN A RAGE...
...AND PULLED OFF MY WIG.
HMM?!
I WAS JUST REHEARSING FOR THE FESTIVAL'S HAUNTED HOUSE.
AND I JUST HAPPENED TO BE YOUR PRACTICE PARTNER.
Mask

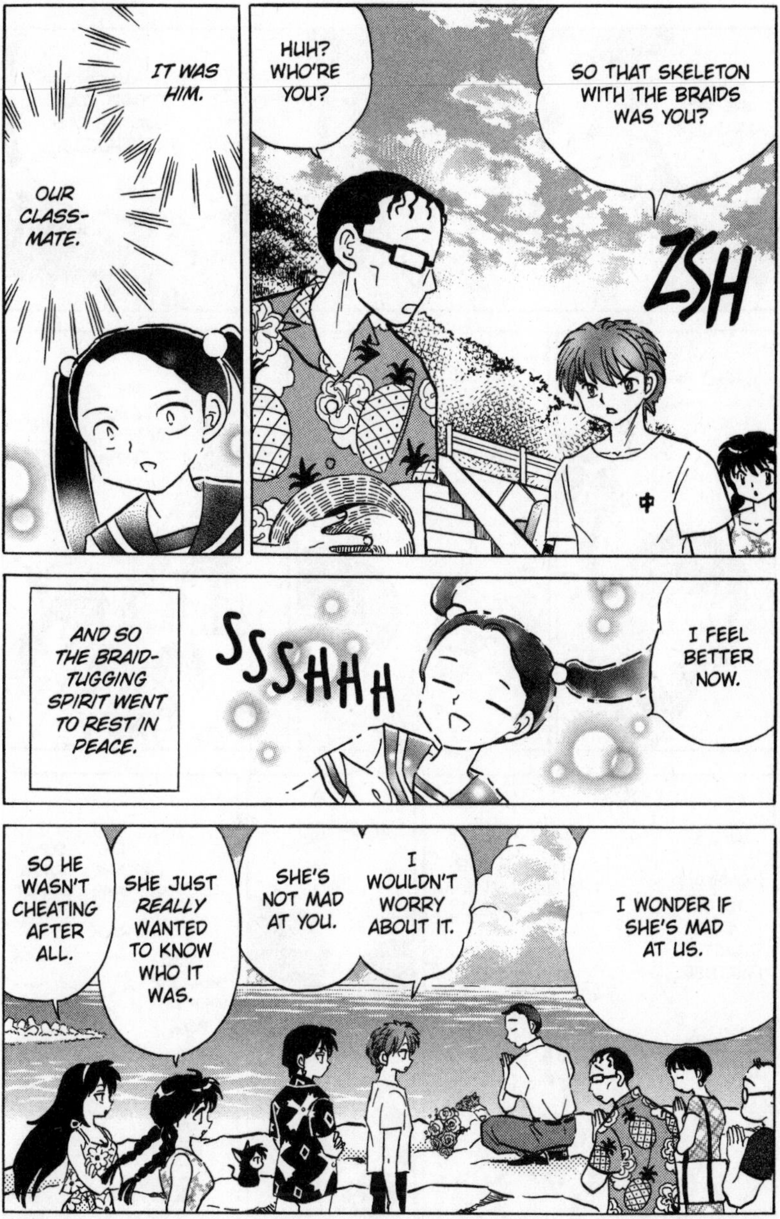
SO THAT SKELETON WITH THE BRAIDS WAS YOU?
ZSH
HUH? WHO'RE YOU?
IT WAS HIM.
OUR CLASSMATE.
I FEEL BETTER NOW.
SSSHHH
AND SO THE BRAID-TUGGING SPIRIT WENT TO REST IN PEACE.
I WONDER IF SHE'S MAD AT US.
I WOULDN'T WORRY ABOUT IT.
SHE'S NOT MAD AT YOU.
SHE JUST *REALLY* WANTED TO KNOW WHO IT WAS.
SO HE WASN'T CHEATING AFTER ALL.

CHAPTER 294: THE GIRLFRIEND IN THE ICE

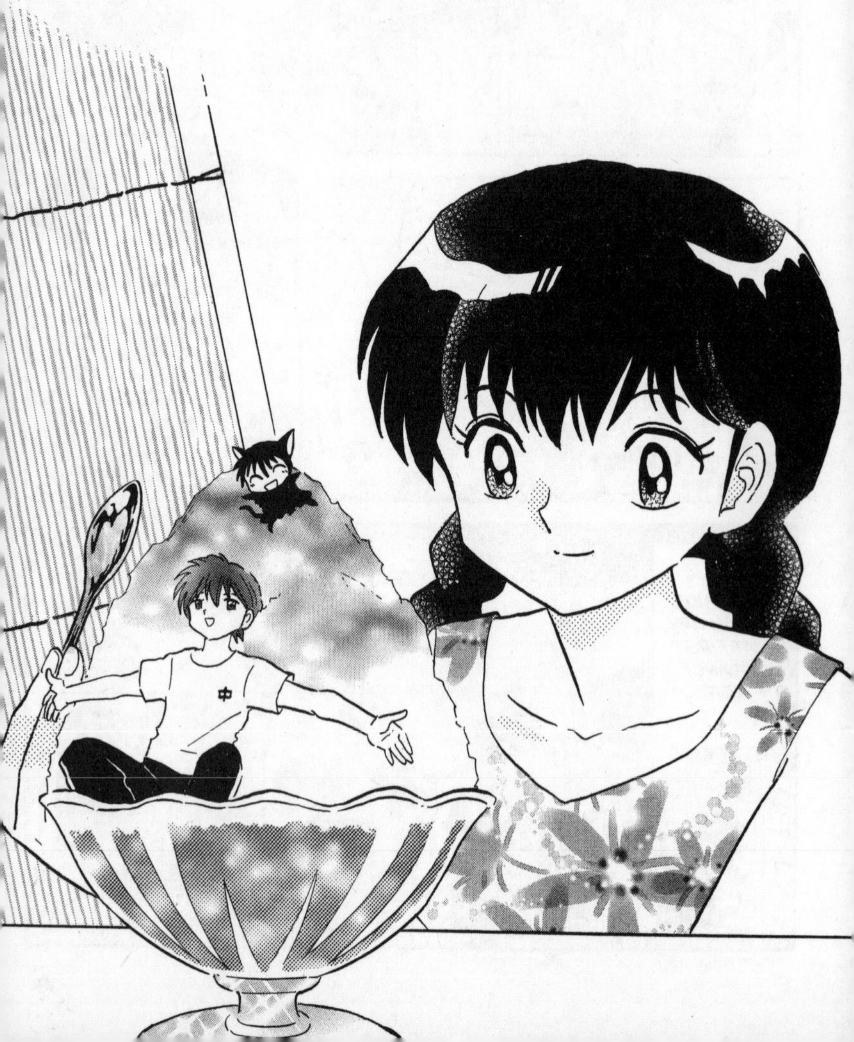

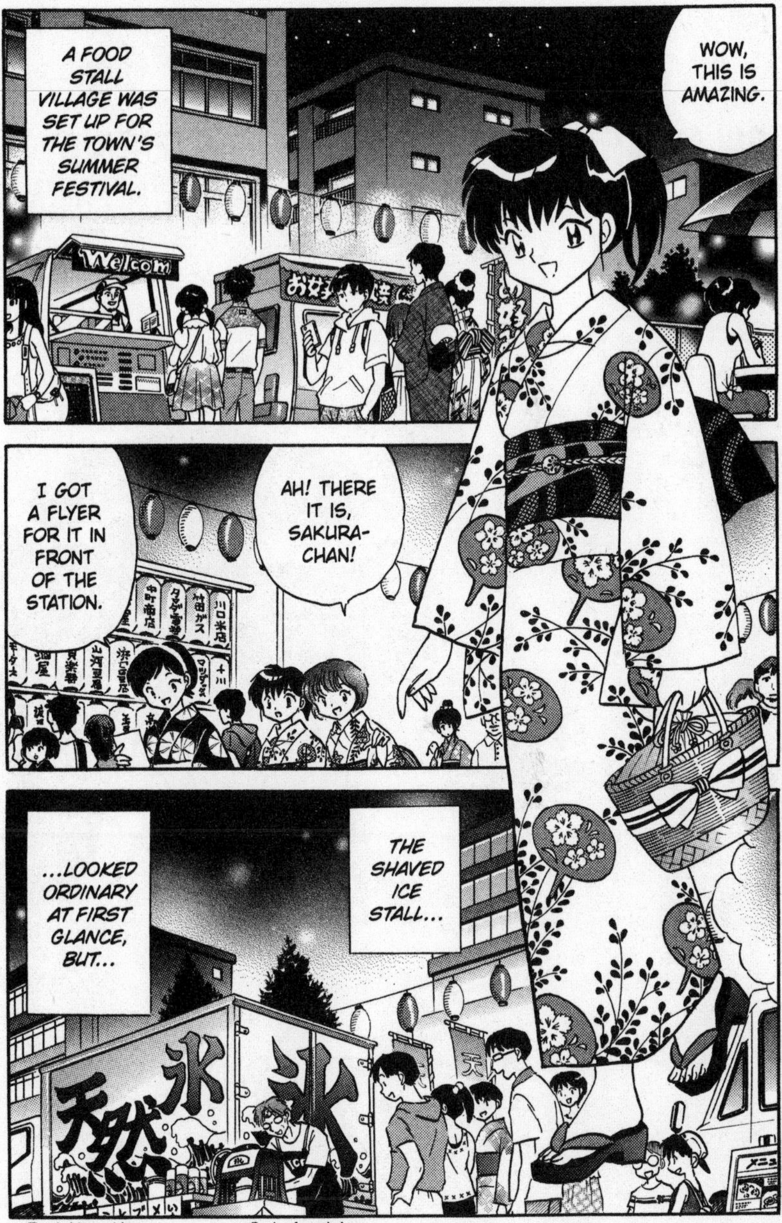
WOW, THIS IS AMAZING.
A FOOD STALL VILLAGE WAS SET UP FOR THE TOWN'S SUMMER FESTIVAL.
AH! THERE IT IS, SAKURA-CHAN!
I GOT A FLYER FOR IT IN FRONT OF THE STATION.
THE SHAVED ICE STALL...
...LOOKED ORDINARY AT FIRST GLANCE, BUT...

Truck: Natural Ice

Back of truck: Ice

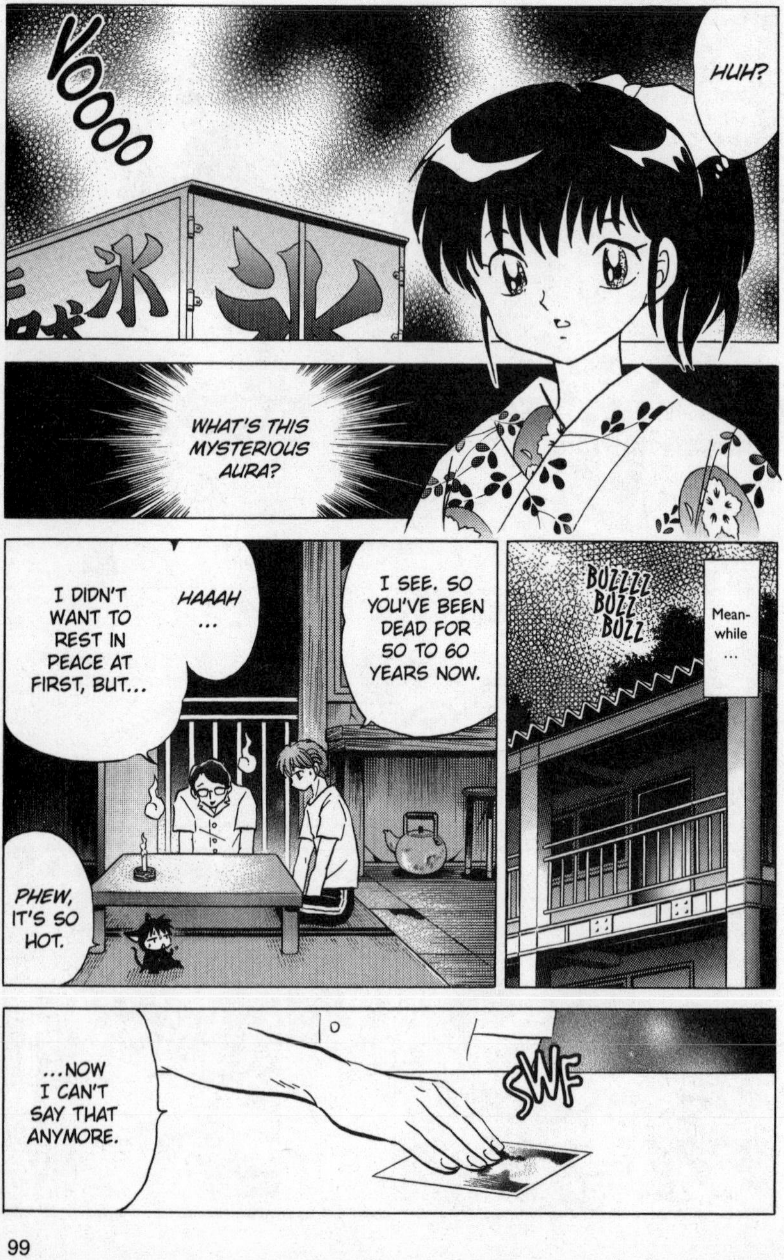
HUH?
VOOOO
WHAT'S THIS MYSTERIOUS AURA?
Mean-while...
BUZZZZ BUZZ BUZZ
I SEE. SO YOU'VE BEEN DEAD FOR 50 TO 60 YEARS NOW.
HAAAH...
I DIDN'T WANT TO REST IN PEACE AT FIRST, BUT...
PHEW, IT'S SO HOT.
SWF
...NOW I CAN'T SAY THAT ANYMORE.

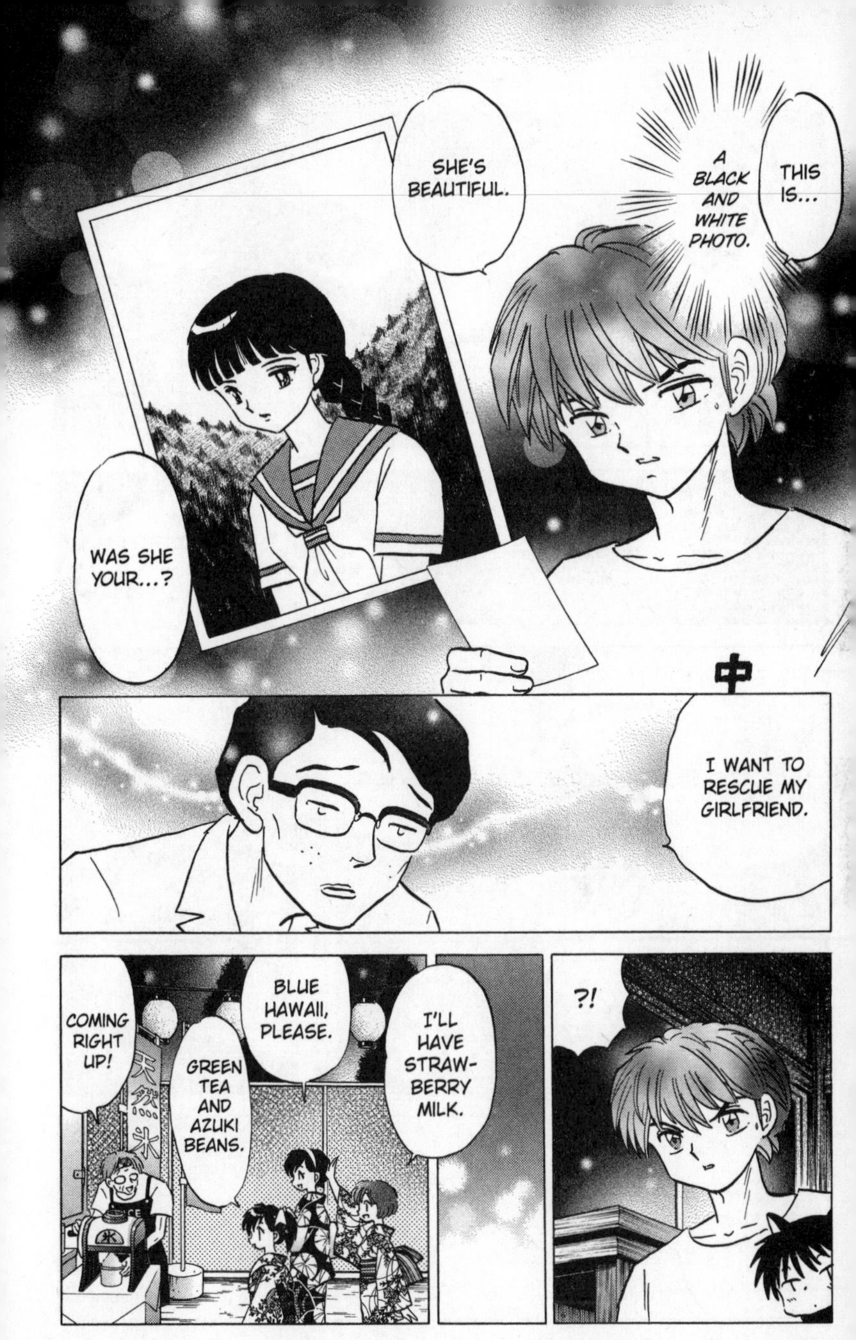
THIS IS...
A BLACK AND WHITE PHOTO.
SHE'S BEAUTIFUL.
WAS SHE YOUR...?
I WANT TO RESCUE MY GIRLFRIEND.
?!
I'LL HAVE STRAW-BERRY MILK.
BLUE HAWAII, PLEASE.
GREEN TEA AND AZUKI BEANS.
COMING RIGHT UP!

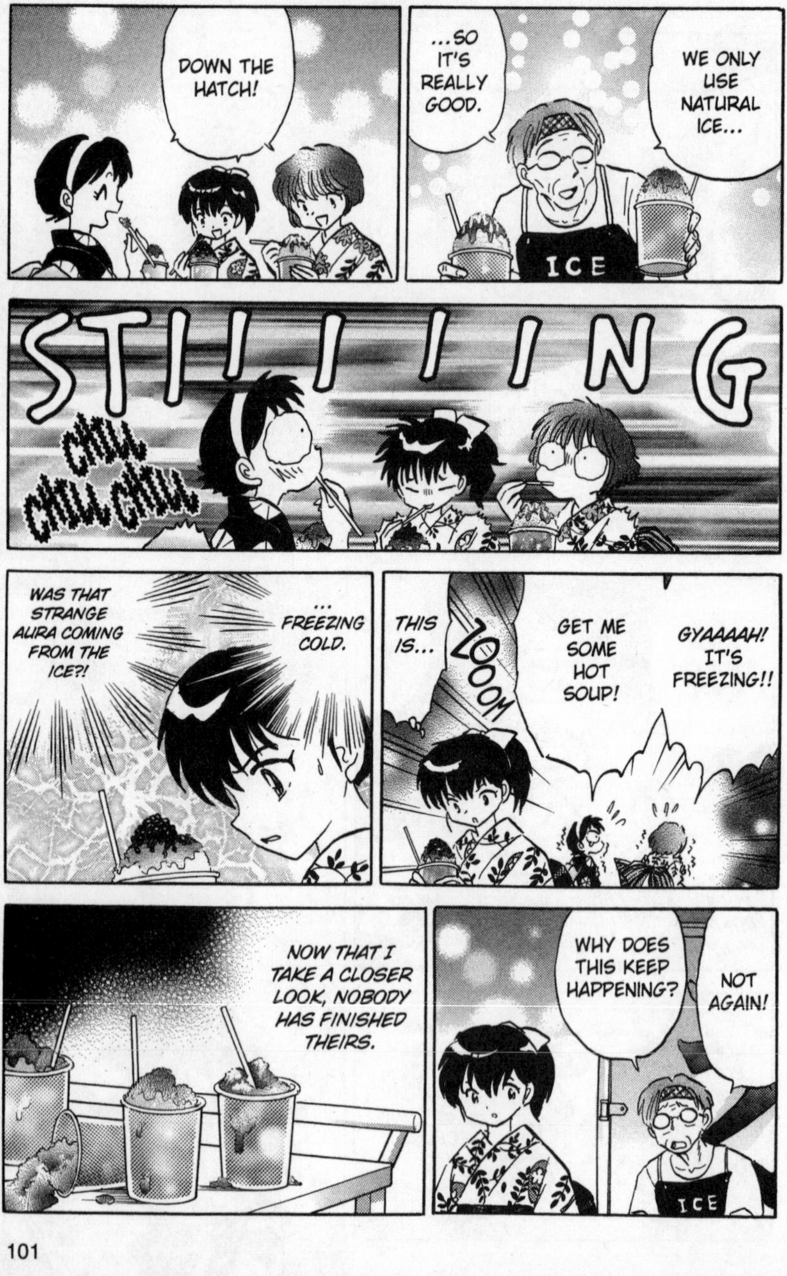
WE ONLY USE NATURAL ICE...
...SO IT'S REALLY GOOD.
ICE
DOWN THE HATCH!
STIIIIING
CHILL CHILL CHILL
GYAAAAH! IT'S FREEZING!!
GET ME SOME HOT SOUP!
ZOOOM
THIS IS...
...FREEZING COLD.
WAS THAT STRANGE AURA COMING FROM THE ICE?!
NOT AGAIN!
WHY DOES THIS KEEP HAPPENING?
ICE
NOW THAT I TAKE A CLOSER LOOK, NOBODY HAS FINISHED THEIRS.

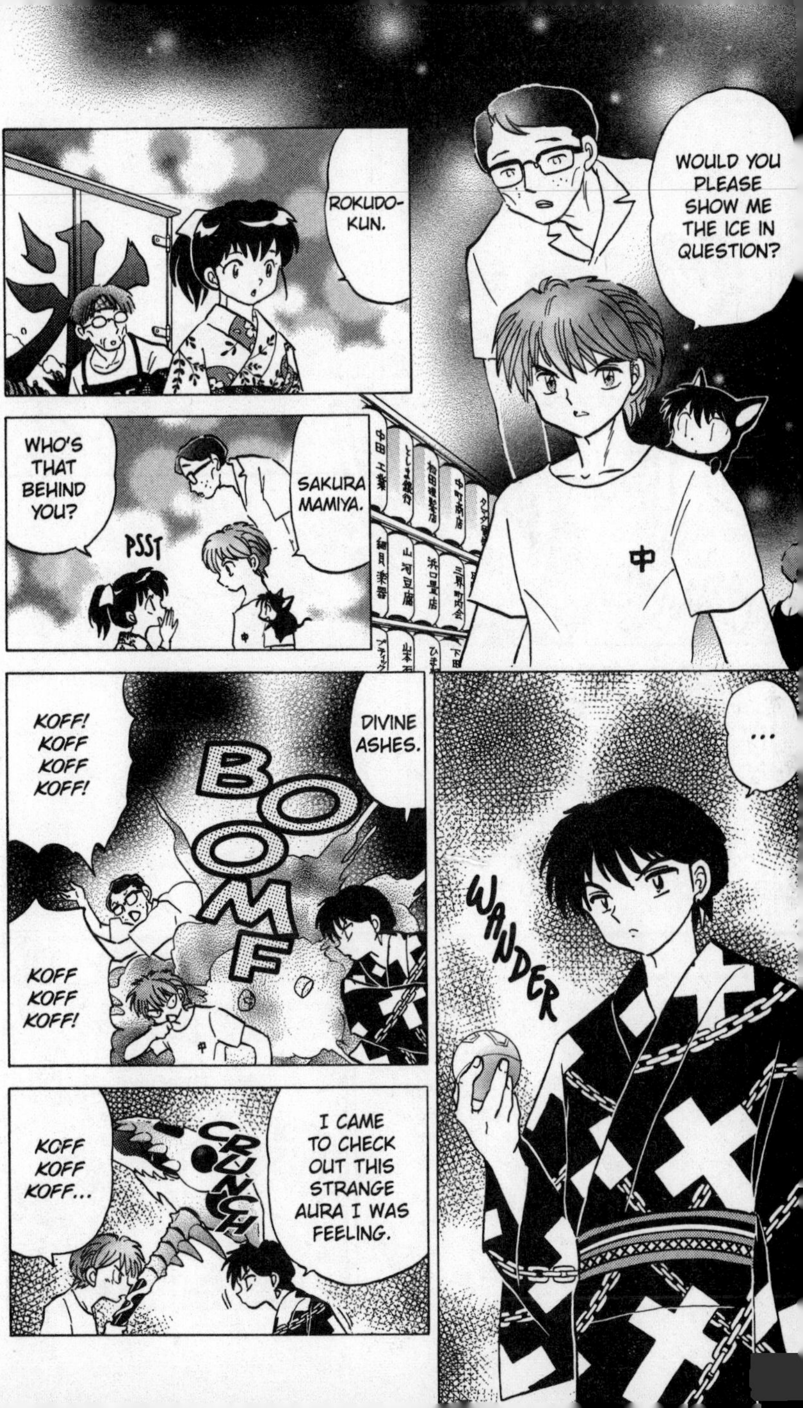
WOULD YOU PLEASE SHOW ME THE ICE IN QUESTION?
ROKUDO-KUN.
WHO'S THAT BEHIND YOU?
PSST
SAKURA MAMIYA.
...
WANDER
DIVINE ASHES.
BOOOMF
KOFF! KOFF KOFF KOFF!
KOFF KOFF KOFF!
I CAME TO CHECK OUT THIS STRANGE AURA I WAS FEELING.
CRUNCH
KOFF KOFF KOFF...

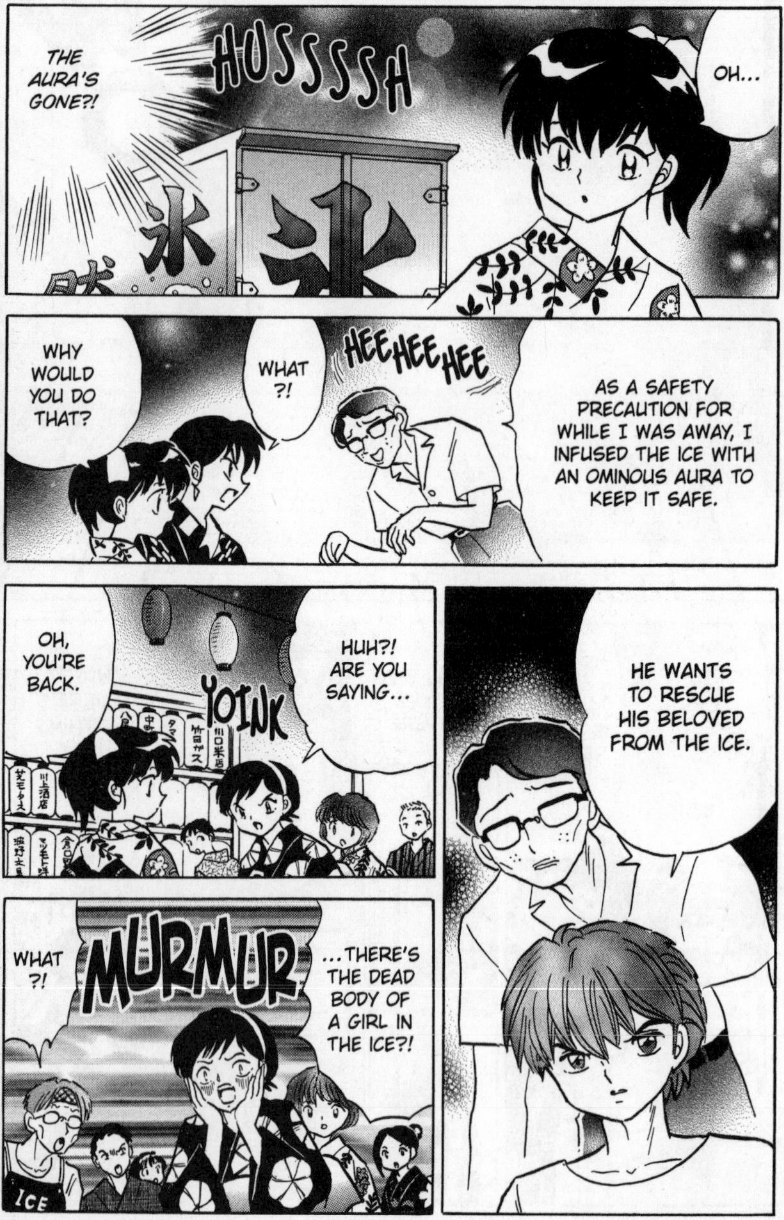
OH...
HUSSSSH
THE AURA'S GONE?!
AS A SAFETY PRECAUTION FOR WHILE I WAS AWAY, I INFUSED THE ICE WITH AN OMINOUS AURA TO KEEP IT SAFE.
HEE HEE HEE
WHAT ?!
WHY WOULD YOU DO THAT?
HE WANTS TO RESCUE HIS BELOVED FROM THE ICE.
HUH?! ARE YOU SAYING...
YOINK
OH, YOU'RE BACK.
...THERE'S THE DEAD BODY OF A GIRL IN THE ICE?!
MURMUR
WHAT ?!
ICE

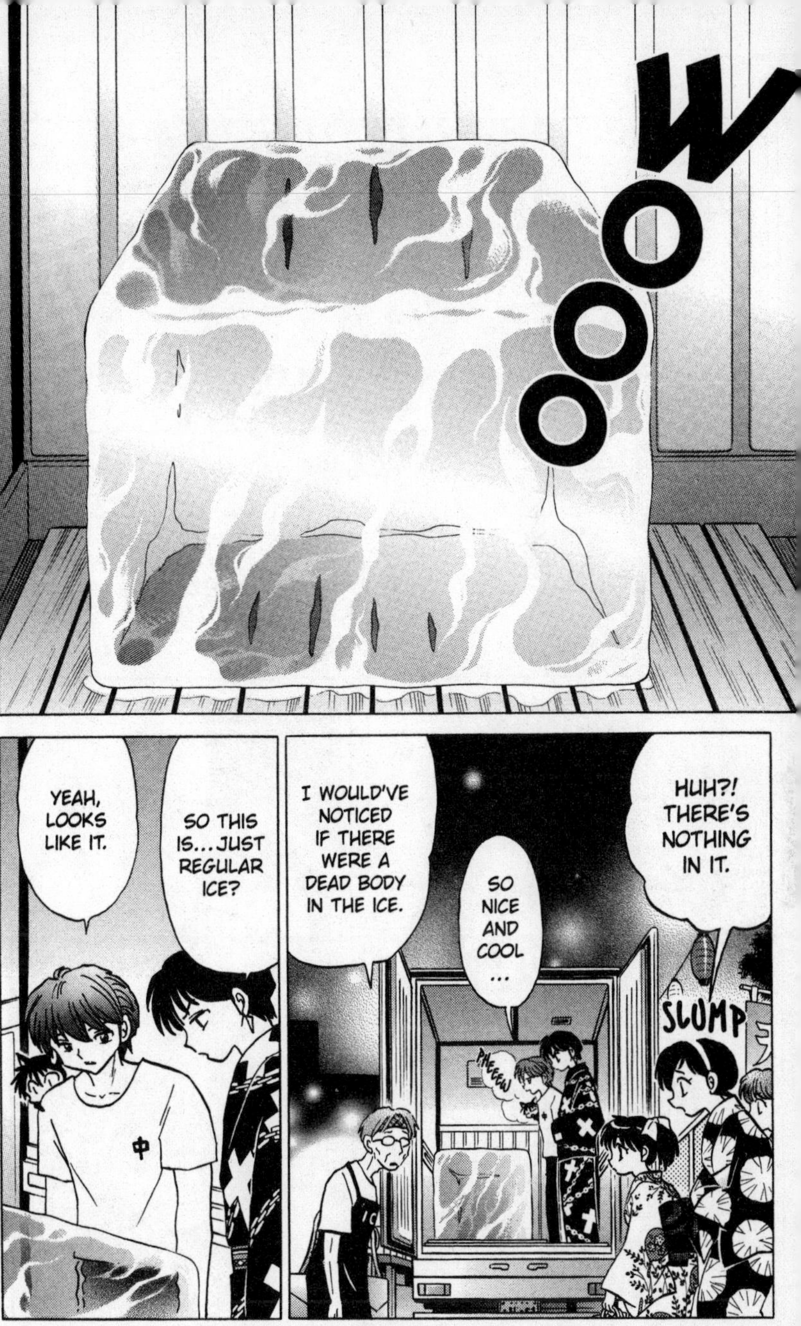
WOOO
HUH?! THERE'S NOTHING IN IT.
SLUMP
SO NICE AND COOL...
PHEEEW
I WOULD'VE NOTICED IF THERE WERE A DEAD BODY IN THE ICE.
SO THIS IS...JUST REGULAR ICE?
YEAH, LOOKS LIKE IT.

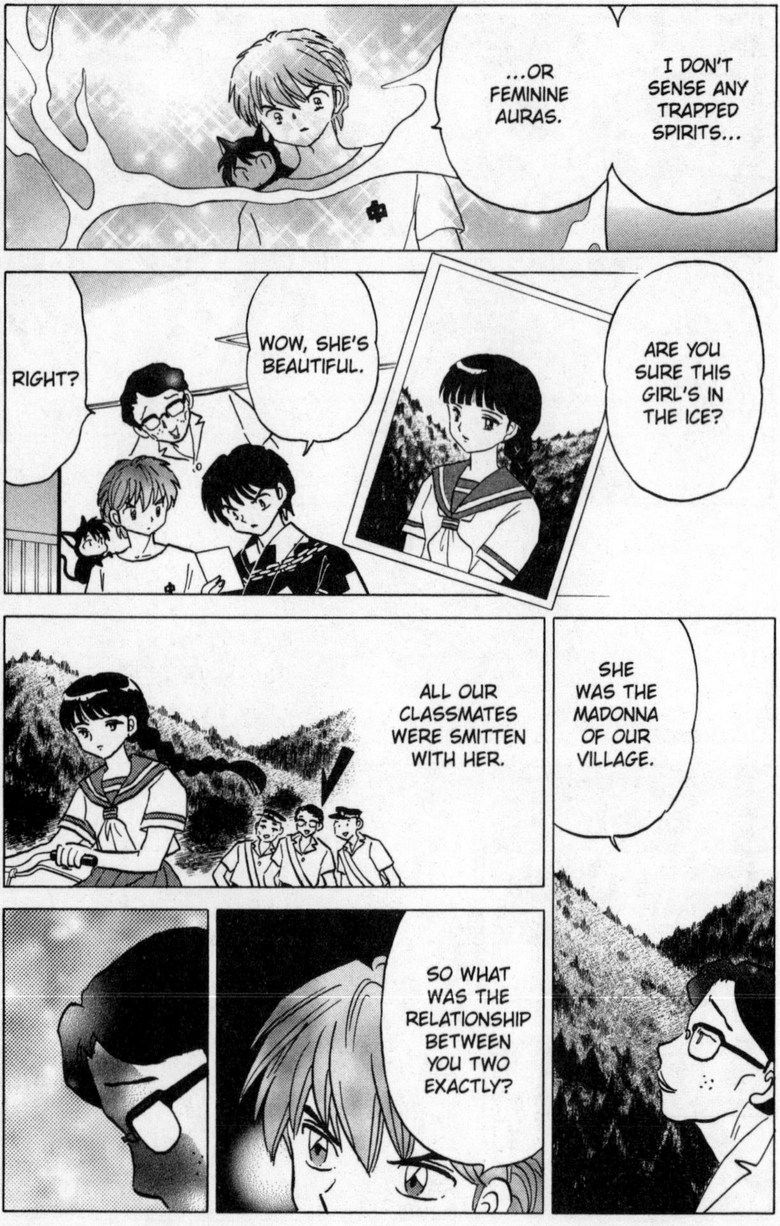
I DON'T SENSE ANY TRAPPED SPIRITS...
...OR FEMININE AURAS.
ARE YOU SURE THIS GIRL'S IN THE ICE?
WOW, SHE'S BEAUTIFUL.
RIGHT?
SHE WAS THE MADONNA OF OUR VILLAGE.
ALL OUR CLASSMATES WERE SMITTEN WITH HER.
SO WHAT WAS THE RELATIONSHIP BETWEEN YOU TWO EXACTLY?

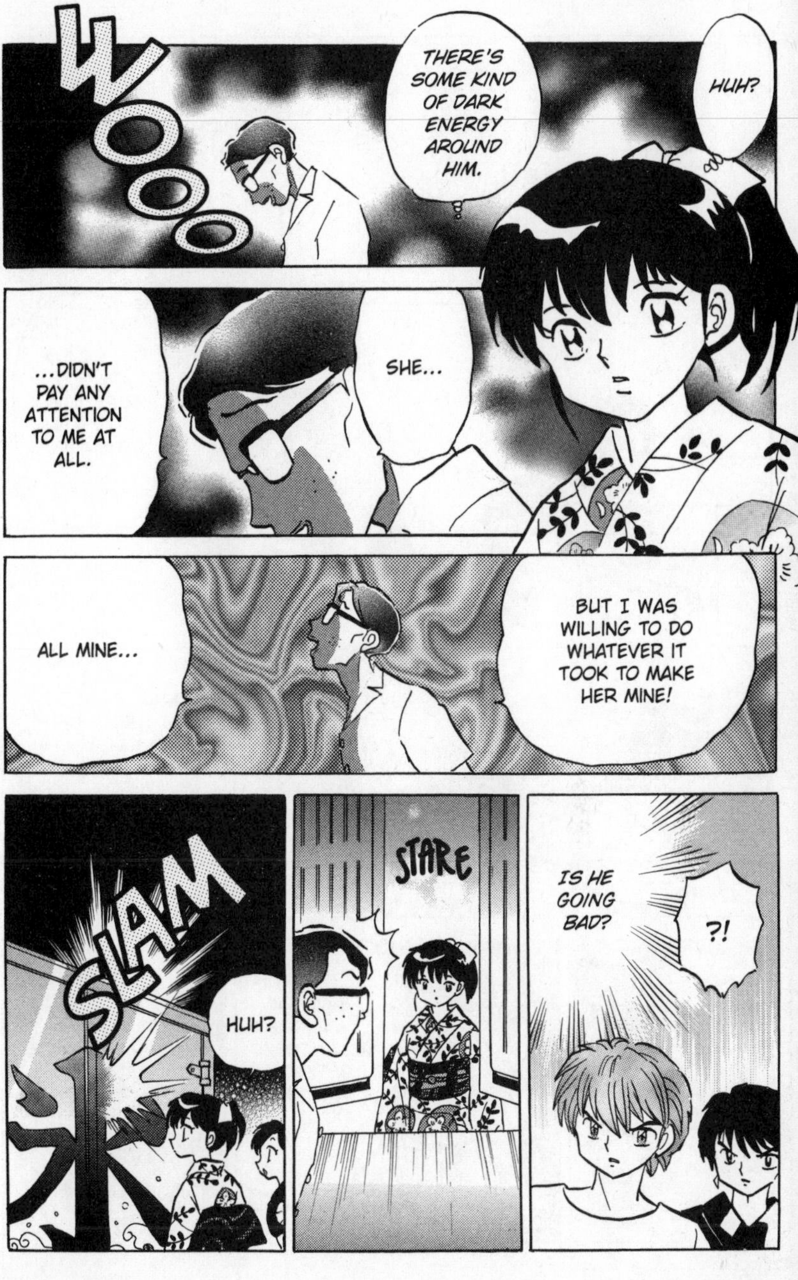
HUH?
THERE'S SOME KIND OF DARK ENERGY AROUND HIM.
WOOOO
SHE...
...DIDN'T PAY ANY ATTENTION TO ME AT ALL.
BUT I WAS WILLING TO DO WHATEVER IT TOOK TO MAKE HER MINE!
ALL MINE...
?!
IS HE GOING BAD?
STARE
SLAM
HUH?

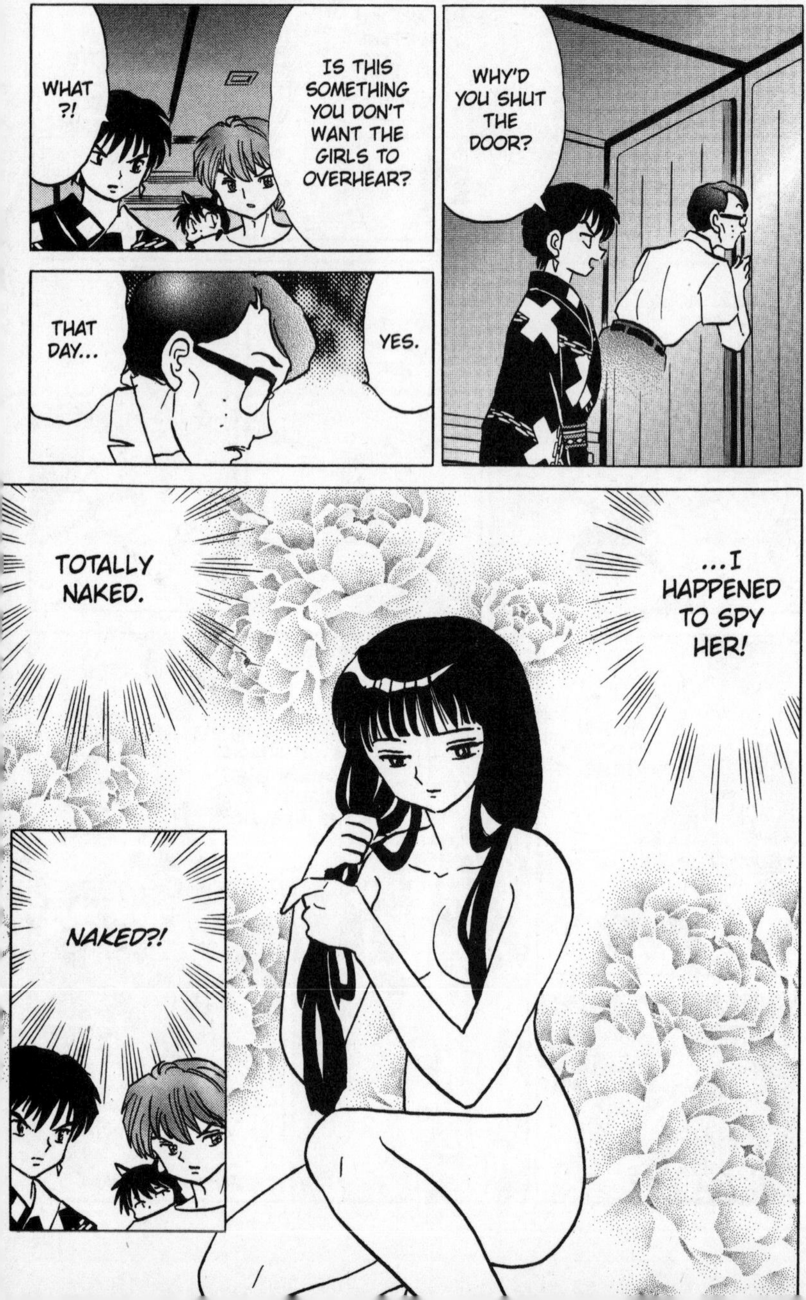
WHY'D YOU SHUT THE DOOR?
IS THIS SOMETHING YOU DON'T WANT THE GIRLS TO OVERHEAR?
WHAT ?!
YES.
THAT DAY...
...I HAPPENED TO SPY HER!
TOTALLY NAKED.
NAKED?!

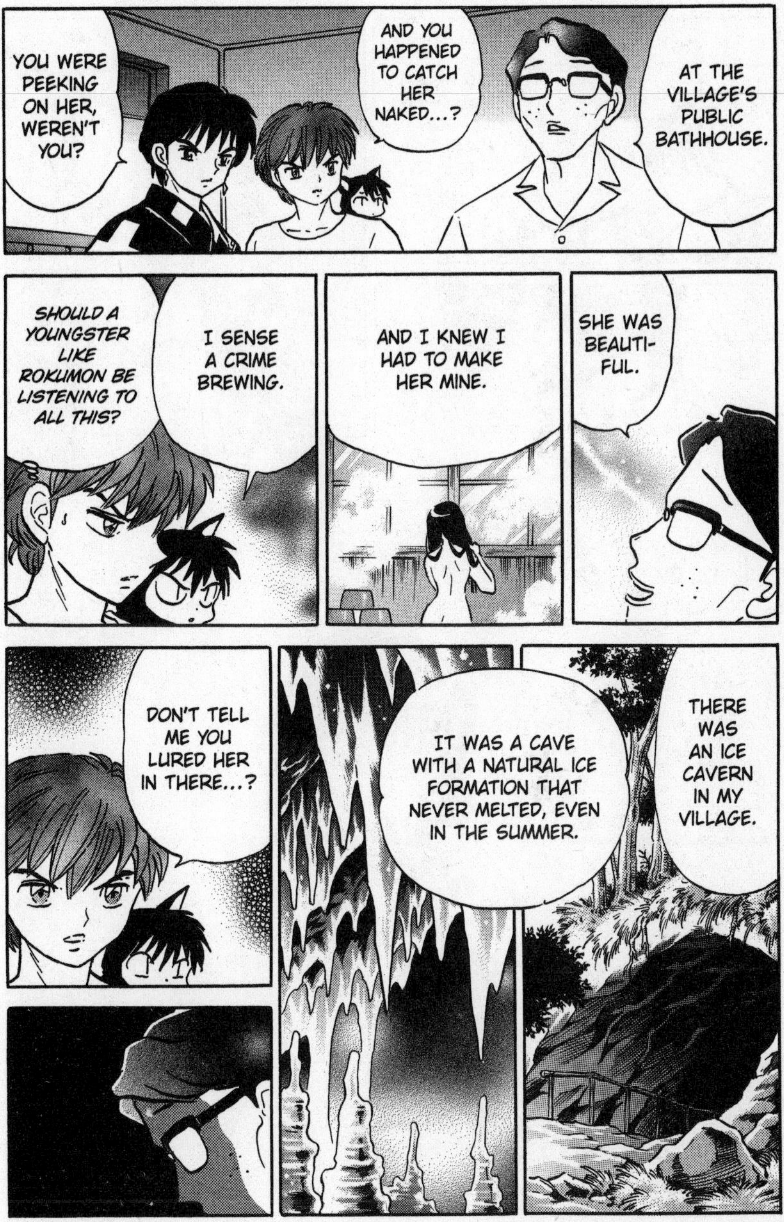
AT THE VILLAGE'S PUBLIC BATHHOUSE.
AND YOU HAPPENED TO CATCH HER NAKED...?
YOU WERE PEEKING ON HER, WEREN'T YOU?
SHE WAS BEAUTI-FUL.
AND I KNEW I HAD TO MAKE HER MINE.
I SENSE A CRIME BREWING.
SHOULD A YOUNGSTER LIKE ROKUMON BE LISTENING TO ALL THIS?
THERE WAS AN ICE CAVERN IN MY VILLAGE.
IT WAS A CAVE WITH A NATURAL ICE FORMATION THAT NEVER MELTED, EVEN IN THE SUMMER.
DON'T TELL ME YOU LURED HER IN THERE...?

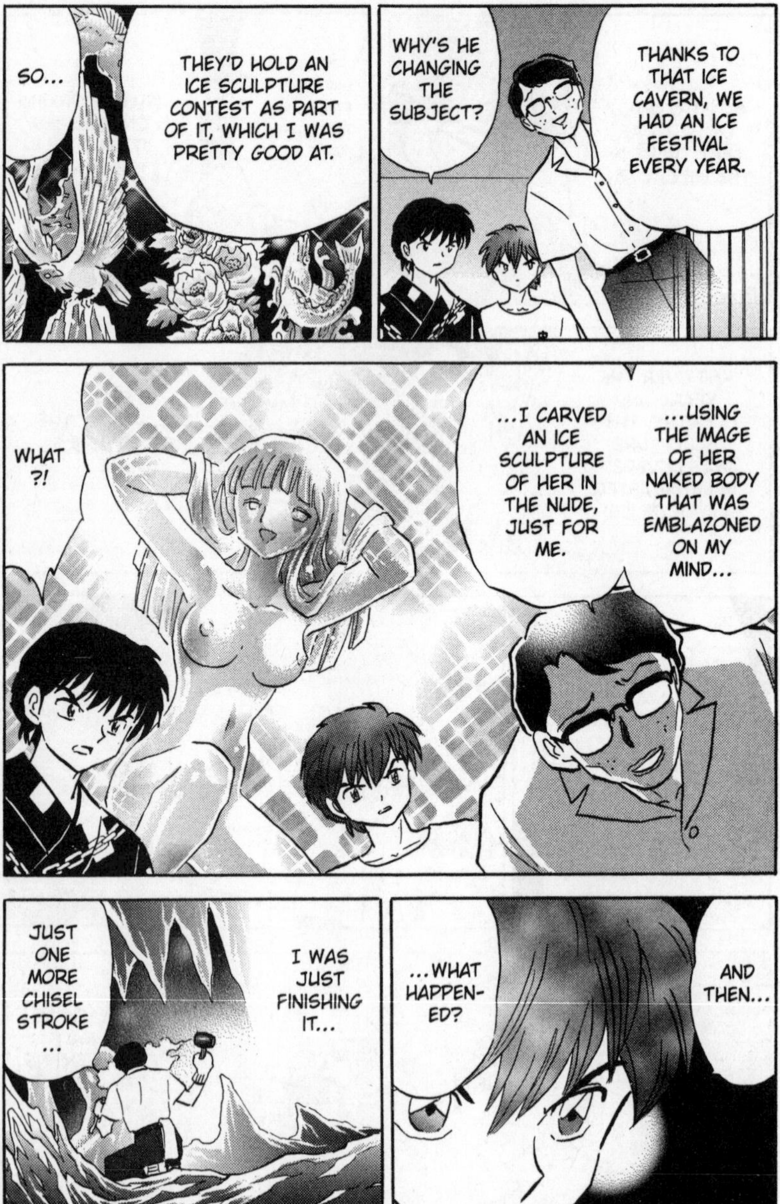
THANKS TO THAT ICE CAVERN, WE HAD AN ICE FESTIVAL EVERY YEAR.
WHY'S HE CHANGING THE SUBJECT?
THEY'D HOLD AN ICE SCULPTURE CONTEST AS PART OF IT, WHICH I WAS PRETTY GOOD AT.
SO...
...USING THE IMAGE OF HER NAKED BODY THAT WAS EMBLAZONED ON MY MIND...
...I CARVED AN ICE SCULPTURE OF HER IN THE NUDE, JUST FOR ME.
WHAT ?!
AND THEN...
...WHAT HAPPEN-ED?
I WAS JUST FINISHING IT...
JUST ONE MORE CHISEL STROKE ...

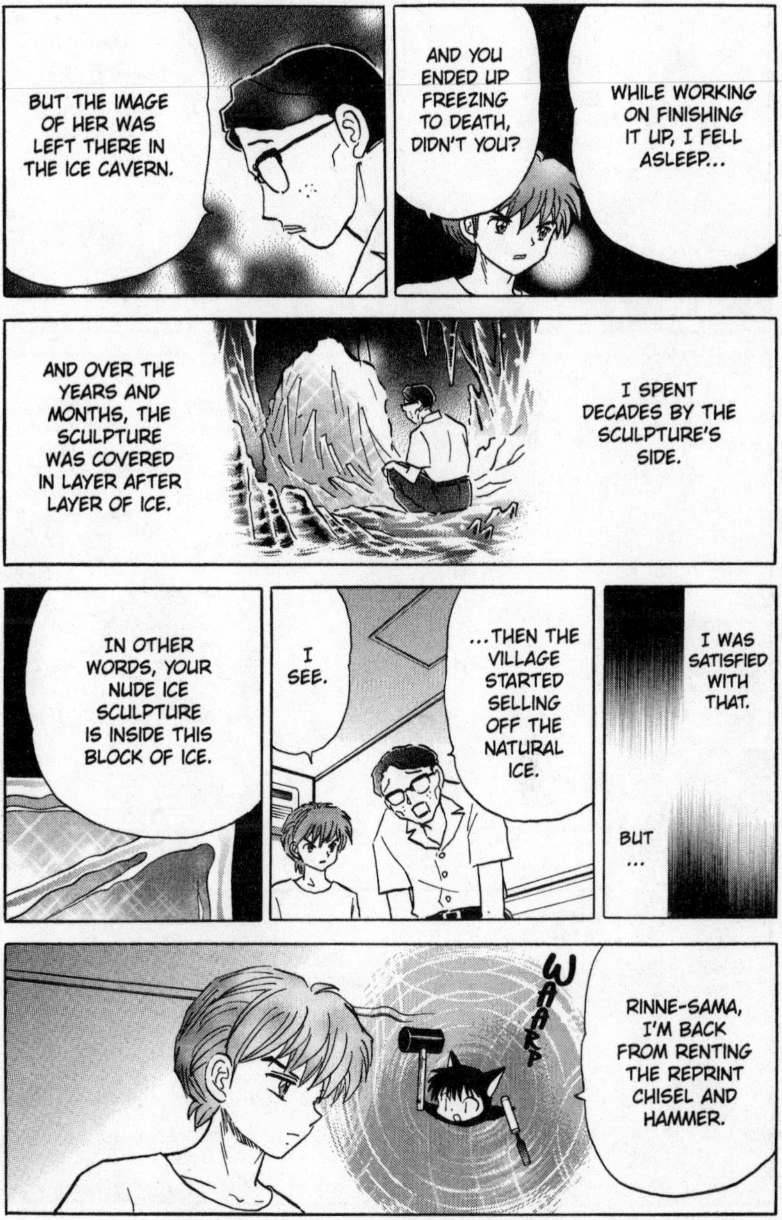
WHILE WORKING ON FINISHING IT UP, I FELL ASLEEP...
AND YOU ENDED UP FREEZING TO DEATH, DIDN'T YOU?
BUT THE IMAGE OF HER WAS LEFT THERE IN THE ICE CAVERN.
I SPENT DECADES BY THE SCULPTURE'S SIDE.
AND OVER THE YEARS AND MONTHS, THE SCULPTURE WAS COVERED IN LAYER AFTER LAYER OF ICE.
I WAS SATISFIED WITH THAT.
BUT ...
...THEN THE VILLAGE STARTED SELLING OFF THE NATURAL ICE.
I SEE.
IN OTHER WORDS, YOUR NUDE ICE SCULPTURE IS INSIDE THIS BLOCK OF ICE.
RINNE-SAMA, I'M BACK FROM RENTING THE REPRINT CHISEL AND HAMMER.
WHAARP

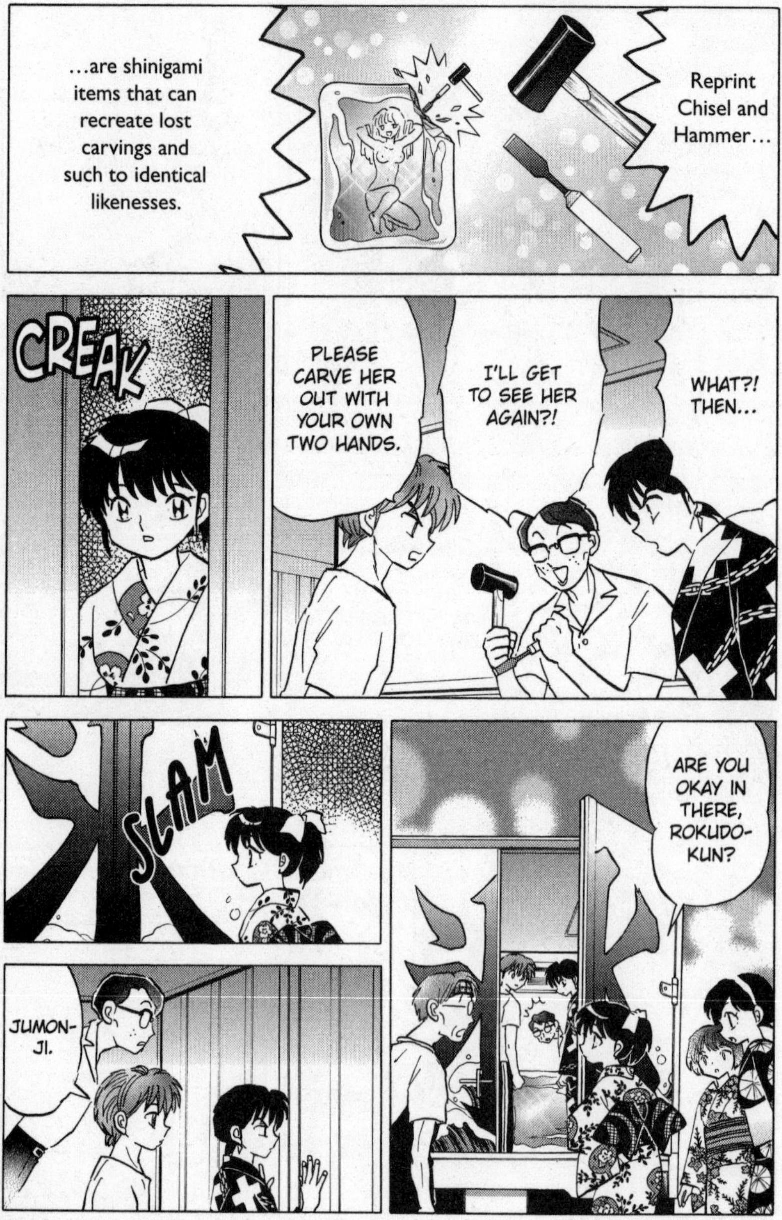
Reprint Chisel and Hammer…
…are shinigami items that can recreate lost carvings and such to identical likenesses.
WHAT?! THEN…
I'LL GET TO SEE HER AGAIN?!
PLEASE CARVE HER OUT WITH YOUR OWN TWO HANDS.
CREAK
ARE YOU OKAY IN THERE, ROKUDO-KUN?
SLAM
JUMON-JI.

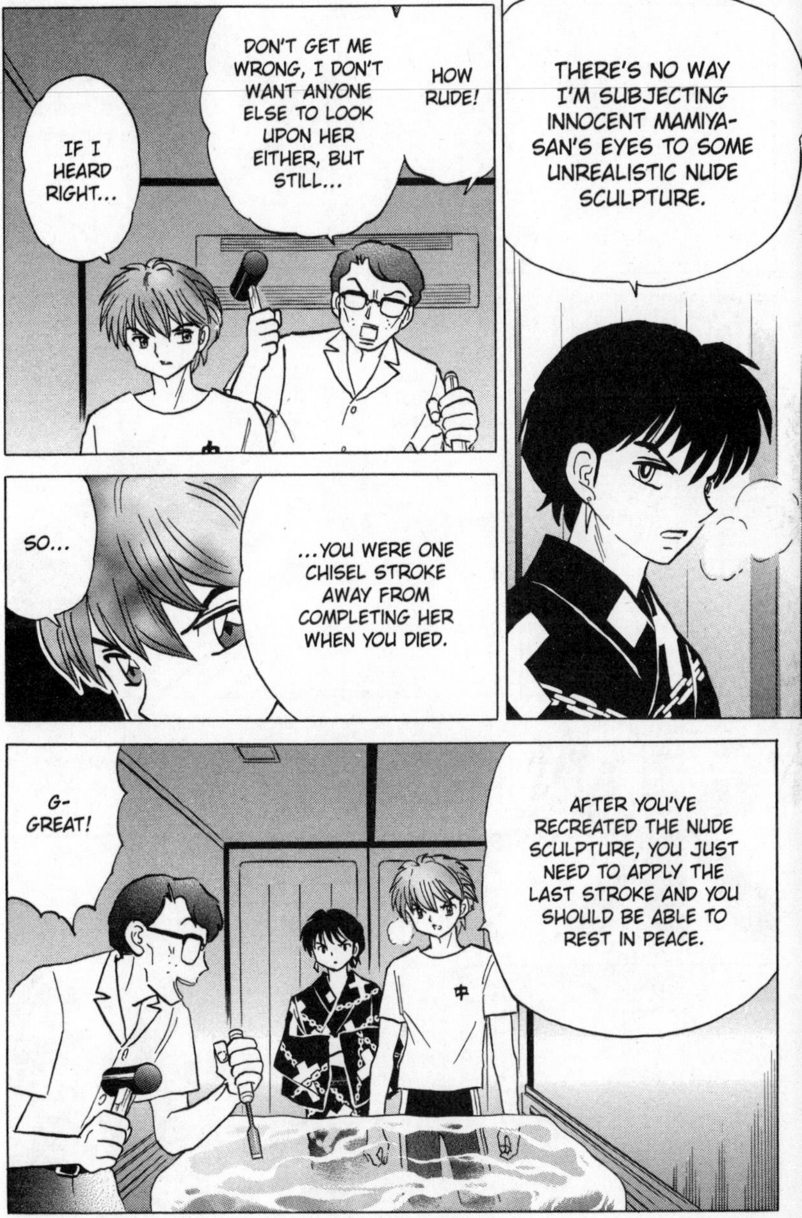
THERE'S NO WAY I'M SUBJECTING INNOCENT MAMIYA-SAN'S EYES TO SOME UNREALISTIC NUDE SCULPTURE.
HOW RUDE!
DON'T GET ME WRONG, I DON'T WANT ANYONE ELSE TO LOOK UPON HER EITHER, BUT STILL...
IF I HEARD RIGHT...
SO...
...YOU WERE ONE CHISEL STROKE AWAY FROM COMPLETING HER WHEN YOU DIED.
AFTER YOU'VE RECREATED THE NUDE SCULPTURE, YOU JUST NEED TO APPLY THE LAST STROKE AND YOU SHOULD BE ABLE TO REST IN PEACE.
G-GREAT!

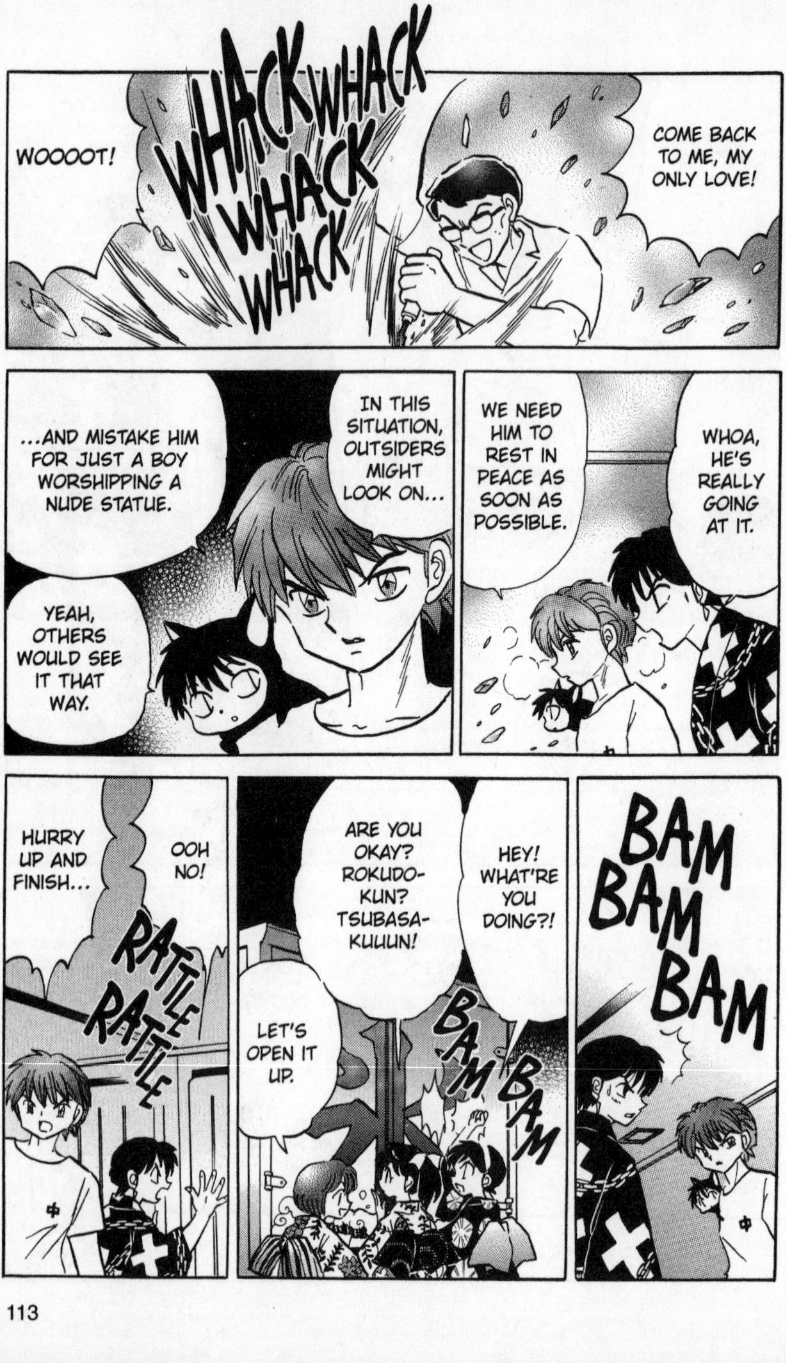
COME BACK TO ME, MY ONLY LOVE!
WHACK WHACK WHACK WHACK WHACK
WOOOOT!
WHOA, HE'S REALLY GOING AT IT.
WE NEED HIM TO REST IN PEACE AS SOON AS POSSIBLE.
IN THIS SITUATION, OUTSIDERS MIGHT LOOK ON...
...AND MISTAKE HIM FOR JUST A BOY WORSHIPPING A NUDE STATUE.
YEAH, OTHERS WOULD SEE IT THAT WAY.
BAM BAM BAM
HEY! WHAT'RE YOU DOING?!
ARE YOU OKAY? ROKUDO-KUN? TSUBASA-KUUUN!
BAM BAM BAM
LET'S OPEN IT UP.
OOH NO!
HURRY UP AND FINISH...
RATTLE RATTLE

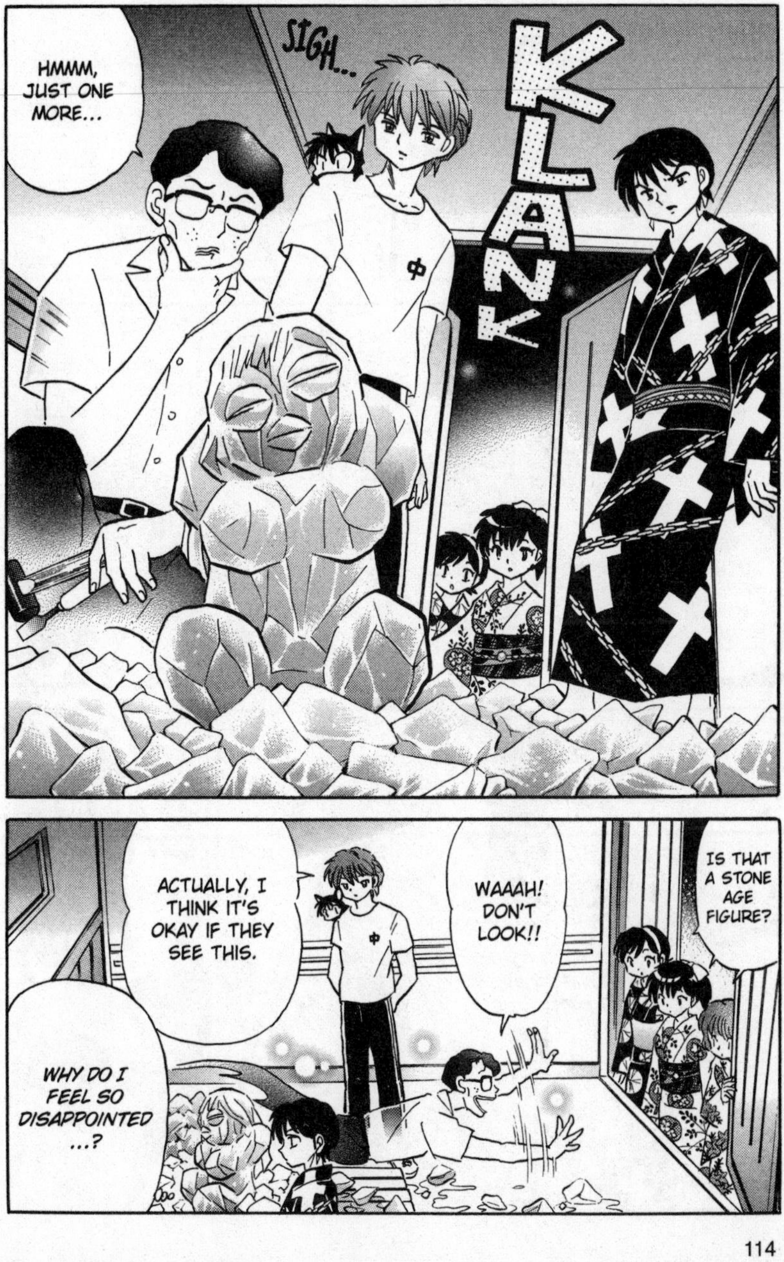
KLANK
SIGH...
HMMM, JUST ONE MORE...
IS THAT A STONE AGE FIGURE?
WAAAH! DON'T LOOK!!
ACTUALLY, I THINK IT'S OKAY IF THEY SEE THIS.
WHY DO I FEEL SO DISAPPOINTED ...?

CHAPTER 295: THE TEACHER AND THE BALLOONS

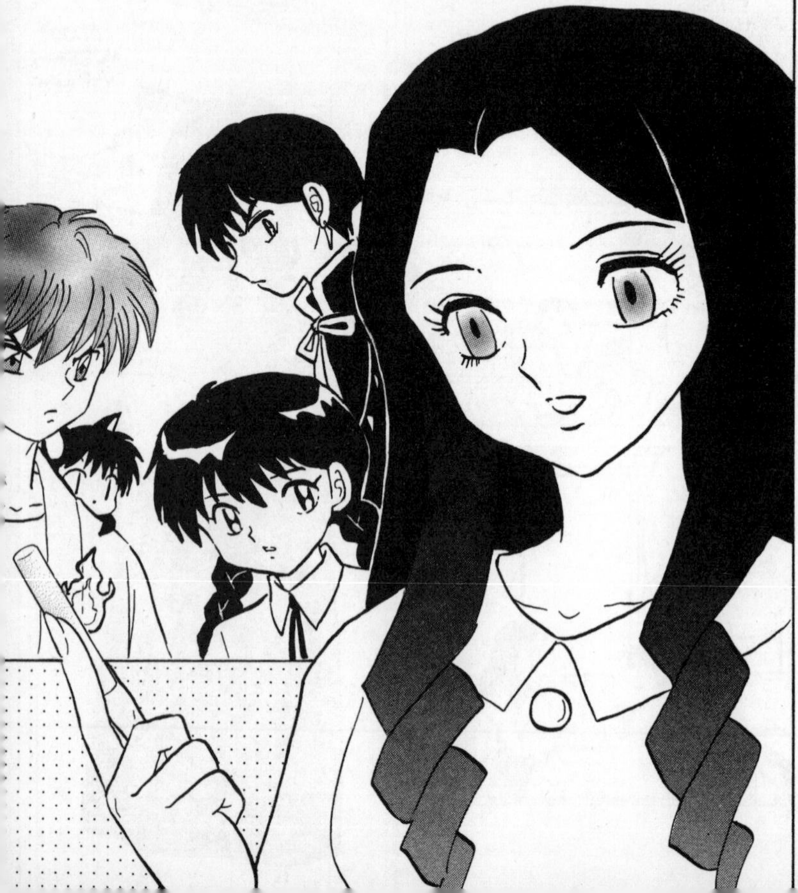

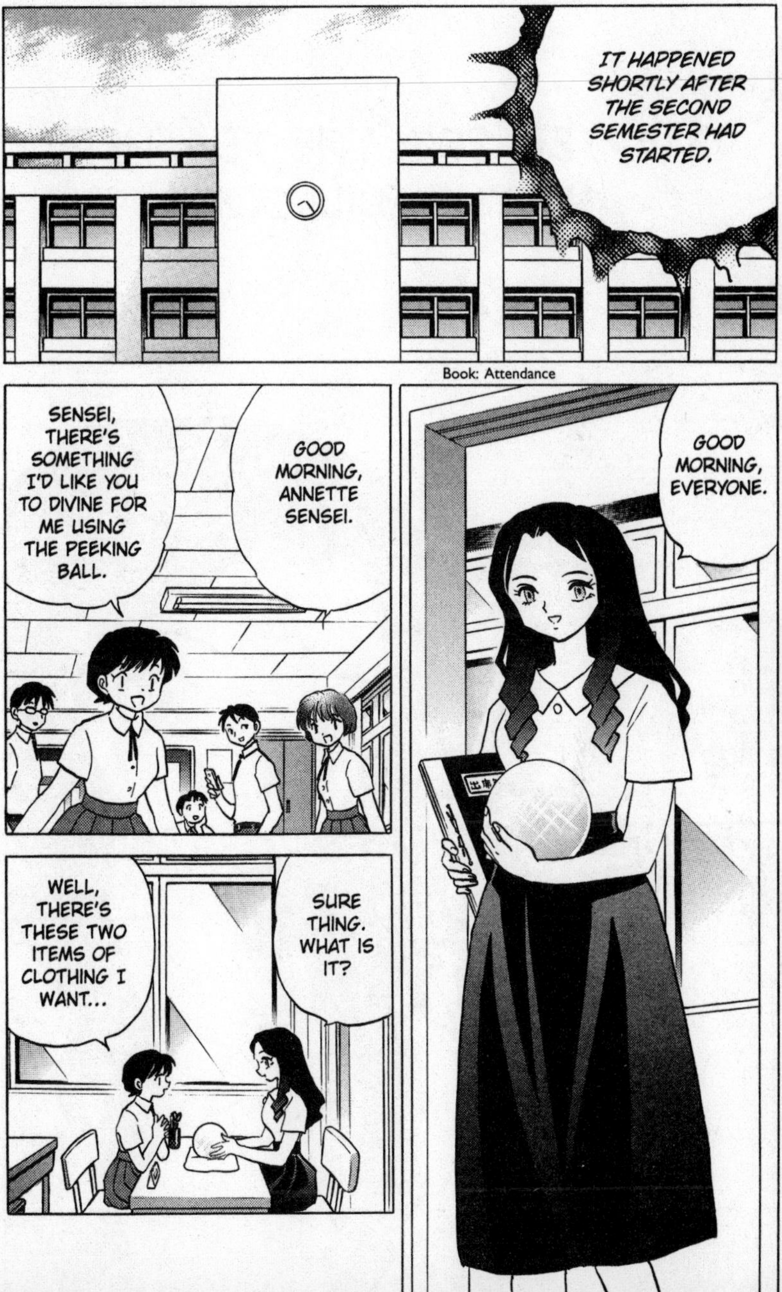
IT HAPPENED SHORTLY AFTER THE SECOND SEMESTER HAD STARTED.
GOOD MORNING, EVERYONE.
GOOD MORNING, ANNETTE SENSEI.
SENSEI, THERE'S SOMETHING I'D LIKE YOU TO DIVINE FOR ME USING THE PEEKING BALL.
SURE THING. WHAT IS IT?
WELL, THERE'S THESE TWO ITEMS OF CLOTHING I WANT...
Book: Attendance

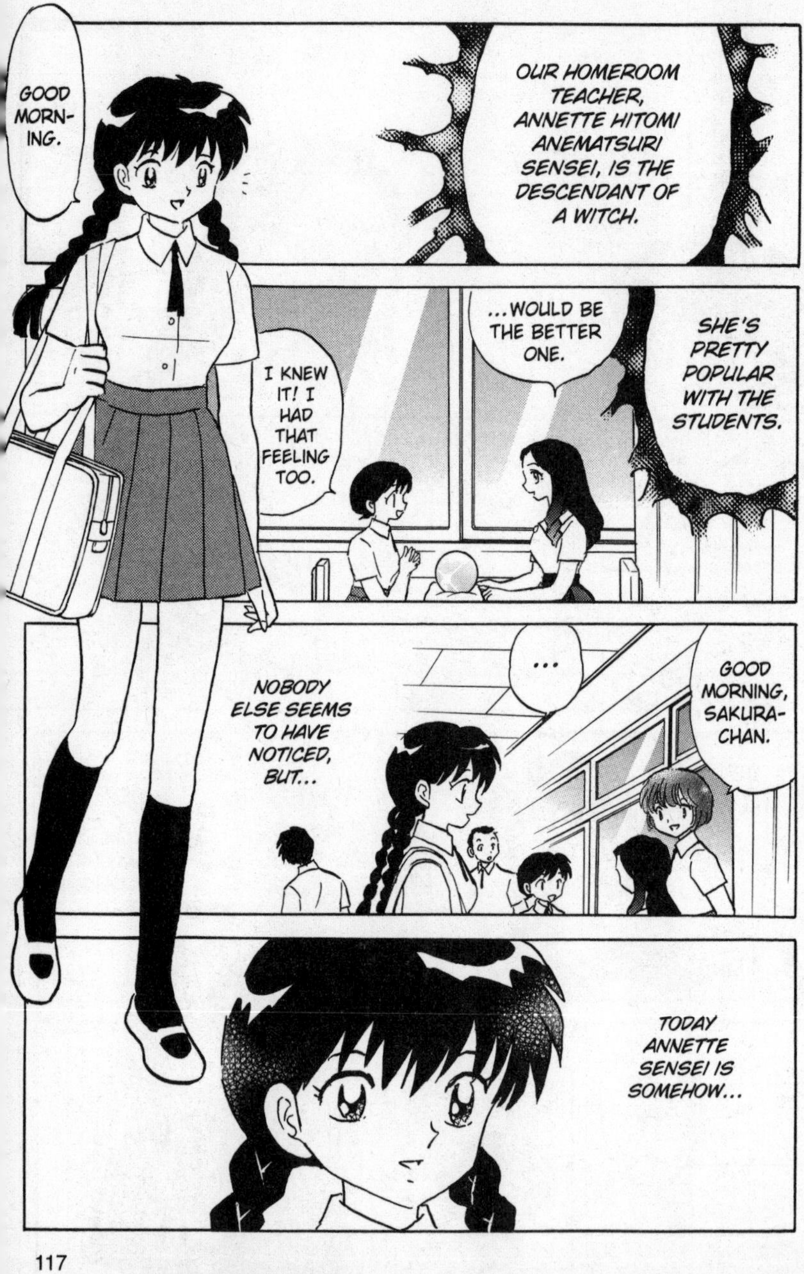
OUR HOMEROOM TEACHER, ANNETTE HITOMI ANEMATSURI SENSEI, IS THE DESCENDANT OF A WITCH.
SHE'S PRETTY POPULAR WITH THE STUDENTS.
...WOULD BE THE BETTER ONE.
I KNEW IT! I HAD THAT FEELING TOO.
GOOD MORNING, SAKURA-CHAN.
...
NOBODY ELSE SEEMS TO HAVE NOTICED, BUT...
GOOD MORN-ING.
TODAY ANNETTE SENSEI IS SOMEHOW...

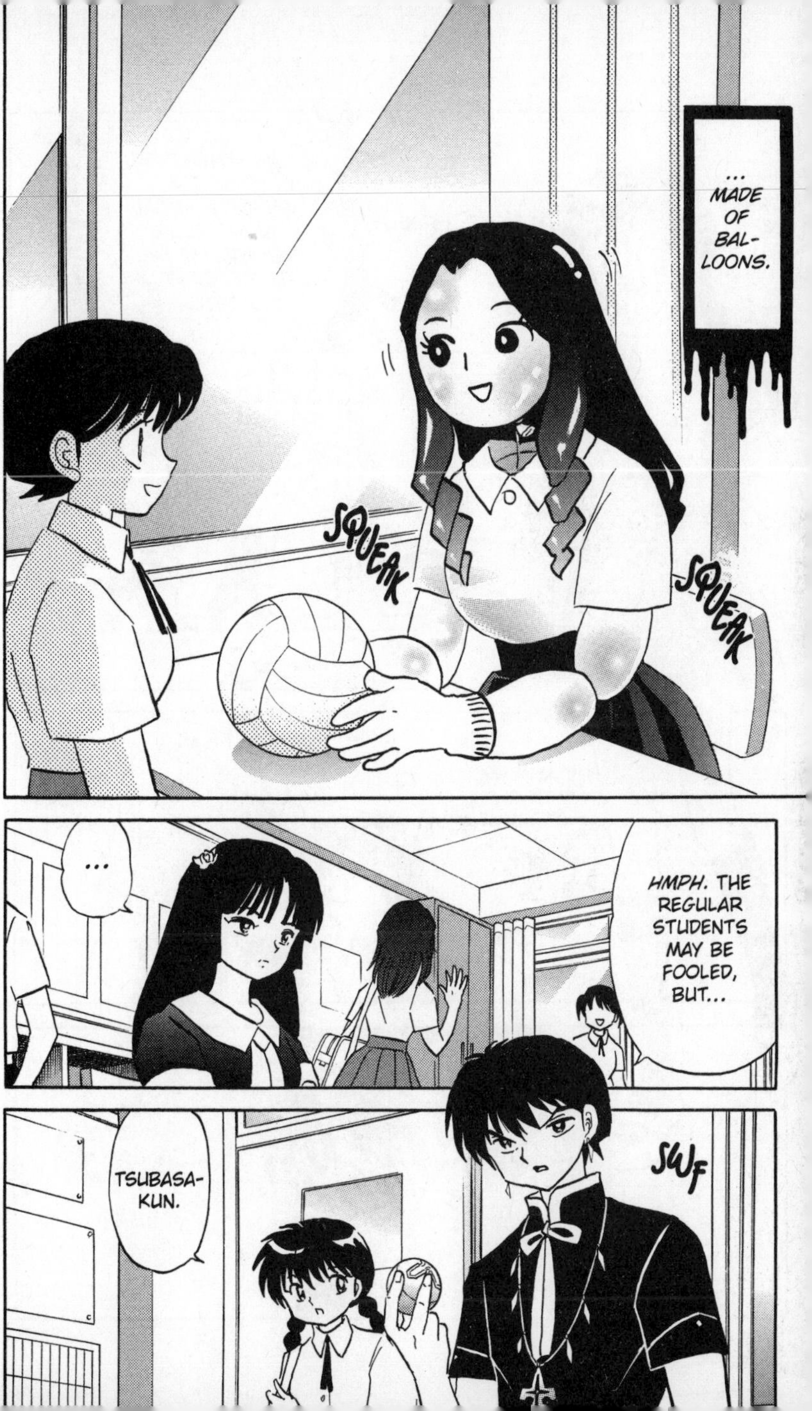

... MADE OF BAL- LOONS.
SQUEAK
SQUEAK
HMPH. THE REGULAR STUDENTS MAY BE FOOLED, BUT...
...
SWF
TSUBASA-KUN.

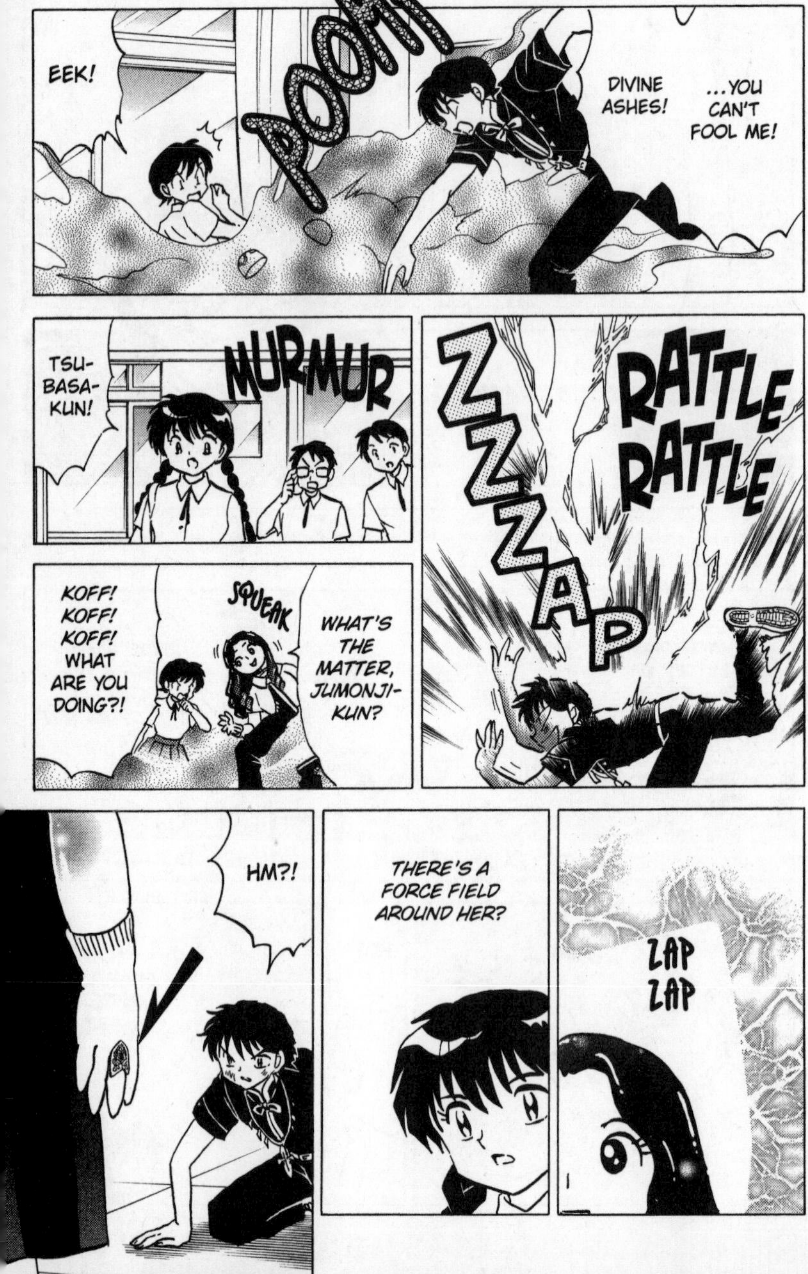
...YOU CAN'T FOOL ME!
DIVINE ASHES!
BOOMF
EEK!
RATTLE RATTLE
ZZZAP
MURMUR
TSU-BASA-KUN!
WHAT'S THE MATTER, JUMONJI-KUN?
SQUEAK
KOFF! KOFF! KOFF! WHAT ARE YOU DOING?!
ZAP ZAP
THERE'S A FORCE FIELD AROUND HER?
HM?!

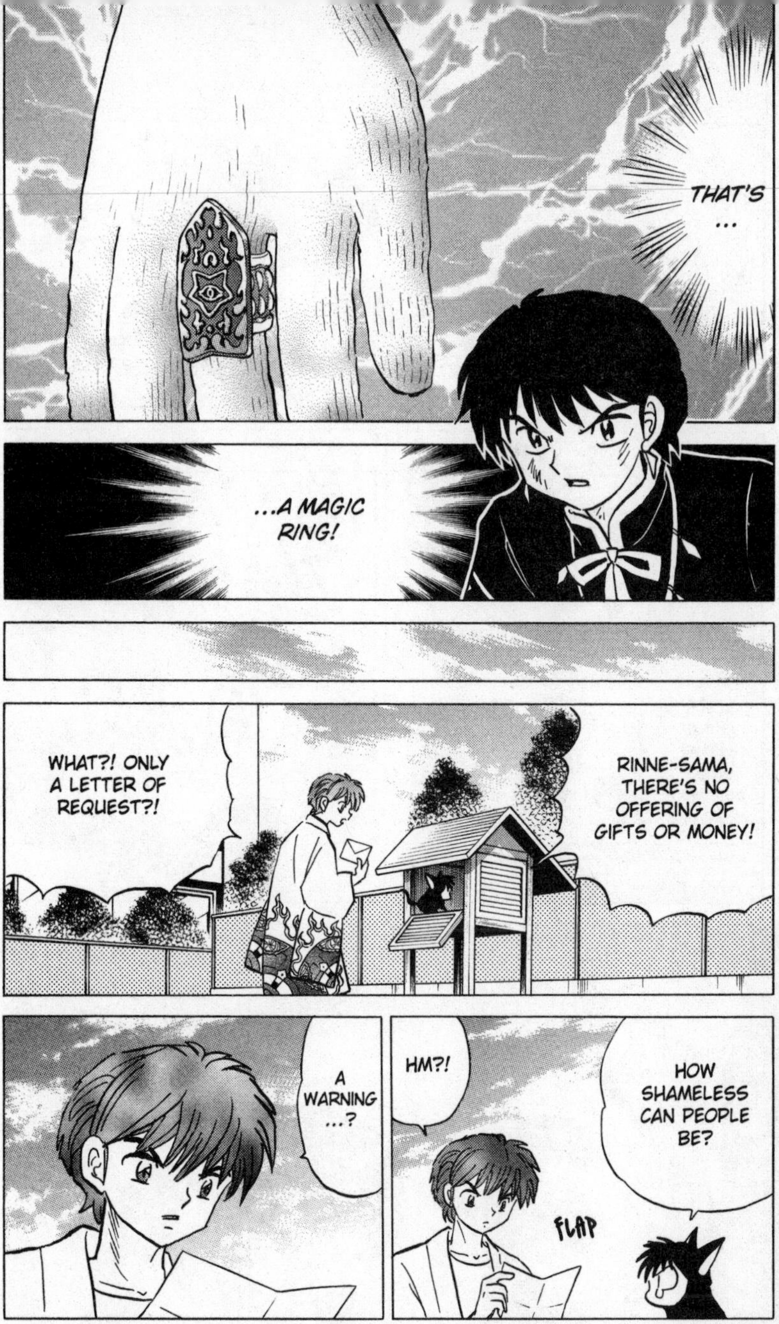
THAT'S ...
...A MAGIC RING!
RINNE-SAMA, THERE'S NO OFFERING OF GIFTS OR MONEY!
WHAT?! ONLY A LETTER OF REQUEST?!
HOW SHAMELESS CAN PEOPLE BE?
FLAP
HM?!
A WARNING ...?

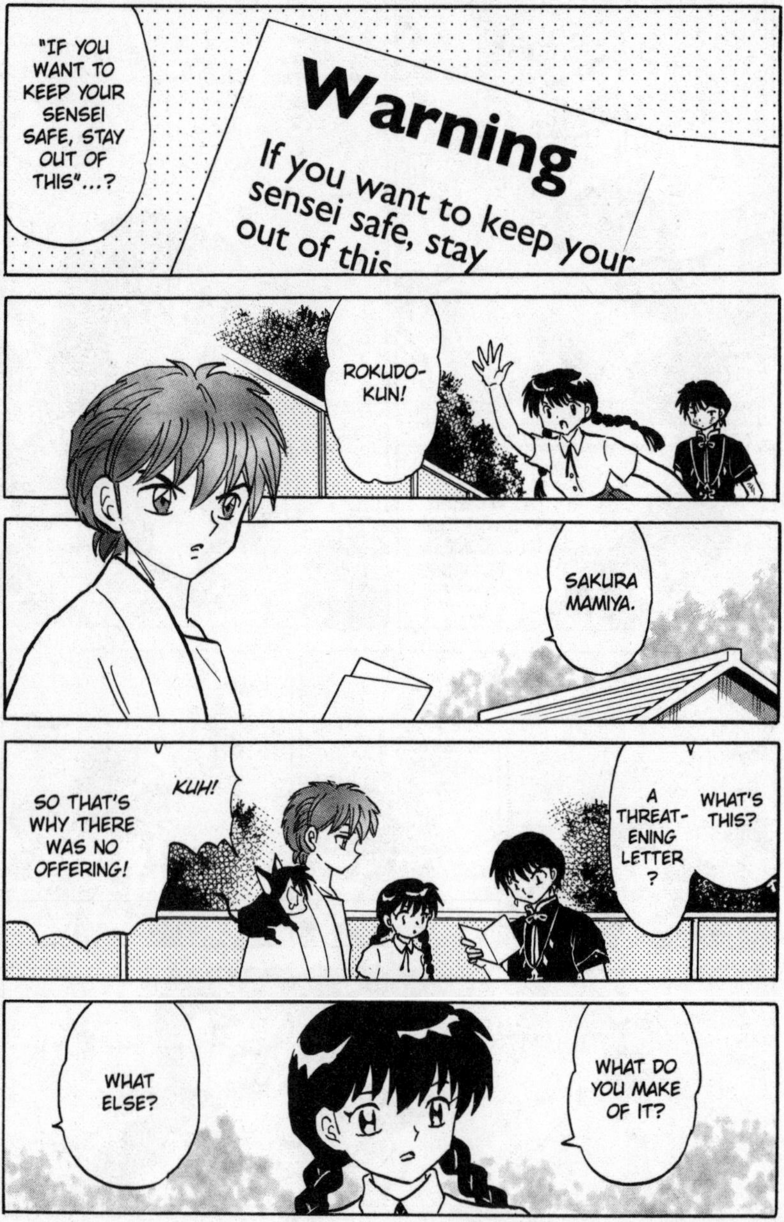
Warning
If you want to keep your sensei safe, stay out of this
"IF YOU WANT TO KEEP YOUR SENSEI SAFE, STAY OUT OF THIS"...?
ROKUDO-KUN!
SAKURA MAMIYA.
WHAT'S THIS?
A THREAT-ENING LETTER?
KUH!
SO THAT'S WHY THERE WAS NO OFFERING!
WHAT DO YOU MAKE OF IT?
WHAT ELSE?

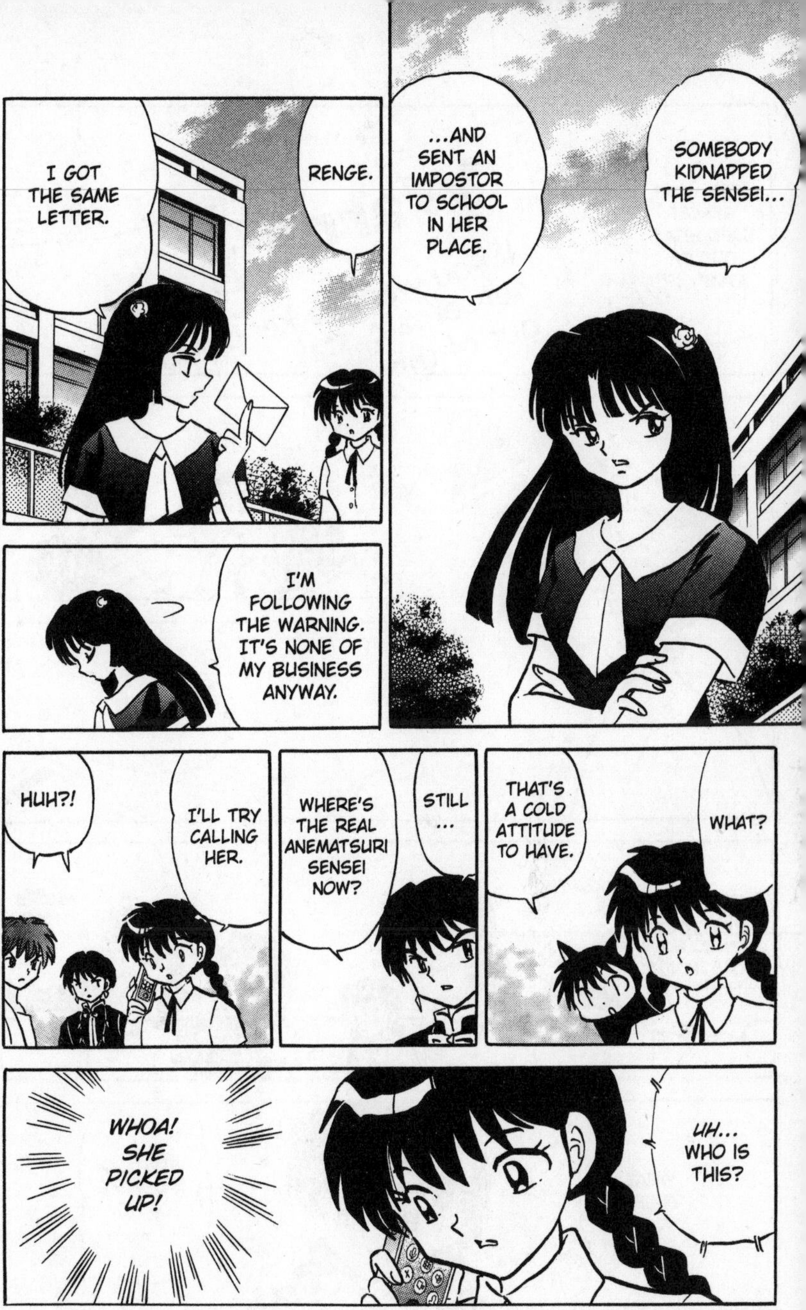
SOMEBODY KIDNAPPED THE SENSEI...
...AND SENT AN IMPOSTOR TO SCHOOL IN HER PLACE.
RENGE.
I GOT THE SAME LETTER.
I'M FOLLOWING THE WARNING. IT'S NONE OF MY BUSINESS ANYWAY.
WHAT?
THAT'S A COLD ATTITUDE TO HAVE.
STILL...
WHERE'S THE REAL ANEMATSURI SENSEI NOW?
I'LL TRY CALLING HER.
HUH?!
UH... WHO IS THIS?
WHOA! SHE PICKED UP!

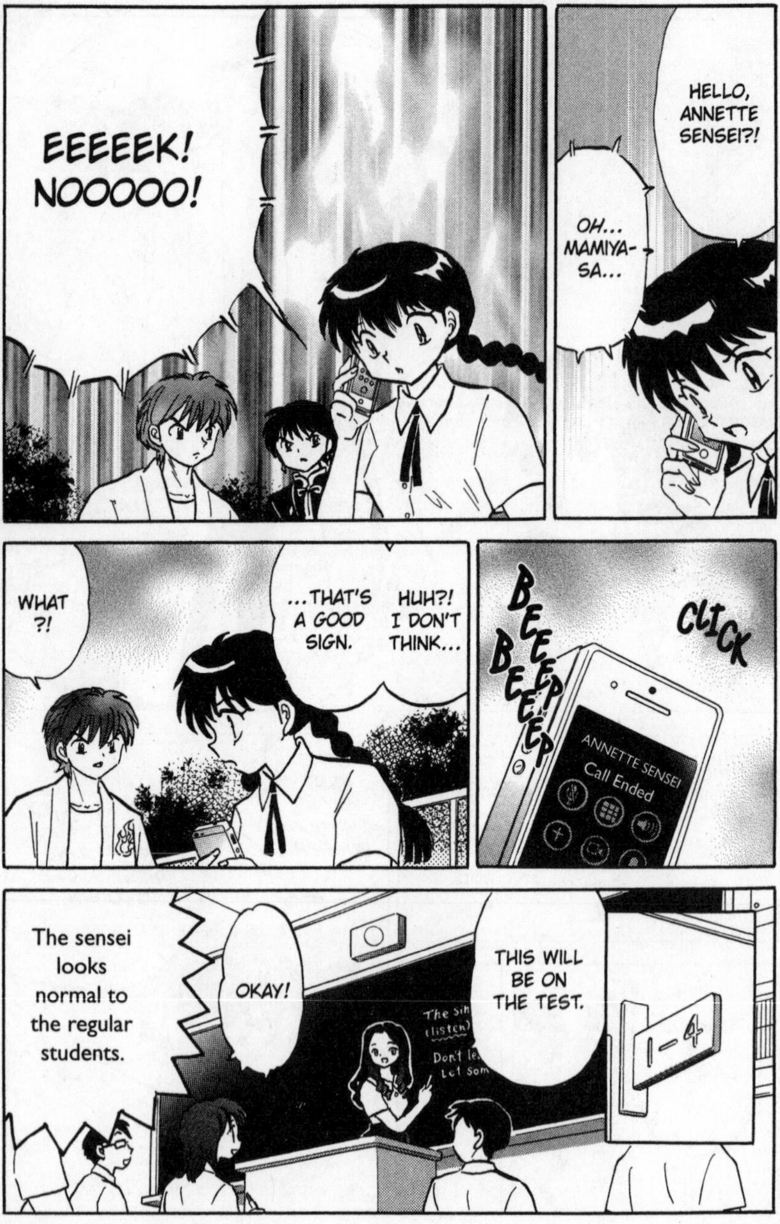
HELLO, ANNETTE SENSEI?!
OH... MAMIYA-SA...
EEEEEK! NOOOOO!
BEEEP BEEEP
CLICK
ANNETTE SENSEI
Call Ended
HUH?! I DON'T THINK...
...THAT'S A GOOD SIGN.
WHAT?!
THIS WILL BE ON THE TEST.
OKAY!
The sensei looks normal to the regular students.
1-4

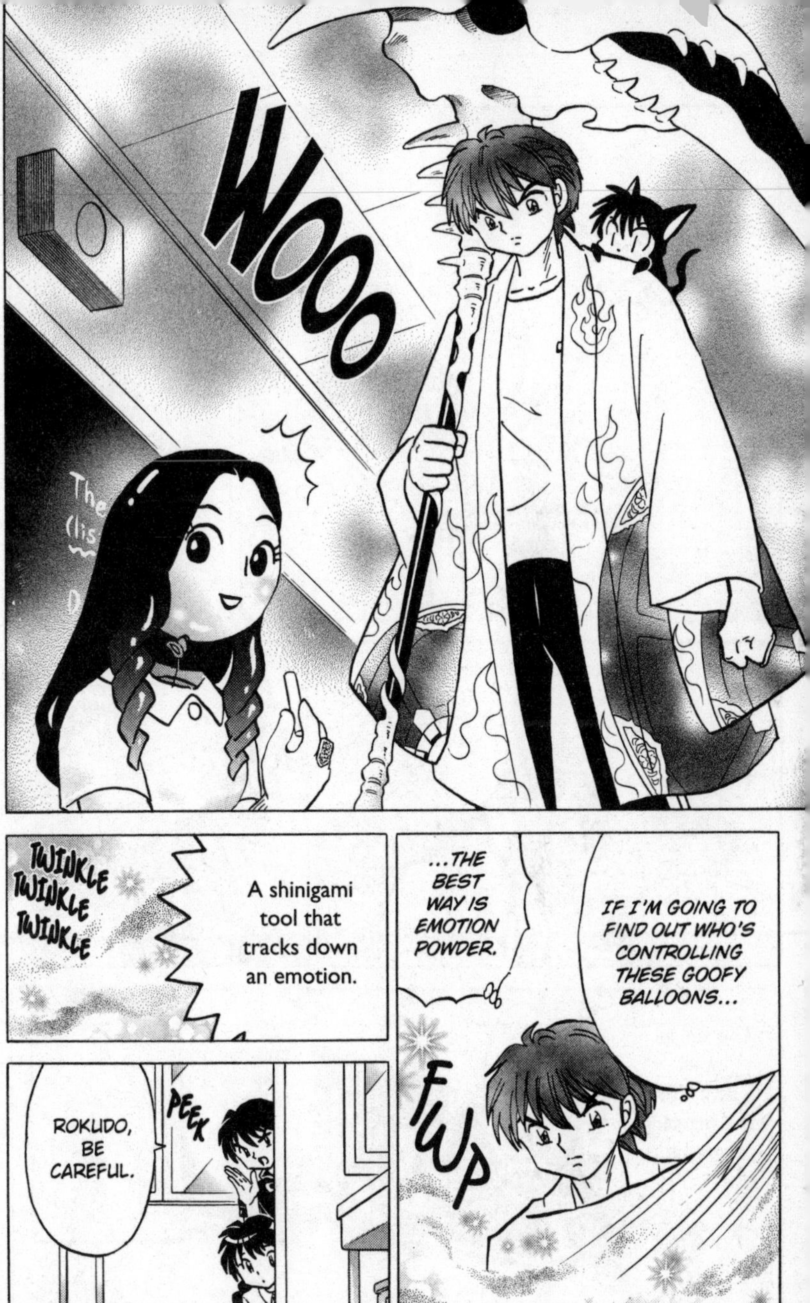
WOOO
IF I'M GOING TO FIND OUT WHO'S CONTROLLING THESE GOOFY BALLOONS...
...THE BEST WAY IS EMOTION POWDER.
FWP
TWINKLE TWINKLE TWINKLE
A shinigami tool that tracks down an emotion.
PEEK
ROKUDO, BE CAREFUL.

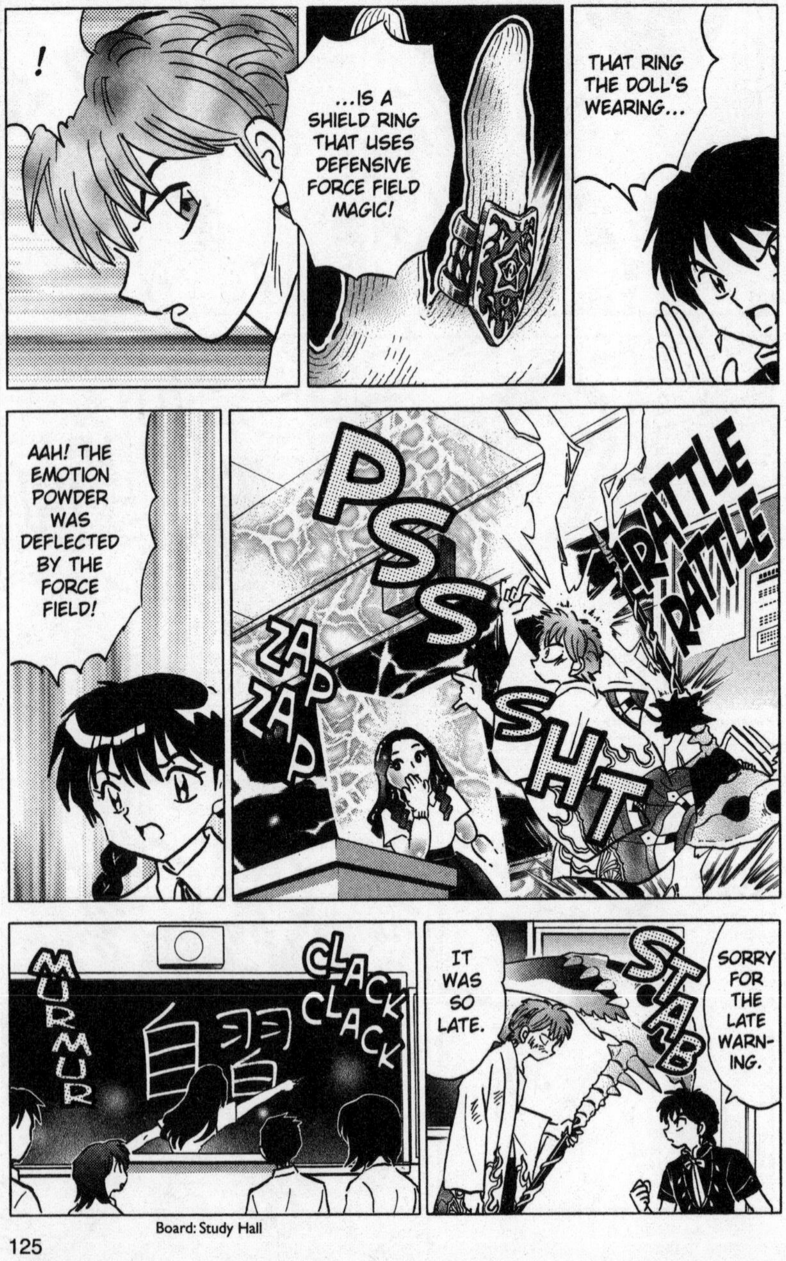
THAT RING THE DOLL'S WEARING...
...IS A SHIELD RING THAT USES DEFENSIVE FORCE FIELD MAGIC!
!
RATTLE RATTLE
PSSSHT
ZAP ZAP
AAH! THE EMOTION POWDER WAS DEFLECTED BY THE FORCE FIELD!
SORRY FOR THE LATE WARN-ING.
STAB
IT WAS SO LATE.
CLACK CLACK
MURMUR
Board: Study Hall

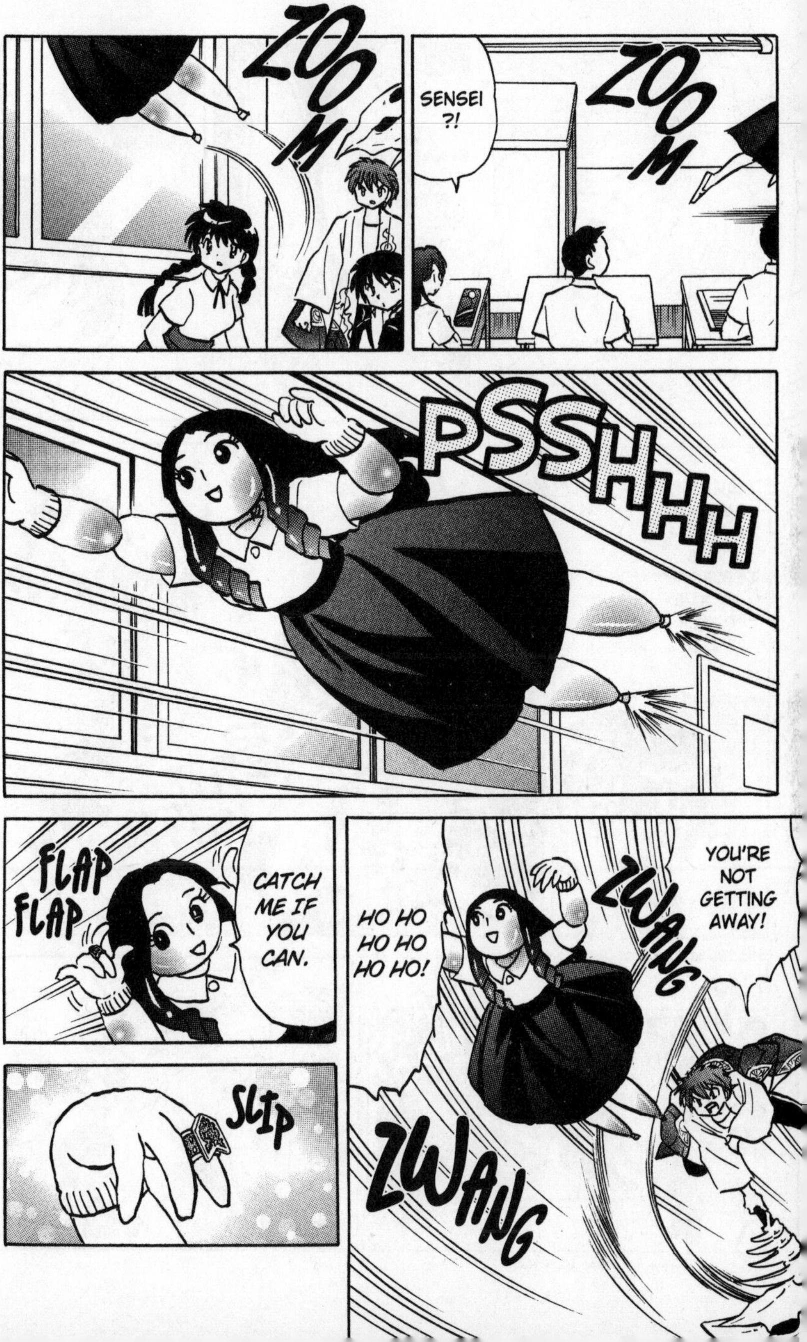
ZOOM
SENSEI ?!
ZOOM
PSSHHHH
YOU'RE NOT GETTING AWAY!
ZWANG
HO HO HO HO HO HO!
ZWANG
FLAP FLAP
CATCH ME IF YOU CAN.
SLIP

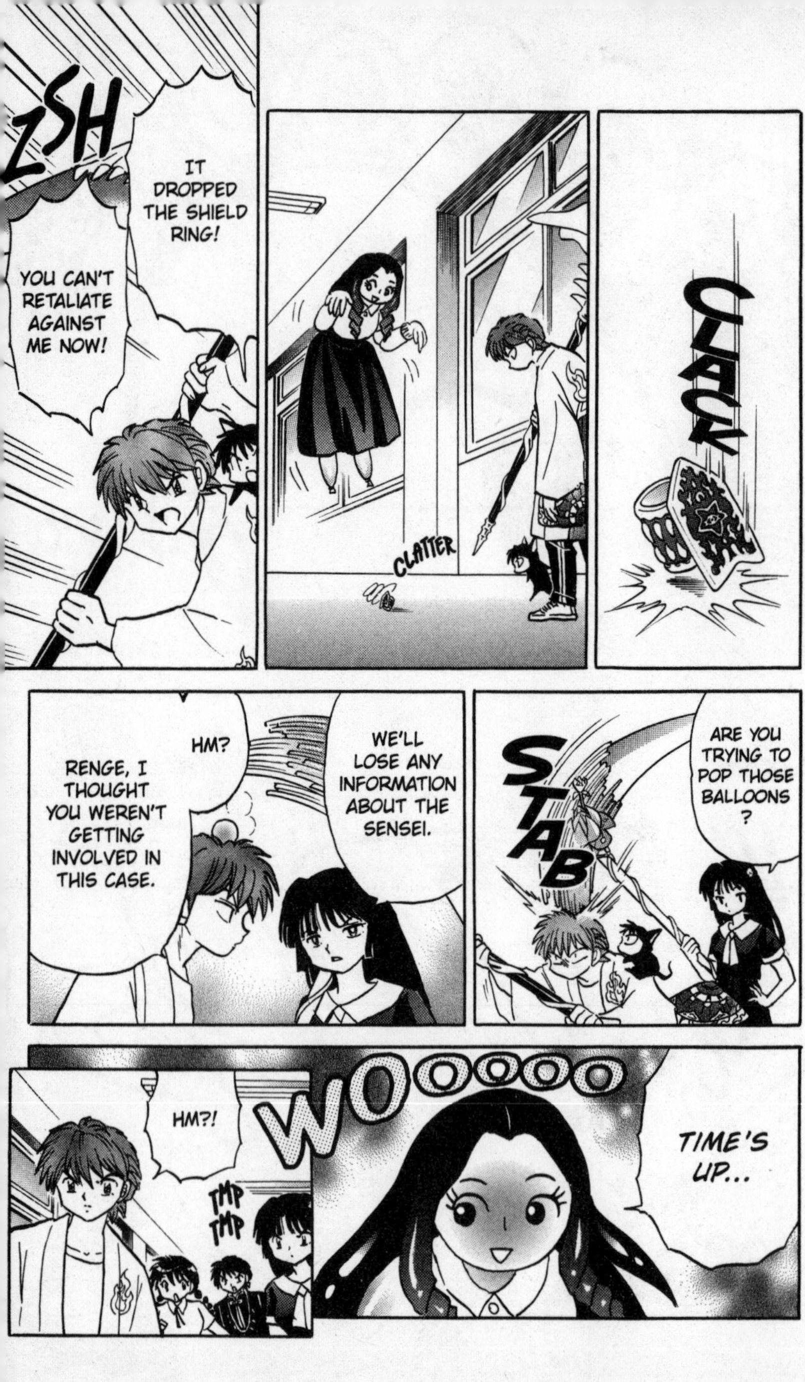
CLACK
CLATTER
ZSH
IT DROPPED THE SHIELD RING!
YOU CAN'T RETALIATE AGAINST ME NOW!
STAB
ARE YOU TRYING TO POP THOSE BALLOONS?
WE'LL LOSE ANY INFORMATION ABOUT THE SENSEI.
HM?
RENGE, I THOUGHT YOU WEREN'T GETTING INVOLVED IN THIS CASE.
WOOOOOO
TIME'S UP...
HM?!
TMP TMP

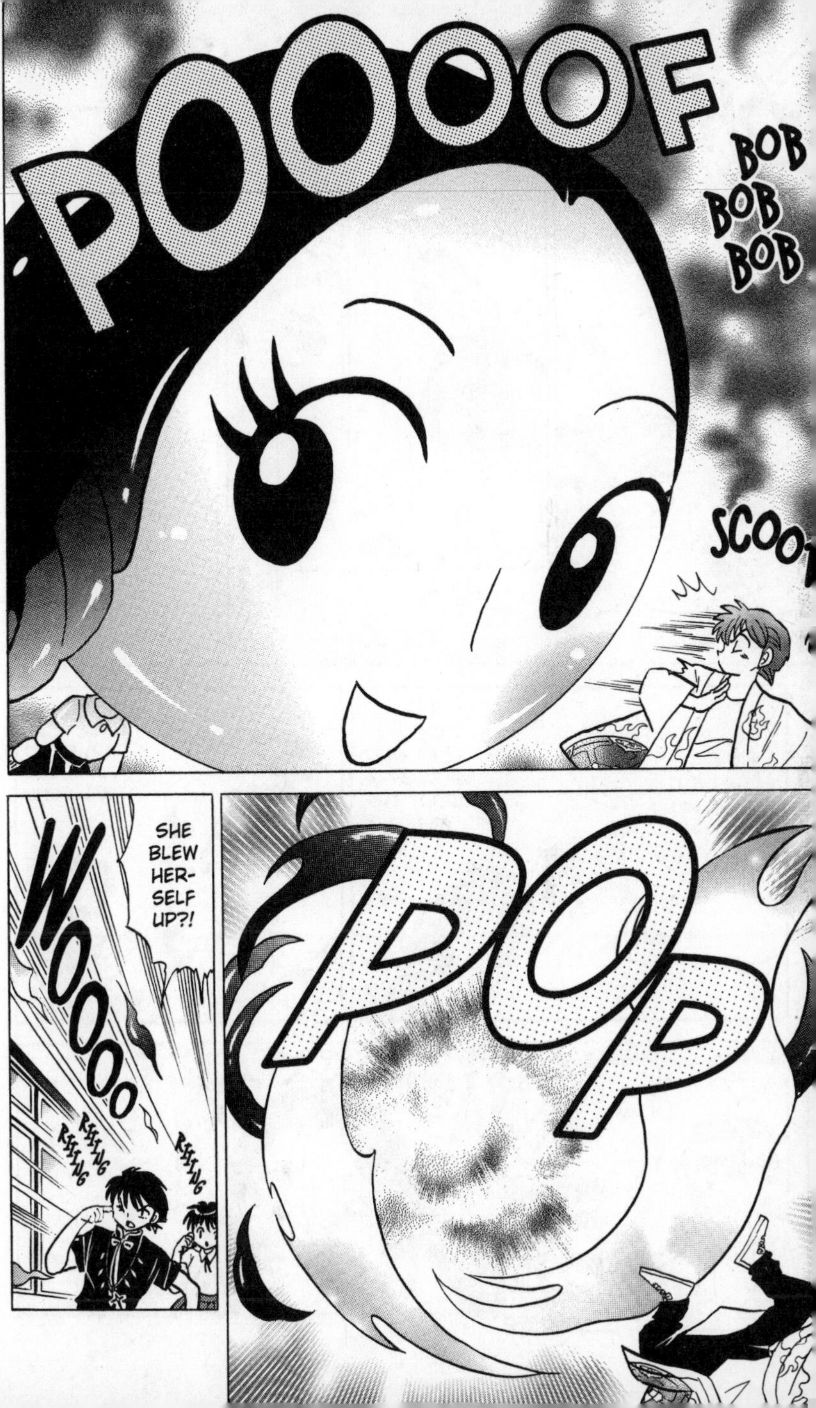
POOOOF
BOB BOB BOB
SCOOT
POP
WOOOOO
SHE BLEW HER-SELF UP?!
RIIING
RIIING RIIING

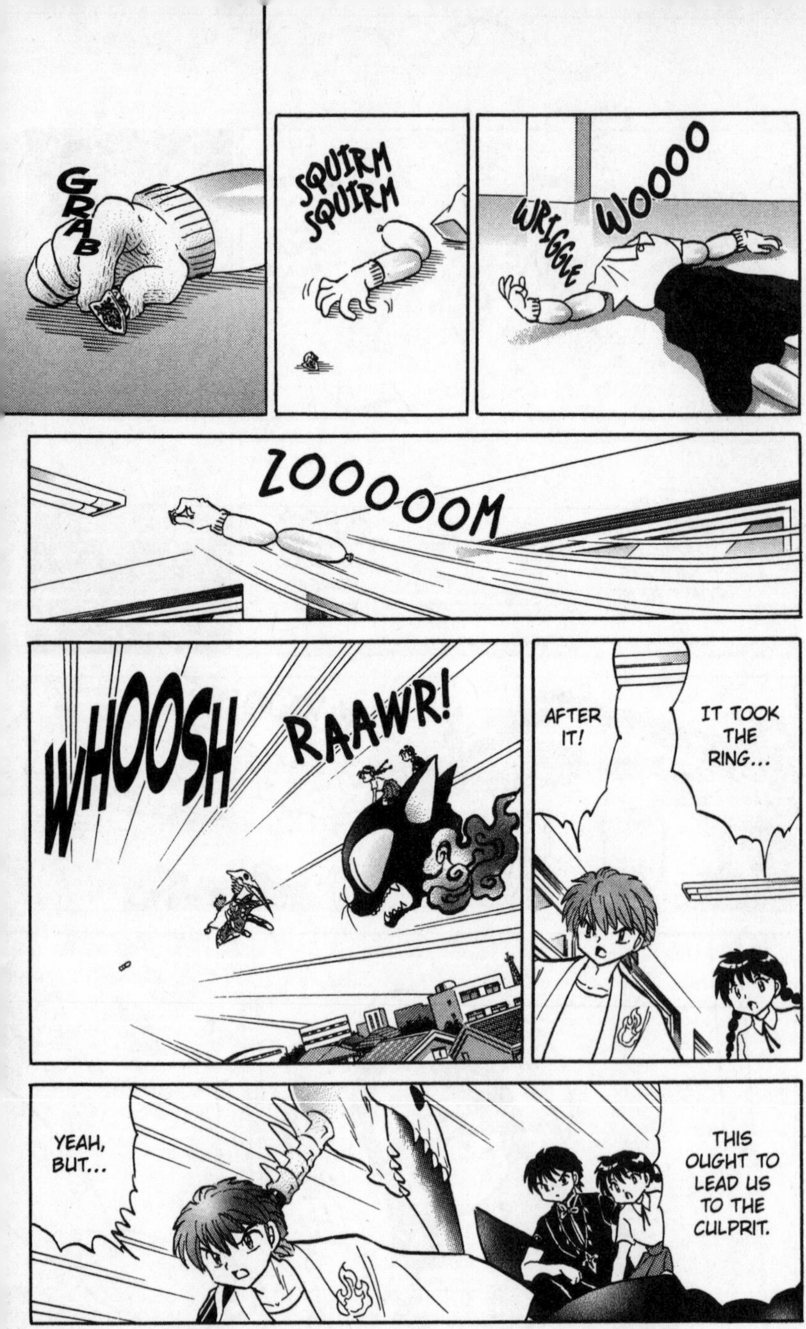
WOOOO
WRIGGLE
SQUIRM SQUIRM
GRAB
ZOOOOOM
IT TOOK THE RING...
AFTER IT!
RAAWR!
WHOOSH
THIS OUGHT TO LEAD US TO THE CULPRIT.
YEAH, BUT...

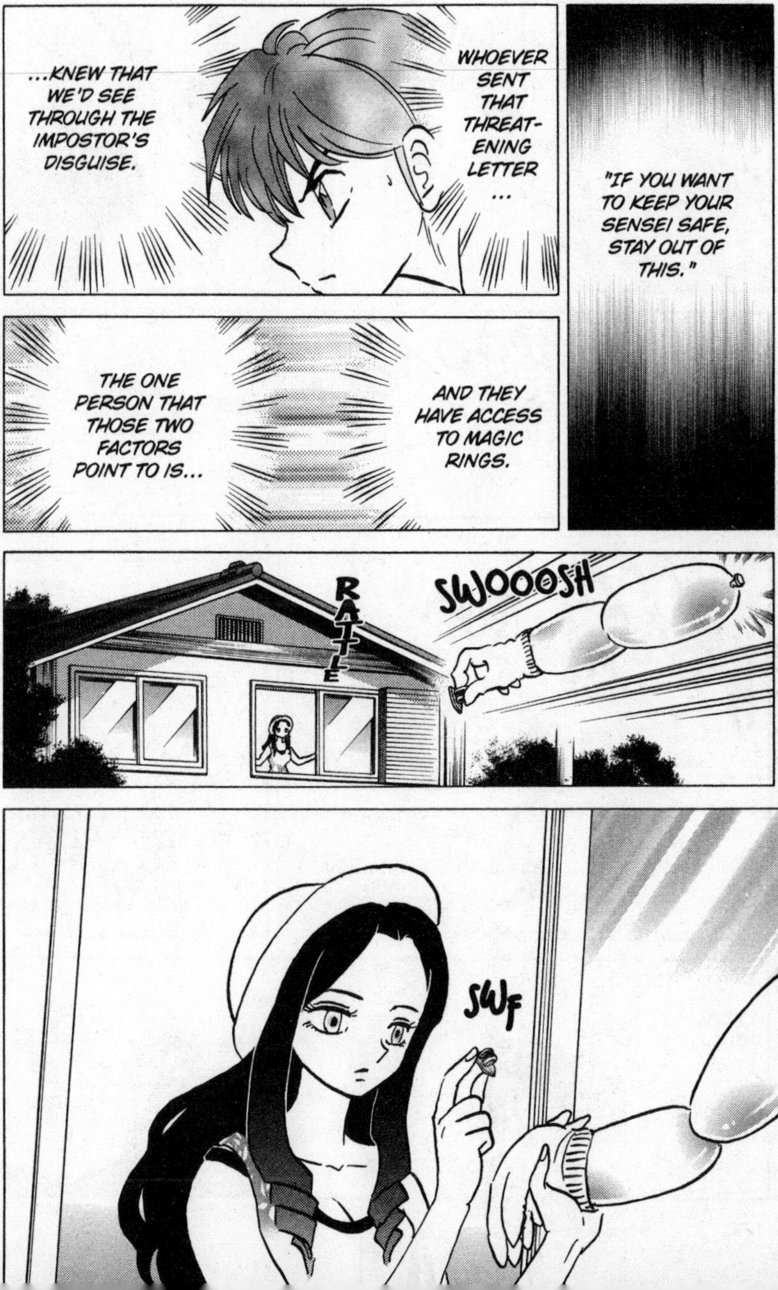
"IF YOU WANT TO KEEP YOUR SENSEI SAFE, STAY OUT OF THIS."
WHOEVER SENT THAT THREAT-ENING LETTER...
...KNEW THAT WE'D SEE THROUGH THE IMPOSTOR'S DISGUISE.
AND THEY HAVE ACCESS TO MAGIC RINGS.
THE ONE PERSON THAT THOSE TWO FACTORS POINT TO IS...
SWOOOSH
RATTLE
SWF

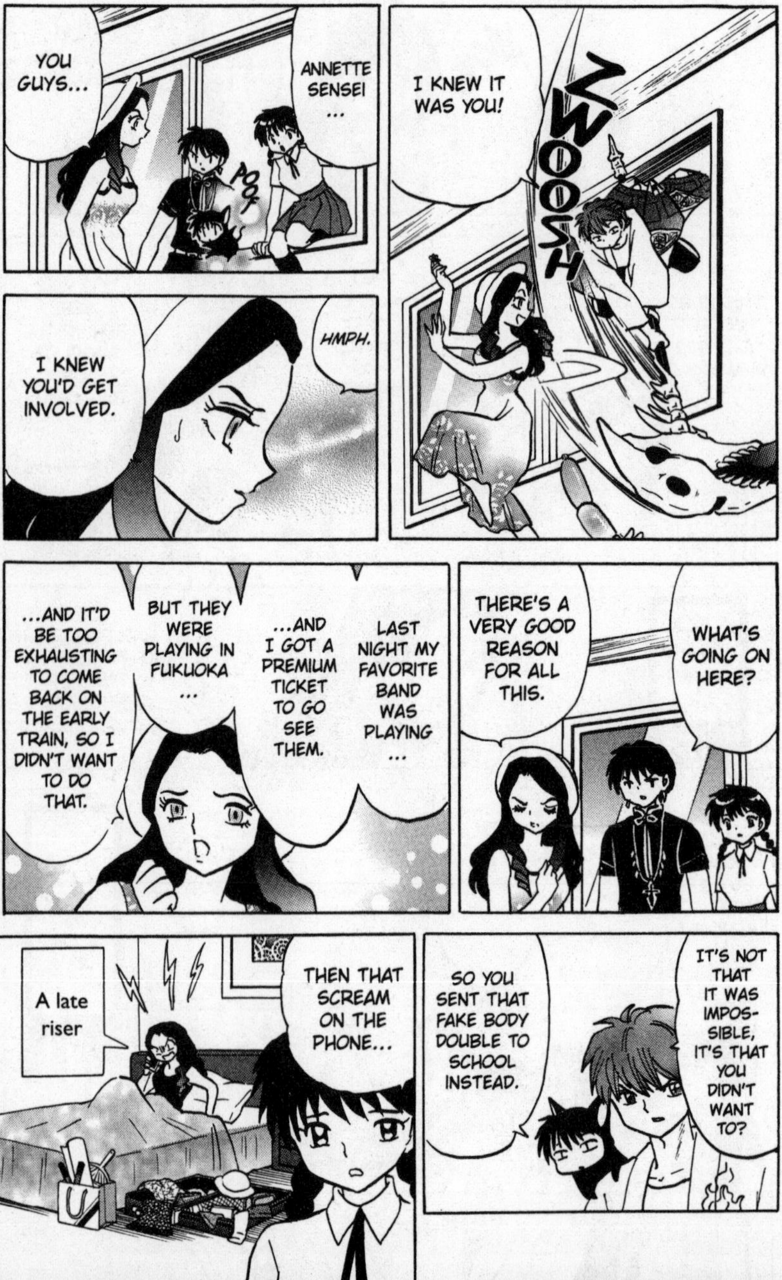
I KNEW IT WAS YOU!
ZWOOOSH
ANNETTE SENSEI ...
YOU GUYS...
POOF
HMPH.
I KNEW YOU'D GET INVOLVED.
WHAT'S GOING ON HERE?
THERE'S A VERY GOOD REASON FOR ALL THIS.
LAST NIGHT MY FAVORITE BAND WAS PLAYING ...
...AND I GOT A PREMIUM TICKET TO GO SEE THEM.
BUT THEY WERE PLAYING IN FUKUOKA ...
...AND IT'D BE TOO EXHAUSTING TO COME BACK ON THE EARLY TRAIN, SO I DIDN'T WANT TO DO THAT.
IT'S NOT THAT IT WAS IMPOS-SIBLE, IT'S THAT YOU DIDN'T WANT TO?
SO YOU SENT THAT FAKE BODY DOUBLE TO SCHOOL INSTEAD.
THEN THAT SCREAM ON THE PHONE...
A late riser

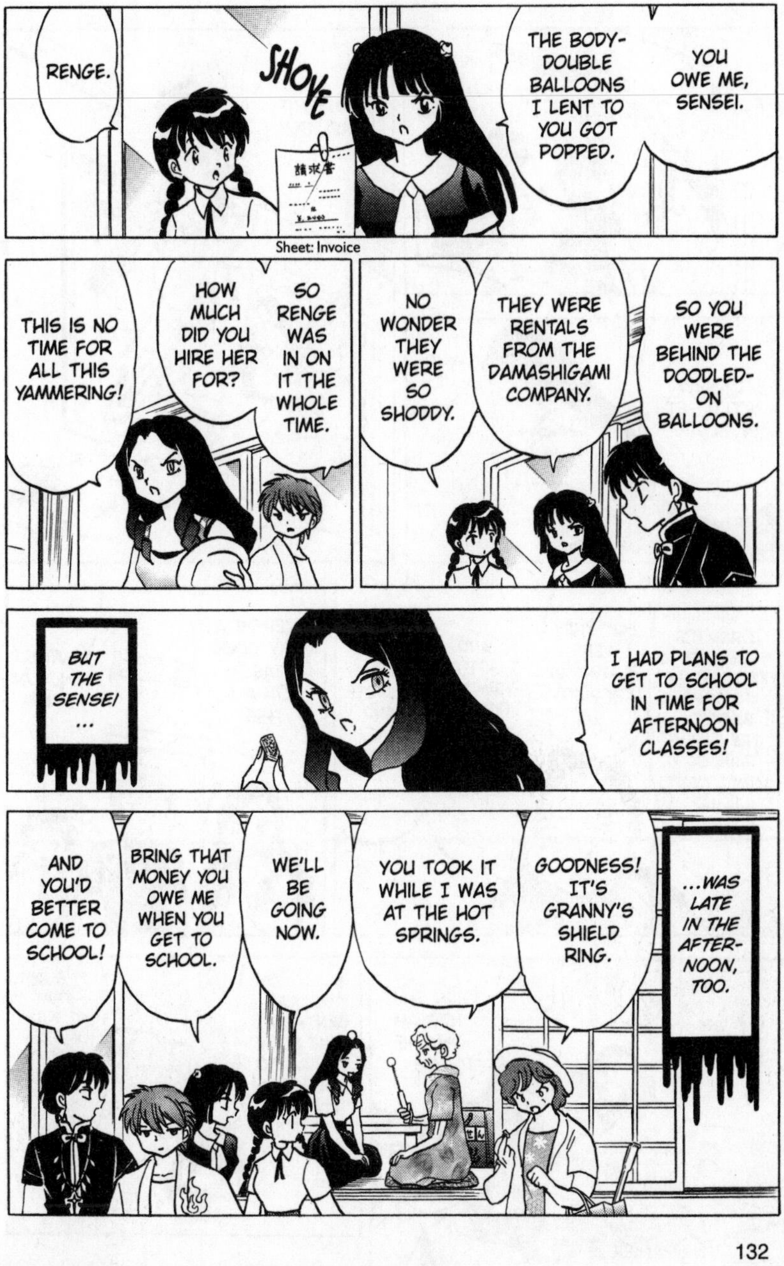
YOU OWE ME, SENSEI.
THE BODY-DOUBLE BALLOONS I LENT TO YOU GOT POPPED.
SHOVE
RENGE.
Sheet: Invoice
SO YOU WERE BEHIND THE DOODLED-ON BALLOONS.
THEY WERE RENTALS FROM THE DAMASHIGAMI COMPANY.
NO WONDER THEY WERE SO SHODDY.
SO RENGE WAS IN ON IT THE WHOLE TIME.
HOW MUCH DID YOU HIRE HER FOR?
THIS IS NO TIME FOR ALL THIS YAMMERING!
I HAD PLANS TO GET TO SCHOOL IN TIME FOR AFTERNOON CLASSES!
BUT THE SENSEI ...
...WAS LATE IN THE AFTERNOON, TOO.
GOODNESS! IT'S GRANNY'S SHIELD RING.
YOU TOOK IT WHILE I WAS AT THE HOT SPRINGS.
WE'LL BE GOING NOW.
BRING THAT MONEY YOU OWE ME WHEN YOU GET TO SCHOOL.
AND YOU'D BETTER COME TO SCHOOL!

CHAPTER 296: SHOW YOUR BACK

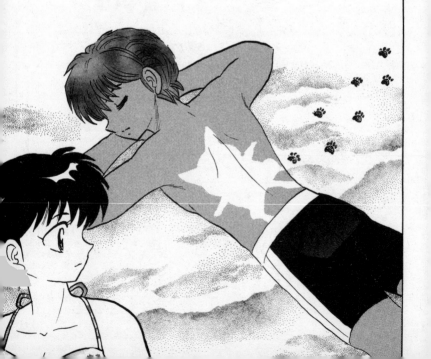

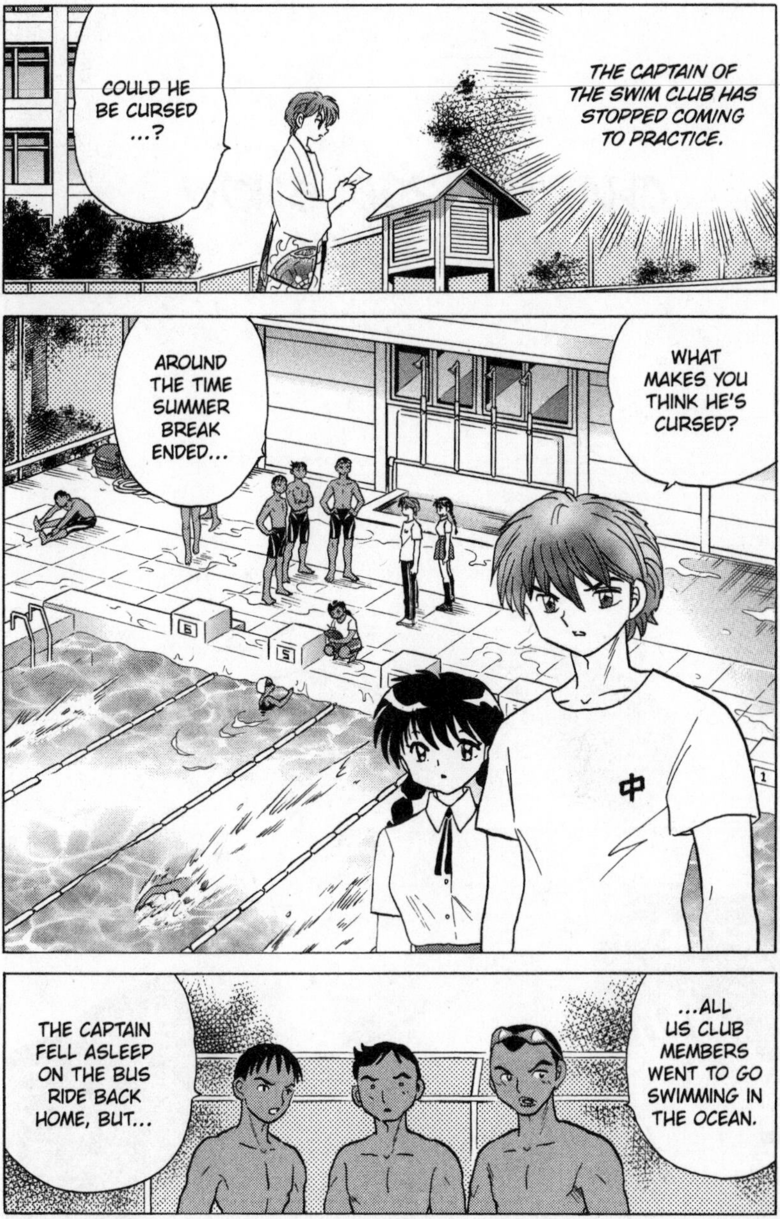
THE CAPTAIN OF THE SWIM CLUB HAS STOPPED COMING TO PRACTICE.
COULD HE BE CURSED ...?
WHAT MAKES YOU THINK HE'S CURSED?
AROUND THE TIME SUMMER BREAK ENDED...
...ALL US CLUB MEMBERS WENT TO GO SWIMMING IN THE OCEAN.
THE CAPTAIN FELL ASLEEP ON THE BUS RIDE BACK HOME, BUT...

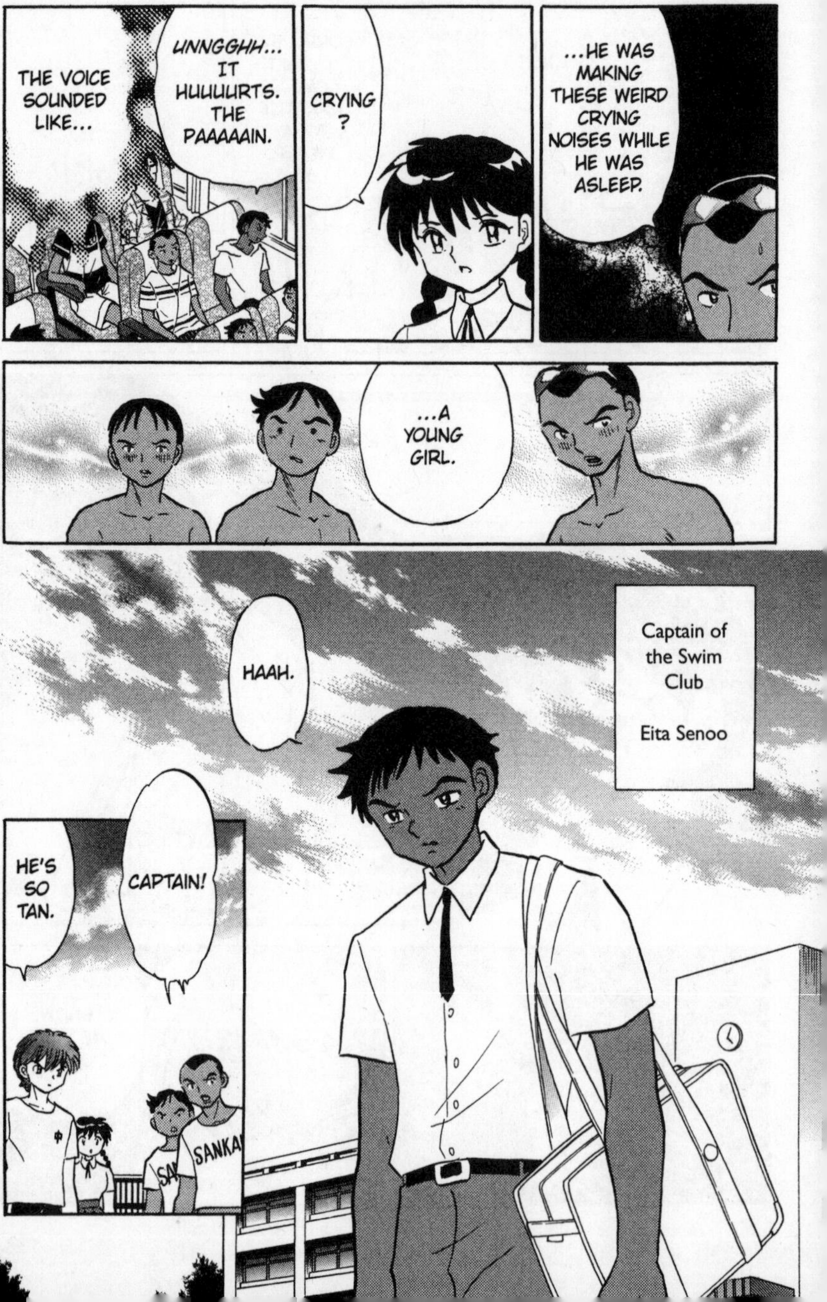
...HE WAS MAKING THESE WEIRD CRYING NOISES WHILE HE WAS ASLEEP.
CRYING ?
UNNGGHH... IT HUUUURTS. THE PAAAAAIN.
THE VOICE SOUNDED LIKE...
...A YOUNG GIRL.
Captain of the Swim Club
Eita Senoo
HAAH.
CAPTAIN!
HE'S SO TAN.

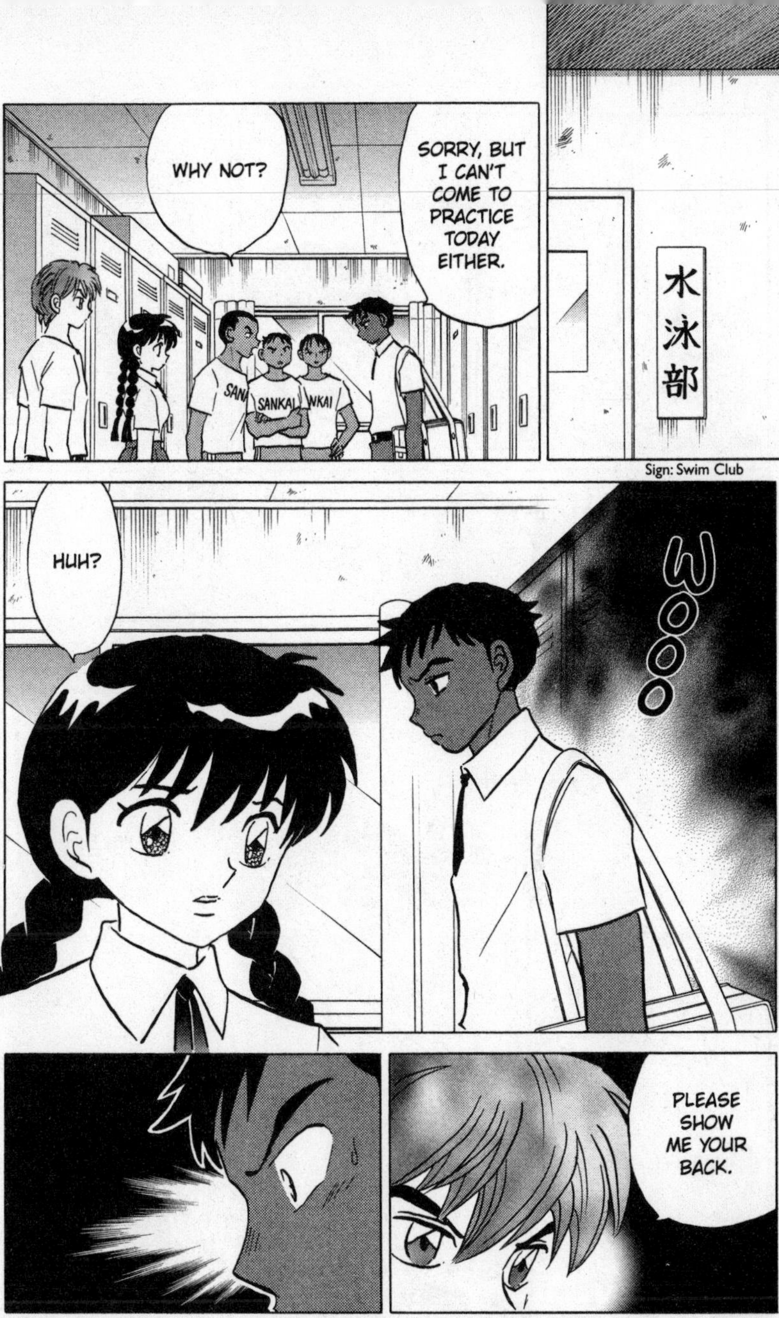
水泳部
SORRY, BUT I CAN'T COME TO PRACTICE TODAY EITHER.
WHY NOT?
SANKAI
SANKAI
WOOOO
HUH?
PLEASE SHOW ME YOUR BACK.

Sign: Swim Club

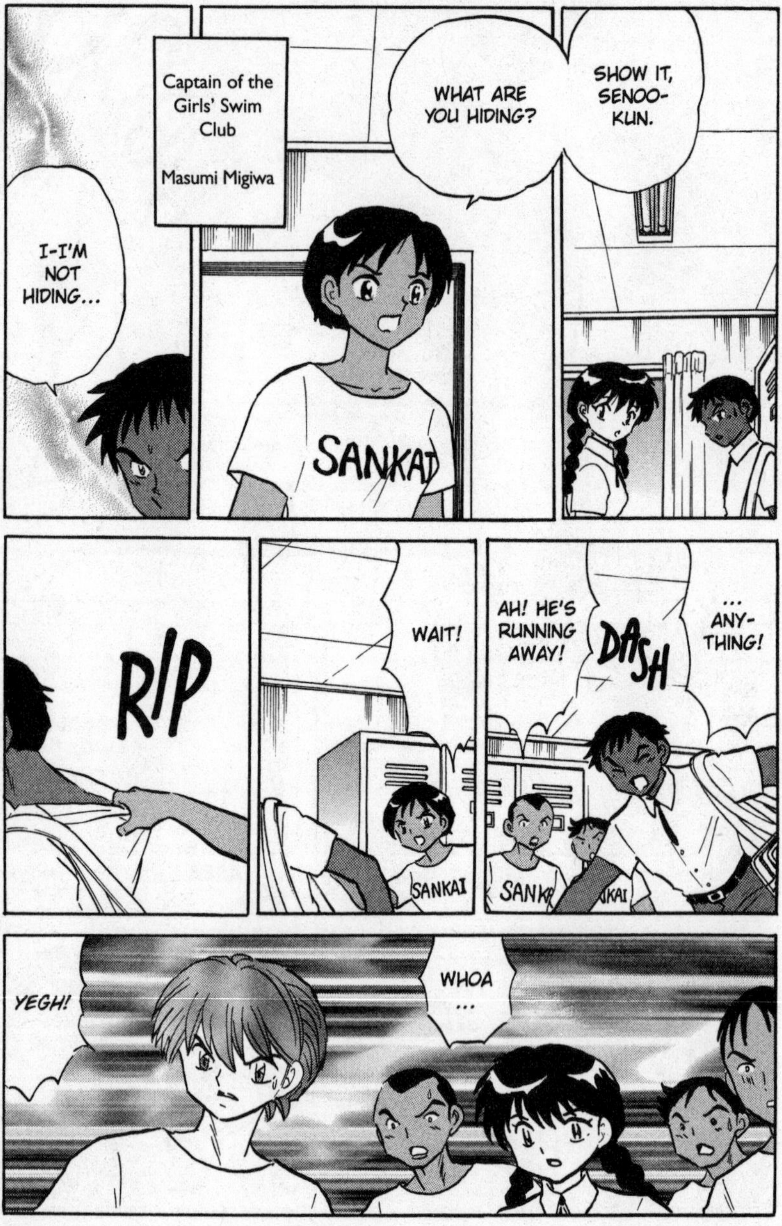
SHOW IT, SENOO-KUN.
WHAT ARE YOU HIDING?
Captain of the Girls' Swim Club
Masumi Migiwa
SANKAI
I-I'M NOT HIDING...
... ANYTHING!
DASH
AH! HE'S RUNNING AWAY!
WAIT!
SANKAI
RIP
WHOA ...
YEGH!

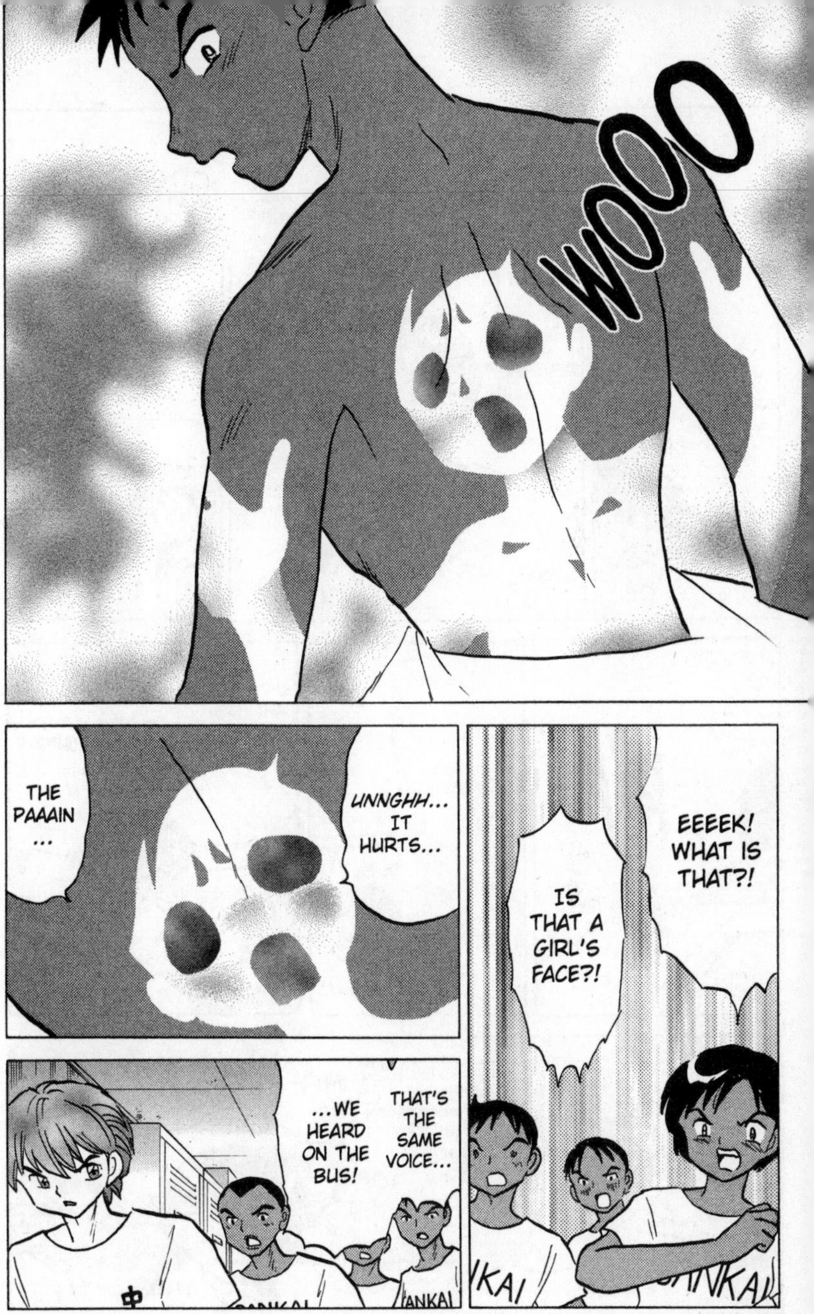
WOOO
EEEEK! WHAT IS THAT?!
IS THAT A GIRL'S FACE?!
UNNGHH... IT HURTS...
THE PAAAIN ...
THAT'S THE SAME VOICE...
...WE HEARD ON THE BUS!

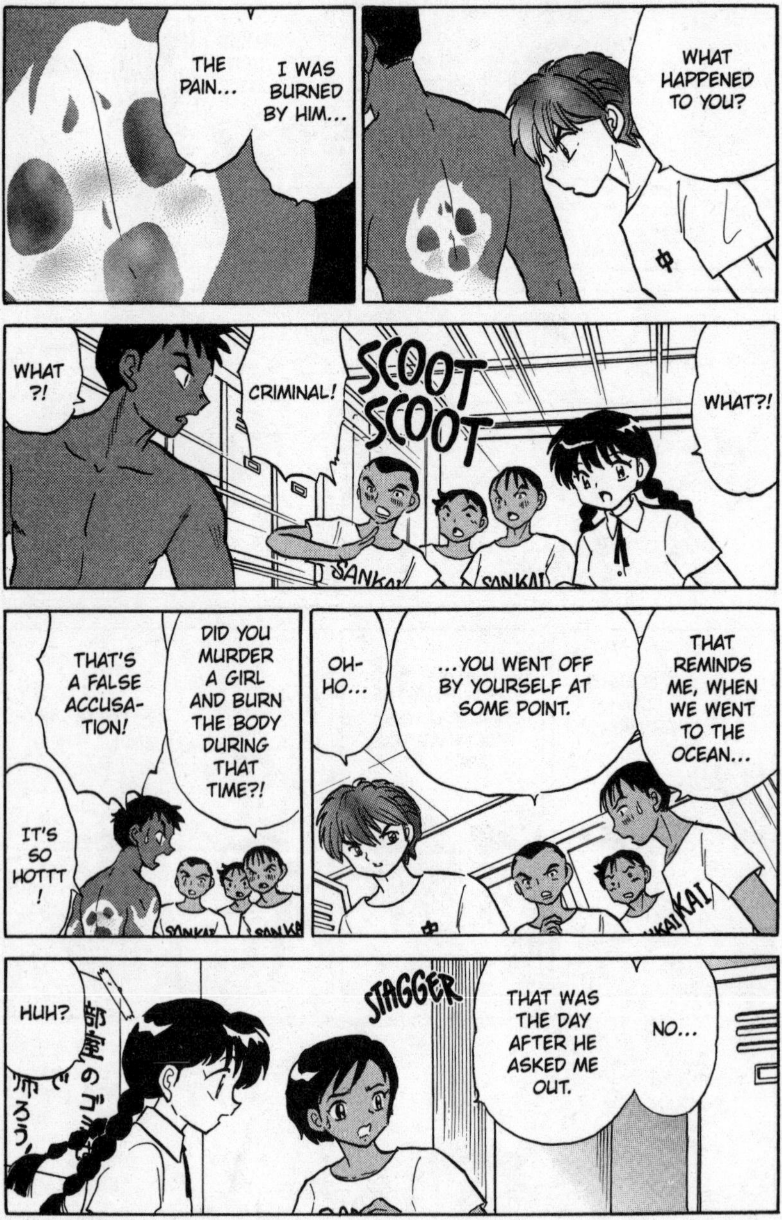
WHAT HAPPENED TO YOU?
THE PAIN... I WAS BURNED BY HIM...
WHAT?!
SCOOT SCOOT
CRIMINAL!
WHAT ?!
THAT REMINDS ME, WHEN WE WENT TO THE OCEAN...
...YOU WENT OFF BY YOURSELF AT SOME POINT.
OH-HO...
DID YOU MURDER A GIRL AND BURN THE BODY DURING THAT TIME?!
THAT'S A FALSE ACCUSATION!
IT'S SO HOTTT!
NO...
THAT WAS THE DAY AFTER HE ASKED ME OUT.
STAGGER
HUH?
Sign: Wet towels in laundry

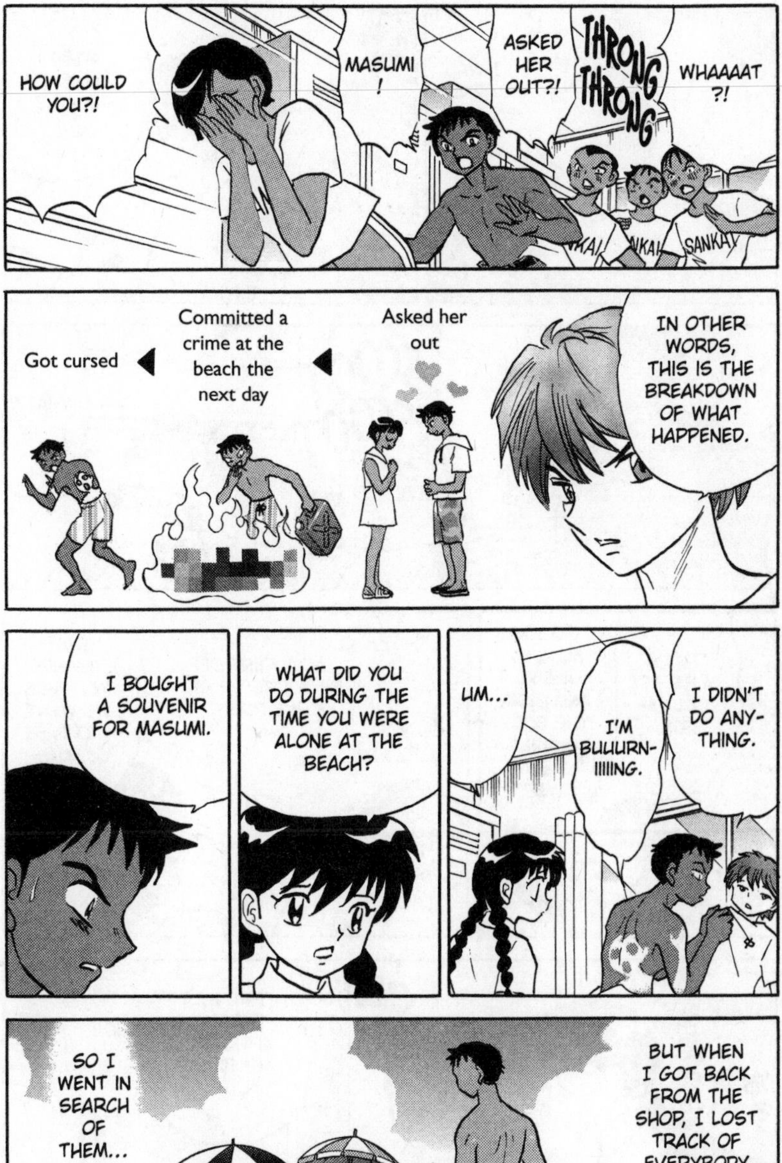
WHAAAAT ?!
THRONG THRONG
ASKED HER OUT?!
MASUMI !
HOW COULD YOU?!
IN OTHER WORDS, THIS IS THE BREAKDOWN OF WHAT HAPPENED.
Asked her out
Committed a crime at the beach the next day
Got cursed
I DIDN'T DO ANYTHING.
I'M BUUURN-IIIIING.
UM...
WHAT DID YOU DO DURING THE TIME YOU WERE ALONE AT THE BEACH?
I BOUGHT A SOUVENIR FOR MASUMI.
BUT WHEN I GOT BACK FROM THE SHOP, I LOST TRACK OF EVERYBODY ELSE...
SO I WENT IN SEARCH OF THEM...

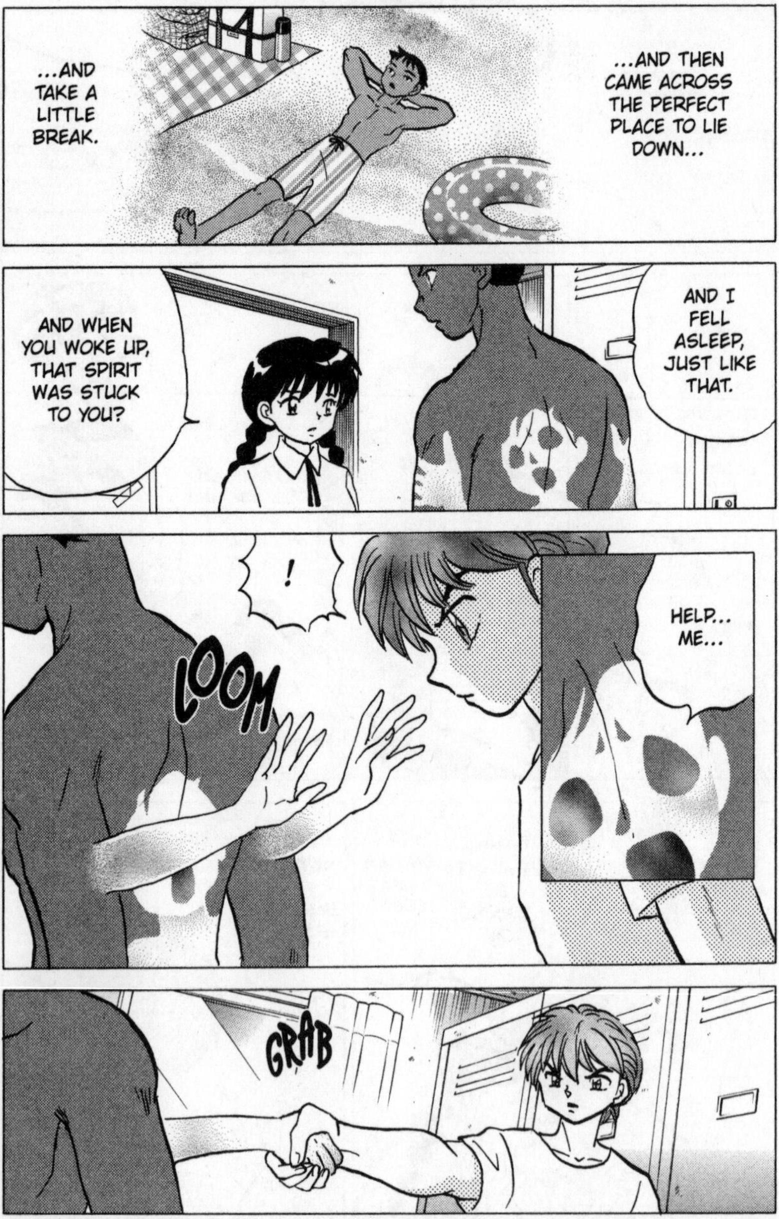
...AND THEN CAME ACROSS THE PERFECT PLACE TO LIE DOWN...
...AND TAKE A LITTLE BREAK.
AND I FELL ASLEEP, JUST LIKE THAT.
AND WHEN YOU WOKE UP, THAT SPIRIT WAS STUCK TO YOU?
HELP... ME...
!
LOOM
GRAB

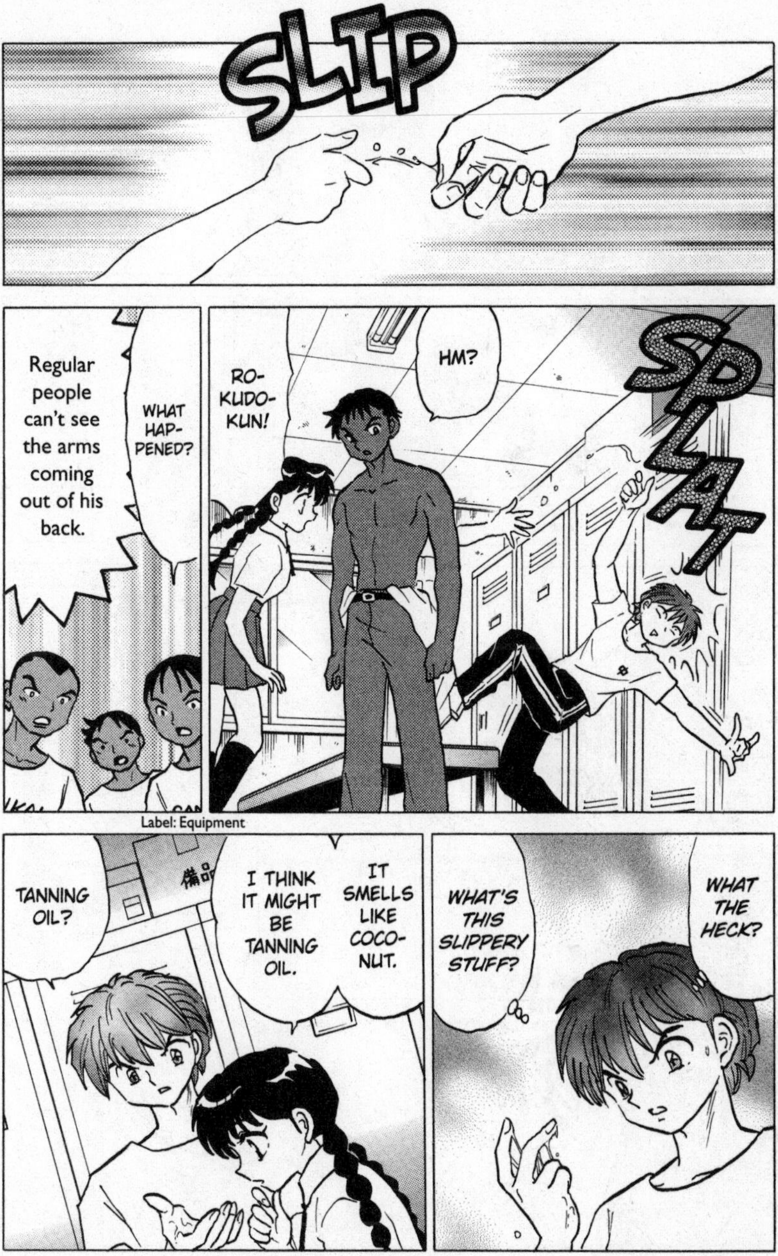
SLIP
SPLAT
HM?
RO-KUDO-KUN!
WHAT HAP-PENED?
Regular people can't see the arms coming out of his back.
WHAT THE HECK?
WHAT'S THIS SLIPPERY STUFF?
IT SMELLS LIKE COCO-NUT.
I THINK IT MIGHT BE TANNING OIL.
備品
TANNING OIL?
Label: Equipment

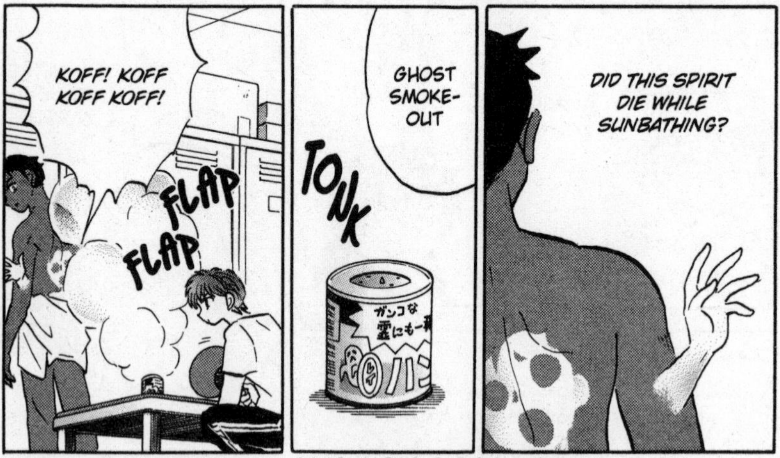
DID THIS SPIRIT DIE WHILE SUNBATHING?
GHOST SMOKE-OUT
TONK
ガンコな
KOFF! KOFF KOFF KOFF!
FLAP
FLAP
Label: Smoke-Out for Really Stubborn Spirits

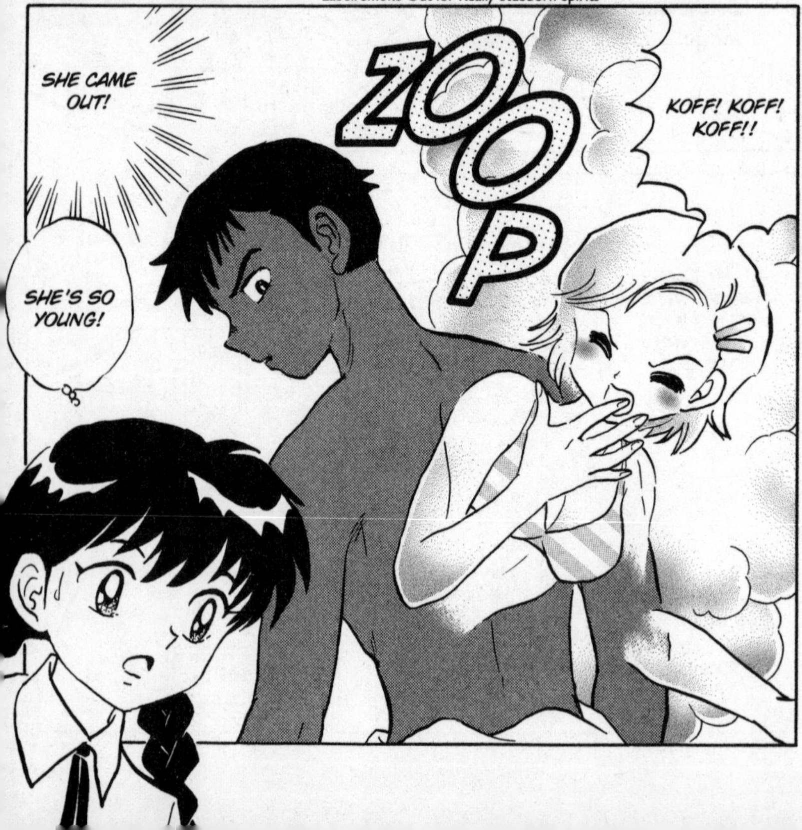
ZOOP
KOFF! KOFF! KOFF!!
SHE CAME OUT!
SHE'S SO YOUNG!

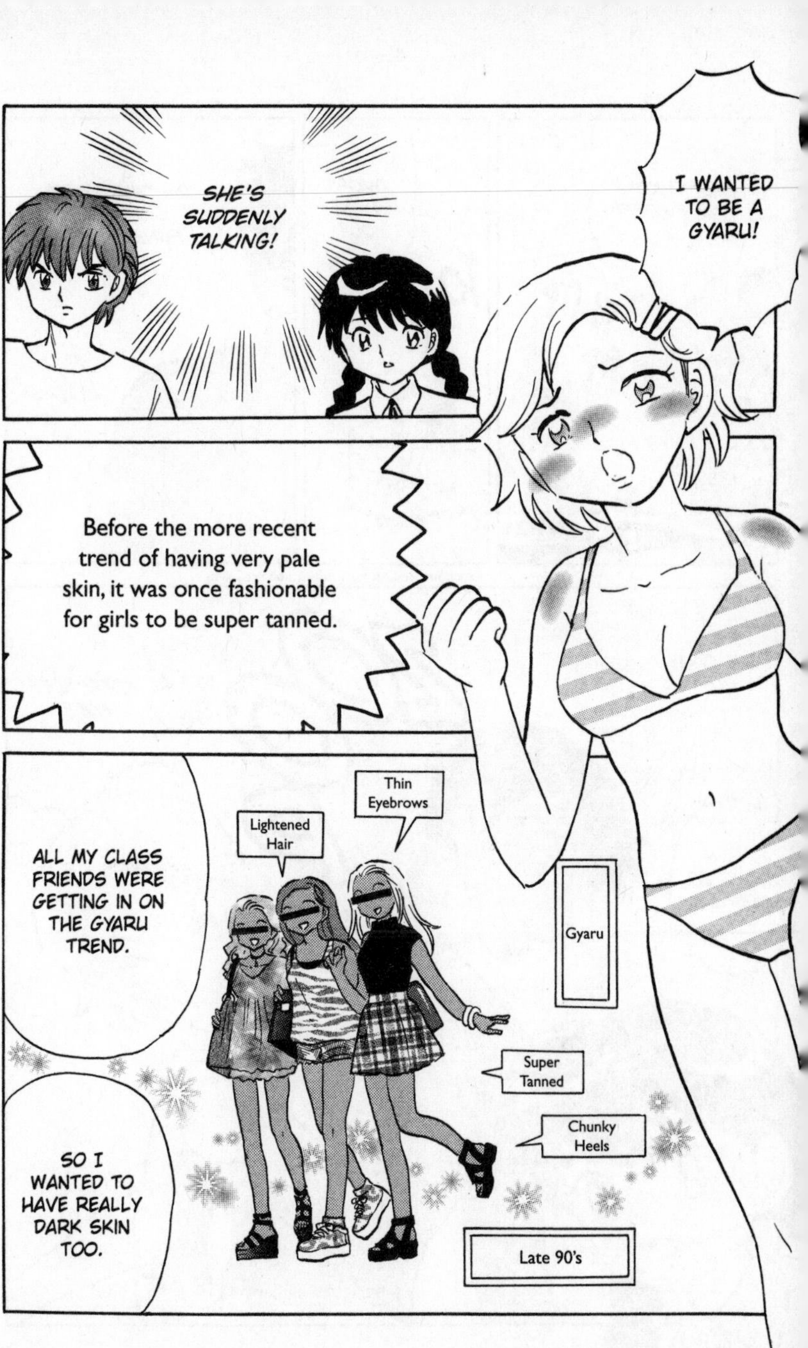
I WANTED TO BE A GYARU!
SHE'S SUDDENLY TALKING!
Before the more recent trend of having very pale skin, it was once fashionable for girls to be super tanned.
Gyaru
Thin Eyebrows
Lightened Hair
ALL MY CLASS FRIENDS WERE GETTING IN ON THE GYARU TREND.
Super Tanned
Chunky Heels
Late 90's
SO I WANTED TO HAVE REALLY DARK SKIN TOO.

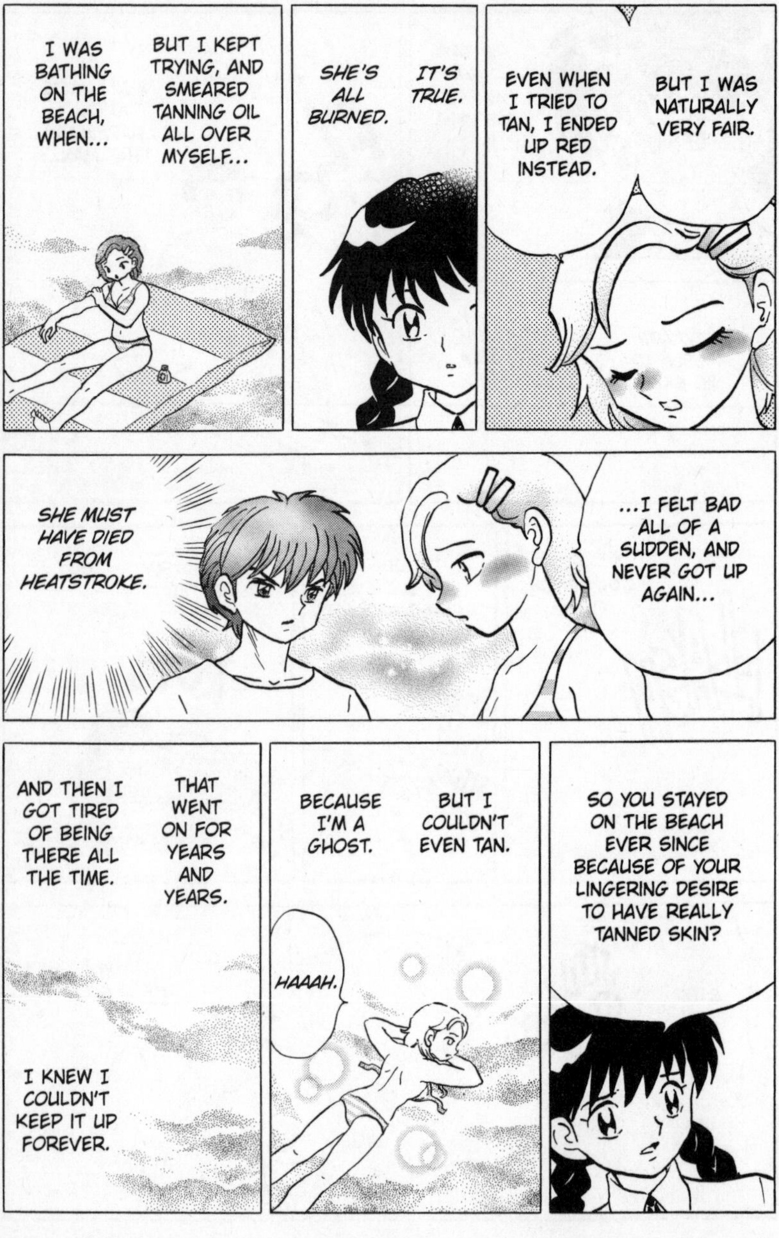
BUT I WAS NATURALLY VERY FAIR.
EVEN WHEN I TRIED TO TAN, I ENDED UP RED INSTEAD.
IT'S TRUE.
SHE'S ALL BURNED.
BUT I KEPT TRYING, AND SMEARED TANNING OIL ALL OVER MYSELF...
I WAS BATHING ON THE BEACH, WHEN...
...I FELT BAD ALL OF A SUDDEN, AND NEVER GOT UP AGAIN...
SHE MUST HAVE DIED FROM HEATSTROKE.
SO YOU STAYED ON THE BEACH EVER SINCE BECAUSE OF YOUR LINGERING DESIRE TO HAVE REALLY TANNED SKIN?
BUT I COULDN'T EVEN TAN.
BECAUSE I'M A GHOST.
HAAAH.
THAT WENT ON FOR YEARS AND YEARS.
AND THEN I GOT TIRED OF BEING THERE ALL THE TIME.
I KNEW I COULDN'T KEEP IT UP FOREVER.

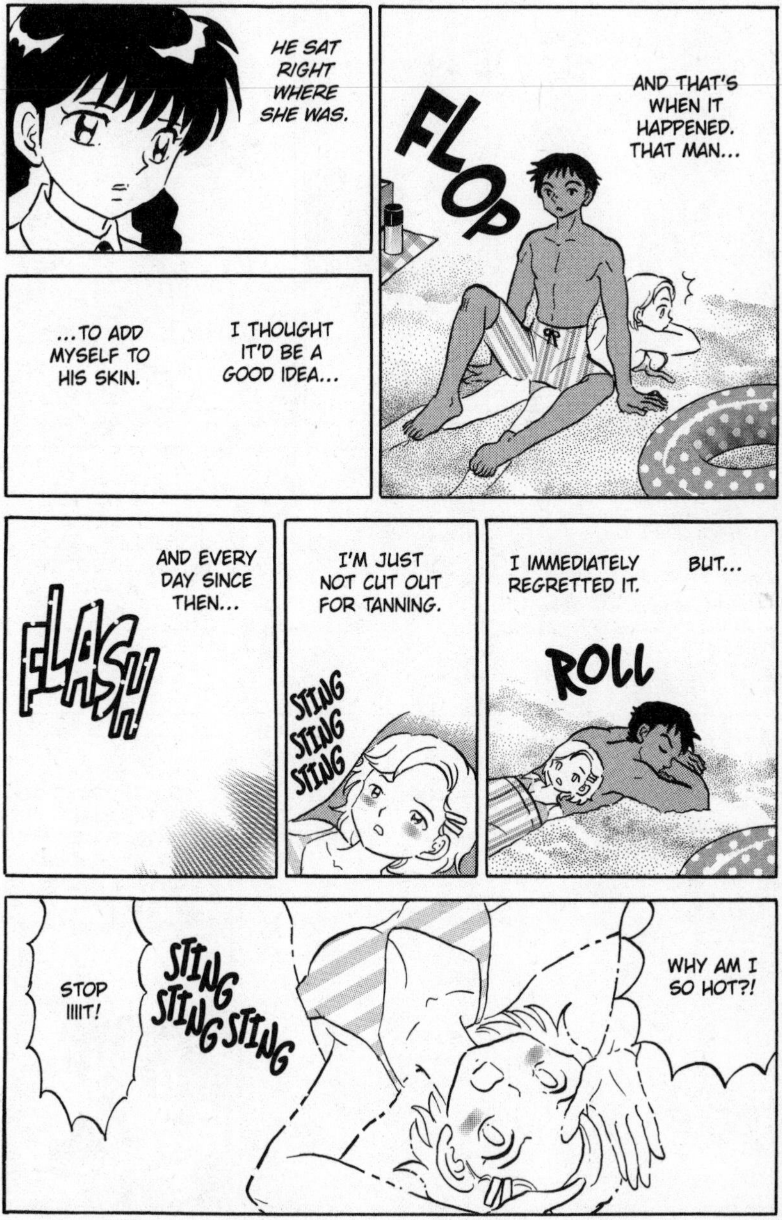
AND THAT'S WHEN IT HAPPENED. THAT MAN...
FLOP
HE SAT RIGHT WHERE SHE WAS.
I THOUGHT IT'D BE A GOOD IDEA...
...TO ADD MYSELF TO HIS SKIN.
BUT...
I IMMEDIATELY REGRETTED IT.
ROLL
I'M JUST NOT CUT OUT FOR TANNING.
STING STING STING
AND EVERY DAY SINCE THEN...
FLASH
WHY AM I SO HOT?!
STING STING STING STING
STOP IIIIT!

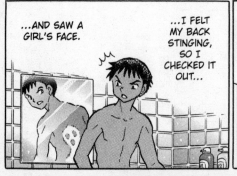

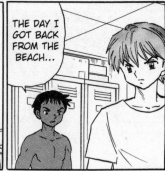

THE DAY I GOT BACK FROM THE BEACH...
...I FELT MY BACK STINGING, SO I CHECKED IT OUT...
...AND SAW A GIRL'S FACE.
I DIDN'T KNOW WHAT IT WAS, BUT I DIDN'T LIKE IT.
SO I RAN TO THE TANNING SALON.
I FIGURED I'D BURN IT OUT. BUT...
...THE MORE I TANNED...
...THE CLEARER THE GIRL'S FACE AND HER EERIE VOICE WERE.
IT HURTS... OWW...
HEEELP...
DO YOU STILL HAVE A LINGERING ATTACHMENT TO THIS WORLD?
HM?!
中
SANKAI
IS THERE SOMETHING THERE?!
Ordinary humans can't see the spirit.

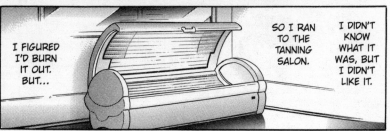

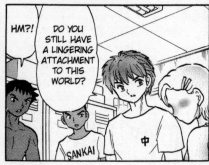

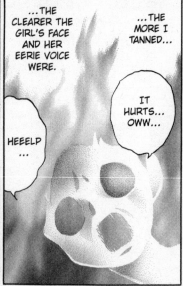

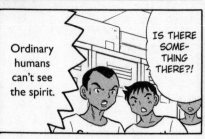

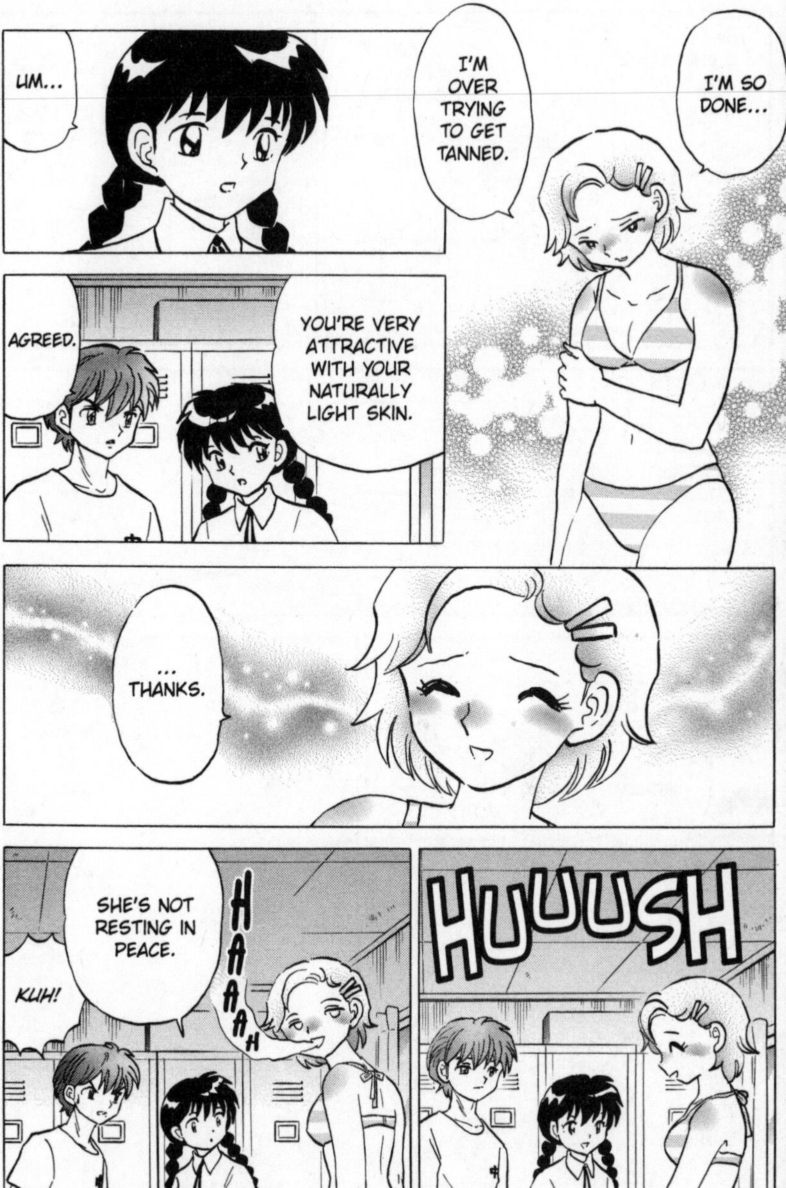
I'M SO DONE...
I'M OVER TRYING TO GET TANNED.
UM...
YOU'RE VERY ATTRACTIVE WITH YOUR NATURALLY LIGHT SKIN.
AGREED.
... THANKS.
HUUUSH
HAAAAH
SHE'S NOT RESTING IN PEACE.
KUH!

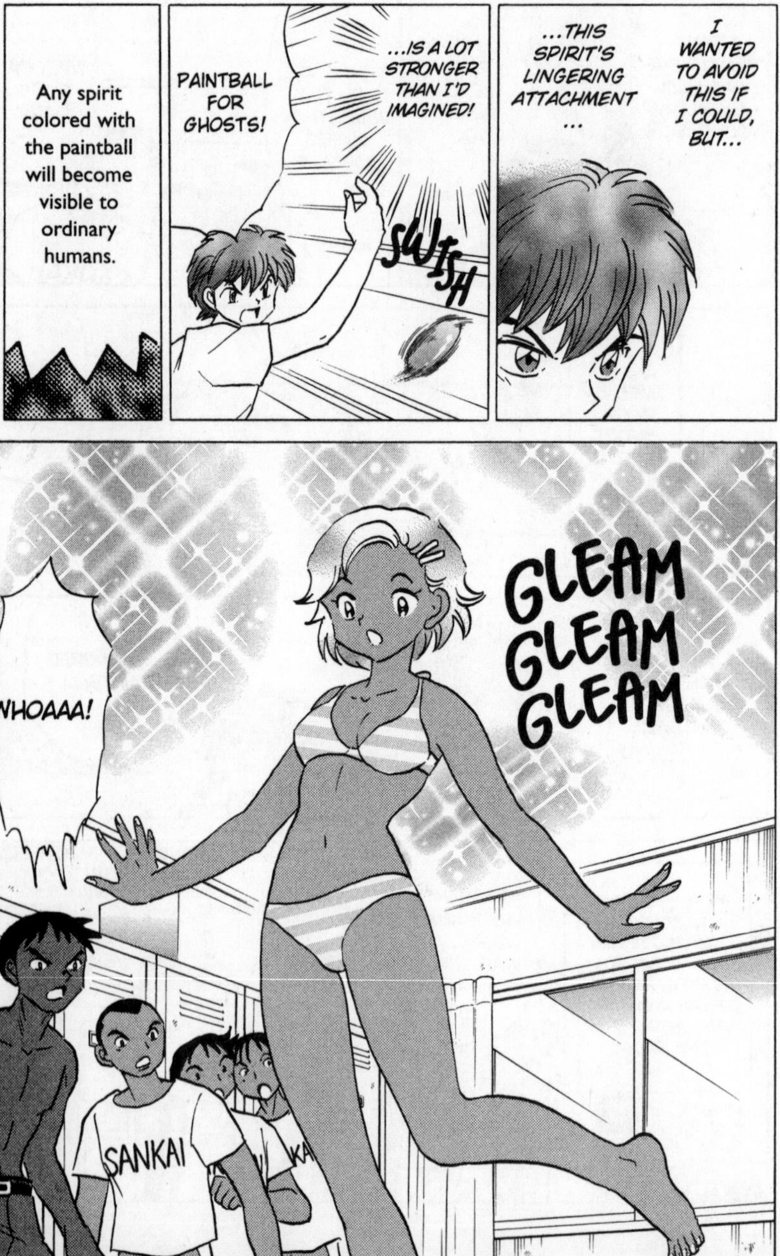
I WANTED TO AVOID THIS IF I COULD, BUT...
...THIS SPIRIT'S LINGERING ATTACHMENT...
...IS A LOT STRONGER THAN I'D IMAGINED!
PAINTBALL FOR GHOSTS!
SWISH
Any spirit colored with the paintball will become visible to ordinary humans.
GLEAM GLEAM GLEAM
WHOAAA!
SANKAI

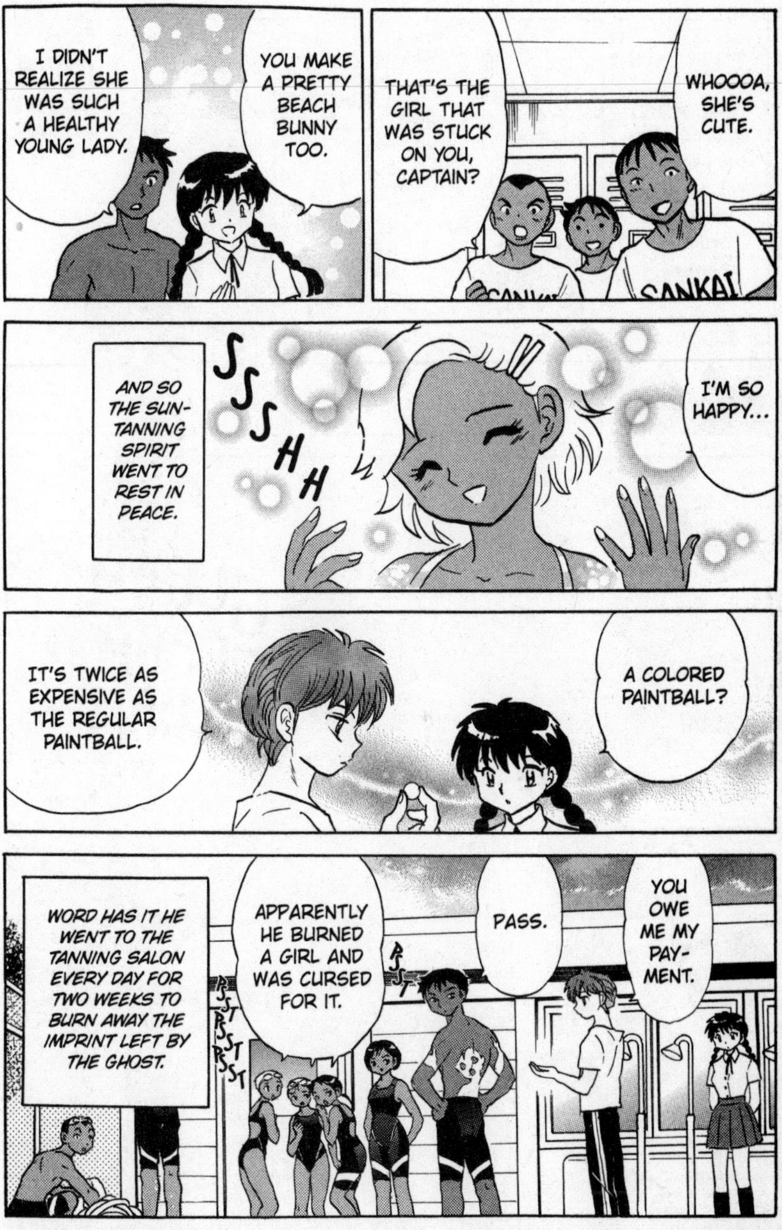
WHOOOA, SHE'S CUTE.
THAT'S THE GIRL THAT WAS STUCK ON YOU, CAPTAIN?
SANKAI
YOU MAKE A PRETTY BEACH BUNNY TOO.
I DIDN'T REALIZE SHE WAS SUCH A HEALTHY YOUNG LADY.
I'M SO HAPPY...
SSSHH
AND SO THE SUN-TANNING SPIRIT WENT TO REST IN PEACE.
A COLORED PAINTBALL?
IT'S TWICE AS EXPENSIVE AS THE REGULAR PAINTBALL.
YOU OWE ME MY PAY-MENT.
PASS.
PSST
APPARENTLY HE BURNED A GIRL AND WAS CURSED FOR IT.
PSST PSST PSST
WORD HAS IT HE WENT TO THE TANNING SALON EVERY DAY FOR TWO WEEKS TO BURN AWAY THE IMPRINT LEFT BY THE GHOST.

CHAPTER 297: THE MASK OF MEDUSA

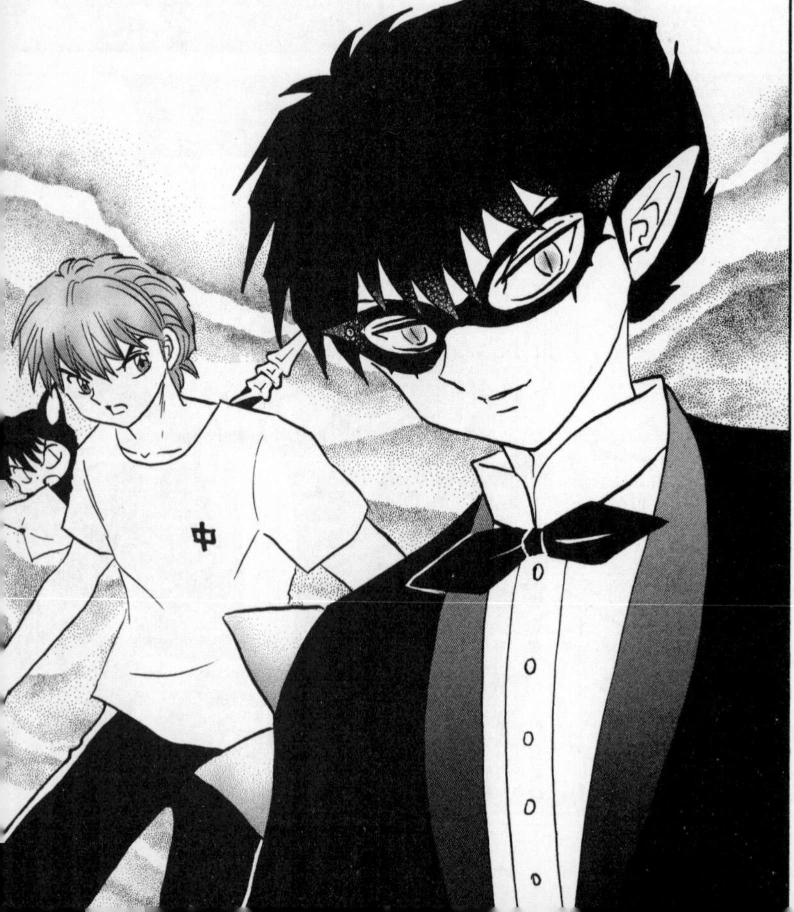
中

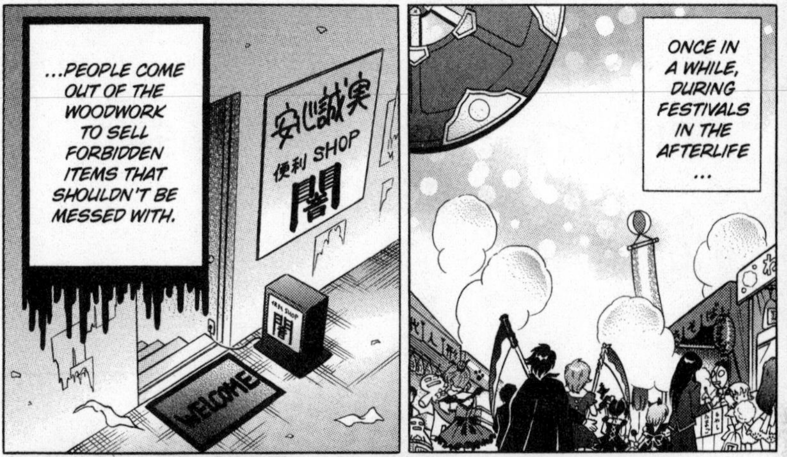
ONCE IN A WHILE, DURING FESTIVALS IN THE AFTERLIFE...
...PEOPLE COME OUT OF THE WOODWORK TO SELL FORBIDDEN ITEMS THAT SHOULDN'T BE MESSED WITH.
安心誠実
便利 SHOP
闇
WELCOME

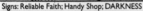

Signs: Reliable Faith; Handy Shop; DARKNESS

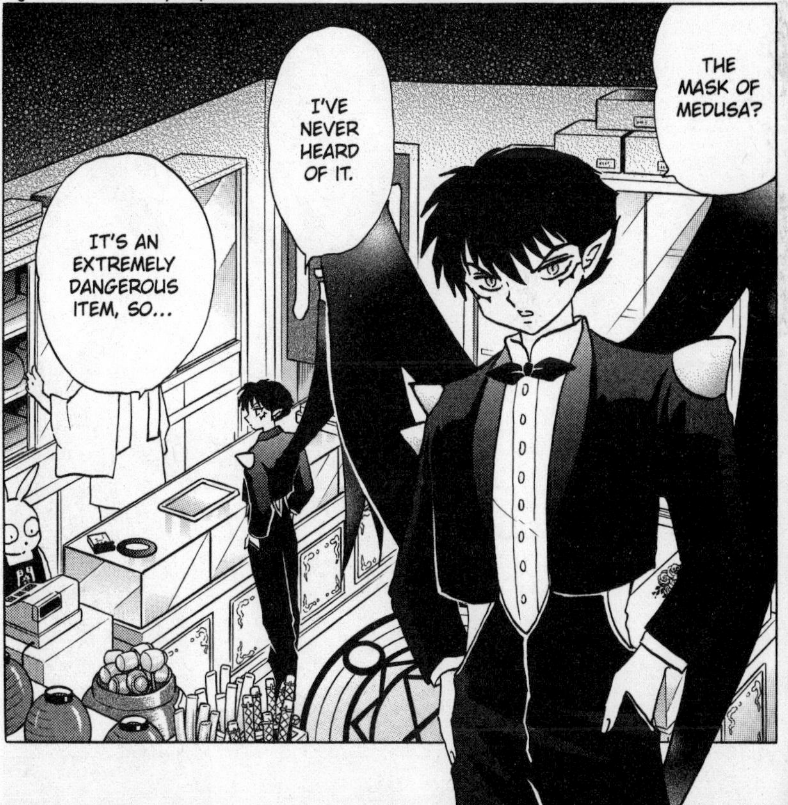
THE MASK OF MEDUSA?
I'VE NEVER HEARD OF IT.
IT'S AN EXTREMELY DANGEROUS ITEM, SO...

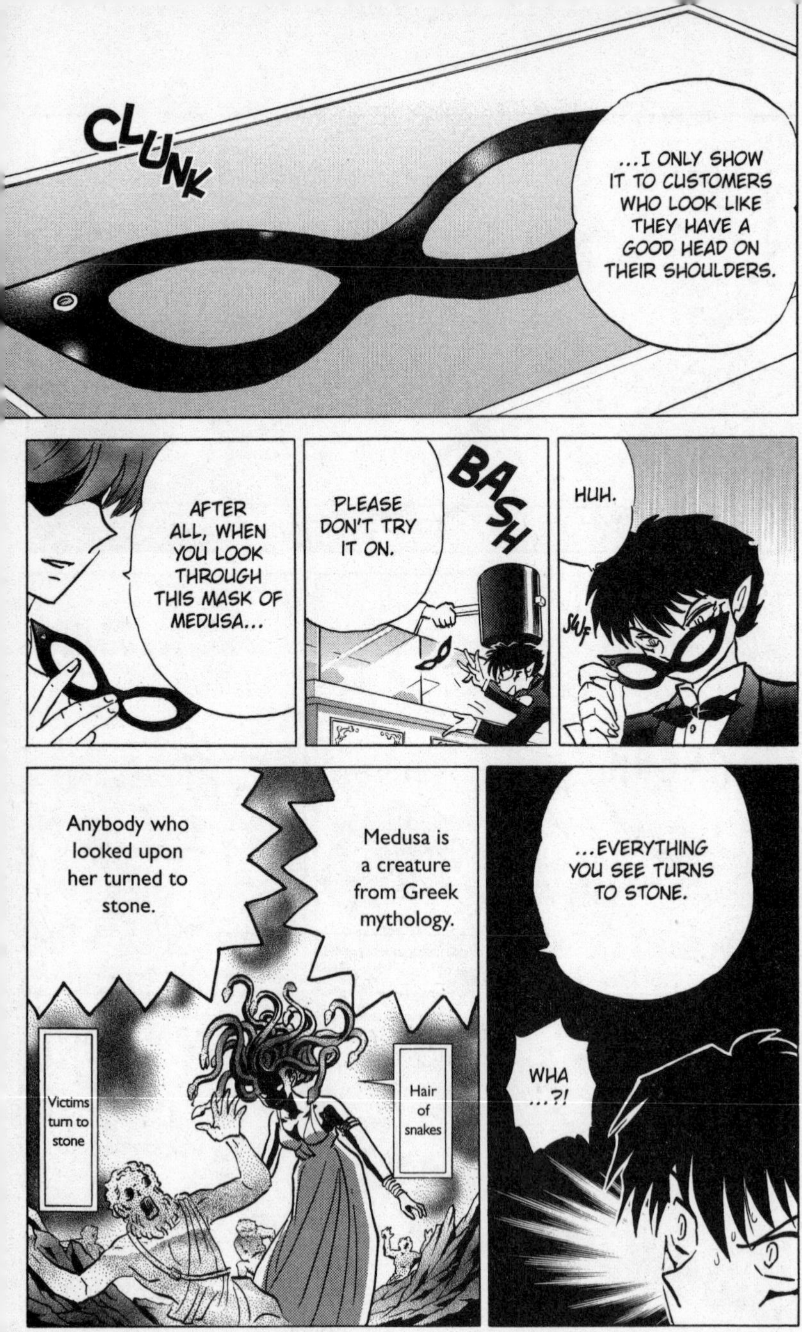
CLUNK
...I ONLY SHOW IT TO CUSTOMERS WHO LOOK LIKE THEY HAVE A GOOD HEAD ON THEIR SHOULDERS.
HUH.
SWF
BASH
PLEASE DON'T TRY IT ON.
AFTER ALL, WHEN YOU LOOK THROUGH THIS MASK OF MEDUSA...
...EVERYTHING YOU SEE TURNS TO STONE.
WHA ...?!
Medusa is a creature from Greek mythology.
Anybody who looked upon her turned to stone.
Hair of snakes
Victims turn to stone

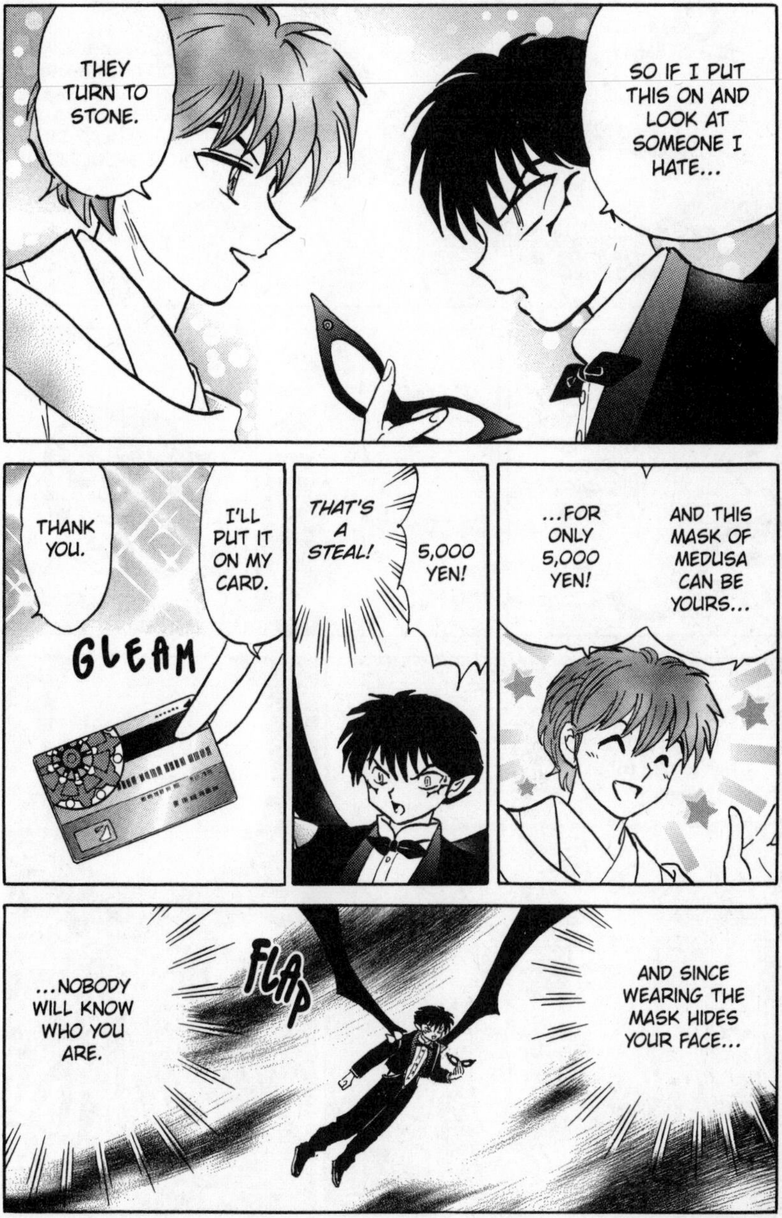
SO IF I PUT THIS ON AND LOOK AT SOMEONE I HATE...
THEY TURN TO STONE.
AND THIS MASK OF MEDUSA CAN BE YOURS...
...FOR ONLY 5,000 YEN!
5,000 YEN!
THAT'S A STEAL!
I'LL PUT IT ON MY CARD.
THANK YOU.
GLEAM
AND SINCE WEARING THE MASK HIDES YOUR FACE...
FLAP
...NOBODY WILL KNOW WHO YOU ARE.

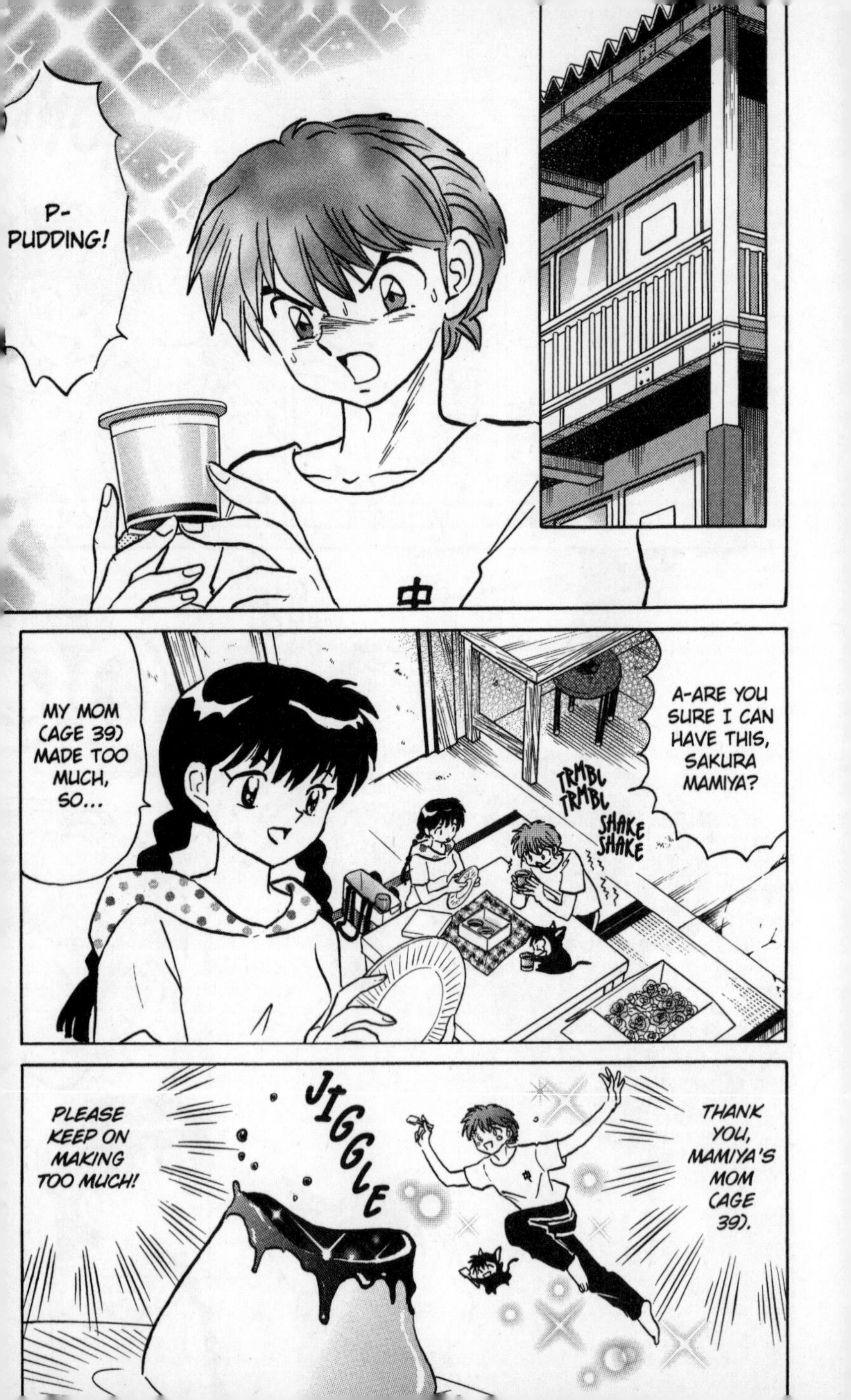
P-PUDDING!
A-ARE YOU SURE I CAN HAVE THIS, SAKURA MAMIYA?
TRMBL TRMBL
SHAKE SHAKE
MY MOM (AGE 39) MADE TOO MUCH, SO...
THANK YOU, MAMIYA'S MOM (AGE 39).
JIGGLE
PLEASE KEEP ON MAKING TOO MUCH!

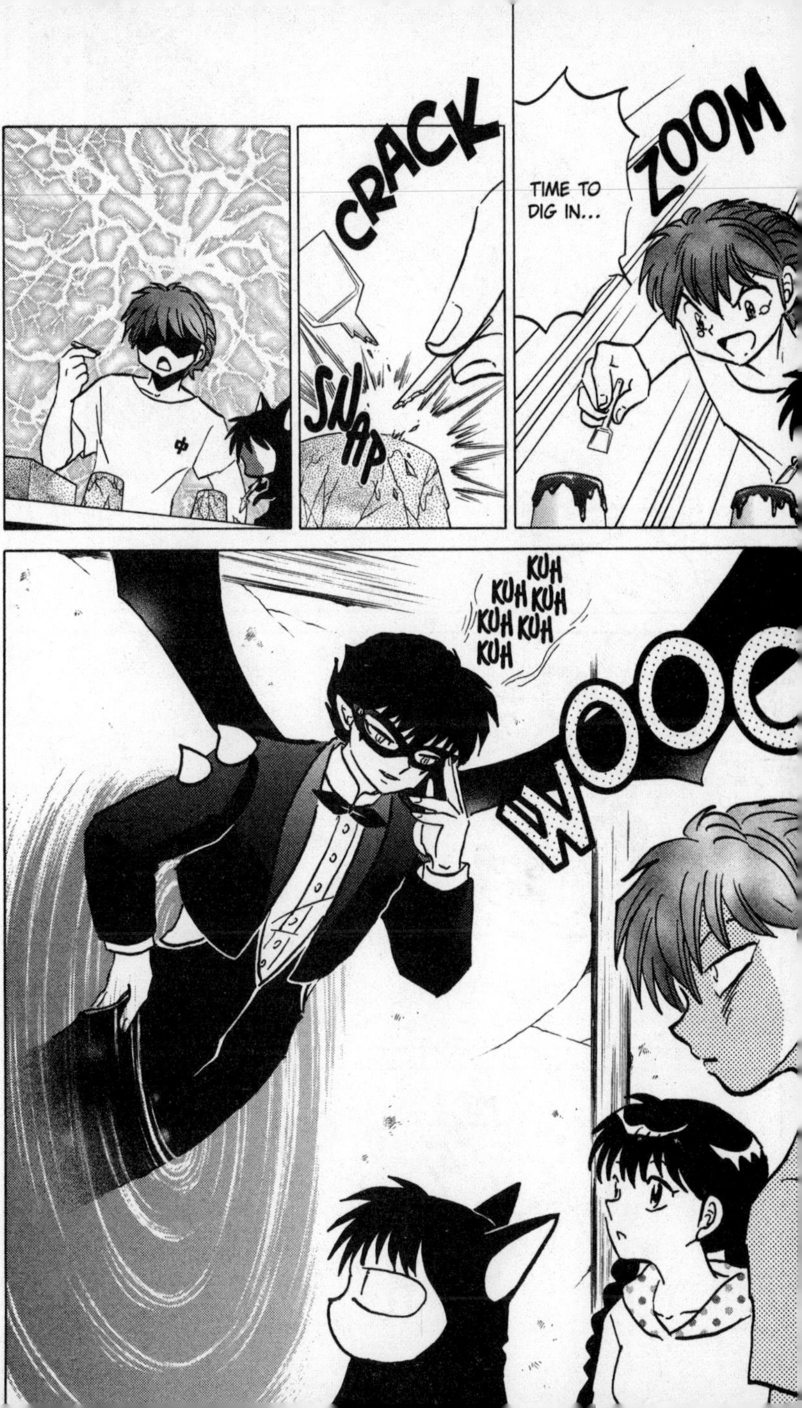
ZOOM
TIME TO DIG IN...
CRACK
SNAP
KUH KUH KUH KUH KUH KUH KUH
WOOO

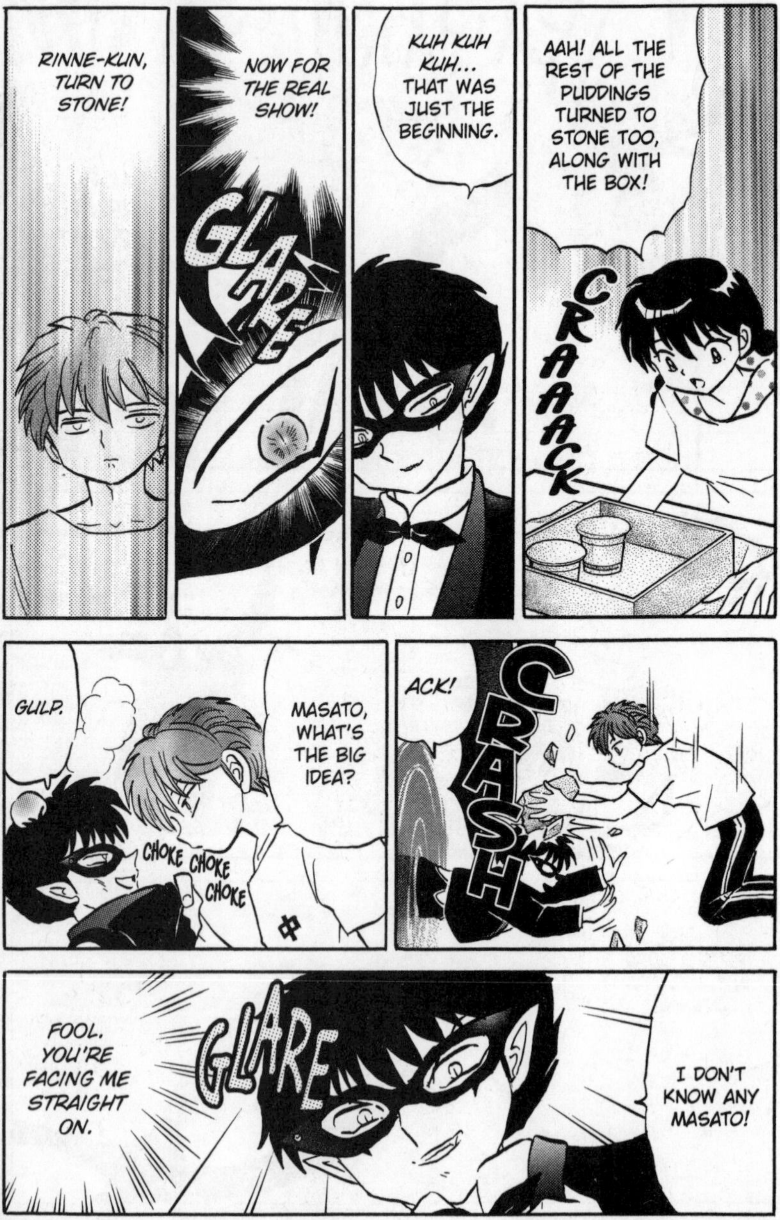
AAH! ALL THE REST OF THE PUDDINGS TURNED TO STONE TOO, ALONG WITH THE BOX!
CRAAACK
KUH KUH KUH... THAT WAS JUST THE BEGINNING.
NOW FOR THE REAL SHOW!
GLARE
RINNE-KUN, TURN TO STONE!
ACK!
CRASH
MASATO, WHAT'S THE BIG IDEA?
GULP.
CHOKE CHOKE CHOKE
I DON'T KNOW ANY MASATO!
GLARE
FOOL. YOU'RE FACING ME STRAIGHT ON.

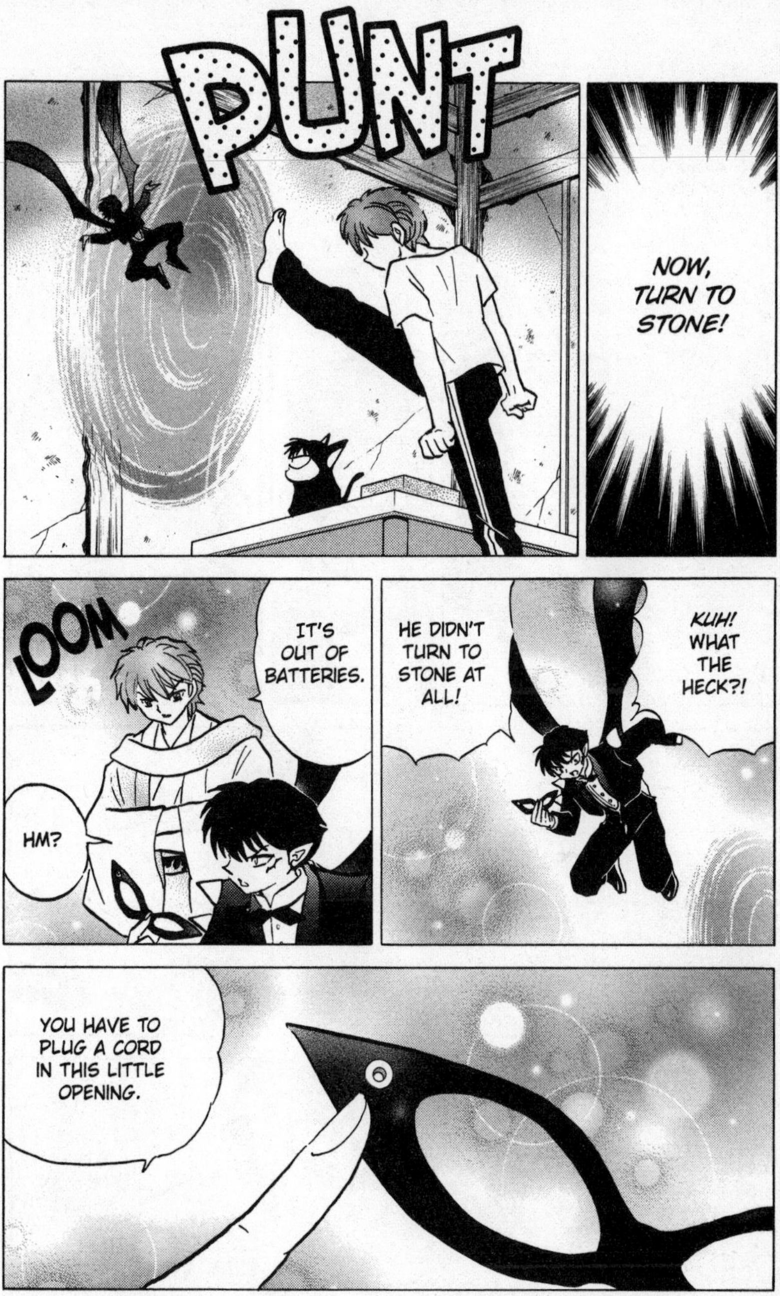
NOW, TURN TO STONE!
PUNT
KUH! WHAT THE HECK?!
HE DIDN'T TURN TO STONE AT ALL!
IT'S OUT OF BATTERIES.
LOOM
HM?
YOU HAVE TO PLUG A CORD IN THIS LITTLE OPENING.

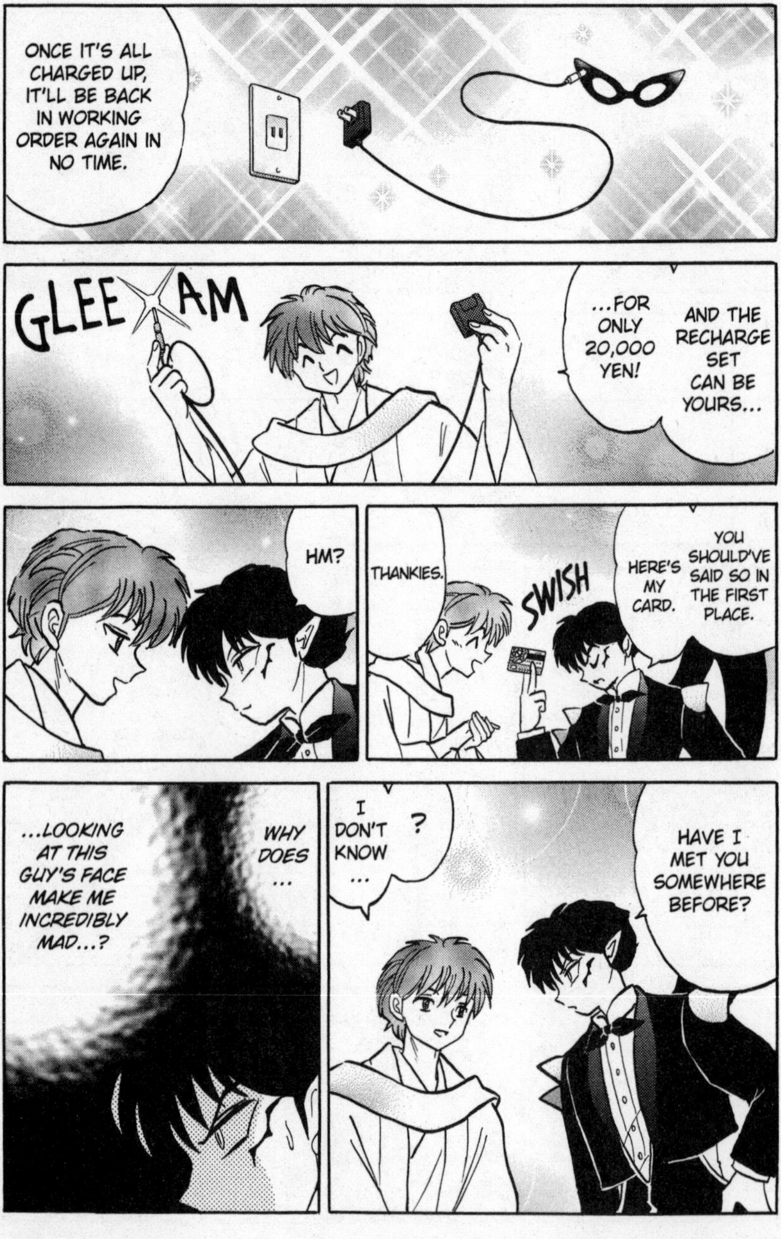
ONCE IT'S ALL CHARGED UP, IT'LL BE BACK IN WORKING ORDER AGAIN IN NO TIME.
AND THE RECHARGE SET CAN BE YOURS...
...FOR ONLY 20,000 YEN!
GLEEAM
YOU SHOULD'VE SAID SO IN THE FIRST PLACE.
HERE'S MY CARD.
SWISH
THANKIES.
HM?
HAVE I MET YOU SOMEWHERE BEFORE?
?
I DON'T KNOW ...
WHY DOES ...
...LOOKING AT THIS GUY'S FACE MAKE ME INCREDIBLY MAD...?

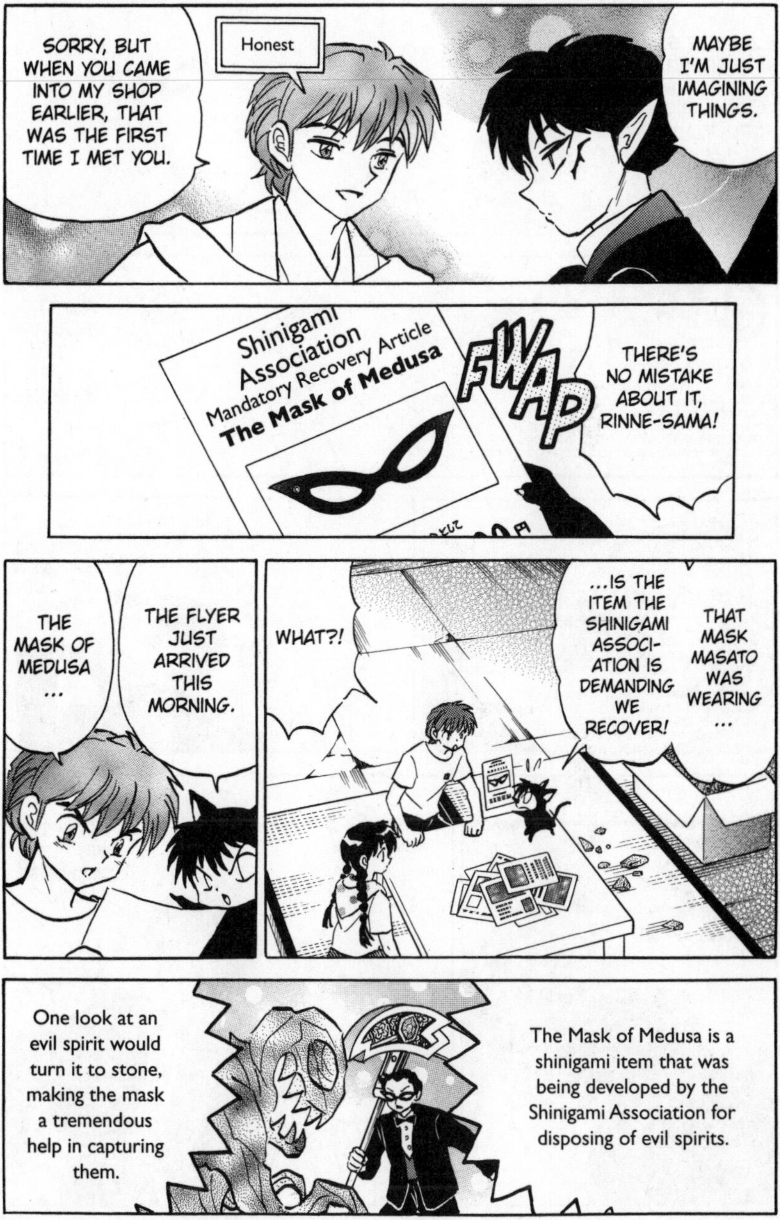
MAYBE I'M JUST IMAGINING THINGS.
Honest
SORRY, BUT WHEN YOU CAME INTO MY SHOP EARLIER, THAT WAS THE FIRST TIME I MET YOU.
THERE'S NO MISTAKE ABOUT IT, RINNE-SAMA!
FWAP
Shinigami Association
Mandatory Recovery Article
The Mask of Medusa
THAT MASK MASATO WAS WEARING ...
...IS THE ITEM THE SHINIGAMI ASSOCIATION IS DEMANDING WE RECOVER!
WHAT?!
THE FLYER JUST ARRIVED THIS MORNING.
THE MASK OF MEDUSA ...
The Mask of Medusa is a shinigami item that was being developed by the Shinigami Association for disposing of evil spirits.
One look at an evil spirit would turn it to stone, making the mask a tremendous help in capturing them.

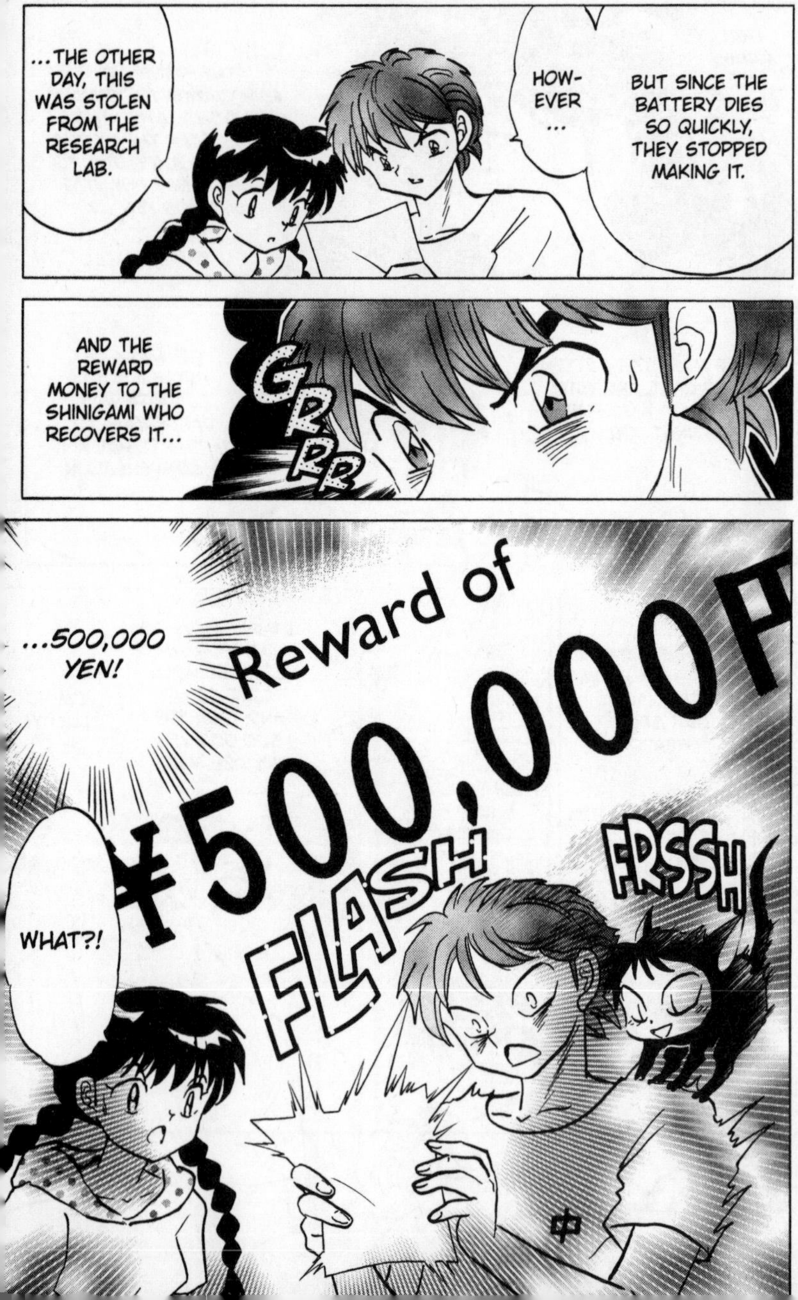
BUT SINCE THE BATTERY DIES SO QUICKLY, THEY STOPPED MAKING IT.
HOW-EVER...
...THE OTHER DAY, THIS WAS STOLEN FROM THE RESEARCH LAB.
GRRR
AND THE REWARD MONEY TO THE SHINIGAMI WHO RECOVERS IT...
Reward of ¥500,000円
...500,000 YEN!
FRSSH
FLASH
WHAT?!

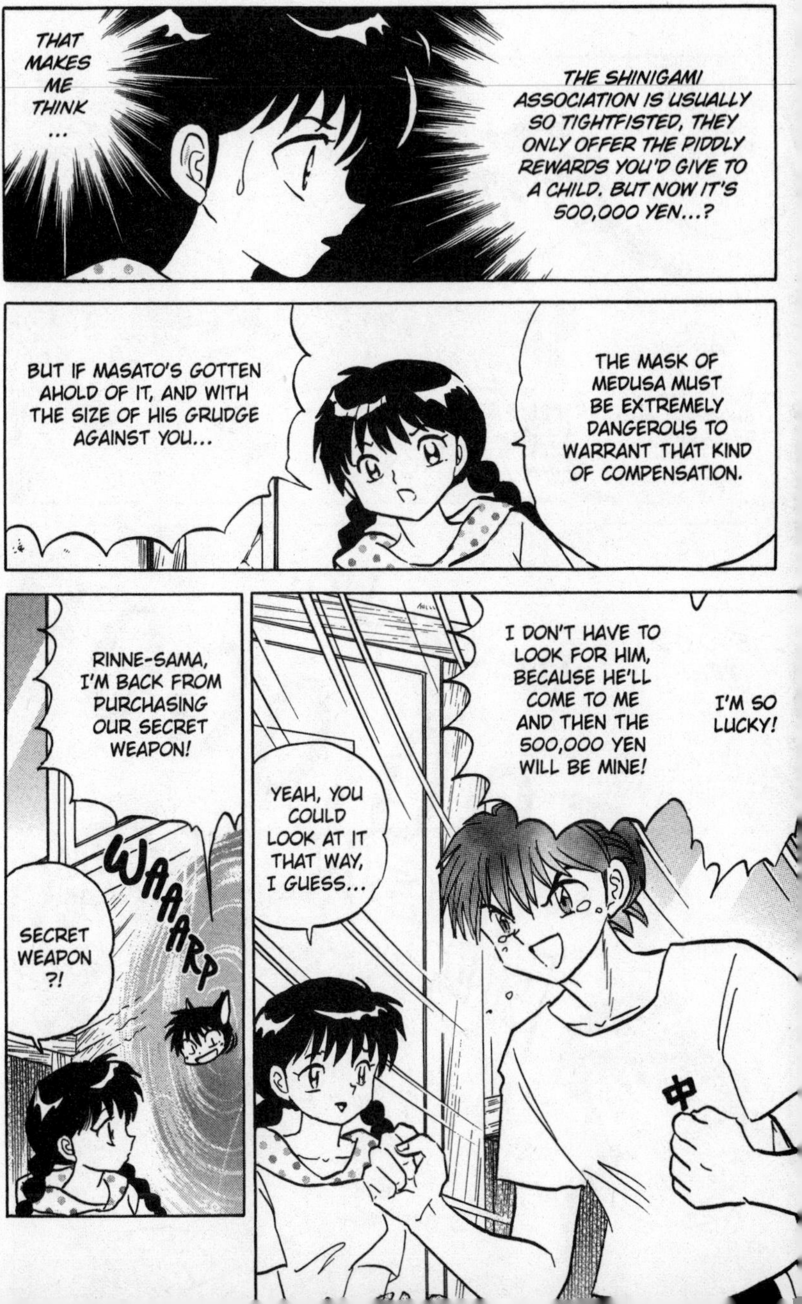
THE SHINIGAMI ASSOCIATION IS USUALLY SO TIGHTFISTED, THEY ONLY OFFER THE PIDDLY REWARDS YOU'D GIVE TO A CHILD. BUT NOW IT'S 500,000 YEN...?
THAT MAKES ME THINK...
THE MASK OF MEDUSA MUST BE EXTREMELY DANGEROUS TO WARRANT THAT KIND OF COMPENSATION.
BUT IF MASATO'S GOTTEN AHOLD OF IT, AND WITH THE SIZE OF HIS GRUDGE AGAINST YOU...
I DON'T HAVE TO LOOK FOR HIM, BECAUSE HE'LL COME TO ME AND THEN THE 500,000 YEN WILL BE MINE!
I'M SO LUCKY!
YEAH, YOU COULD LOOK AT IT THAT WAY, I GUESS...
RINNE-SAMA, I'M BACK FROM PURCHASING OUR SECRET WEAPON!
WAAAARP
SECRET WEAPON?!

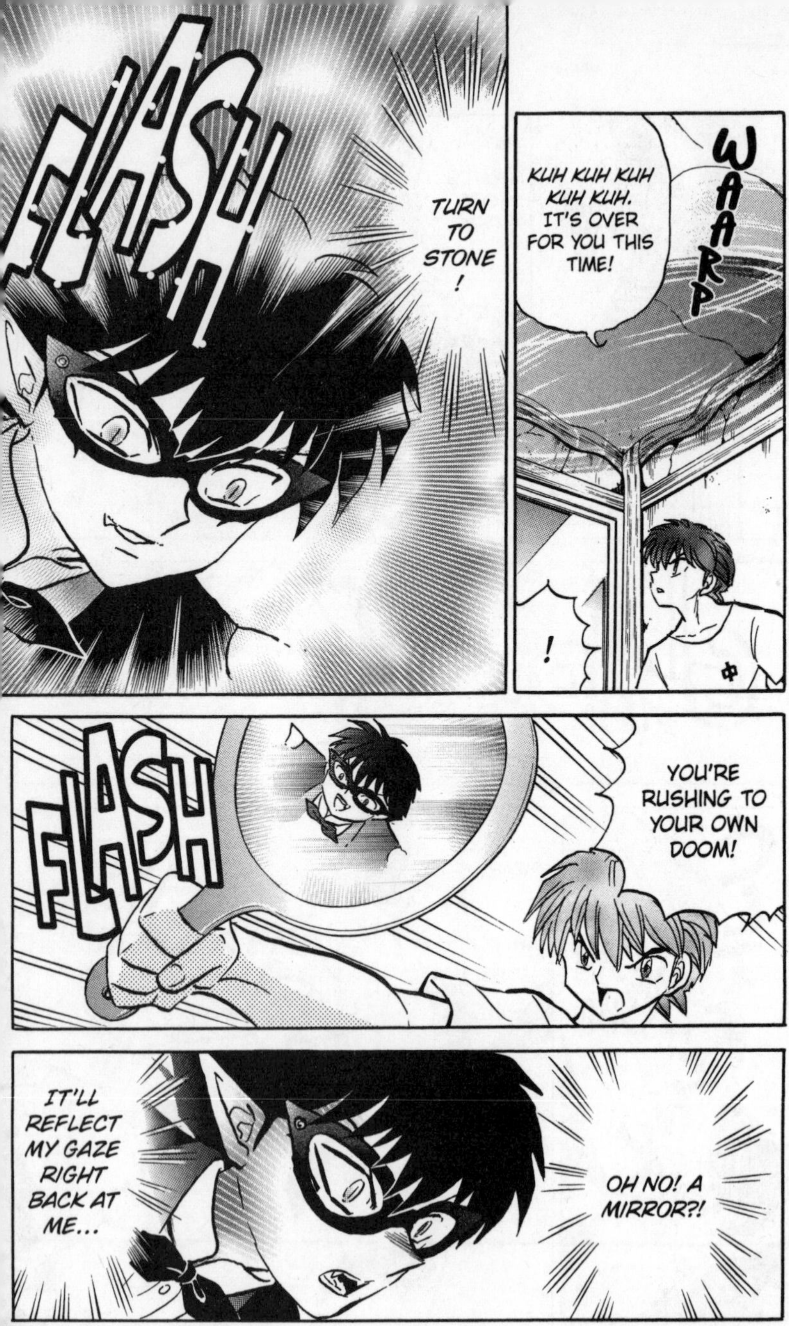
WAARP
KUH KUH KUH KUH KUH. IT'S OVER FOR YOU THIS TIME!
!
FLASH
TURN TO STONE!
YOU'RE RUSHING TO YOUR OWN DOOM!
FLASH
OH NO! A MIRROR?!
IT'LL REFLECT MY GAZE RIGHT BACK AT ME...

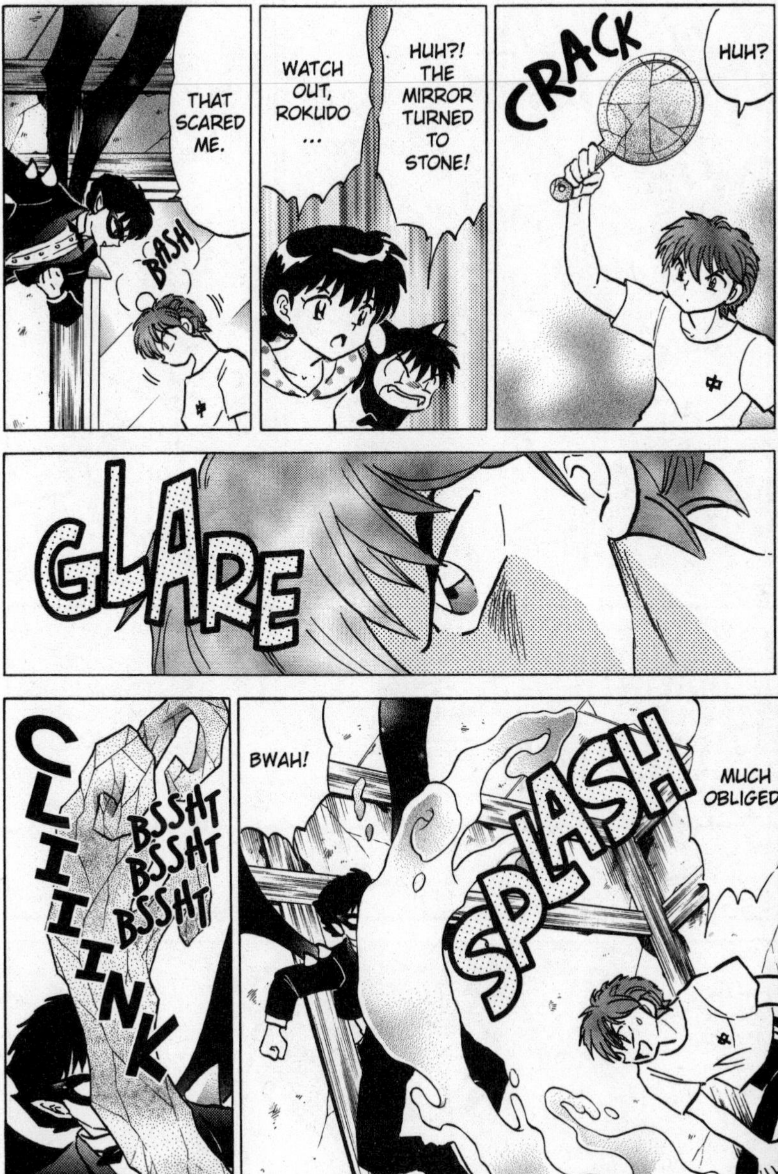
CRACK
HUH?
HUH?! THE MIRROR TURNED TO STONE!
WATCH OUT, ROKUDO ...
THAT SCARED ME.
BASH
GLARE
SPLASH
MUCH OBLIGED!
BWAH!
CLIIIINK
BSSHT BSSHT BSSHT

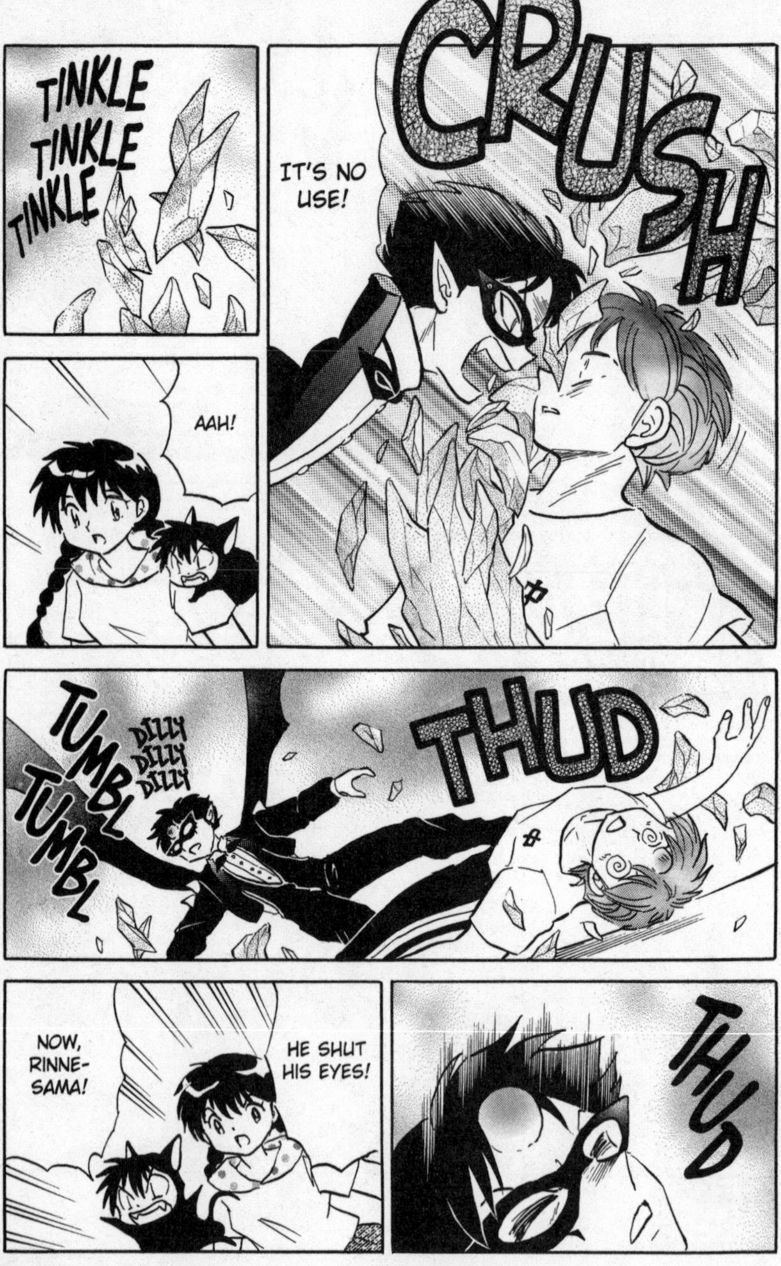
CRUSH
IT'S NO USE!
TINKLE TINKLE TINKLE
AAH!
THUD
DILLY DILLY DILLY
TUMBL TUMBL
THUD
HE SHUT HIS EYES!
NOW, RINNE-SAMA!

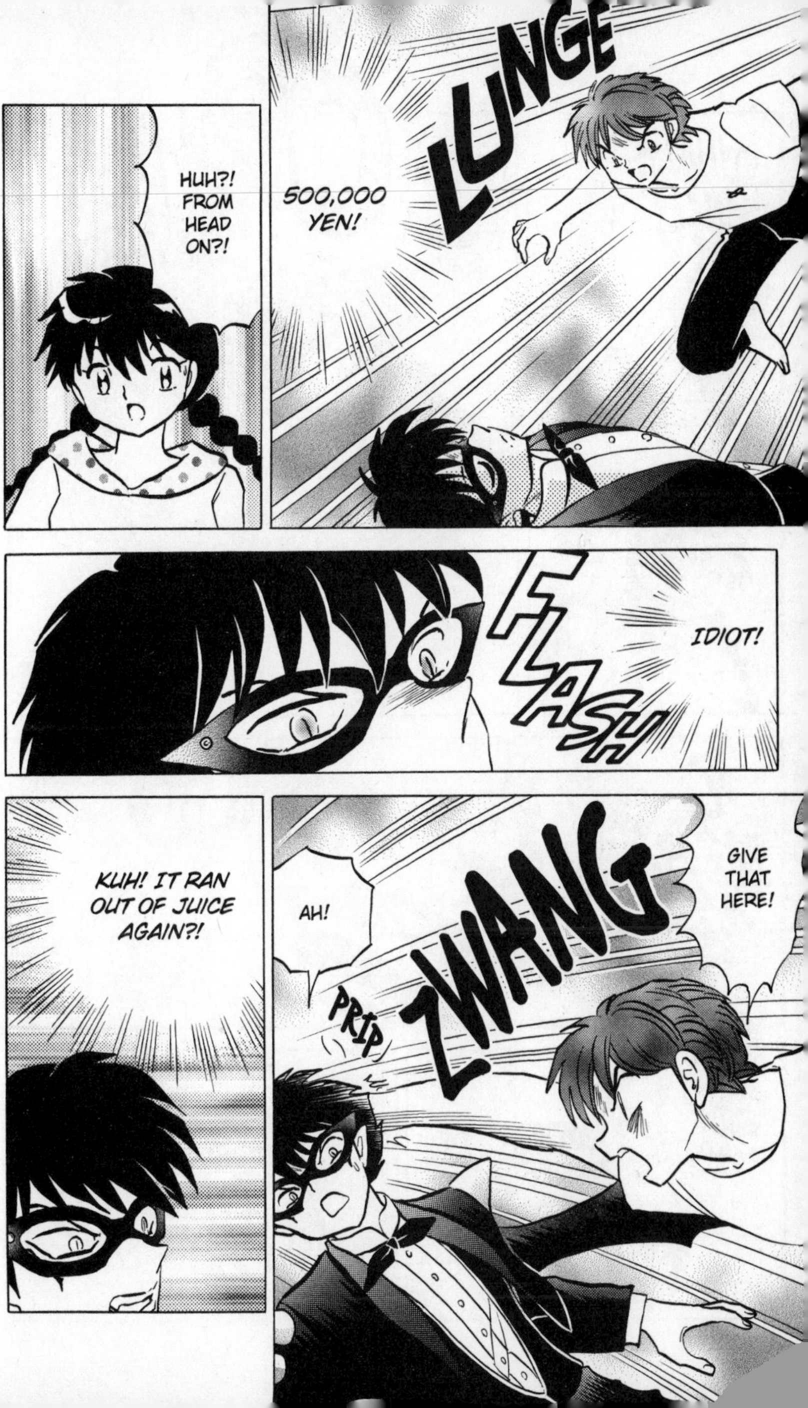
LUNGE
500,000 YEN!
HUH?! FROM HEAD ON?!
IDIOT!
FLASH
GIVE THAT HERE!
ZWANG
AH!
PRIP
KUH! IT RAN OUT OF JUICE AGAIN?!

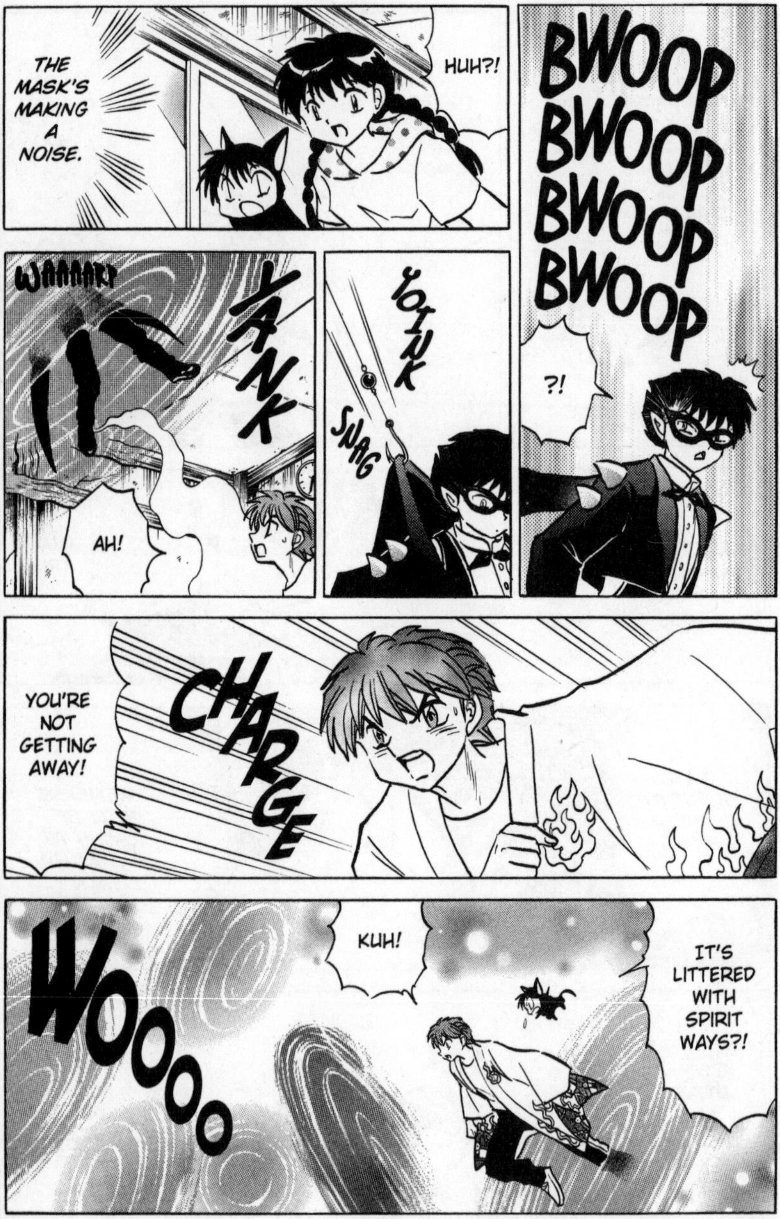
BWOOP BWOOP BWOOP BWOOP
?!
HUH?!
THE MASK'S MAKING A NOISE.
YOINK
SNAG
YANK
WAAAARP
AH!
CHARGE
YOU'RE NOT GETTING AWAY!
IT'S LITTERED WITH SPIRIT WAYS?!
KUH!
WOOOOO

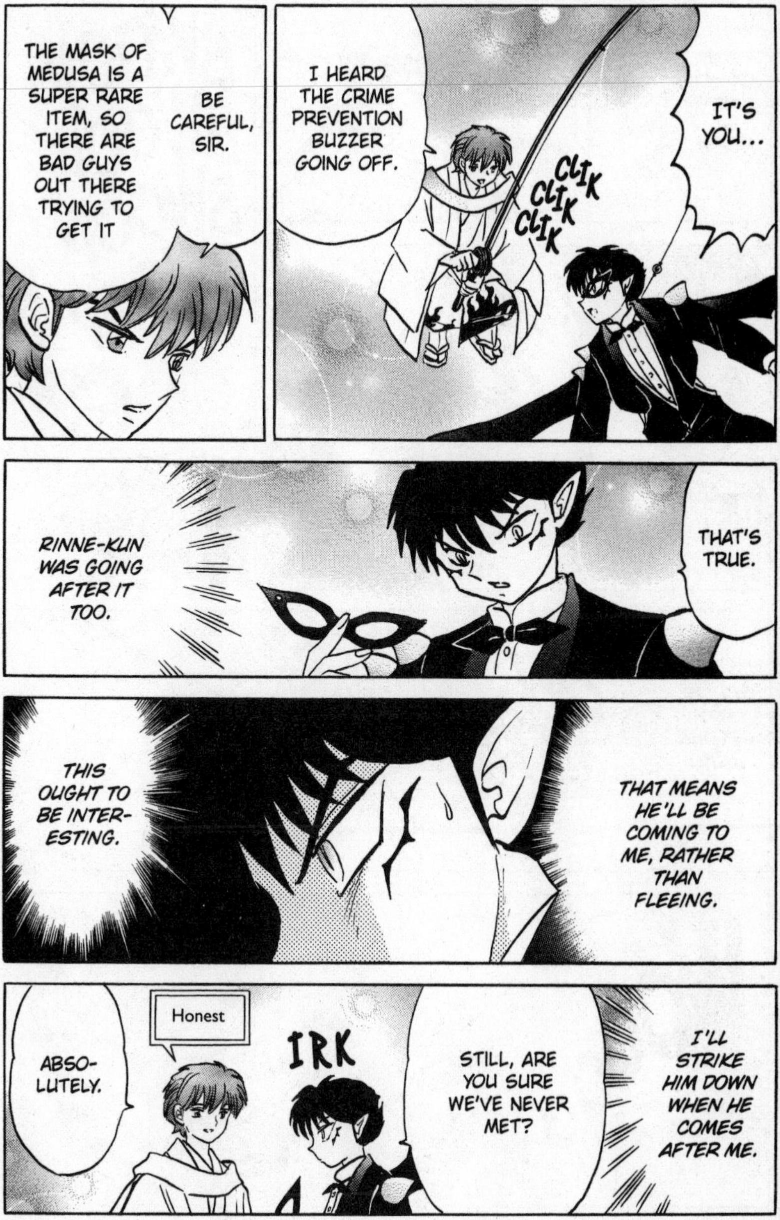
IT'S YOU...
I HEARD THE CRIME PREVENTION BUZZER GOING OFF.
CLIK CLIK CLIK
BE CAREFUL, SIR.
THE MASK OF MEDUSA IS A SUPER RARE ITEM, SO THERE ARE BAD GUYS OUT THERE TRYING TO GET IT
THAT'S TRUE.
RINNE-KUN WAS GOING AFTER IT TOO.
THAT MEANS HE'LL BE COMING TO ME, RATHER THAN FLEEING.
THIS OUGHT TO BE INTER-ESTING.
I'LL STRIKE HIM DOWN WHEN HE COMES AFTER ME.
STILL, ARE YOU SURE WE'VE NEVER MET?
IRK
Honest
ABSO-LUTELY.

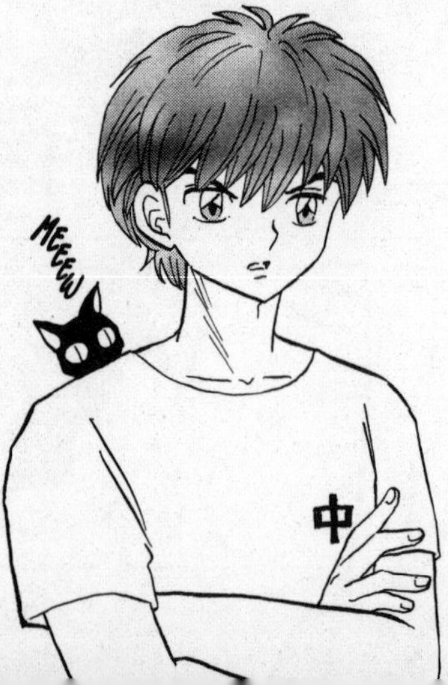
MEEEW
中

CHAPTER 298: TURN TO STONE!

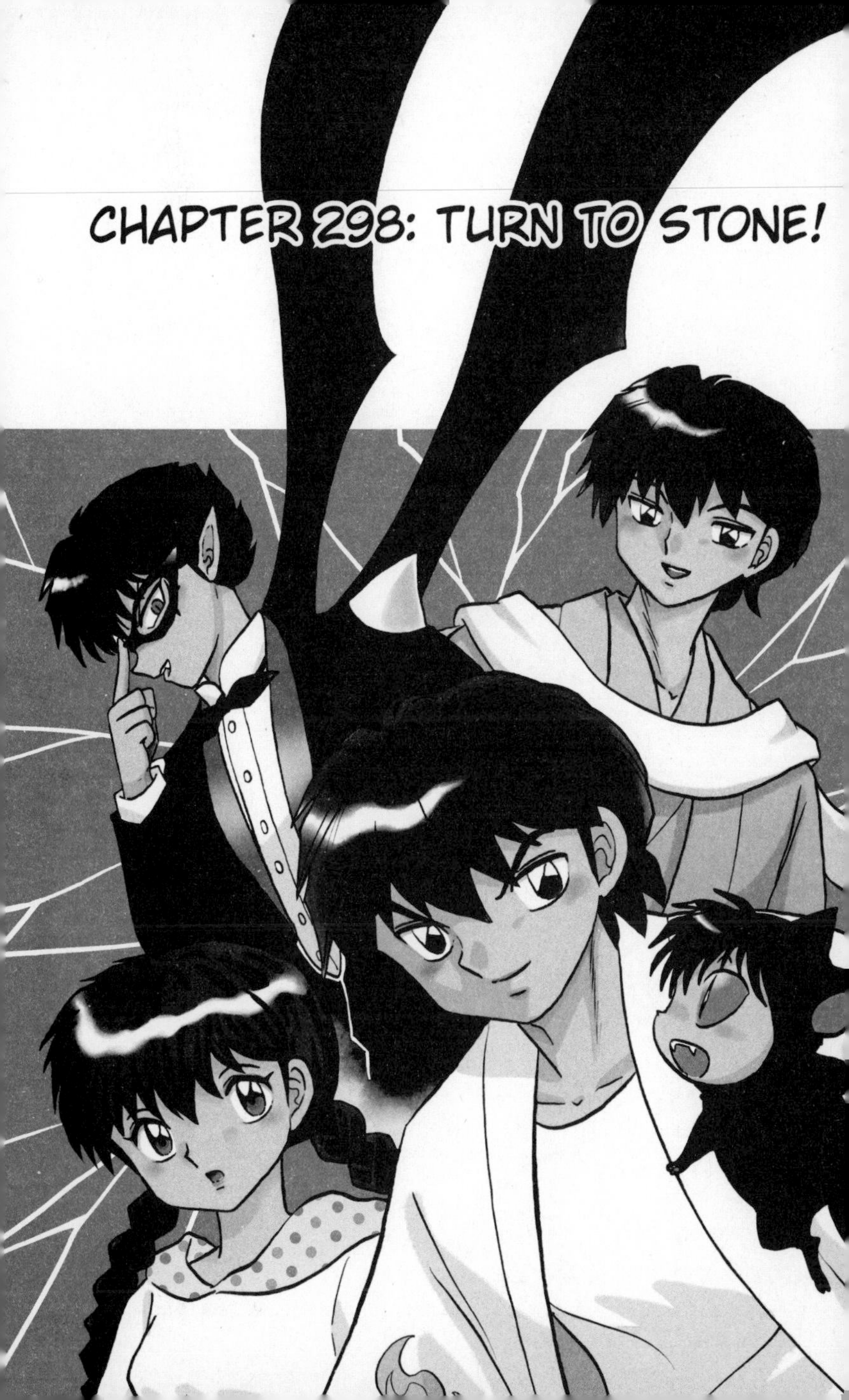

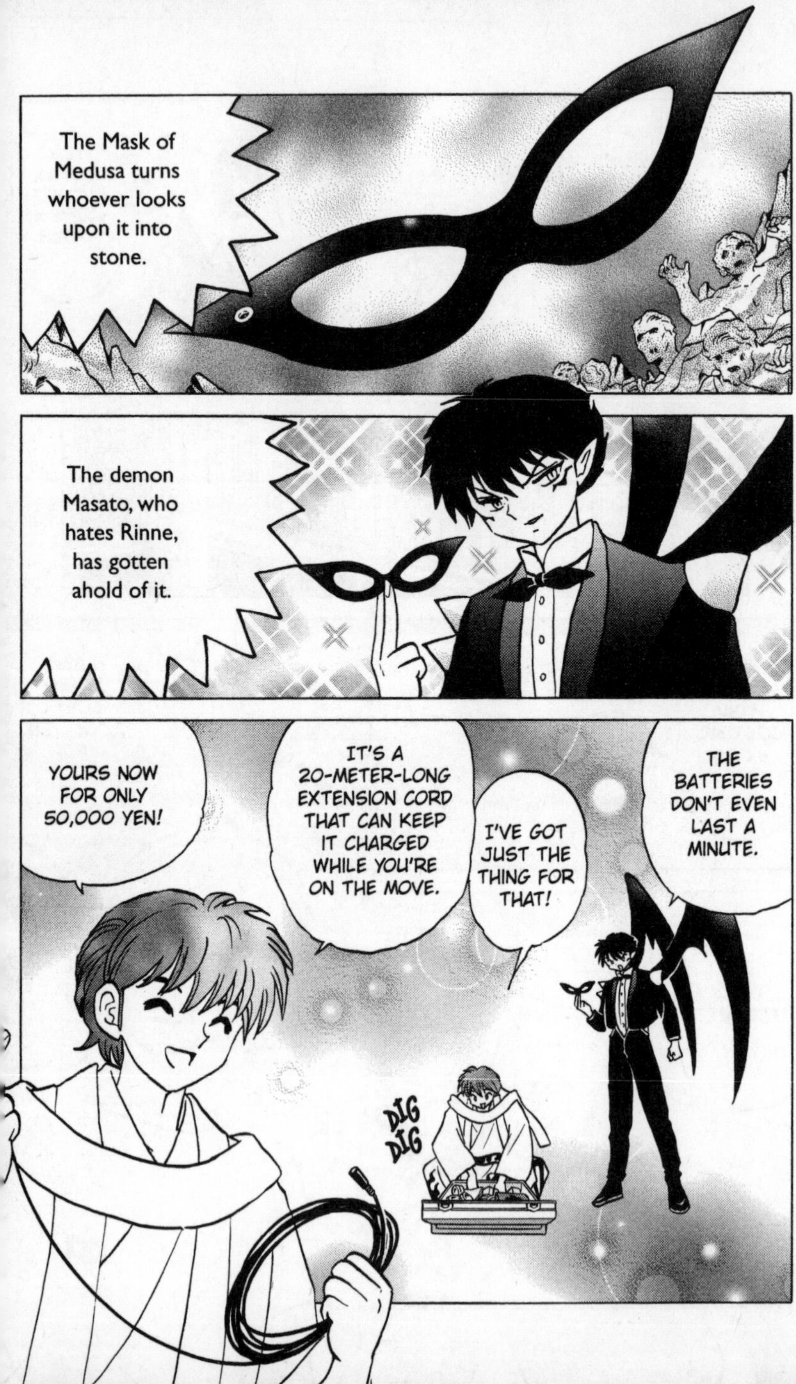
The Mask of Medusa turns whoever looks upon it into stone.
The demon Masato, who hates Rinne, has gotten ahold of it.
THE BATTERIES DON'T EVEN LAST A MINUTE.
I'VE GOT JUST THE THING FOR THAT!
IT'S A 20-METER-LONG EXTENSION CORD THAT CAN KEEP IT CHARGED WHILE YOU'RE ON THE MOVE.
YOURS NOW FOR ONLY 50,000 YEN!
DIG DIG

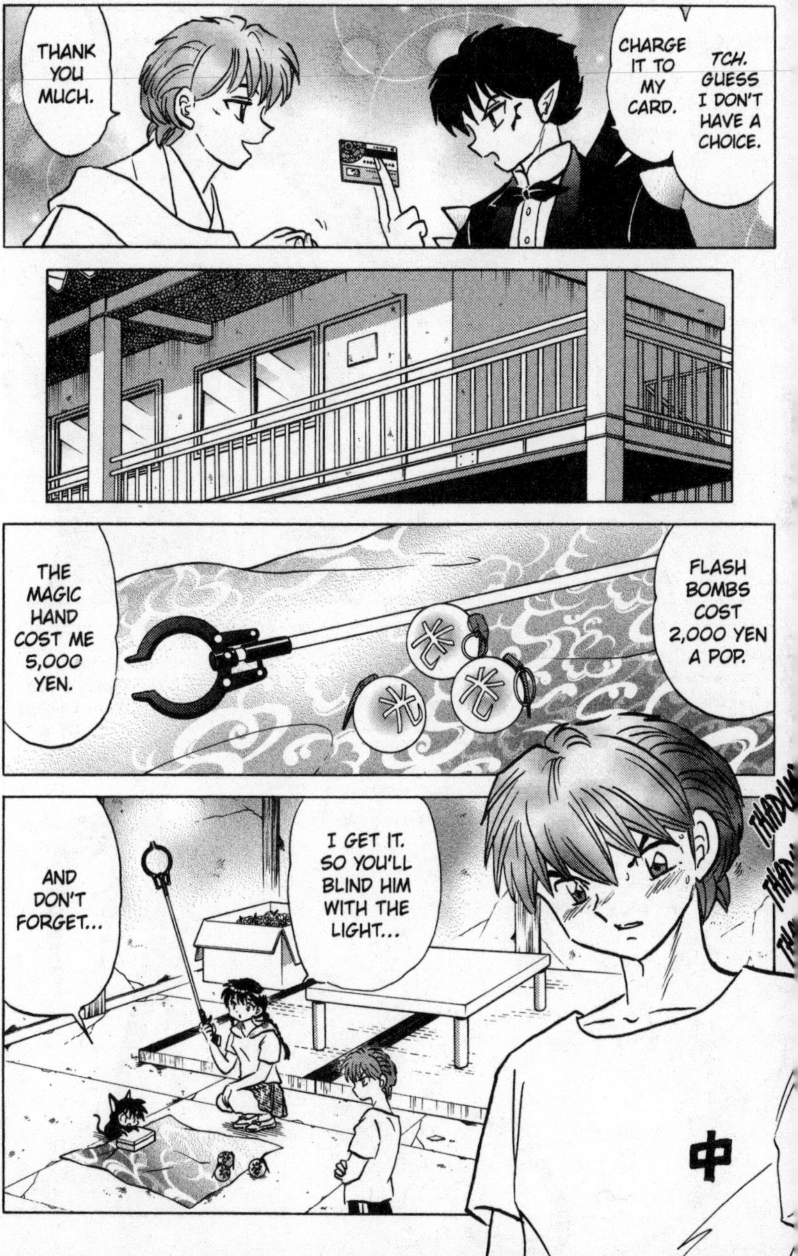
TCH. GUESS I DON'T HAVE A CHOICE.
CHARGE IT TO MY CARD.
THANK YOU MUCH.
FLASH BOMBS COST 2,000 YEN A POP.
THE MAGIC HAND COST ME 5,000 YEN.
I GET IT. SO YOU'LL BLIND HIM WITH THE LIGHT...
AND DON'T FORGET...

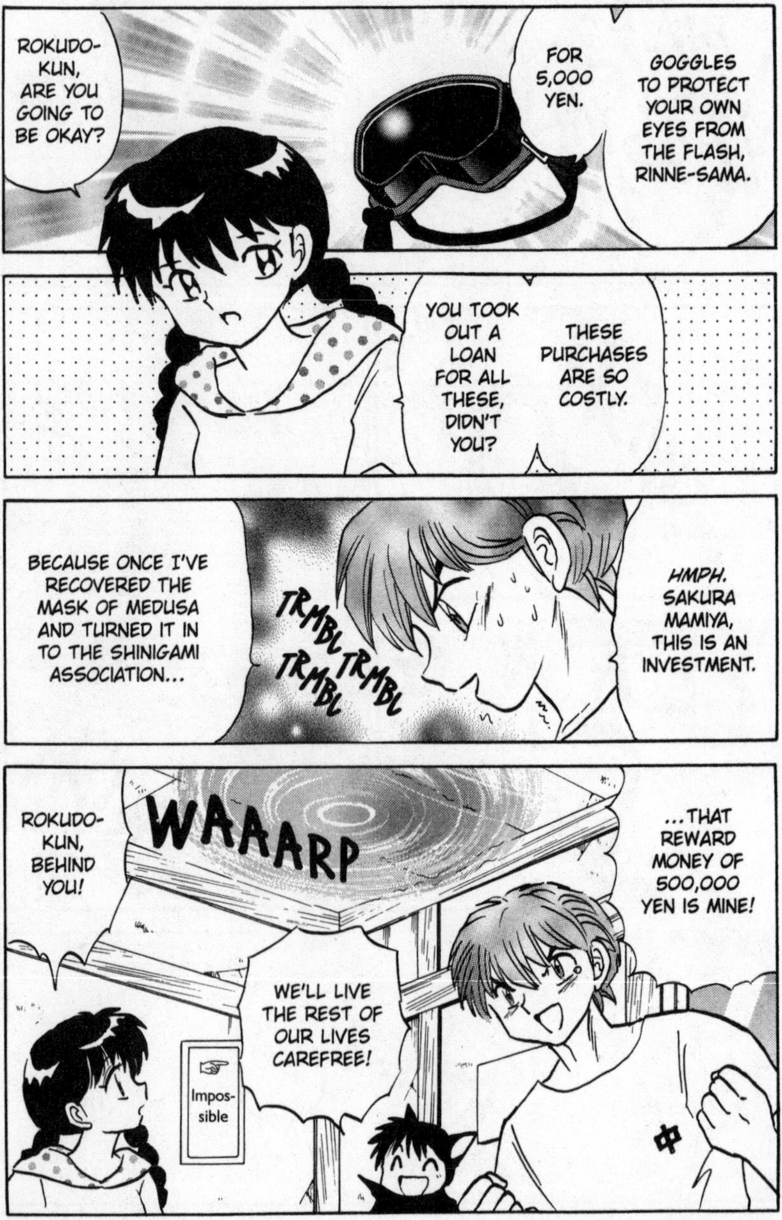
GOGGLES TO PROTECT YOUR OWN EYES FROM THE FLASH, RINNE-SAMA.
FOR 5,000 YEN.
ROKUDO-KUN, ARE YOU GOING TO BE OKAY?
THESE PURCHASES ARE SO COSTLY.
YOU TOOK OUT A LOAN FOR ALL THESE, DIDN'T YOU?
HMPH. SAKURA MAMIYA, THIS IS AN INVESTMENT.
TRMBL TRMBL TRMBL
BECAUSE ONCE I'VE RECOVERED THE MASK OF MEDUSA AND TURNED IT IN TO THE SHINIGAMI ASSOCIATION...
...THAT REWARD MONEY OF 500,000 YEN IS MINE!
WAAARP
ROKUDO-KUN, BEHIND YOU!
WE'LL LIVE THE REST OF OUR LIVES CAREFREE!
Impos-sible

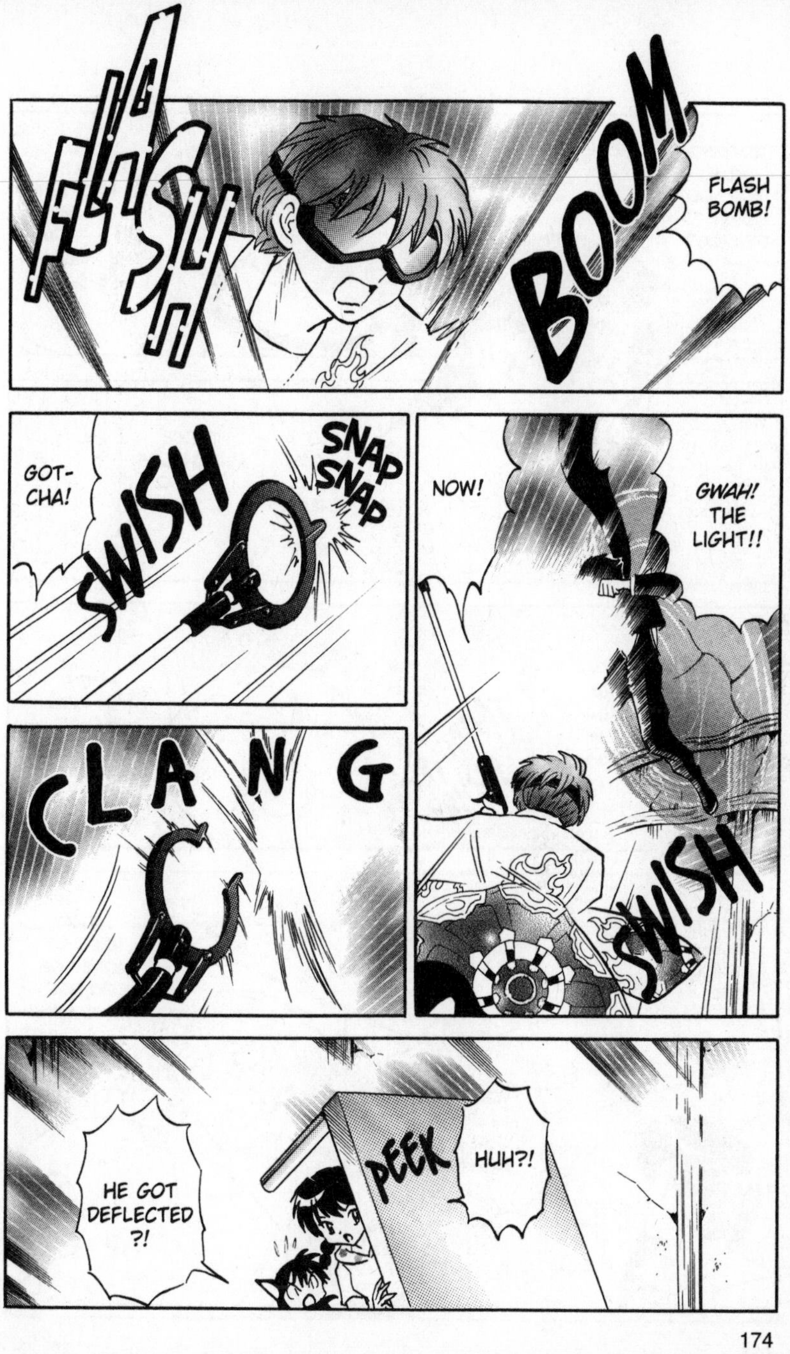
FLASH BOMB!
BOOM
FLASH
GWAH! THE LIGHT!!
NOW!
SWISH
SNAP SNAP SNAP
SWISH
GOT-CHA!
CLANG
HUH?!
PEEK
HE GOT DEFLECTED ?!

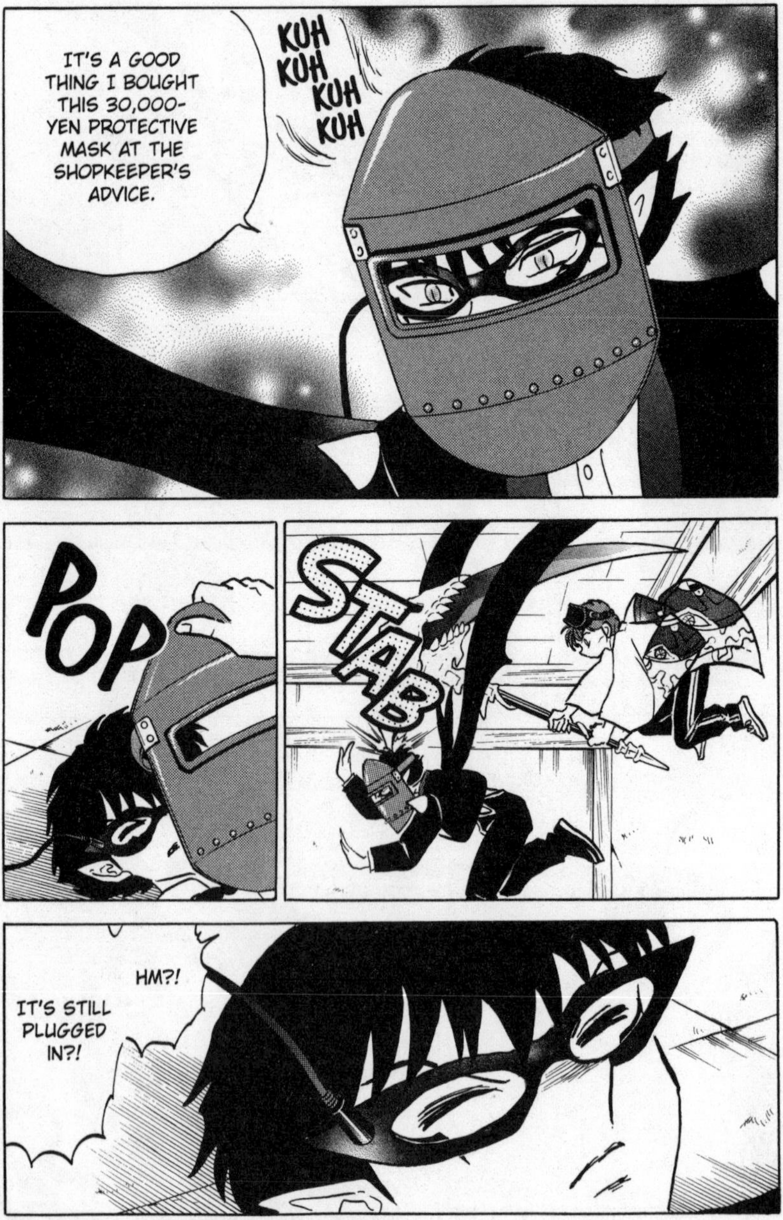
KUH KUH KUH KUH
IT'S A GOOD THING I BOUGHT THIS 30,000-YEN PROTECTIVE MASK AT THE SHOPKEEPER'S ADVICE.
STAB
POP
HM?!
IT'S STILL PLUGGED IN?!

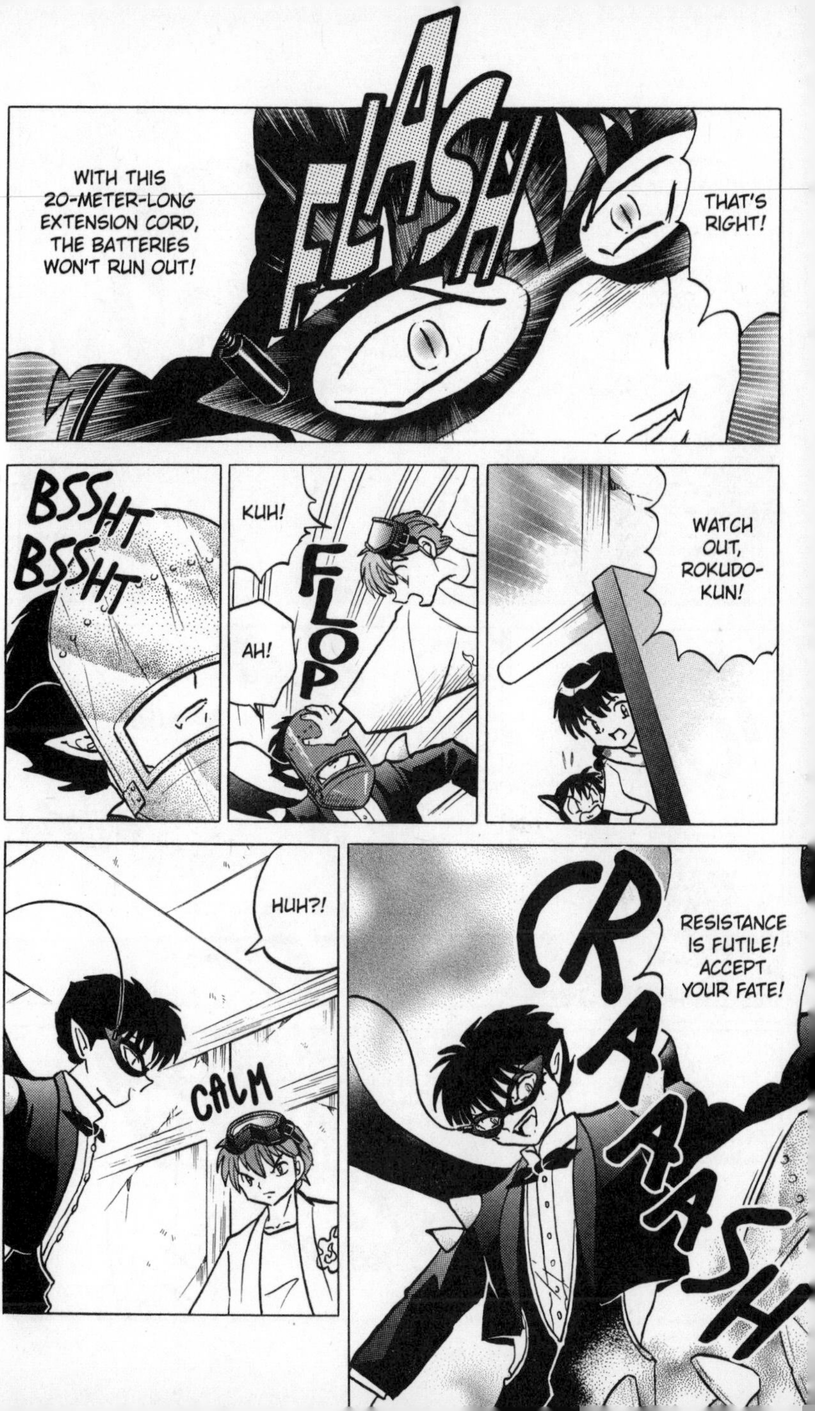
THAT'S RIGHT!
FLASH
WITH THIS 20-METER-LONG EXTENSION CORD, THE BATTERIES WON'T RUN OUT!
WATCH OUT, ROKUDO-KUN!
KUH!
FLOP
AH!
BSSHT BSSHT
CRAAASH
RESISTANCE IS FUTILE! ACCEPT YOUR FATE!
HUH?!
CALM

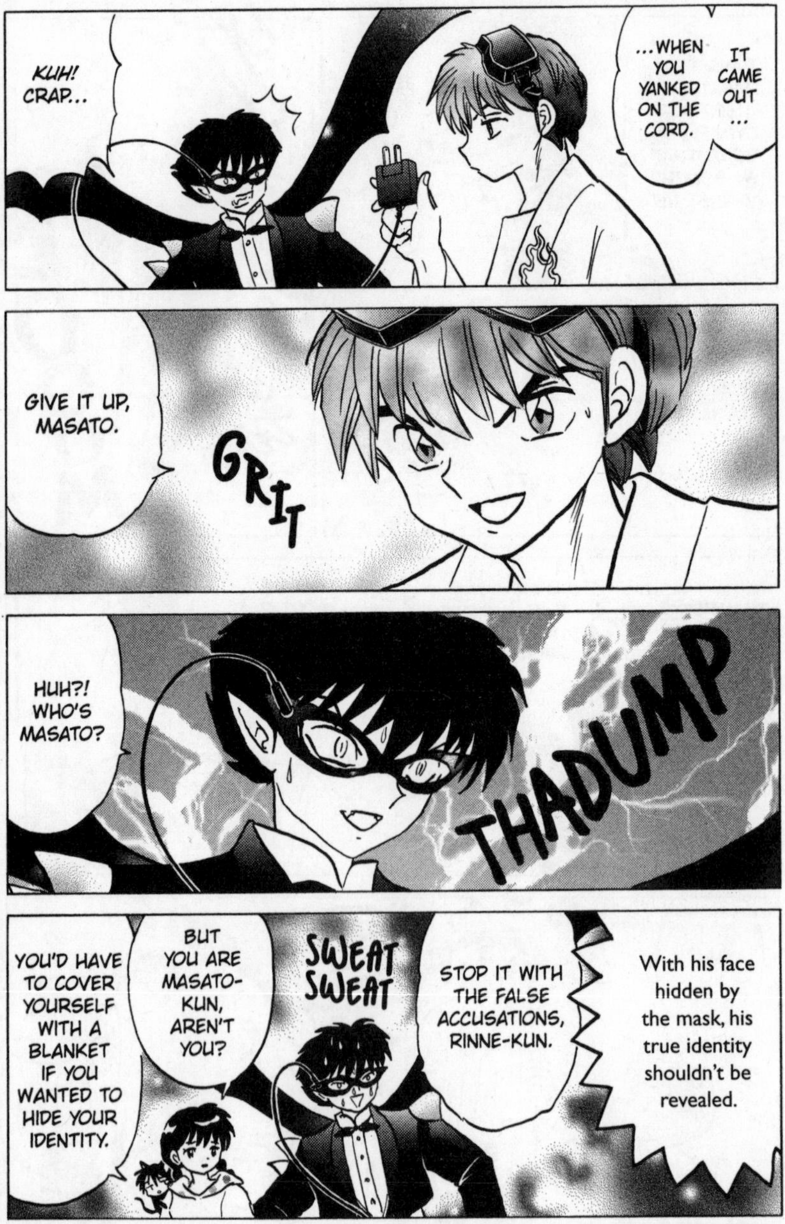
IT CAME OUT...
...WHEN YOU YANKED ON THE CORD.
KUH! CRAP...
GRIT
GIVE IT UP, MASATO.
THADUMP
HUH?! WHO'S MASATO?
With his face hidden by the mask, his true identity shouldn't be revealed.
STOP IT WITH THE FALSE ACCUSATIONS, RINNE-KUN.
SWEAT SWEAT
BUT YOU ARE MASATO-KUN, AREN'T YOU?
YOU'D HAVE TO COVER YOURSELF WITH A BLANKET IF YOU WANTED TO HIDE YOUR IDENTITY.

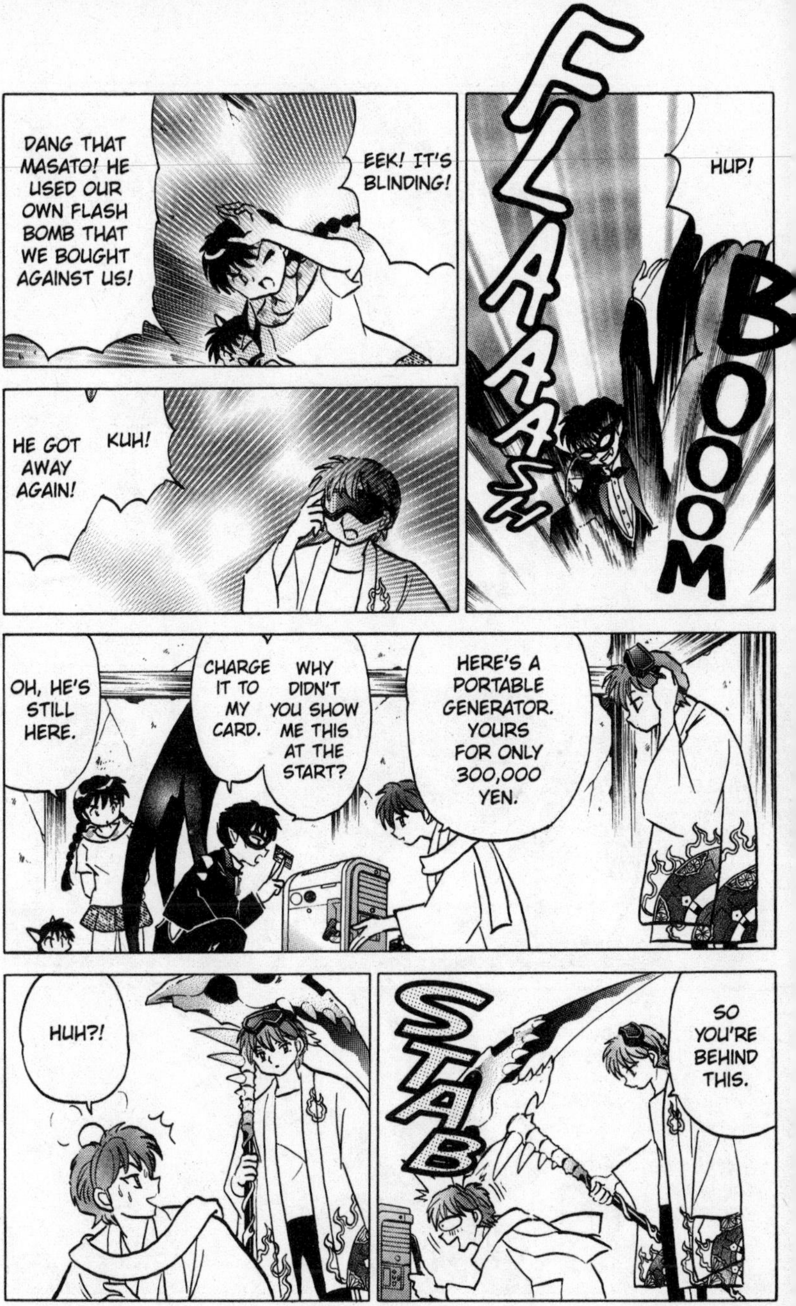
HUP!
BOOOM
FLAAASH
EEK! IT'S BLINDING!
DANG THAT MASATO! HE USED OUR OWN FLASH BOMB THAT WE BOUGHT AGAINST US!
KUH!
HE GOT AWAY AGAIN!
HERE'S A PORTABLE GENERATOR. YOURS FOR ONLY 300,000 YEN.
WHY DIDN'T YOU SHOW ME THIS AT THE START?
CHARGE IT TO MY CARD.
OH, HE'S STILL HERE.
SO YOU'RE BEHIND THIS.
STAB
HUH?!

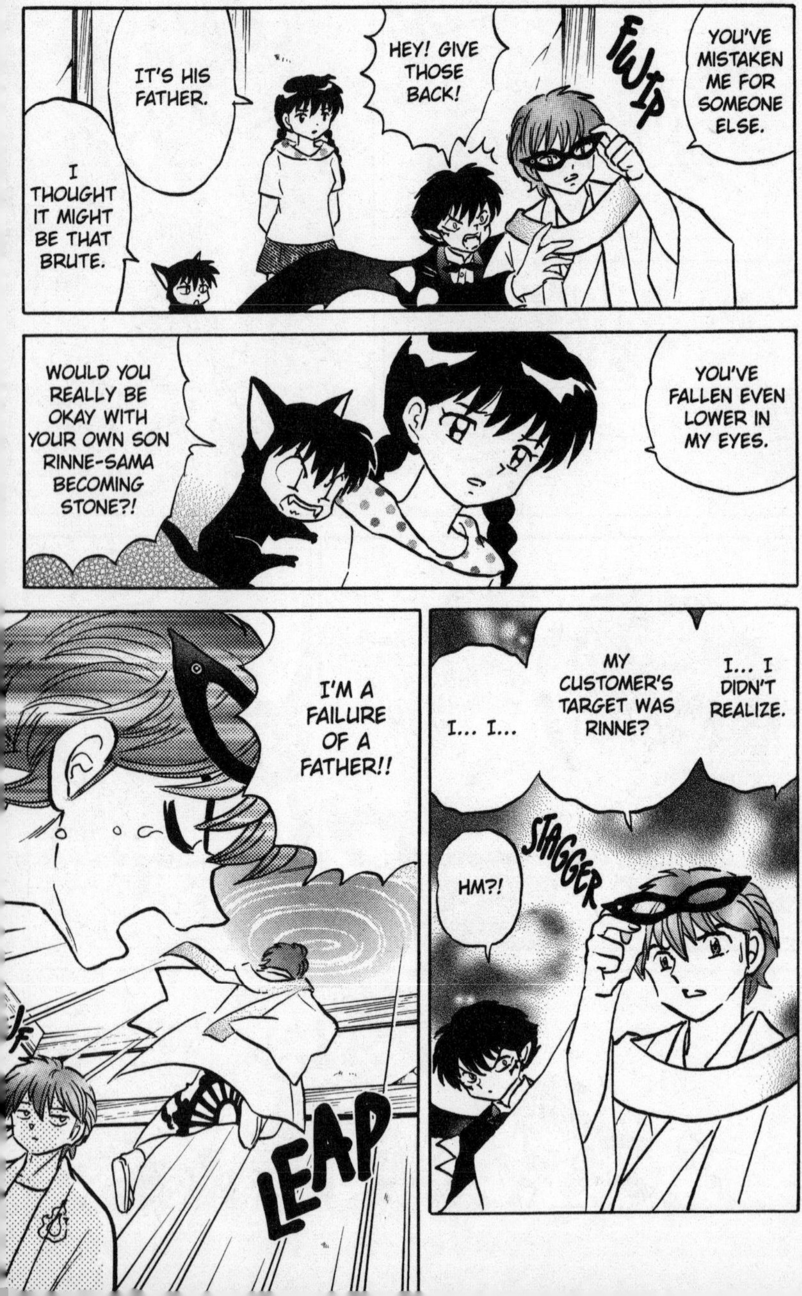
YOU'VE MISTAKEN ME FOR SOMEONE ELSE.
FWIP
HEY! GIVE THOSE BACK!
IT'S HIS FATHER.
I THOUGHT IT MIGHT BE THAT BRUTE.
YOU'VE FALLEN EVEN LOWER IN MY EYES.
WOULD YOU REALLY BE OKAY WITH YOUR OWN SON RINNE-SAMA BECOMING STONE?!
I... I DIDN'T REALIZE.
MY CUSTOMER'S TARGET WAS RINNE?
I... I...
STAGGER
HM?!
I'M A FAILURE OF A FATHER!!
LEAP

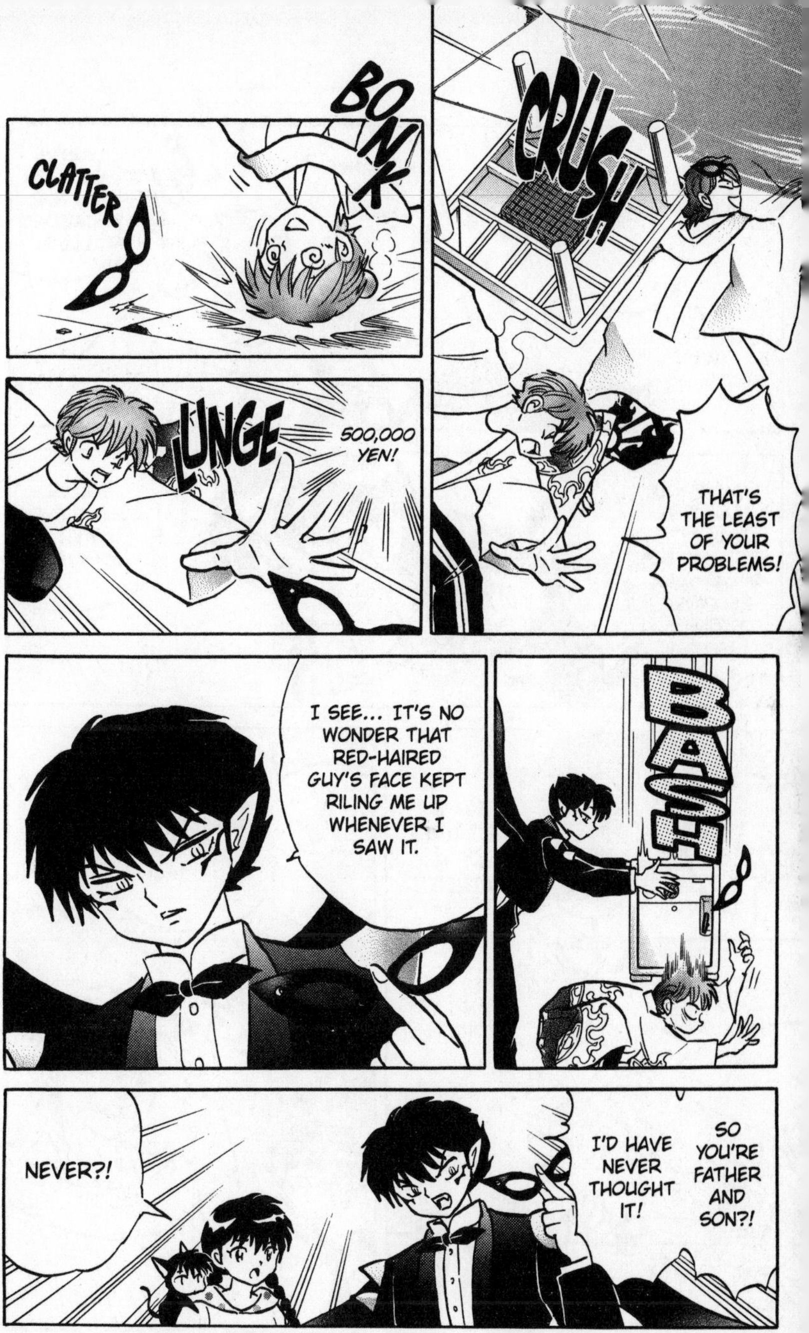
CRUSH
THAT'S THE LEAST OF YOUR PROBLEMS!
BONK
CLATTER
LUNGE
500,000 YEN!
BASH
I SEE... IT'S NO WONDER THAT RED-HAIRED GUY'S FACE KEPT RILING ME UP WHENEVER I SAW IT.
SO YOU'RE FATHER AND SON?!
I'D HAVE NEVER THOUGHT IT!
NEVER?!

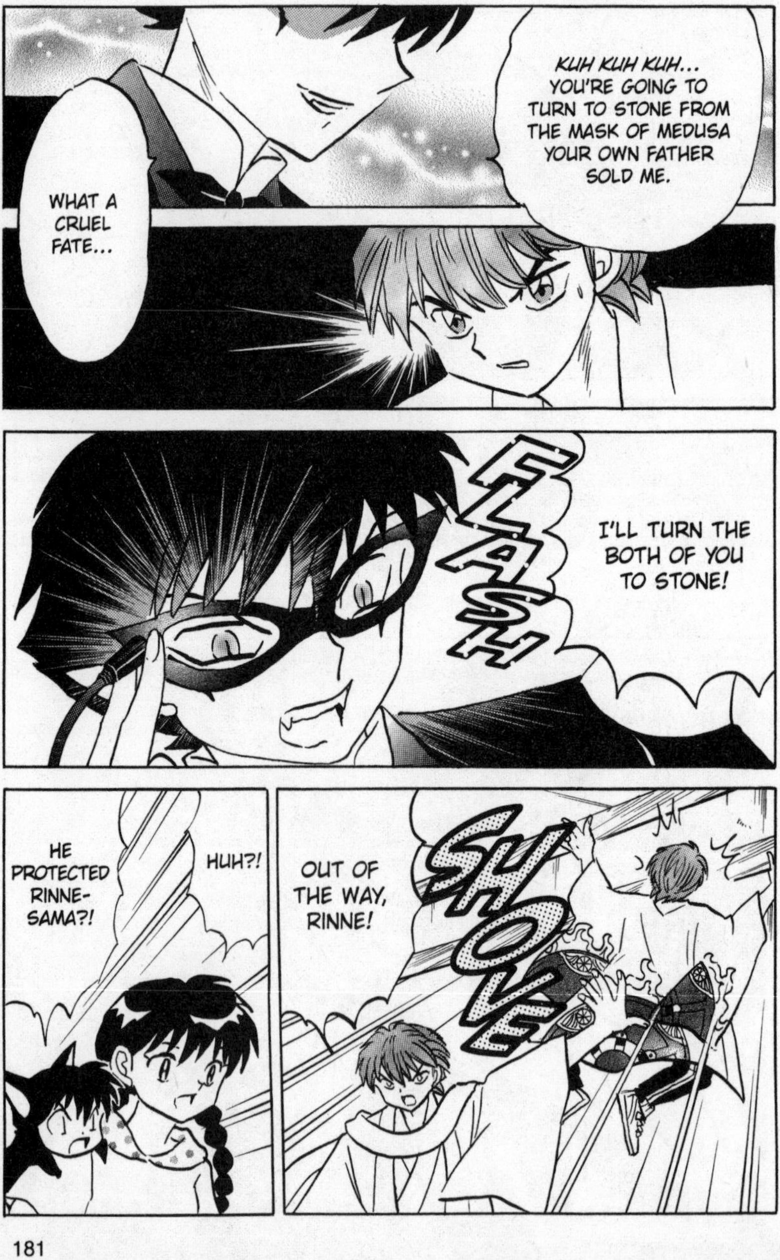
KUH KUH KUH... YOU'RE GOING TO TURN TO STONE FROM THE MASK OF MEDUSA YOUR OWN FATHER SOLD ME.
WHAT A CRUEL FATE...
I'LL TURN THE BOTH OF YOU TO STONE!
FLASH
SHOVE
OUT OF THE WAY, RINNE!
HUH?!
HE PROTECTED RINNE-SAMA?!

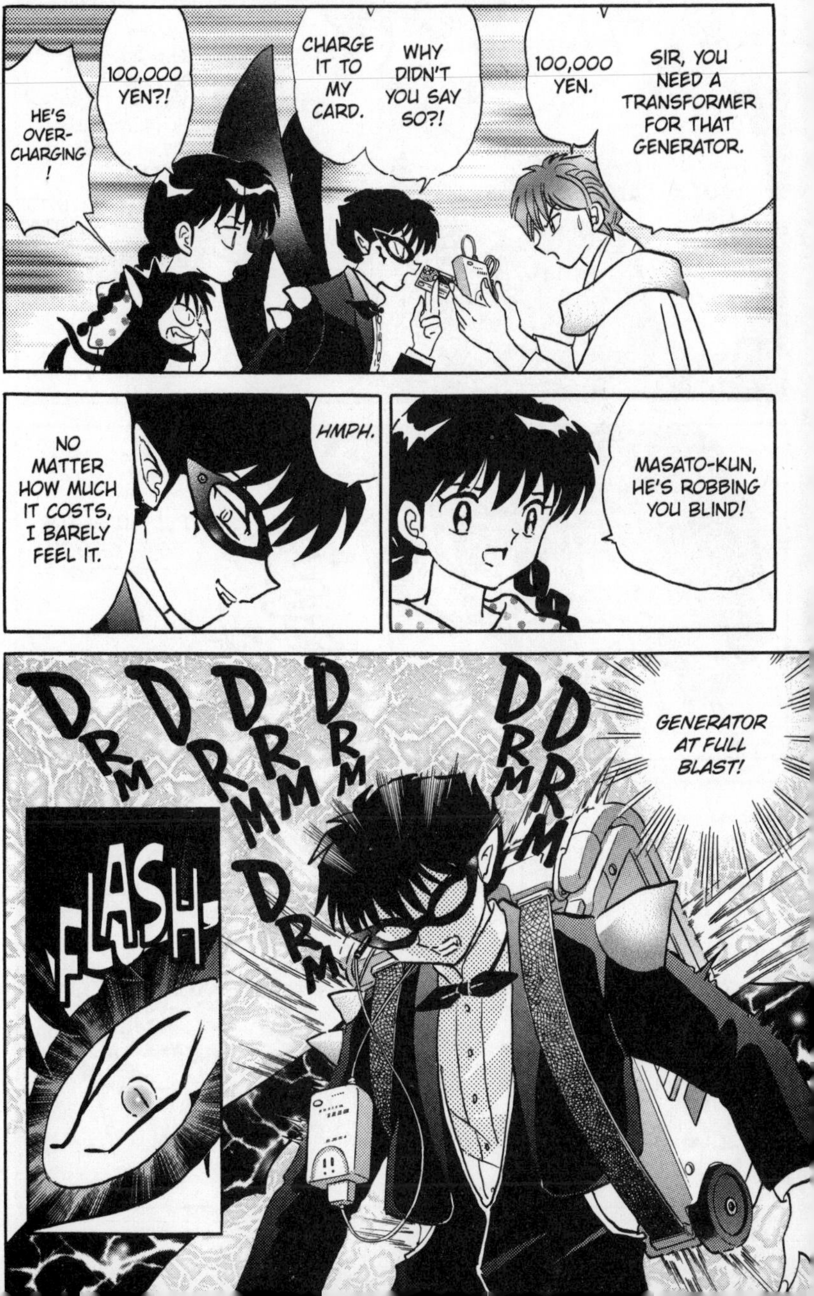
SIR, YOU NEED A TRANSFORMER FOR THAT GENERATOR.
100,000 YEN.
WHY DIDN'T YOU SAY SO?!
CHARGE IT TO MY CARD.
100,000 YEN?!
HE'S OVER-CHARGING!
MASATO-KUN, HE'S ROBBING YOU BLIND!
HMPH.
NO MATTER HOW MUCH IT COSTS, I BARELY FEEL IT.
GENERATOR AT FULL BLAST!
DRM
DRRMM
DRRMM
DRM
DRM
DDRRM
FLASH

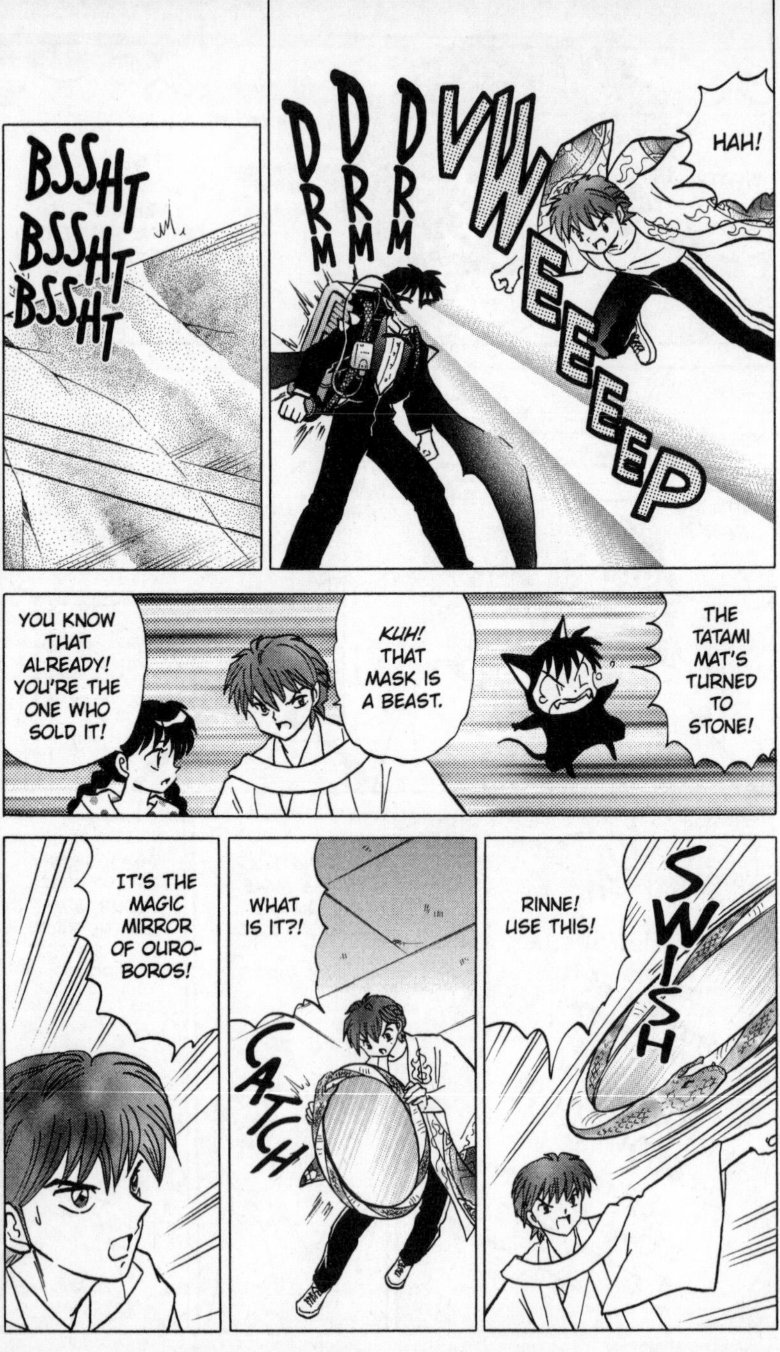
HAH!
VWWEEEEEP
DRM
DRM
DRM
BSSHT
BSSHT
BSSHT
THE TATAMI MAT'S TURNED TO STONE!
KUH! THAT MASK IS A BEAST.
YOU KNOW THAT ALREADY! YOU'RE THE ONE WHO SOLD IT!
SWISH
RINNE! USE THIS!
WHAT IS IT?!
CATCH
IT'S THE MAGIC MIRROR OF OURO-BOROS!

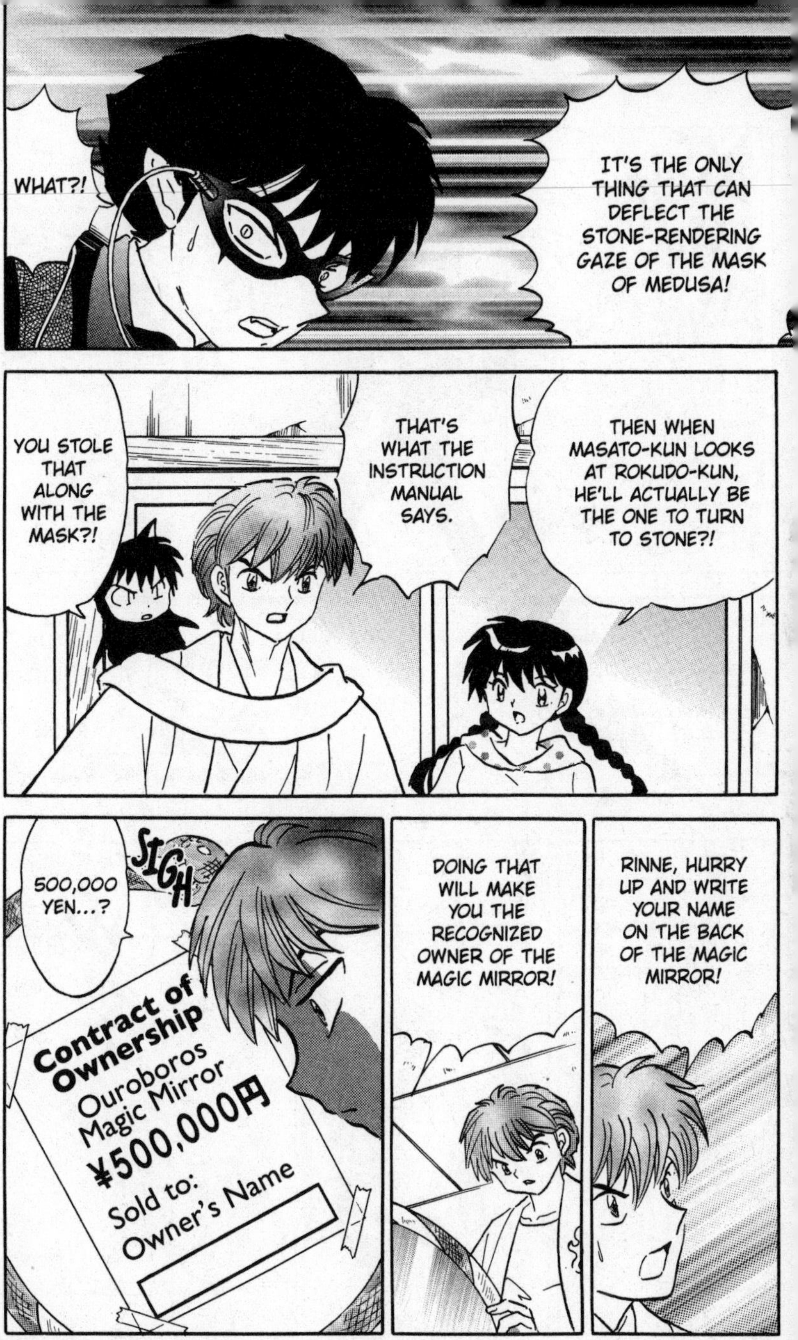
IT'S THE ONLY THING THAT CAN DEFLECT THE STONE-RENDERING GAZE OF THE MASK OF MEDUSA!
WHAT?!
THEN WHEN MASATO-KUN LOOKS AT ROKUDO-KUN, HE'LL ACTUALLY BE THE ONE TO TURN TO STONE?!
THAT'S WHAT THE INSTRUCTION MANUAL SAYS.
YOU STOLE THAT ALONG WITH THE MASK?!
RINNE, HURRY UP AND WRITE YOUR NAME ON THE BACK OF THE MAGIC MIRROR!
DOING THAT WILL MAKE YOU THE RECOGNIZED OWNER OF THE MAGIC MIRROR!
SIGH
500,000 YEN...?
Contract of Ownership
Ouroboros Magic Mirror
¥500,000円
Sold to:
Owner's Name

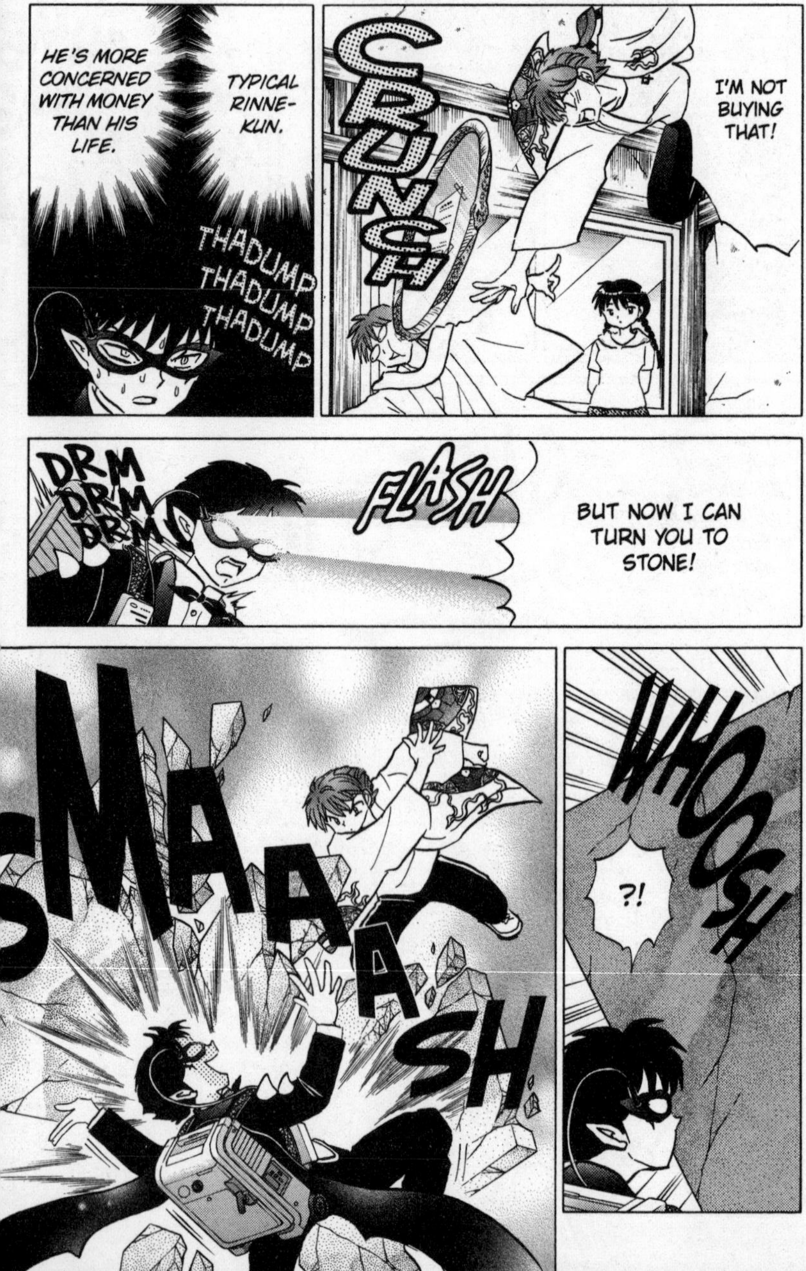
CRUNCH
I'M NOT BUYING THAT!
TYPICAL RINNE-KUN.
HE'S MORE CONCERNED WITH MONEY THAN HIS LIFE.
THADUMP THADUMP THADUMP
BUT NOW I CAN TURN YOU TO STONE!
FLASH
DRM DRM DRM
WHOOSH
?!
SMAAAASH

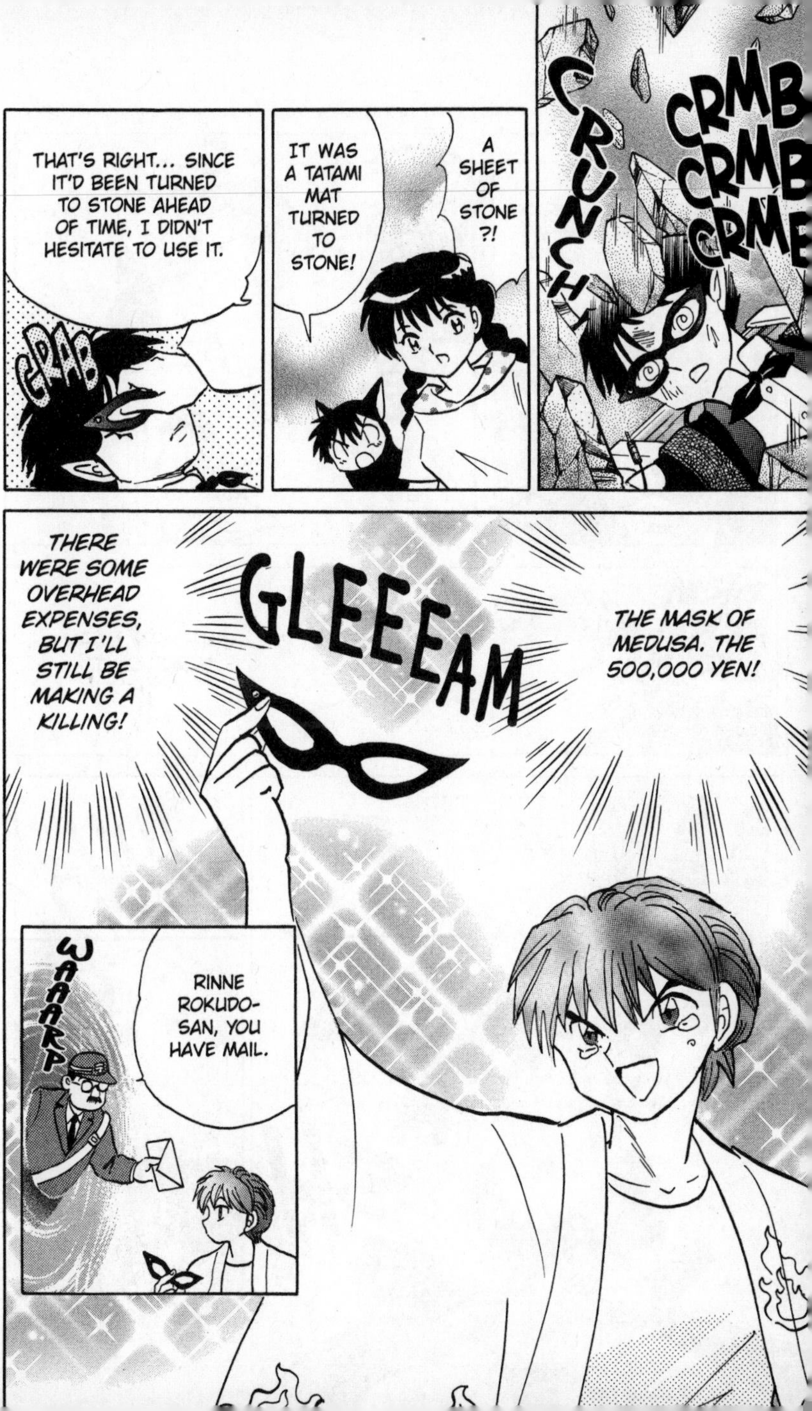
CRUNCH
CRMB CRMB CRM
A SHEET OF STONE?!
IT WAS A TATAMI MAT TURNED TO STONE!
THAT'S RIGHT... SINCE IT'D BEEN TURNED TO STONE AHEAD OF TIME, I DIDN'T HESITATE TO USE IT.
GRAB
THE MASK OF MEDUSA. THE 500,000 YEN!
GLEEEAM
THERE WERE SOME OVERHEAD EXPENSES, BUT I'LL STILL BE MAKING A KILLING!
WAAAARP
RINNE ROKUDO-SAN, YOU HAVE MAIL.

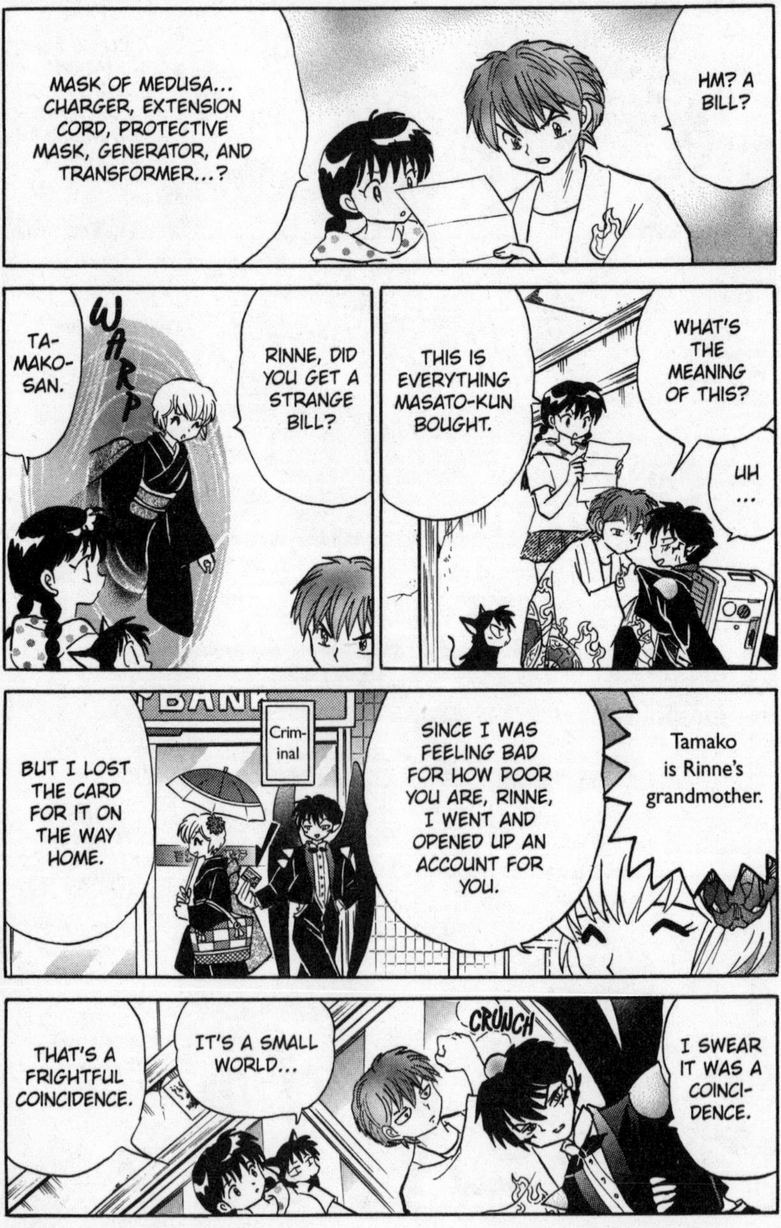
HM? A BILL?
MASK OF MEDUSA... CHARGER, EXTENSION CORD, PROTECTIVE MASK, GENERATOR, AND TRANSFORMER...?
WHAT'S THE MEANING OF THIS?
UH ...
THIS IS EVERYTHING MASATO-KUN BOUGHT.
RINNE, DID YOU GET A STRANGE BILL?
WARP
TA-MAKO-SAN.
Tamako is Rinne's grandmother.
SINCE I WAS FEELING BAD FOR HOW POOR YOU ARE, RINNE, I WENT AND OPENED UP AN ACCOUNT FOR YOU.
Crim-inal
BUT I LOST THE CARD FOR IT ON THE WAY HOME.
I SWEAR IT WAS A COINCI-DENCE.
CRUNCH
IT'S A SMALL WORLD...
THAT'S A FRIGHTFUL COINCIDENCE.

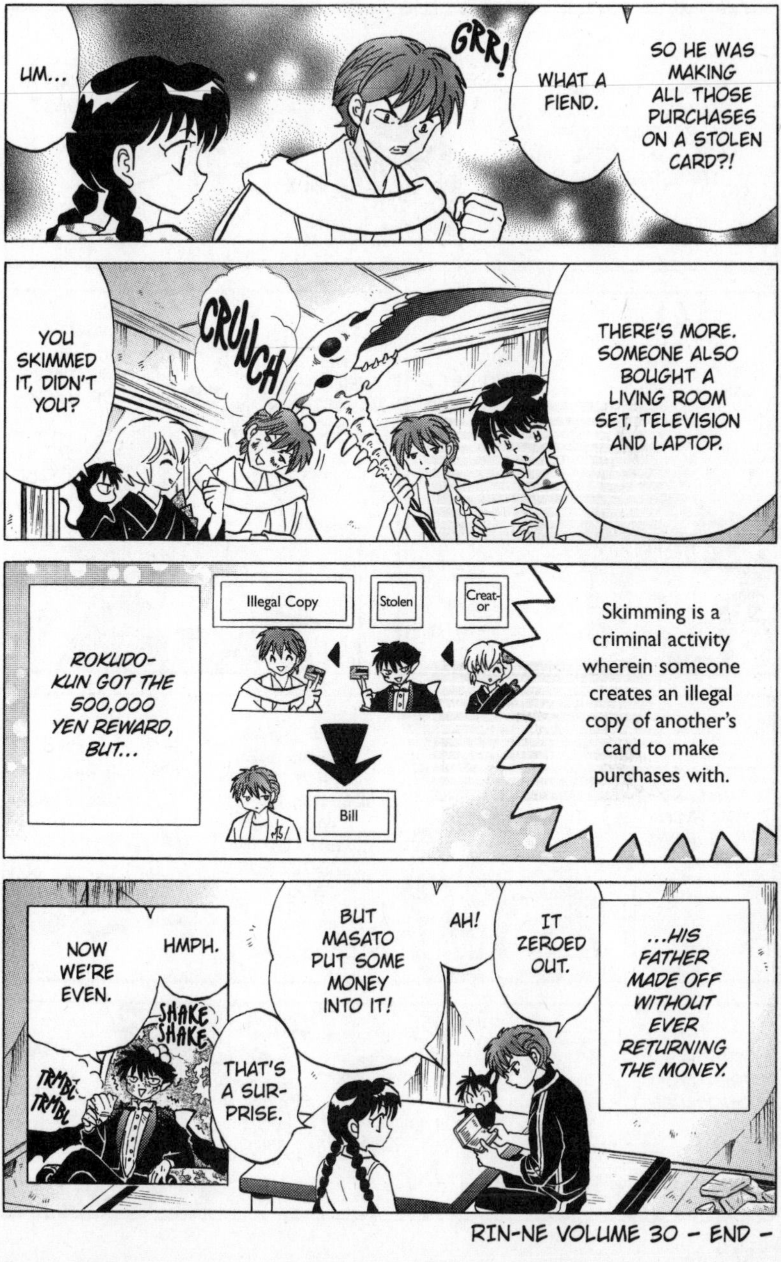
SO HE WAS MAKING ALL THOSE PURCHASES ON A STOLEN CARD?!
GRR!
WHAT A FIEND.
UM...
THERE'S MORE. SOMEONE ALSO BOUGHT A LIVING ROOM SET, TELEVISION AND LAPTOP.
CRUNCH
YOU SKIMMED IT, DIDN'T YOU?
Skimming is a criminal activity wherein someone creates an illegal copy of another's card to make purchases with.
Creat-or
Stolen
Illegal Copy
Bill
ROKUDO-KUN GOT THE 500,000 YEN REWARD, BUT...
...HIS FATHER MADE OFF WITHOUT EVER RETURNING THE MONEY.
IT ZEROED OUT.
AH!
BUT MASATO PUT SOME MONEY INTO IT!
THAT'S A SURPRISE.
HMPH.
NOW WE'RE EVEN.
SHAKE SHAKE
TRMBL TRMBL

RIN-NE VOLUME 30 - END -

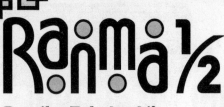
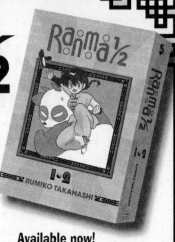

Hey! You're Reading in the Wrong Direction!

This is the end of this graphic novel!

To properly enjoy this VIZ graphic novel, please turn it around and begin reading from right to left. Unlike English, Japanese is read right to left, so Japanese comics are read in reverse order from the way English comics are typically read.

This book has been printed in the original Japanese format in order to preserve the orientation of the original artwork. Have fun with it!

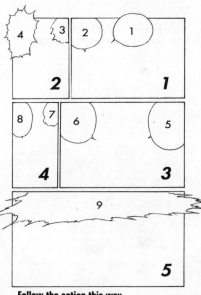

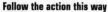

Follow the action this way

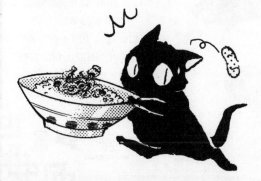

Rumiko Takahashi

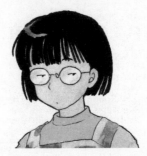

The spotlight on Rumiko Takahashi's career began in 1978 when she won an honorable mention in Shogakukan's prestigious New Comic Artist Contest for *Those Selfish Aliens*. Later that same year, her boy-meets-alien comedy series, *Urusei Yatsura*, was serialized in *Weekly Shonen Sunday*. This phenomenally successful manga series was adapted into anime format and spawned a TV series and half a dozen theatrical-release movies, all incredibly popular in their own right. Takahashi followed up the success of her debut series with one blockbuster hit after another—*Maison Ikkoku* ran from 1980 to 1987, *Ranma ½* from 1987 to 1996, and *Inuyasha* from 1996 to 2008. Other notable works include *Mermaid Saga*, *Rumic Theater*, and *One-Pound Gospel*.

Takahashi was inducted into the Will Eisner Comic Awards Hall of Fame in 2018. She won the prestigious Shogakukan Manga Award twice in her career, once for *Urusei Yatsura* in 1981 and the second time for *Inuyasha* in 2002. A majority of the Takahashi canon has been adapted into other media such as anime, live-action TV series, and film. Takahashi's manga, as well as the other formats her work has been adapted into, have continued to delight generations of fans around the world. Distinguished by her wonderfully endearing characters, Takahashi's work adeptly incorporates a wide variety of elements such as comedy, romance, fantasy, and martial arts. While her series are difficult to pin down into one simple genre, the signature style she has created has come to be known as the "Rumic World." Rumiko Takahashi is an artist who truly represents the very best from the world of manga.

RIN-NE

VOLUME 30
Shonen Sunday Edition

STORY AND ART BY
RUMIKO TAKAHASHI

KYOKAI NO RINNE Vol. 30
by Rumiko TAKAHASHI
© 2009 Rumiko TAKAHASHI
All rights reserved.
Original Japanese edition published by SHOGAKUKAN.
English translation rights in the United States of America,
Canada, the United Kingdom, Ireland, Australia and New
Zealand arranged with SHOGAKUKAN.

Translation/Christine Dashiell
Touch-up Art & Lettering/Evan Waldinger
Design/Yukiko Whitley
Editor/Megan Bates

Printed in the U.S.A.

Published by VIZ Media, LLC
P.O. Box 77010
San Francisco, CA 94107

10 9 8 7 6 5 4 3 2 1
First printing, July 2019

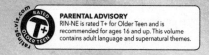

viz.com

shonensunday.com